CREATIVE ADMINISTRATION IN
RECREATION AND PARKS

Creative administration in recreation and parks

RICHARD G. KRAUS

Professor and Coordinator, Recreation Program,
Herbert H. Lehman College,
City University of New York,
New York

JOSEPH E. CURTIS

Director of Recreation and Parks,
City of New Rochelle,
New York

SECOND EDITION

with 113 *illustrations*

THE C. V. MOSBY COMPANY

Saint Louis   1977

SECOND EDITION

Copyright © 1977 by The C. V. Mosby Company

All rights reserved. No part of this book may be reproduced in any manner without written permission of the publisher.

Previous edition copyrighted 1973

Printed in the United States of America

Distributed in Great Britain by Henry Kimpton, London

The C. V. Mosby Company
11830 Westline Industrial Drive, St. Louis, Missouri 63141

Library of Congress Cataloging in Publication Data

Kraus, Richard G
   Creative administration in recreation and parks.

   Bibliography: p.
   Includes index.
   1. Recreation—Administration. 2. Parks—Management. I. Curtis, Joseph E., 1922-
joint author. II. Title.
GV182.15.K72 1977   658'.91'79   76-29696
ISBN 0-8016-2739-7

CB/CB/B 9 8 7 6 5 4 3 2 1

To two great pioneers in parks development and recreation administration:

ROBERT F. MOSES

of New York

and

ROBERT W. CRAWFORD

of Philadelphia

PREFACE

During the past several decades, the operation of recreation programs and park facilities has become a major responsibility of American government and voluntary agencies on all levels. Today, it represents a growing area of career service, demanding a high level of leadership, training, and professional expertise, in both the United States and Canada.

This book is designed to serve as a basic text for those who seek to enter this field and are enrolled in college programs of professional preparation as well as a useful reference in the professional libraries of recreation and park administrators. Although it gives primary emphasis to the administration of public departments, it also provides numerous illustrations and guidelines for the management of voluntary agencies and therapeutic recreation programs. In addition to background information on the scope of recreation and leisure in modern life and an analysis of current administrative theory, it also describes (1) the structure and legal basis of recreation and park departments, (2) personnel management, (3) budget making and fiscal management, (4) planning, design, and maintenance of facilities, (5) program development, (6) public relations and community relations, and (7) the process of evaluation and research.

We have coupled modern theory related to administrative goals and methodology with realistic information about the administrator's role. In this second edition, we have stressed such up-to-date concerns as personnel development practices, grantsmanship and new fund-raising methods, new approaches to public relations and evaluation, and innovative program development. In addition, we present the problem of operating within a political framework in community life and reconciling conflicting priorities and demands.

In writing this text, we have relied heavily on three major sources of information.

First, we have drawn on our professional experience, in one case as a veteran administrator of municipal recreation and parks who has been commissioner in one of the largest cities of the United States and in the other as a college educator, researcher, and consultant.

Second, we have made extensive use of published materials on recreation and park management found in professional publications, reports, bulletins, and conference proceedings.

Third, we have gathered hundreds of annual reports, manuals, personnel codes, planning studies, and similar documents from cities, counties, and townships throughout the United States and Canada. Although it is not possible to acknowledge all the departments that provided such materials, some of the leading sources of information were public recreation and park officials in the following:

Albuquerque, New Mexico
Asheville, North Carolina
Atlanta, Georgia
Amarillo, Texas
Boston, Massachusetts
Cedar Rapids, Iowa
Chicago, Illinois
Columbus, Ohio
Dallas, Texas
Detroit, Michigan
Edmonton, Alberta, Canada
El Segundo, California
Eugene, Oregon
Evansville, Indiana
Flint, Michigan
Fort Wayne, Indiana
Huntington Beach, California
Kansas City, Missouri
Lakewood, California
Las Vegas, Nevada
Lincoln, Nebraska
Los Angeles, California
Milwaukee, Wisconsin

Minneapolis, Minnesota
Moline, Illinois
Montreal, Quebec, Canada
Nassau County, New York
New Haven, Connecticut
New York, New York
Oak Park, Illinois
Oakland, California
Oklahoma City, Oklahoma
Omaha, Nebraska
Ontario, Canada
Orlando, Florida
Phoenix, Arizona
Richmond, Virginia
San Francisco, California
Spokane, Washington
St. Louis, Missouri
St. Petersburg, Florida
Taft, California
Tulsa, Oklahoma
Vancouver, British Columbia, Canada
Washington, D.C.
White Plains, New York

In addition, increased illustrative material is provided in this edition based on programs operated by voluntary organizations and therapeutic recreation agencies, including the Athens, Ohio, Mental Health Center; Boy Scouts of America; Boys' Clubs of America; Children's Village, Dobbs Ferry, New York; Campfire Girls; Girl Scouts of the U.S.A.; Penetanguishene Mental Health Centre, Ontario, Canada; San Francisco Recreation Center for the Handicapped; Spring Grove State Hospital, Maryland; and the Young Men's and Young Women's Christian Associations.

Increased information is included about Canadian recreation and park programs. Among those who assisted in this regard were Elliott Avedon and David Ng of the University of Waterloo, Ontario; David Parker of Mt. Royal College in Calgary, Alberta; Al Sinclair, recreation director of the Midwestern Regional Centre in Palmerston, Ontario; and especially William Knott, a leading Canadian recreation research specialist. The assistance of Henry Dunow, who did much of the research for the first edition of this text, should also be acknowledged.

We have sought to avoid the inclusion of lengthy and repetitious laws, organizational charts, or other overwhelming masses of detailed information. Instead, we have tried to present down-to-earth, realistic, and practical materials that reflect the contemporary administrative scene as concisely as possible.

We have also presented an image of the recreation and park administrator as far more than a routine functionary, custodian of facilities, or games leader. Instead, the administrator must be a confident and eloquent individual, a community catalyst and leader, a man or woman who can communicate with all levels of the public and provide forceful direction within an increasingly important sphere of modern life, the constructive and creative use of our growing leisure.

No one imagines that a student can become an effective administrator of this type simply by reading a book. Realistically, most individuals learn the nuts and bolts of their profession by on-the-job experience under capable supervision. However, a textbook can provide a clear analysis of the administrator's function, as well as a full range of operational guidelines and strategies and, finally, a vision of the significant goals of the recreation and park field.

We hope that we have achieved our goal of providing such a book. It will be up to the teachers, students, and professional leaders who will use this book throughout the United States and Canada to determine whether we have succeeded.

RICHARD G. KRAUS
JOSEPH E. CURTIS

CONTENTS

CREATIVE ADMINISTRATION IN
RECREATION AND PARKS

CHAPTER 1

RECREATION SERVICE TODAY

This book is concerned with the effective organization and administration of recreation and park departments and agencies in the United States and Canada today. Its purposes are twofold: (1) to provide a broad, theoretical understanding of the management process as it applies to public, voluntary, private, and therapeutic recreation agencies and (2) to present effective policies and procedures within major functional areas, such as personnel and budget management, program development, or facilities design, construction, and maintenance.

We seek to be both *realistic* and *practical* in our analysis of management practices and *visionary* in our view of the role of recreation service in American life. Recreation can be a vital force in healthy human development and constructive community life, and it is the administrator's responsibility to work aggressively and vigorously to create favorable public understanding and support for this field.

PUBLIC ACCEPTANCE OF RECREATION TODAY

Although the comment is frequently made that recreation is at the low end of the totem pole when compared to other municipal services, it is clear that Americans and Canadians value it greatly and are prepared to spend lavishly to obtain and enjoy it. Estimates of leisure spending in the United States range as high as $200 billion a year, and involvement in a great number of recreational pursuits has reached a new high.

For example, it was recently estimated that in the United States alone, there are almost 55 million hunters or fishermen, who spend over $7 billion a year on their recreational interests. Expenditures on domestic vacation travel amount to $40 billion or more a year, with an additional $7.5 billion spent on vacations abroad. Since World War II, there has been an enormous rise in the number of cultural arts programs in the United States. Today, there are over 1,000 orchestras and 6,000 museums, with many additional thousands of community theaters and operatic, choral, and dance companies.

Recreation and park departments have been established in several thousand cities, counties, towns, and villages in the United States. All fifty states today operate park systems, promote tourism vigorously, provide recreation services in state-operated institutions, and assist and guide local departments in the provision of leisure services. Billions of dollars are spent and hundreds of millions of visitor- or user-days recorded in federal recreation programs sponsored by

1

the National Park Service, the Forest Service, the Army Corps of Engineers, and the armed forces.

In Canada there has been a comparable growth of publicly sponsored recreation agencies, facilities, and programs. Municipal and provincial recreation, sports, and cultural programs and therapeutic organizations serve many millions each year. Four new Canadian national parks were established in 1974 alone; today there are twenty-four such parks, stretching from Newfoundland to Vancouver Island. Each province assists and coordinates local recreation departments, promotes amateur sport through liaison with athletic federations, and provides funding assistance for the development of recreation facilities. In Canada, as in the United States, there has been a rapid growth of professional employment and training, with dozens of 2-year and senior colleges offering specialized higher education in recreation and leisure services.

THE MEANING OF RECREATION SERVICE: DEFINITIONS

As recreation has become an increasingly important professional service, it has gradually developed its own national or regional professional organizations, system of higher education, research, publications, and standards. A key element in this process has been the definition of recreation as a form of community service. At the outset, recreation tended to be thought of as any activity carried on for its own sake and without extrinsic motivation or purpose. A typical early definition of recreation was

> . . . any activity pursued during leisure, either individual or collective, that is free and pleasureful, having its own immediate appeal, not impelled by a delayed reward beyond itself or by any immediate necessity.[1]

Conceptualized in this way, recreation encompasses a wide range of leisure pursuits, including many constructive activities, such as sports, camping and hiking, and social or cultural and artistic involvement. However, it might also consist of drug or alcohol abuse, compulsive gambling, or sexual promiscuity. Thus it has become recognized that when recreation is provided by community agencies and funded by taxes or voluntary giving, it must be conceptualized differently. A contemporary definition of recreation would therefore include the following elements:

> Recreation consists of activities or experiences carried on by individuals in their free time, either for pleasure or to achieve certain desirable physical, social, or emotional outcomes. When it is sponsored by public or voluntary community agencies, recreation must be couched within a framework of constructive and socially acceptable moral values and designed to achieve worthwhile goals for participants and for the community at large.

Recently, some authorities have suggested that recreation should be regarded not as activity or experience but rather as the psychological or emotional outcome of participation. Gray and Greben have written:

> Recreation is an emotional condition within an individual human being that flows from a feeling of well-being and self-satisfaction. It is characterized by feelings

of mastery, achievement, exhilaration, acceptance, success, personal worth, and pleasure. It reinforces a positive self-image. Recreation is a response to aesthetic experience, achievement of personal goals, or positive feedback from others. It is independent of activity, leisure, or social acceptance.[2]

Although this interpretation has received widespread support, it is somewhat narrow and limited as a concept of recreation. Recreation and park practitioners must realize that to bring about such desirable outcomes, it is necessary for them to provide appropriate facilities, programs, and services that people may enjoy in their leisure. Recreation in this sense must be regarded as a form of community institution and administrative responsibility. In this light, it encompasses sponsors of many types, who provide a broad spectrum of leisure opportunities to meet the needs and interests of people young and old, healthy and disabled, as individuals or in groups, and of varying racial, religious, and socioeconomic backgrounds.

CATEGORIES OF ORGANIZED RECREATION SERVICE

The field of organized recreation service has become extremely complex and diverse in the United States and Canada today. In addition to programs offered by the federal, state, or provincial governments, local communities are served by four major categories of sponsors: public, voluntary, private, and commercial.

Public recreation and park departments

This type of organization is responsible for providing recreation facilities and programs as a primary function. Recreation and park authorities are branches of local government, supported primarily by tax funds, and usually operating within the civil service personnel structure. Customarily, they provide year-round programs for all age groups, in both indoor and outdoor settings, including day camps, community center activities, Golden Age Clubs, arts workshops and classes, sports instruction and competition, and a host of other activities. In addition to such familiar facilities as parks and playgrounds, many community recreation and park departments also operate such varied types of facilities as marinas, ski centers, indoor skating rinks, pools, tennis courts, sportsmen's centers, cultural complexes, and golf courses.

A second type of local public agency has recreation as a secondary function. Thus municipal youth authorities, police departments, welfare agencies, housing authorities, or hospitals provide recreation as part of a multiservice operation designed to achieve certain beneficial social objectives.

In many cases, recreation has become a vital part of local community-school operations. In others, it has been provided by the joint efforts of government and groups of private citizens. For example, in Vancouver, British Columbia, a large Community Centre movement got under way in the years after World War II. At first, Centres were built and managed through the initiative of local citizen groups. By the 1960s, however, they were administered and funded jointly by the Vancouver Board of Parks and Public Recreation and neighborhood Community Centre Associations.

Voluntary social and recreation agencies

A second major category of community recreation organization consists of so-called voluntary social and recreational agencies. These are sponsored and directed by private citizens, with funding derived primarily from charitable giving, memberships and registration fees, and other nongovermental sources. They include both independent organizations and others that are part of larger national movements, such as the Boy Scouts, Girl Scouts, Young Men's or Young Women's Christian Association, Boys' Clubs, Girls' Clubs, and a host of similar agencies. Such organizations tend to regard themselves as character-building or youth-service bodies, rather than primarily as recreation agencies, although they regard recreation as one of their key program elements. Voluntary agencies often operate their own buildings or centers but usually do not also provide a network of outdoor recreation facilities.

Private recreation organizations

A third category of community recreation organizations is the private, closed-membership organization. This includes thousands of social, athletic, country, golf, tennis, beach, or yacht clubs, as well as other special-interest groups that are not usually open to the public at large. Private recreation groups tend to cater to the upper socioeconomic classes and to be more socially exclusive and expensive than public or voluntary agencies.

In many cases, real estate developments (private apartment or condominium complexes, leisure villages, or suburban home developments) include elaborate athletic, aquatic, and social recreation facilities for their residents. Another form of private recreation organization is the industrial recreation program, which is usually intended to serve only the employees of a company or their immediate families. Private recreation organizations are usually managed by committees or boards representing the total membership and are supported financially by annual dues and fees, although some are commercially owned and operated for profit.

Commercial recreation

The largest single category of recreation sponsor today is the commercial recreation organization. These are profit-making bodies, usually incorporated under state law, that provide entertainment, instruction, and a variety of other services or leisure activities. They cover an extremely broad range, from movie houses, bowling alleys, and dance halls to sports stadiums, race tracks, night clubs, and bars. Their income is derived from admission fees, instructional charges, rental fees, memberships or registrations, sales of equipment, food service, and a variety of other charges. They may represent small single-attraction businesses or, as in the case of large-scale amusement complexes, provide entertainment and sports facilities, housing, food services, sales outlets, and a variety of other activities. Although they do not usually have the sharply defined social goals of public or voluntary agencies, commercial recreation sponsors often provide socially desirable and constructive activity for all age groups and for families in particular.

Purpose of recreation agencies

What is the common denominator of these four different kinds of recreation agencies? It is—or should be—to provide joyous, absorbing, and challenging recreation activities that will contribute significantly to individual well-being and the overall social needs of the community. Put another way, they provide a zestful accent on life, a challenge, and an opportunity for personal, creative involvement in an increasingly depersonalized, technological society.

FACTORS SUPPORTING THE RECREATION MOVEMENT

What are the key social factors that have encouraged the growth of the recreation movement during the past several decades and that will continue to support it in the future? They include the following.

Growth of leisure

During the twentieth century, there has been a steady expansion of free time for workers in both industry and agriculture as a consequence of improved technological means of production. In addition to the gradual decline of the work week, particularly for white-collar and blue-collar workers, many companies have initiated 4-day or even 3-day workweeks. Mobley and Hellreigel point out that the 4-day week, almost unknown in the early 1960s, had become adopted by several hundred companies by 1971.[3] The American Management Association has estimated that between sixty and seventy new companies are adopting this employment system each month.

Greatly expanding numbers of holidays and longer vacations also have added greatly to the average worker's discretionary time. The United States is not unique in this respect; indeed, it lags considerably behind other industrial nations. To illustrate, the average American worker today has about 3 weeks of vacation each year, after having been employed for several years. In contrast, all French workers, from clerks to factory supervisors, are given 4 weeks of vacation starting with the first year of work, and many Frenchmen take holidays of up to 7 weeks a year. In the Scandinavian countries, vacation policies are even more liberal.

Improved Social Security or company retirement plans and longer life expectancy have also provided a great increase of new leisure for many older citizens. For example, a government report revealed in 1975 that only 22% of men in the United States remain in the work force after the age of 65, compared with 42% just two decades earlier. Various reputable economists have predicted that within the next 15 to 20 years we will see a 4- to 5-hour working day, a 22-hour work-week, and retirement in the forties, or some combination of these factors.

This increased leisure, combined with such factors as a climbing standard of living and greater affluence (despite cyclical periods of recession and continuing inflation), has created an even greater demand for organized recreation services. Even during severe economic slumps, as in 1974-1975, leisure spending has remained high, with tourism reaching new records. Even though the rate of population growth has leveled off, this growth also has expanded the need for varied leisure services. In particular, emphasis is now being given to those groups in the population that have enforced leisure, such as aged or retired, physically or mentally handicapped, unemployed, and institutionalized people. For them, recreation is not seen merely as a complement to work. They have nothing *but* free time and have a crucial need for recreation as a means of enriching otherwise barren lives.

National support of recreation and parks

In both the United States and Canada, the federal governments have given substantial support to meeting national recreation needs, particularly in the area of outdoor recreation. Today, in the United States, there are over eighty federal agencies, commissions, committees, and councils involved in 300 separate outdoor recreation programs, which range from the management of parklands to providing technical and financial assistance, planning, research support, resource use, and regulation of other agencies. The major federal land-managing agencies operate a total of 755 million acres, and three agencies alone (the National Park Service, Forest Service, and U.S. Army Corps of Engineers) have been responsible for as many as 619 million visitor days a year at sites they have developed. Through the Bureau of Outdoor Recreation, hundreds of millions of dollars derived from the sale of offshore oil leases and surplus lands, federal recreation area revenues, and motorboat fuel tax have been allocated to helping states and local agencies develop outdoor recreation resources through matching grants.

The federal government has also given substantial funds to programs for the handicapped and socially disadvantaged and to inner-city community action programs and public housing and Model Cities recreation programs. United States government funding for the arts rose from $2.5 million per year in the mid-1960s to $82 million in fiscal 1976 through a funding program administered by the National Endowment for the Arts. A number of major federal support programs, particularly those dealing with antipoverty needs, have been cut in recent years years (Chapter 8), and there has been strong criticism of the government's lack of full commitment and coordination in this field. Nonetheless, it is clear that the federal government has taken on an increasing responsibility for recreation and park development in recent years.

Ironically, the major emphasis of federal assistance to state and local recreation and park agencies has been in land acquisition and recreation resource development. However, federal policy has ignored the glaring weakness of inadequate maintenance capability in many large cities. Major investments in land and equipment are accompanied by an unwillingness to provide adequate day-by-day maintenance funds. Politicians on the federal, state, and local levels find the temptation irresistible to build golf courses, swimming pools, ice rinks, community centers, and stadiums costing huge sums. Bands play, ribbons are cut, and the public marches in to find skeleton caretaker forces that let grass grow long, lights burn out, trees die, and toilets clog up. Clearly, fuller support in this area is needed!

In Canada, the federal government has assumed an increasingly greater responsibility for promoting and assisting recreation on all levels. Although its major direct responsibility has been the operation of national parks, it has also provided considerable assistance to programs of competitive sport, physical recreation, and fitness, through the Fitness and Amateur Sport Branch of the Canadian government and its two subdivisions, Recreation Canada and Sport Canada. The federal government also provides substantial support to the arts and to cultural exchange programs through the Canada Council and has a wide variety of special programs designed to promote tourism, environmental needs, wildlife propagation and protection, youth job opportunities and travel, and other recreation-related projects. Similarly, such provinces as Alberta, Nova Scotia, and Ontario have provided strong leadership in such areas as community education, amateur sport development, construction of local recreation facilities, special services to youth and aging persons, and cultural recreation (Chapter 8).

Changing social attitudes on work and leisure

Another important social factor supporting the growth of the recreation movement has been the shift of public attitudes toward work and leisure. In past generations, the industrial nations have been strongly work-oriented, and in no nation was the Protestant work ethic as strongly rooted as in the United States. In recent years, however, many young Americans and some middle-aged ones have developed new values that reject work for its own sake and that stress personal creativity and a leisurely way of life. Many people today have embraced alternative life-styles, taking up simple crafts, living close to the soil and raising organic foods, and rejecting high-pressure, nose-to-the-grindstone careers. Increasingly, they are coming to value leisure because of the potential it offers for individuality and self-expressiveness.

In part, this change of attitude has resulted in the growing conviction that recreation and leisure are essential parts of life in modern society, and that a high priority of our educational system must be to educate for leisure. Many public schools not only provide facilities, such as gymnasiums, swimming pools, or craft and music rooms, that are used for community recreation programs, but also are cooperating directly with municipal agencies in the sponsorship of recreation programs (Chapter 9). Community schools are providing, among other programs, continuing education classes in hobbies, sports, languages, arts and crafts, music, dance, and a host of other leisure-oriented skills that are being taken today by as many as 30 million adult Americans. In a number of Canadian provinces, educational authorities are working directly with local school systems to promote such activities and related youth services.

Similarly, the major religious denominations, which once disapproved of play and sought to limit it, today regard leisure as an important spiritual concern and directly sponsor many recreational programs. Individual churches and synagogues frequently operate youth programs, adult couples clubs, and senior centers. Organizations such as the Catholic Youth Organization (CYO), the Young Men's and Young Women's Christian and Hebrew Associations (YMCA, YWCA, and YM-YWHA), and the Baptist and Methodist youth fellowships offer extensive recreation programs for their members, including sports and cultural and social activities. Other religious organizations assist member agencies, such as nursing homes, child-care centers, or other treatment institutions in the development of recreation and group work services.

As a consequence, recreation and leisure are regarded today as increasingly important public concerns and are receiving a higher level of public support.

Emergence of other sponsors

In addition to the programs described earlier, recreation has become fully established in a number of other kinds of settings.

Industrial recreation programs offer a leading example. A 1968 study examined 132 major industrial firms with over 570,000 employees in eleven midwestern states. It found that 118 (89%) of these companies provided recreation programs for their employees. About half of these companies had employee recreation associations; many of them operated their own parks, golf courses, or other special recreation facilities. In 1975, the National Industrial Recreation Association reported that 50,000 companies in the United States were spending a total of $2 billion a year to "entertain, exercise and educate" their workers with a wide variety of hobby classes, clubs, sports leagues, and travel programs.[4]

Another area of recreation service that has grown rapidly in recent years is the field of therapeutic recreation. Today, programs of recreational or activity therapy are provided in both institutions and community settings for the mentally ill and mentally retarded, the physically disabled, dependent aging persons, and similar special populations. A recent study of recreation services for disabled children, funded by the Children's Bureau of the United States Department of Health, Education, and Welfare, revealed that 94% of the public recreation and park departments in ten large metropolitan areas around the country provided recreation for the handicapped.

For all these reasons, it is clear that recreation has become an ever more important service in communities large and small throughout the United States and Canada. At the same time, it is also apparent that a number of other social trends or problems have presented the recreation and park movement with serious obstacles that must be overcome in the years ahead.

CHALLENGES TO THE RECREATION AND PARK MOVEMENT

Changing leisure tastes and values. Recreation and park administrators must face the need to make their programs relevant and vital, without sacrificing their standards, in an era of rapid change in leisure interests and social values. The forms of recreation people enjoy have been transformed in recent years. Inventive technology has made possible entirely new kinds of play: rock music, scuba diving, snowmobiling, indoor ice skating, powerboating, skydiving, and the like. Television itself, as a manifestation of modern technology, has become the most popular use of leisure time. Alcoholism and drug addiction pose serious problems, particularly for millions of young people, and changing moral standards have altered sexual behavior in modern society. Within this context, many public recreation and park departments have changed little in recent years, continuing to offer the same basic programs as in the past. If they are to keep abreast of the times and to offer programs that will be meaningful to all age groups today, it will be necessary for many recreation programs to be radically revised.

Economic recession and budget cutbacks. In contrast to the 1950s and 1960s, which were decades of economic growth with rapidly expanding recreation and park facilities and programs, the 1970s marked a period of severe economic recession, caused by growing inflation, unemployment, the energy crisis, and sharp cutbacks in government spending. In the United States particularly, many state and local governments have been forced to freeze manpower and to reduce capital expenditures. Growing welfare, environmental, and law enforcement costs in

Fig. 1-1. A, Top civic officials often become involved in recreation programs. Here, Washington, D.C.'s Mayor Walter Washington opens Summer United States Youth Games. **B,** In many large cities, mayors have initiated youth opportunity programs, closely tied in to summer recreation projects. Such programs combine play, education, jobs, and other youth services. **C,** Nassau County, New York, Executive Ralph Caso discusses recreation and park development on a television program with administrators Richard Fitch and Francis Cosgrove. **D,** County Executive Caso chats with Russian Olympic wrestling team before meet with American wrestlers in county sports center.

the larger cities have in many cases compelled the firing of large numbers of civil service workers and the closing of schools, libraries, hospitals, and day care centers. The obvious challenge to recreation and park administrators has been the need for them to justify their program priorities at a time of fiscal crisis and to maintain the optimum level of service possible within existing budget limits.

Need to unify community groups. During the 1960s, in many American cities, there was unparalleled turmoil and militance of radical political groups, generational conflict, racial antagonism, and antiwar activism. Campuses were taken over, and whole sections of some cities were put to the torch. Parks became a center of controversy; they were a focal point for drug users and hippies, and frequently they were the scene of violent protests, police "busts," and other forms of social disturbance. Recreation and park directors were faced by the need to provide improved facilities and services to low-income, minority-group neighborhoods and were often charged with lack of relevance or with nonsensitivity. Although such problems passed their peak by the early 1970s, their lesson remains clear: recreation and park authorities cannot afford to regard themselves as agencies concerned only with fun or pleasure. Instead, they must have a meaningful social impact, particularly for disadvantaged and minority-group populations. As part of this responsibility, a key purpose must be to build bridges among community groups and to unify residents from many neighborhoods and socioeconomic, racial, or religious backgrounds through sports programs, social activities, cultural events, and volunteer service projects.

Physically restoring the cities. In addition to the social turmoil and financial difficulty just described, many great cities have also suffered from marked physical deterioration. One critic has written:

> They are physically obsolete, financially unworkable, crime-ridden, garbage strewn, polluted, torn by racial conflicts, wallowing in welfare, unemployment, despair and official corruption. As they exist at present they are unsalvageable, destined to join the dinosaur in deserved extinction.[5]

There *is* hard statistical evidence of the decline of cities. For the first time in the history of the United States, more people live in suburban communities (75.6 million) than in central cities (63.8 million), with the remainder in smaller cities and the countryside. A major cause of this population shift has been the physical deterioration of the central cities themselves. They suffer from smog, dirt, garbage, abandoned housing, clogged traffic arteries, disused waterfronts, and a host of other physical ills. Recreation and park departments must play a vital role in the effort to reverse this situation by renewing the physical vitality and beauty of our cities. New and more attractive waterfront areas, plazas, and parks are contributing to the visual appeal of many cities around the nation. Revised zoning codes, programs of neighborhood renewal, and imaginative forms of urban design that include shopping malls, bicycle paths, sports stadiums, and similar facilities must contribute to the coming urban renaissance. In addition to playing a key role in their physical redevelopment, recreation and parks must provide cultural, historical, athletic, and social events that create a feeling of vitality and excitement in the urban environment.

Needs of suburban communities and smaller cities. Most suburban communities and smaller cities have not undergone the stresses of the central cities. Typically, they have attracted substantial amounts of business and industry, have developed strong networks of parks and other recreation facilities, and have instituted extensive systems of fees and charges, which have kept their recreation budgets on the plus side of the ledger. In such communities, the social goals described earlier in this chapter are not as obvious. Administrators tend to give chief priority to providing the kinds of recreation programs and facilities that are wanted by middle-class and upper-class residents within a context of recreation as an amenity.

Yet even in suburban communities and smaller cities, there are substantial numbers of handicapped or economically disadvantaged persons who need to be provided with special services. Drug abuse, juvenile delinquency, and similar problems are not unknown, and recreation administrators must devise meaningful programs to attack them. In many suburban townships that are threatened by the disappearance of open space, recreation and park authorities have collaborated with planning boards to ensure that substantial portions of land are set aside as permanent open space in all new residential or industrial projects, often through zoning changes or requirements that developers contribute pieces of land for parkland. A final crucial problem in many suburban areas is the proliferation of governmental units (counties, townships, municipalities, school boards, and even special park districts) that tend to overlap and conflict with each other in metropolitan regions. Increased coordination and more effective planning must be developed by recreation administrators to solve this problem.

Other critical problems. Several other issues and challenges pose day-by-day difficulties for recreation and park administrators. The energy crisis, which has escalated the costs of facilities, maintenance, and program operation, demands entirely new planning approaches, particularly during a period of budget crisis. The term *affirmative action*, which has in the past referred chiefly to the hiring of members of racial minority groups, is today being applied more and more to the elimination of sexism in public and private employment. It poses a critical problem to recreation and park executives, in terms of both nondiscriminatory personnel policies and the enrichment of program opportunities for girls and women.

The need to expand programs of physical fitness and active sports participation must be a key priority of community recreation agencies. A recent study of physical recreation and fitness in the United States, sponsored by the President's Council on Physical Fitness and Sport, found that:

> Forty-nine million adults do not engage in exercise for physical fitness, and those who do take it so easy . . . and participate for such a short period of time . . . that they hardly increase their heart and breathing rates. In addition, they engage in these activities only once or twice a week. Also, in spite of the upsurge in the number of health, trimline, and fitness clubs and programs, only three out of every one hundred Americans participate in an organized fitness program. . . .[6]

Since schools and colleges tend to serve only the younger age groups in modern society, it is clearly the responsibility of recreation and park departments to provide much wider segments of the adult population with attractive and well-organized opportunities for sports and physical fitness–oriented activities. A related concern is the need to promote desirable social values in the sponsorship of competitive sports programs. It is clear that, despite our widespread acceptance of the value of sports in building desirable social attitudes and values of citizenship, we have overglamorized the high-level professional and de-emphasized programs for the true amateur and have corrupted the true purposes of play in our emphasis on winning at all costs. A top priority is the need for public and voluntary recreation agencies to promote a philosophy of play that will be healthier and that will restore sport to its proper role in modern society (Chapter 6).

RESPONSIBILITIES OF RECREATION AND PARK ADMINISTRATORS

How must today's recreation and park administrator regard his or her function in community life? The executive's task is to provide philosophical direction for the department, to represent it well with other community agencies and with the public at large, and to manage its operation to ensure maximum productivity, economy, and effectiveness. Specifically, the following eight responsibilities may be identified:

1. *Goal-setting.* It is the task of the administrator to provide leadership in formulating the philosophy and goals of the recreation and parks department and then to gain understanding and support for them within the staff of his department, among other department heads, boards and commissions, and among the public at large.

2. *Maintenance of effective relationships.* The administrator must maintain effective cooperative relationships with other municipal departments, with the mayor, city manager, and city council, and with representatives of relevant state and federal agencies.

3. *Financial planning and control.* A key responsibility of the administrator is to formulate financial priorities and policies, develop budgetary plans, and maintain control of the system of revenue management, expenditures, and overall fiscal management.

4. *Personnel management.* The administrator must develop a job classification system for full-time and part-time personnel, and must recruit, hire, and be responsible for the training, assignment, and supervision of personnel, usually within the civil service structure imposed by the community, county, or state.

5. *Program development.* This is the heart of the administrator's overall responsibility: to conceptualize and put into action a varied range of recreation program activities, to meet the needs of all groups in the community, and to achieve the established departmental objectives.

6. *Facilities management.* The administrator must coordinate the planning, acquisition, design, construction, and maintenance of recreation and park resources and facilities. In a broader sense, he must also be a forceful community spokesman for environmental protection, open-space planning, and effective land-use policies.

7. *Public and community relations.* It is the administrator's task to establish a meaningful two-way process of public relations, including the effective use of publicity media to tell the department's story, as well as the fullest possible involvement of community groups in planning and consultation, joint program efforts, fund-raising, and volunteer service projects.

8. *Evaluation.* Finally, the administrator must take the lead in establishing a meaningful process of regular evaluation of all program elements, including leadership, program effectiveness, facilities maintenance, and similar functions; in addition, he must maintain a comprehensive system of reports and records of the department's operation.

These functions have been presented with emphasis on the roles played by recreation and park administrators in *public* departments. They would vary somewhat for directors of *voluntary* agencies or in *therapeutic* settings. However, the basic tasks tend to be the same in all organizations concerned with recreation and related community services. In addition to them, there *is* one further challenge that is faced by all professional personnel in this field. It is the need to contribute to professional advancement in recreation. Although the field itself has made tremendous progress in terms of material growth, recreation is still not widely understood or supported by the American public as a specialized area of professional service. Too often, the image of the recreation and park worker tends to be the outmoded image of the playground leader; few citizens are fully aware of the complex and important task played by professionals in this field.

To improve this situation, it is necessary that progress be made on two fronts: new and more creative uses of recreation and park personnel must be devised, and the field itself must be upgraded, in terms of recognition, public influence, and status.

Particularly within the bureaucratic hierarchies of large-city recreation and park departments, the job of recreation line personnel (both leaders and supervisors) has tended to be frozen in outmoded patterns of assignments. Increasingly, the profession is becoming aware of the need for recreation leaders and supervisors to play an effective role as planners, organizers, and catalysts within the community, working with people and organizations on all levels. In some cities strenuous efforts are being made to retrain personnel and to assign them to new, more flexible, and varied responsibilities.

On the administrative level, it is essential that every effort be made to strengthen the status of recreation and park executives and their influence in community life. This implies the need for them to become increasingly competent within the technical areas of service, such as program development, budget planning and management, personnel selection and supervision, intragovernmental relationships, facilities development, and community relations.

But beyond this, if recreation is to become more highly regarded and influential in community life, its leaders must have a new and expanded view of their own function.

Recreation and park administrators must develop a new sense of the possible, of innovation, of the potential role of leisure programs in urban and suburban society. They must generate a sense of mission. They must become movers and shakers—the kinds of people who are able to communicate with and influence business executives, religious leaders, civic officials, college, university, and school system administrators, and people in every walk of life. They must be able to mobilize newspaper editors, television producers, spokesmen for the poor, officers of civic clubs, agencies serving the handicapped, conservationist and environmental groups, and a host of other forces in American communities to support a common effort to meet the leisure needs and related social concerns of all groups in society. They must be able to challenge apathy and be daring and imaginative in their approaches to solving the problems of their community.

Only if its leaders are able to move forcefully in such directions will the recreation and park profession—including administrators in voluntary and therapeutic as well as public service—be able to gain fuller status and the support needed to promote their programs successfully in American communities.

Suggested topics for class discussion or examination questions

1. Compare the range and amount of spending by Americans and Canadians on organized recreation services (to support *public* recreation and park departments or voluntary agencies) with expenditures on *private* or *commercial* recreation. What implications do you find for society, in terms of meeting the overall leisure needs of the nation? What are the unique ways in which only government can provide adequate recreation opportunity for the mass of people?

2. What are the key factors in Western society today that promote the growth of public recreation and park agencies? What are the most difficult problems and issues facing the administrators of such departments?

3. Contrast the goals, programs, and facilities of typical *inner-city* and *small-town* or *suburban* recreation and park departments. In what ways are they similar? In what ways are they radically different?

REFERENCES

1. Neumeyer, Martin H., and Neumeyer, Esther: *Leisure and Recreation,* New York, 1958, The Ronald Press Co., p. 19.
2. Gray, David E., and Greben, Seymour: "Future Perspectives," *Parks and Recreation,* July, 1974, p. 49.
3. Mobley, Tony A., and Hellreigel, Don: "The Four-Day Work-Week," *Parks and Recreation,* November, 1974, p. 17.
4. "Company Recreation: Now It's More Than Softball," *The New York Times,* November 26, 1975, p. 34.
5. Raskin, Eugene: "Are Our Cities Doomed?" *The New York Times,* May 2, 1971, sect. 8, p. 1.
6. Bucher, Charles: "National Adult Physical Fitness Survey," *Journal of Health, Physical Education and Recreation,* January, 1974, p. 25.

CHAPTER 2

THE ADMINISTRATIVE PROCESS

Administration is a process common to a variety of human organizations and institutions—governmental, educational, and industrial. Large hospitals, public service corporations, the armed forces, and companies of every type are only a few of the settings in which it must operate. Whenever men and women join together in group endeavors to accomplish certain goals, the administrative process is at work.

In general usage, the term *management* has become widely accepted in recent years as synonymous with *administration*. This is particularly true with respect to business administration, where management is viewed as including not only the top-level executive but also division heads and middle-level supervisory personnel who have responsibility for controlling and directing company operations. McFarland writes:

> Management is defined for conceptual, theoretical and analytical purposes as that process by which managers create, direct, maintain and operate purposive organizations through systematic, coordinated, cooperative human effort.[1]

Regardless of whether the task involves an informal social enterprise or a highly structured agency of government, the key to successful performance is the efficient and well-planned use of human and physical resources. The basic element of administration is the dynamic and changing process by which the activities and material resources of the group are assembled and coordinated toward accomplishing its objectives. Kast and Rosenzwieg state:

> Managers are needed to convert the disorganized resources of men, machines, material, money, time and space into a useful and effective enterprise. Essentially, administration is a process whereby these unrelated resources are integrated into a total system for objective accomplishment.[2]

Normally, administration is only one part of a much larger system, whether it be in the field of government, social service, or business. However, it is the most vital element in that it guides and coordinates all the others. The process itself may vary considerably in different administrative structures. The director of a large hospital will have different objectives and goals from the director of a small community center or day camp. However, it is possible to draw a number of key generalizations about the administrative process. Usually, it is believed to include three major steps or functions: planning, organizing, and controlling.

PLANNING, ORGANIZING, AND CONTROLLING

Planning is the preliminary, conceptual phase of the administrative process, in which the dimensions of the task of administration are established and in which fundamental goals and objectives are decided on. Preliminary decisions regarding the administrative structure of the organization, the assignment of responsibility, the allocation of resources, and the general policies of operation are elements in planning.

Organizing is the phase of administration in which action is taken and the operation is gotten under way. This might involve actually setting up organizational units or departmental divisions to provide direct services, build and maintain facilities, or develop favorable public and community relations. It includes allocating resources and assignments to personnel, establishing program schedules, and providing channels of communication among the various branches or departments of an agency.

Controlling implies the task of overseeing the operation. It may involve giving orders, directing, observing how assigned tasks are being carried out, and evaluating the degree to which objectives are being met.

Within a time sequence, the administrative process might be said to have the following five elements:

1. Establishing goals and objectives through a decision-making process
2. Planning and managing the work of others to achieve these objectives
3. Organizing the work and allocation of material and physical resources so that the program is carried out most efficiently and successfully
4. Guiding and motivating personnel to carry out their assignments within the total administrative operation
5. Controlling, evaluating, and reporting on the performance and outcomes of the total effort[3]

THEORY AND PRACTICE IN ADMINISTRATION

Public administration is a field of human endeavor that requires the combination of theoretical analysis with practical accomplishment. This duality of focus is common to all large-scale administrative operations. Dimock states:

> Public administration must be sufficiently practical to accomplish the many complex responsibilities of organizations, and it must also develop a body of theory as a guide to the most effective accomplishment possible.[4]

The practical responsibilities of recreation and park administrators include such elements as setting up specific levels of responsibility, developing a network of parks, playgrounds, and other facilities, hiring and supervising full-time and part-time recreation leaders, planning and submitting annual budgets, and other comparable tasks. The theoretical aspect is concerned with the way in which this is carried on and the framework of values or human relationships within which tasks are assigned and carried out. These two contrasting ingredients of administration must be blended in a harmonious relationship.

In the field of public administration and business management, a number of approaches to effective administrative practice have been developed during the past several decades. At the outset, these models sought to define principles or laws under which organizations might be administered most productively. In more recent years, the emphasis has been on the scientific analysis of human relationships and organizational processes and on new systems-oriented approaches to planning and control. The most influential of these approaches to administration, past and present, are described in the following pages.

Scientific management model

Under the leadership of Frederick W. Taylor, a number of leading engineers and business theorists developed the *scientific management* approach to administration. Although it was most popular during the first three decades of this century, this model is still influential today; a number of its basic principles are still widely accepted. Often referred to as the *machine-model* theory, this approach held that there were certain laws and principles that might be discovered through an engineering-based analysis of organization.

The scientific management model was addressed primarily to business enterprise. Orderliness was its primary focus, and it saw workers as only one component in a much larger system. They had to be managed, and it was essential that the most efficient and productive work procedures be determined by industrial engineers and then followed exactly by all employees.

Nigro writes that the individual had to adjust to the total structure of the organization and had little free choice with respect to his own functioning:

> . . . the anatomy of the organization came first and . . . was the principal consideration. . . . Efficiency depended upon the proper initial arrangement and later readjustment of the "parts," that is, the organization subdivisions. Taylor knew that the cooperation of the employees was essential, but he assumed that their cooperation would be a by-product of the scientific approach.[5]

A number of important principles of administrative theory were evolved as part of the scientific management approach.

Division of labor and task specialization. Under this principle, the operational functions of an organization must be sharply identified and placed in separate departments. Departments in turn are subdivided into separate units or sections. Work assignments are differentiated according to specialized functions. New departments or units are added and old ones subdivided as the organization expands. The appropriate departmentalization of the organization and the efficient arrangement of its parts are crucial to successful operation.

Unified command and centralized decision making. It is essential that the decision-making power be tightly restricted to the administrators of the organization or the heads of departments or subdivisions. Each subadministrator or supervisor must exert direct and strong leadership over each unit of the organization. Responsibility must flow directly down the chain of command, from the head of the organization down through the hierarchy, through those in charge of each of the departments.

Span of control. This principle refers to the number of immediate subordinates that an administrator can effectively supervise. This may be demonstrated diagrammatically by showing a narrow or *tall* span of control, as contrasted with a broad or *flat* span of control. In the narrow structure, the administrator exerts a tight command over a limited number of subordinates, as contrasted with a broad structure, in which he cannot give as direct and intensive supervision over a larger number of subordinates.

Summary. The scientific management approach did not represent a complete and consistent body of theory based on truly scientific research and empirical observation. However, in its central goal of efficiency and in its convincing guidelines for organizing productive enterprises, it had a great deal of appeal for business administrators, industrial engineers, and college educators in this field. Its weakness was that it failed to consider the human factor in organizational life. People were regarded as cogs in a machine, with little concern for the elements of human motivation, group process, or individual creativity. The machine model was therefore most useful in those operations where tasks were mechanical and repetitive and least useful in situations where the management process had to deal with varied or rapidly changing tasks and functions.

Human relations model

As its name suggests, the *human relations* model conceived of management as a social system in which the attitudes and relationships of workers toward each other and toward the total organization strongly influence their job output. This approach was most influential during the period from about 1930 to the 1950s. It stemmed initially from the famous Hawthorne studies in which Elton Mayo explored the effect of changing working conditions at a large Western Electric Company plant.

It was discovered that any change in working conditions tended to increase worker productivity. The key factor was that when employees thought their needs were being considered, they responded with a higher level of individual and group motivation. The experimenters concluded that workers within any organization tended to coalesce into groups that developed their own strong values and codes. These in turn influenced the extent to which each worker would cooperate with management and the effort he would make to meet production goals. Thus, rather than focus on a mechanical analysis of work assignments, the human relations approach dealt with the lower levels of organization and stressed such elements as communication, leadership, interpersonal processes, and their effects on closely knit groups of employees.

As a consequence of this approach, the view that management should be based on rigid laws and principles that ignored the human element was challenged. For the first time, the human substructure within management systems was recognized, and supervisory and managerial human relations skills were developed. However, this approach continued to retain much of the paternalism of the machine model. It was still management-oriented and assumed that workers would have to adjust to the organization and its goals, rather than the reverse.

Industrial humanism model. In the development of the human relations approach, behavioral scientists such as psychologists and anthropologists became influential. As they continued to study work environments, a number of leading investigators, including Douglas McGregor, Abraham Maslow, Rensis Lickert, and Chris Argyris formed what has been called a *behavioral school* of industrial and management theory. Their approach, the *industrial humanism* model, represents a radical extension of the human relations approach. Sometimes called the *man-centered* model, it stresses the need to consider all aspects of human personality in the design of job functions and the work environment.

Golembiewski[6] describes some of the fundamental tenets of this administrative theory:

1. Work must be made psychologically acceptable, rather than threatening or boring to the individual.

2. Work must permit the employee to develop his individual faculties, creativity, and sense of responsibility. It must allow him the opportunity for self-determination.

3. The worker must have the possibility of controlling, in a meaningful way, the environment in which he functions.

4. The organization should no longer be the sole and final decision-making agent; instead, this power should be shared more widely, and both the organization and the individual should be subject to an external code of values and moral order.

Proponents of the industrial humanism model take the position that it is counterproductive to specialize job assignments so highly that they are repetitive and boring. In terms of worker satisfaction and job output, better results can be obtained when individuals are given responsibility for more than one operation or are able to vary their tasks from day to day.

The industrial humanism theory also takes the position that close supervision, a narrow span of control, and highly centralized decision-making do not contribute to efficiency. Worker performance is improved when individuals are given latitude for using their own discretion and elbow room on the job. Power should be delegated more freely to subordinates; creative problem-solving is encouraged on all levels, rather than bucking even the most minor problems up the hierarchy to department heads.

Organization theorists today have not entirely abandoned the scientific management theory. In practice, many large organizations continue to operate on the basis of the task specialization, unified command, and span of control principles. However, the more recent industrial humanism approach has had considerable influence on those organizations that face nonroutine tasks, particularly in the realm of human services and social agency programs.

Management science approach to administrative structure

The most recent trend in management theory has been described as the *management science* approach. Although this title is similar to that of the first approach described, it represents a far more complex analysis of administrative structure and process. It includes detailed exploration of such elements as the formal and informal structure of organizations, the role of authority, line and staff personnel groups, vertical and horizontal subsystems, and program management. New approaches to planning and control functions have included the use of electronic data processing in systems analysis, PERT and the Critical Path Method, PPBS (Planning-Programming-Budgeting-Systems), MBO (Management by Objectives), and conflict resolution theory. Several of these innovative approaches are described in the following section of this chapter, beginning with an analysis of administrative structure.

The term *administrative structure* refers to the tangible framework of role assignments, titles, functions, and relationships through which an organization is administered. Structure provides for channels of communication and coordination and has a considerable effect on the actual performance of the organization. It may be regarded as the established arrangement of the components and subsystems of a system through which all decisions and actions must flow.

A logically organized structure is essential to efficient operation; a poorly built one hampers performance at every level. The ultimate purpose of a structural plan is to ensure the most smoothly operating day-by-day organizational functioning. Management experts point out that structures are established on two levels: formal and informal.

The *formal* structure of an organization consists of explicitly stated rules, operating policies, work procedures, and other devices that are put into effect by management to organize all the components of the work enterprise to meet established goals. Particularly when it deals with the functioning of personnel, it may reflect not only administrative decisions but union contracts that regulate hours, leaves, disciplinary action and arbitration of disputes, and even work output. It is usually reflected within an organization chart, job descriptions, personnel manuals or regulations, and similar formal documents.

In contrast, the *informal* structure of an organization does not appear in writing and represents a fluid and dynamic process of interpersonal behavior and decision-making. It represents the way in which the formal code of operations is realistically adapted to the day-by-day problems of administrative management and in which personnel on all levels actually carry out their functions, communicate with each other, and contribute to organizational goals.

Organization chart. An organization chart presents in pictorial form a somewhat simplified and abstract model of the formal structure, showing each level of administrative responsibility as well as the various departments that assume specialized functions. Normally, each position or department would have a title and placement on the chart indicating its specific areas of responsibility, with those placed closer to the top of the chart having higher status and those closer to the bottom having lower status. Lines connecting various sections of an organization chart indicate channels of authority or administrative relationships. Examples of organization charts are provided in Chapter 3.

Organization charts usually fail to give a full and realistic picture of the actual working of an organization. They do not measure the degree of authority individuals have over subordinate employees, nor do they describe the precise relationship between departments, particularly on comparable levels within the organization. However, the organization chart is a useful device for indicating the overall hierarchical nature of an operating structure and the specific assignments of administrative responsibility.

It is essential that organization charts be *credible,* that is, that they reflect the actual structure of the department or agency rather than an idealized version of the way the administrator would like it to look. They should be simple and understandable rather than cluttered up with myriad titles, complicated connecting lines and arrows, and excessive detail. If a chart is too complicated, it suggests that the organization itself is chaotic or confused. Charts should be updated regularly and should be displayed in appropriate places or publications to be most useful in providing needed information about the organization.

Within most departmental structures today, certain general principles of organization are followed. These tend to reflect, at least outwardly, the influence of the scientific management approach to administrative theory.

Division of labor and task specialization. This principle, as described earlier, divides all work into specialized tasks and organizes the total effort of an organization into separate departments. Within a recreation and park department, it means that there are several divisions, bureaus, or units—usually concerned with direct program services, the development and management of physical facilities, personnel, budget, public relations, and similar major functions.

Scalar principle. According to this principle, authority is established at the top of the organization chart and flows in a vertical line down to the lower levels of the structure. Emphasis is given to the concept of *unity of command,* under which each subordinate should have only one superior to whom he is directly responsible.

In many recreation and park systems this principle is not fully applicable. For example, an arts and crafts specialist employed in a large community center would normally be regarded as being responsible directly to the center director. However, if there is a city-wide director of cultural programs or arts activities, he might also function under the leadership of that individual. He might also be responsible, in planning arts programs or festivals, to the district supervisor who coordinates various projects within a geographical area of the community. Thus, realistically, the vertical line of authority may also include diagonal lines, in which subordinates operate under other supervisors, or even horizontal lines to parallel services or units in the structure.

Assignment of authority. The overall administrative structure is generally dependent on the principle that authority is legitimatized—that is, that superiors have the right to command others to take certain actions and that subordinates must obey these commands. Accompanying this principle is the tenet of accountability; once an individual has been given an assignment, he must carry it out and is responsible for its outcome. This principle is fundamental to the operation of *all* large organizations of bureaucratic structures.

In practice, however, it is not always carried out in an autocratic way. Intelligent administrators and supervisors normally seek the views of their subordinates or develop a team-planning process in which decisions are arrived at based on the views of all. Nonetheless, in all structures, if there is disagreement, the superior has the *right* to impose orders on his subordinates, provided that these do not violate personnel policies or other departmental regulations.

Span of control. As described earlier in this chapter, this principle relates to the ability of a single individual to supervise the work of several subordinates. Generally, as applied within a recreation and park structure, it would mean that the top administrator would have several department heads who would be directly responsible to him; these individuals, in turn, would exert control over *their* subordinates. Traditional theory suggests that the narrower the span of control (that is the smaller the number of individuals for which an administrator is responsible), the more efficient the operation. However, this implies creating a number of intermediate levels of supervision over whom the administrator has no direct influence. Both the process of communication and the task of decision-making may be hampered when the span of control is too narrow, unless effective channels for vertical communication are established and meaningful policy-making responsibilities are assigned throughout the structure.

Some authorities have indicated that the maximum number of employees that a manager can supervise directly is between six and ten. However, no rigid standard can be applied in this area. Instead, the optimum span of control is influenced by (1) the capability of the manager or supervisor, (2) the skills and commitment of the workers being supervised, (3) the level of difficulty and degree of similarity of the tasks assigned, and (4) the overall managerial process and the extent to which it is willing to trust subordinate employees with decision-making or other critical responsibilities.

Line and staff organization. This principle is drawn from classical organization theory and makes a distinction between two types of job functions. *Line* employees are generally regarded as those responsible for the central mission of the agency; in a recreation and park department, they would be the administrators, supervisors, leaders, specialists, foremen, and laborers. The line structure is usually perceived as a set of direct vertical relationships, or chain of command, through which authority flows. It is often considered to be the basic framework of the organization, since it is directly concerned with getting the job done.

In contrast, *staff* workers are not responsible for carrying out the central mission. In military units, for example, staff members are generally regarded as aides to executive officers rather than as attached to fighting units. Staff personnel are often given important advisory or consultative functions. In a given department, they might be involved in tasks related to public relations, research, systems analysis, budget development, and similar tasks. Usually they work directly with the administrator or his deputies and do not give orders or deal directly with personnel in lower line positions. Seen in another light, line workers are in a direct *vertical* line that is concerned with action and the delivery of services, whereas staff workers are generally placed in a *horizontal* position on an organization chart.

In the past, staff workers have often been regarded as subordinate to line personnel because of their advisory role. However, in recent years, their status has grown to the point where they often become responsible for initiating action. Typically, in a recreation and park system, the staff workers responsible for carrying out an analysis of maintenance operations may develop a report that leads to direct action, including the reassignment of personnel or phasing out of maintenance units.

In some large municipal recreation departments, because of civil service or union regulations that limit his flexibility in appointing line personnel, the administrator may choose to appoint advisors or consultants on fairly high levels of authority. Ostensibly, their role is to assist him as staff workers. However, in reality, they may serve as action deputies, playing an administrative rather than advisory role.

Within smaller recreation and park departments, the distinction between line and staff personnel is often blurred. Often, the department may have no workers who play a purely staff function; such roles may be filled by individuals employed by the municipal government itself (such as a budget analyst), rather than within the actual department.

Vertical and horizontal subsystems. Organizations are normally divided on the basis of both vertical and horizontal subsystems. The *vertical* division of personnel reflects the hierarchy of power—the basic chain of command. Position in the vertical structure generally determines the status, responsibilities, and rewards given to each employee. The *horizontal* differentiation of personnel is carried out through departmentalization. Normally, within productive enterprises, departmentalization is based on three factors: function, product, and location.

Function is used as a basis for departmentalization, when divisions are established on the basis of their fundamental assignment. In a recreation and park department, they are normally based on such elements as programs, facility development and maintenance, budget, personnel, or public relations.

Product departmentalization obviously would reflect responsibility for different products within a manufacturing company. In a large recreation and park department, it might be based on responsibility for different program elements, such as athletics, aquatics, cultural arts, programs for the handicapped, or playgrounds and day camps.

Location departmentalization is normally based on bringing all the administrative responsibilities within a geographical area into a single unit for effective management. It is illustrated in the customary division of a large city into several major districts or areas, each under the jurisdiction of an area supervisor.

Traditional administrative theory was primarily concerned with the chain of command and with the flow of power up and down the vertical structure of an organization. It tended to pay little attention to horizontal relationships between departments, administrative units, or individuals at approximately the same level.

However, as organizations have become more complex in their operations, it has become increasingly difficult to provide the needed coordination of various services within the vertical hierarchy.

To illustrate, a recreation and park agency might wish to initiate a major new program in a large community center. Several departments might be involved: the recreation program department (in the person of recreation leaders or supervisors), the maintenance department (representing building custodians and park foremen who would be responsible for maintaining indoor and outdoor facilities), the personnel department (which would have to assign full- and part-time additional personnel to the center), and the public relations department (which might wish to publicize the program or to consult with local residents in planning specific activities).

If full reliance were placed on the vertical structure for planning and decision-making, each responsible individual within each department in the center would have to go to his district superior, and so on up the chain of command, to obtain approval of specific plans for his department. Only at the top of the hierarchy would there be likely to be a process of joint planning. The decisions would then flow down the vertical chain of command to the line personnel responsible for taking action. If there were contradictions or problems in the operation, the process would have to be repeated.

In the past, it was recognized that problems of horizontal coordination by individuals on the same level but in different departments might be handled through the informal structure—that is, by personal contacts and agreements. However, these generally are not adequate to deal with major problems; in any case, they are dependent on the good will of all parties and have no binding effect.

Contemporary administrative theory therefore stresses the need to develop more effective coordinating mechanisms between the separate departments of an organization on the same horizontal level without having to resort to the vertical chain of command. Increasingly, this has been brought about by developing devices for improving interdepartmental communication and planning. These may include committees, task forces, coordinating teams, interdepartmental advisory staffs, and program managers. Increasingly, new operational units such as operations research teams and data processing centers for monitoring activity are being established.

Program management. Within large industrial or governmental organizations, a recent approach has been to develop formal managerial groups to provide integration of the diverse operations of the total organization. Program management is concerned with organizing and controlling all activities involved in attempting to reach organizational goals. To do this, it may find itself in conflict with the normal organizational structure and may require the elimination or addition of departmental components or the modification of existing patterns of information sharing or decision-making. Cleland writes:

> The program manager acts as a focal point for the concentration of attention on the major problems of the project. This concentration forces the channeling of major

program considerations through an individual who has the proper perspective to integrate relative matters of costs, time, technology and total project compatibility.[7]

Dynamic structure of organizations. Much current administrative theory is based on the growing realization of management experts that dramatic changes in the nature of organizations occur rapidly and that administration must be flexible enough to respond quickly and intelligently to such changes. Kast and Rosenzwieg comment:

> Increasingly, administrative organizations are accepting the necessity for changing their structure as a fact of life and are establishing permanent departments charged with the responsibility for organizational analysis and planning.[8]

In contrast to the carefully planned and rigid structure envisioned by scientific management theorists, many management experts today believe that large organizations must be less structured and must permit more frequent change of human roles and responsibilities, as well as more dynamic interaction among personnel on all levels. Within such a system, which Kast and Rosenzweig call the "adaptive-organic" structure, executives play less of a commanding role and instead become coordinators or links between different project groups or departments. They must be familiar with research and able to mediate effectively between different interests. "People will be differentiated not vertically according to rank and role, but flexibly according to skill and professional training."[9]

Current administrative theory thus borrows from both the past and the present. Such key principles as departmentalization, span of control, and differentiation of staff and line functions are still operative in most areas of public administration or industrial concerns. However, there is a new flexibility in terms of structure, communication, decision making, and the willingness to change in response to program needs.

Management science approach to administrative process

In terms of administrative *process* as opposed to organizational *structure*, the most recent innovations have been concerned with new methods of planning, decision-making, controlling and monitoring expenditures, work flow, and production, chiefly through the use of electronic data-processing equipment. Particularly in large industrial concerns and governmental operations, the computer has become a key administrative tool. It was indispensable, for example, in the development of so-called systems theory, which is central to most contemporary management innovation.

Systems theory. This approach is based on the view that organizations are complex systems comprised of subsystems with many interdependent parts and variations. In turn, the organizations are also parts themselves of larger governmental or economic systems. To administer an organization today, it is necessary to clearly understand these relationships and processes.

Since systems theory emphasizes the totality of internal and external systems and influences, models must be built to demonstrate these relationships. Two key aspects of these models are *equilibrium* and *feedback*.

The concept of equilibrium implies that most human or natural processes tend to achieve a state of relative balance or steadiness. This centers around a fixed point or level of balance, which is the normal state. When external forces are brought to bear on the system, modifications occur. If the system is a highly stable one, the forces needed to create change must be powerful. If it is unstable or precarious, even small outside forces may affect the equilibrium.

The concept of feedback refers to the process through which diagnostic information is gathered about the effects of various inputs or influences on the system. In highly automated systems, feedback may be used as a self-regulating device to control the rate or volume of production, as in the simple example of a home-heating thermostat. In more complex systems analysis operations, feedback is used to monitor the operation, providing a flow of information useful in modifying a model or actual on-the-job performance.

Systems analysis takes the position that to make intelligent decisions or to carry out the controlling function of administration, business or public administration planners must develop careful analyses of all the elements within the system and their relationships with and effects on each other. All parts of the operation must be integrated into a functional whole. Different courses of action that the administrator is considering must be analyzed systematically in terms of their relative costs and benefits and in terms of how they affect the entire system. Usually this is done by developing an analytical sequence or model for better understanding the problem. Timms[10] suggests a six-part sequence as a systems approach to problem-solving:

1. *Appraise the problem.* This involves stating the nature of the problem concisely and comprehensively.

2. *Analyze the problem.* Here all the elements of the problem and their implications or relationships are identified and measured.

3. *Develop a conceptual model of system.* This stage might involve identifying alternative courses of action but would end by proposing an ideal structure for dealing with the problem.

4. *Test the model.* This involves going back over the findings, reanalyzing the systems, evaluating conclusions, and developing the basis for a new and improved model.

5. *Propose a new model.* This may be repeated several times, each time with a model being developed that is believed to come closer to the ideal structure.

6. *Apply the model to quantitative systems analysis.* Here, appropriate mathematical techniques are used to analyze the proposed model, usually through computer study.

After each stage, the systems analyst may return to the start of the previous step to retrace his study, reevaluate the system in terms of new data, and ultimately propose an acceptable model. Obviously, this is a complicated process, demanding considerable expertise, particularly in terms of the mathematical analysis that is carried out on proposed models. Many large companies and governmental agencies have systems analysts or engineers who apply this approach to various aspects of the organization's operation.

Use in recreation and park administration. The systems approach is applied in many areas of government, especially in those fields in which a substantial number of different activities or operating units must be integrated into a common effort. The fields of transportation, pollution control, urban renewal, and space exploration are examples of such complex enterprises. It is particularly useful in large organizations, such as major urban, state, and federal agencies. In such settings, systems analysis may be used to establish priorities and planning needs, identify task components, and determine the most effective means of achieving objectives. Work flow is monitored and regulated, periodic performance reports are made, and the effectiveness of employees is precisely measured and graded. Broadly applied, the systems approach seeks to:

1. Establish detailed work objectives that specifically determine what, when, where, and how work is to be accomplished
2. Develop effective schedules for maintenance and repairing; group functions together for efficient performance
3. Develop standardized methods for job performance in which work routines are programmed, with time standards for completion

Fig. 2-1. Park Board members in Vancouver, British Columbia, **A,** examine the model of a model village development and **B,** make a field visit to a site for a potential new park with recreation and park planners. **C,** Favorable publicity is a key concern for recreation and park administrators. An attractive conservatory in the Vancouver Park System is used as a setting for television programs.

4. Provide instruments and techniques for effectively measuring and determining the cost of job performance to assist in evaluating employee work output and assigning tasks or planning budgets

To illustrate how systems analysis might apply in the recreation and park field, one might consider a problem in facilities maintenance. Traditionally, many small parks or large playground complexes have been assigned to a single custodian or gardener for year-round maintenance. Would a network of parks and other recreation facilities maintained on this basis (with larger parks divided into smaller 3- or 4-acre tracts, each with its own gardener) be efficiently managed?

The systems analysis approach would suggest that it would not be. Instead, a model of effective and economical maintenance would have to be developed, considering the different tasks that would have to be accomplished, the effects of different seasons of the year, and the work capabilities of men and machines. Each element in the process of park maintenance would be identified and analyzed: seeding, weeding, cutting and watering lawns, planting and pruning shrubs and flowers, litter control, tree care, and care of benches and other equipment. The rate of growth of each form of vegetation, the effects of use by city residents, and similar factors would be measured.

These different tasks would vary greatly. Some might have to be done on a daily basis, some weekly or monthly, and some only once or twice a year. Some might require roving teams of workers using heavy equipment, others might be done by automated equipment (daily watering of lawns, for example), and still others might continue to be carried on by single workers. All such factors would be examined, as well as the effect of imposing a different type of work assignment on individuals, before decisions for changing the maintenance system would be made. Ultimately, however, the final maintenance model would be developed, and it would, presumably, provide more effective maintenance on a year-round basis at lesser cost to the department.

More specific examples of how systems theory may be used in recreation and park administration are provided in Chapter 10, which demonstrates its application in the development of therapeutic recreation programs, and in resource planning.

PPBS. PPBS (*Planning-Program-Budgeting-Systems*), a specific method of applying systems theory, was developed in the early 1960s by the U.S. Department of Defense. It represents an attempt to build a planning mechanism that integrates information of all kinds into a single, coherent management system, with special emphasis on budgetary planning. PPBS requires the careful and precise development of goals and objectives, the preliminary evaluation of each program intended to meet these goals (measuring the projected benefits against the estimated costs), and the shaping of budget requests on the basis of this analysis and developing justification for the requests within the context of a long-range program and budgetary plan.

More broadly, PPBS may be used to deal with any aspect of governmental responsibility. Its key aspect is a systematic analysis of alternatives. This consists of:

1. Careful identification and description of governmental objectives, covering the range of agencies and programs
2. Projection of needs to future years
3. Explicit, systematic identification of alternative ways of reaching the objectives
4. Estimation of the total cost implications of each alternative, including capital and noncapital costs, as well as nondirect charges such as employee benefits or vehicle replacement and building maintenance costs
5. Estimation of the expected results of each alternative
6. Presentation of the resulting major cost and benefit trade-off among the alternatives, along with the identification of major assumptions and uncertainties, over the period of time ahead

In some cases, PPBS outlines several possible courses of action that may depend on other factors that cannot readily be predicted, such as economic growth or recession, population trends, and similar factors. The advantages of PPBS are that, when it is fully implemented by all government agencies in a city, it provides administrators, planners, legislators, budget personnel, and residents alike with a wide range of alternatives with respect to budget and program decision-making. Although PPBS is costly at the outset (computer analysis is a necessary element), it is believed that in the end the efficiency and rational contribution it makes to planning are worth the cost in terms of contemporary planning needs.

MBO. MBO (*Management By* Objectives) represents one of the most useful planning-and-control approaches to have been introduced in the past two decades. It emphasizes the joint involvement of supervisors and subordinate employees in the careful establishment of goals and in the regular evaluation of performance. Lower-level workers are given a much greater degree of responsibility and opportunity for showing initiative than in traditional job settings. Carroll and Tosi[11] report the observed effects of MBO:

1. Work activity is directed toward meeting organizational goals, and there is less likelihood of drifting into unessential directions.

2. Periodic MBO planning and review meetings force managers to think in terms of organization progress and to consider how all personnel decisions, schedules, and assignment of resources are affecting success in achieving goals.

3. It establishes useful criteria for control.

4. MBO encourages achievement-oriented behavior; employees become more fully involved in working toward goals they have set themselves, thus improving motivation.

5. Since objectives set by each manager reflect his or her personal styles and strengths, MBO is believed to make better uses of human resources within the organization.

6. Since MBO reduces uncertainty by clarifying what a manager is supposed

to accomplish and how his work will be measured, it reduces role conflict and improves morale.

7. Through work-review discussions held by managers and subordinate workers, problems in the system are quickly identified, and efforts are made to solve them.

PERT and CPM. PERT (*Program Evaluation Review Technique*) is one of the most significant recent developments in management science. Essentially it is a system of planning and control that uses mathematical concepts and computers to identify all key activities that must be carried out to accomplish a given project successfully. These are outlined in advance through the CPM (*Critical Path Method*) approach, which arranges each activity in a complicated flow sequence, showing the amount of time, kinds of resources, and human performance that will be required to accomplish each task. Dearden sums up PERT as "the science of using network techniques for the maximum utilization of manpower, machinery, and time in the accomplishment of a project."[12]

To do this, a "network" of essential activities is established in a logical time sequence. Starting and completion times for each task component (called *events*) are plotted to create a pictorial description of the time relationships involved in the total project. Through a system of arrows, it is shown which activities can be begun, based on which earlier ones have been completed. Every event in this network is assigned a number to simplify references to specific activities. The entire sequence is adapted to mathematical and computer analysis, and estimates are made as to its time demands (PERT-TIME) and financial requirements (PERT-COST).

The chief purpose of PERT-TIME analysis is to keep management informed about the progress of a project. By sharply identifying each activity and expected time of accomplishment as well as which activities are essential before beginning other activities, it provides a means of monitoring and planning project time schedules effectively. In summary, Dearden[13] indicates that PERT-TIME will:

1. Present an organized plan for the project's completion
2. Provide an estimated time of completion
3. Identify the critical activities
4. Identify those activities whose completion can be stretched out and the maximum time they can be extended
5. Provide a means for making economic trade-offs between the cost penalties of being late, and the cost penalties for reducing the scheduled time

In general, both PERT-TIME and PERT-COST are seen as having the advantages of forcing planners to consider and carefully plan all the elements of projects well in advance, to recognize their relationships, and to test out alternative ways of completing a project. During the process of implementation, it provides immediate feedback on progress and allows management to divert resources from activities that have slack time to others.

Because of its complexity and expense, the full PERT system is not used by many recreation and park agencies. However, its basic principles may be used effectively in planning and carrying out recreation programs or major facilities development projects.

Conflict resolution. Unlike MBO and PERT, which are rather complex planning systems, conflict resolution grows out of a recent trend in administrative theory. The traditional view of conflict within any governmental or business organization was that it was harmful and should be avoided or prevented at all costs. It was thought that any employee who caused conflict was a troublemaker, and authoritarian or legalistic means were used to deal with such workers. It was the major responsibility of administrators to *prevent* conflict.

In modern administrative theory, a somewhat different view prevails. Many experts believe that conflict is not only inevitable but that it is desirable and may be used to constructive ends. This is based on the view that it is necessary for organizations to adapt and change to survive. Conflict, which often stems from sharply contrasting points of view or from individuals or groups who refuse to accept traditional or establishment approaches, may lead to problem-solving or other adjustments that help the organization move more effectively toward its goals.

The effort then must *not* simply be to reduce or eliminate conflicts when they appear. Instead, the creative administrator may actually encourage them to some degree and should certainly seek to use them to benefit and support the goals of the organization. Conflict management and resolution, seen in this light, become important responsibilities in modern management practice.

THE HUMAN SIDE OF ADMINISTRATION

More than any other responsibility, modern management science must be understood as having a significant concern with the problem of human relations. McFarland makes this point strongly:

> The process of management is largely a social one, since it so largely involves the interrelationships of people at work. There is a base of technology, machinery, engineering processes, physical properties, financial assets, and other non-human elements that are an important part of management. Yet it is through the human effort called management that these non-human resources are made to provide for our needs and wants. Management integrates the efforts of individuals and groups; it operates as a process whereby the organization comes to function as a whole.[14]

Although a number of researchers have contributed to the development of the industrial humanism approach described earlier in this chapter, one more than any other focused his attention on the human side of the professional manager's role. Douglas McGregor, a leading social psychologist, was deeply concerned with problems of human motivation and incentive and with the effects of different types of reward and punishment systems on productivity and morale. He stressed that the traditional reliance on extrinsic rewards as a means of promoting interest and effort is not as effective as developing a sense of internal commitment and satisfaction and thus providing intrinsic rewards for personnel.

Based on recent studies in industrial social psychology, McGregor laid bare the effects of group influence on worker behavior and the nature of interpersonal transactions on various levels of management. Unlike earlier spokesmen for the human relations approach to management, it was his view that conventional organization theory is meaningless and that human beings in organizations do not behave the way theory says they should:

> . . . it would not, in any sense, be an exaggeration to assert that any large organization would come to a grinding halt within a month if all its members began behaving strictly in accordance with the structure of responsibility and authority defined by the formal organization chart, the position descriptions, and the formal controls.[15]

Instead, McGregor held that the actual working of large organizations involves many more complex relationships and roles, realistic accommodations, problem-solving, and forms of cooperative behavior on many levels than is implied in the simplistic models of formal organizational structure. It was his concern to develop the highest possible level of sensitivity and openness on the part of managers and to help them rely less on the formal authority invested in them than on their own capabilities with respect to technical knowledge and management skills.

Generally, McGregor's approach was to urge that people be freed to operate more fully in an atmosphere of self-direction, autonomy, and trust. He cited much evidence to show that, although this method of management appears to involve serious risks of failure, it yields both a better emotional climate and higher levels of production when put into effect. On the other hand, reliance on rigid authority, threats, rewards, and punishments as aspects of a manager's style generally results in resistance, insecurity, and poor performance by subordinates.

McGregor described the characteristics of a managerial team (considered to be the top management of any major subsystem in business of government) to include the following, when intelligently directed:

1. *Understanding, mutual agreement, and identification with respect to the primary task.* It is essential that all members of the team agree on their priorities and fundamental responsibilities.

2. *Open communications.* It is essential that sound decisions must depend on full awareness of all the relevant facts—including not only information or logistical knowledge but also feelings and emotions. "Genuinely open expression of ideas *and* feelings—what some have referred to as leveling—is a necessary condition for effective functioning in a managerial team."[16]

3. *Mutual trust.* Recognizing that trust is a delicate property of human relationships, McGregor said that it must exist among all members of a managerial team if it is to be successful. Essentially it implies that people must have confidence in each other and willingness to rely on each other for support in matters of crucial self-concern. Trust, he points out, can best be built by consistent action over a period of time, rather than by words.

4. *Mutual support.* Mutual support, which is closely related to the need for open communications and trust, implies that members of a managerial unit should be freed from the need to defend or protect themselves and able to contribute their abilities more fully to the overall task of the team.

5. *Management of human differences.* Inevitably, in any group effort, there will be disagreements and conflicts, based on different points of view or perceptions of self-interest or on personality disputes. The successful management of such disagreements, rather than simply attempting to suppress them, is essential if decisions are to be reached that can be carried out rather than sabotaged. At the same time, imposing a conformity of belief or denying the managerial team the right to move for creative solutions to problems harms overall morale and effort. Therefore, McGregor stressed the need to work through differences through a genuine interchange of views and a meaningful group process.

Beyond these guidelines, McGregor also argued for *selective use of the team* in appropriate task situations; for encouraging and developing *appropriate member skills* in terms of working effectively as members of the managerial team; and, finally, for extending the *leadership* (the personal qualifications, skills, role, and strategy) of the team manager. The T-group method of social interaction in a learning situation has become widely used in managerial and other personnel training programs and has led to a proliferation of so-called encounter groups, sensitivity groups, and similar approaches to improving human relationships in social or business situations.

How relevant is this approach to recreation and park administrative concerns? On two levels, it would appear to be extremely important. First, recreation and park administrators must work closely with the heads of various departments—both within their own organization and elsewhere in the municipal government structure. Second, within any large bureaucratic structure, there frequently is the problem of a substantial number of line personnel who are relatively autonomous and who, if their sense of morale and personal commitment is poor, are likely to make only limited contributions to the total enterprise.

Generally, more intensive supervision and threats of punishment for nonperformance do not result in improving the situation; instead, a more creative approach is likely to be effective. Finally, for the recreation and park administrator or supervisor who attempts to work with advisory councils or groups of local citizens, it is essential that there be an understanding of human dynamics, group behavior, and open communication and trust.

Suggested topics for class discussion or examination questions

1. Define the essential nature of administration in governmental agencies or business enterprises, and outline the major elements or stages involved in the administrative process.
2. Compare the fundamental principles or philosophy of the *scientific management* or *machine model* approach to administration to the *industrial humanism* model. Which, in your judgment, prevails in large business concerns today? In governmental service?
3. What are the key elements required to establish an emotional climate among workers in a large bureaucratic system that will promote high morale and maximum work output? What factors militate against establishing such a climate?

REFERENCES

1. McFarland, Dalton E.: *Management: Principles and Practices,* New York, 1970, Macmillan, Inc., p. 5.
2. Kast, Fremont E., and Rosenzwieg, James F.: *Organization and Management, a Systems Approach,* New York, 1970, McGraw-Hill Book Co., p. 7.
3. Rodney, Lynn S.: *Administration of Public Recreation,* New York, 1964, The Ronald Press Co., pp. 27-52.

4. Dimock, Marshall E., and Dimock, Gladys O.: *Public Administration,* New York, 1969, Holt, Rinehart & Winston, Inc., p. 5.
5. Nigro, Felix A.: *Modern Public Administration,* New York, 1970, Harper & Row, Inc., p. 87.
6. Golembiewski, Robert T.: *Men, Management and Morality: Toward a New Organizational Ethic,* New York, 1965, McGraw-Hill Book Co., p. 65.
7. Cleland, David I.: "Why Project Management?" *Business Horizons,* Winter, 1964, p. 83.
8. Kast and Rosenzweig, *op. cit.:* pp. 203-205.
9. Bennis, Warren G.: *Changing Organizations,* New York, 1966, McGraw-Hill Book Co., p. 12.
10. Timms, Howard L.: Introduction to Operations Management, Homewood, Ill., 1967, Richard D. Irwin, Inc., pp. 92-94.
11. Carroll, Stephen, and Tosi, Henry, Jr.: *Management by Objectives: Applications and Research,* New York, 1973, Macmillan, Inc.
12. Dearden, John: *Computers in Business Management,* Homewood, Ill., 1966, Dow Jones-Irwin, Inc., p. 203.
13. *Ibid.:* p. 211.
14. McFarland, *op. cit.:* p. 5.
15. McGregor, Douglas: *The Professional Manager,* New York, 1967, McGraw-Hill Book Co. Used with permission of McGraw-Hill Book Co.
16. McGregor, *ibid.:* p. 36.

CHAPTER 3

STRUCTURE AND ORGANIZATION OF RECREATION AND PARK AGENCIES

The previous chapters have described the current scope of recreation and park departments and agencies in the United States and Canada and have presented a number of the basic concepts of modern administrative practice. This chapter is primarily concerned with the structure and organization of public recreation and park departments, although it also provides illustrations of several major types of voluntary, commercial, and therapeutic agencies. It includes the following:

1. The legal basis for the establishment of public recreation and park departments on the local level
2. The major types of municipal, town, or county public recreation departments
3. The composition and function of recreation and park boards and commissions
4. Examples of organization charts of public recreation and park agencies
5. Examples of voluntary, commercial, and therapeutic organizations: governance and structure

LEGAL BASIS FOR LOCAL RECREATION AND PARK AGENCIES

Local government—viewed here as cities, counties, towns, boroughs, townships, school districts, or park and recreation districts—must normally function within a framework of enabling legislation.

In the early decades of the recreation movement, many playgrounds and summer programs for youth were carried on by private initiative and with the support of charitable funds. As local governments began to assume the responsibility for operating recreation facilities and programs, they often did so on the basis of the police powers granted them by their states. Providing local government "the right to frame and enforce reasonable measures for the protection of health, life, property, and morals," these were frequently used to justify governmental functions intended to serve the common welfare. In other cases, local government action was based on general welfare clauses or the provisions of local home-rule charters provided for in state constitutions.

However, as this became a more important function and the range of facilities and services increased, there began to develop a need for special legislation that would give municipalities the requisite powers for operating recreation and park programs. It is important to understand that local governments are not autonomous units; they are governmental units created by their states and must normally have legal authorization to carry out specific acts.

Special recreation and park laws. One approach to state legislation supporting local recreation and park functions was the *special law*. These were laws passed by state legislatures, many of which are operative today, empowering individual cities or towns to sponsor recreation and park facilities and programs. Usually they dealt with specific types of facilities, such as auditoriums, community buildings, stadiums, swimming pools, or golf courses and provided legal authorization for taxing, floating bonds, or otherwise funding such ventures. In some cases they were passed to permit such program features as band concerts, music or opera programs, or Sunday recreation programs.

Regulatory laws. A second type of state legislation affecting recreation was the *regulatory law*. These represent laws passed by state governments that seek to control, license, censor, or supervise recreation programs to protect the public's health, safety, and general well-being. They usually apply not only to governmental agencies but to voluntary, commercial, and private organizations as well. For example, most states have laws controlling the sale of liquor or admission to bars, the speed of motorboats and licensing of pilots, the length of hunting seasons, the sanitary conditions of swimming pools or other facilities, and similar matters.

Enabling laws. The major type of state legislation affecting recreation and parks is the *enabling law*. These state laws empower local units of government to acquire, develop, and maintain recreation and park areas and to operate programs under leadership. Such laws vary from state to state. In some cases they apply only to certain types of municipalities, but in others they include county government and school districts as well. Some briefly describe the performance of the function and authorize the expenditure of tax funds for it. Others list the powers, structure, and procedures of the managing agency in detail. Butler[1] suggests that state enabling acts should include the following provisions, unless they are already included in other state laws:

1. Enabling legislation for recreation and parks should apply to all cities, towns, villages, counties, school districts, and other governmental units in the state.

2. It should permit any two or more such units to combine in the administration and financing of recreation facilities and programs.

3. Governing bodies of local political units should be allowed to dedicate and set aside for recreation use any lands or buildings owned or leased by them and not already assigned to other public use.

4. Municipalities should have the power to acquire and spend money for land and buildings or other recreation facilities, both within and outside their boundaries. This includes the right to initiate bonding programs for the acquisition of land or buildings.

5. Municipalities should be specifically authorized to establish, operate, and maintain playgrounds, recreation centers, and other facilities and to operate programs in them, with tax monies taken from general or special funds or both.

6. Municipalities should be permitted to assign responsibility for operating such facilities or programs to existing school boards, park boards, or other bodies or to establish separate recreation boards or commissions, as they choose.

7. They should be authorized to equip and maintain areas and facilities, conduct a variety of recreation programs for all the people in a community, employ professional and other workers, and cooperate with other public or private agencies in providing programs.

Butler also suggests that enabling laws should contain provisions stipulating whether a recreation board or commission must be established by the local community and, if so, the manner of its appointment, number of members, and responsibilities. Other provisions may have to do with the power to reject or accept real estate or other gifts or bequests and to use the facilities of other municipal or county agencies, provided such use does not conflict with their programs.

It is important to understand that state law is *permissive* rather than *mandatory* in this respect. It permits local communities to pass their own laws or ordinances establishing recreation and park programs, but it does not compel them to do so.

Park or recreation district laws. In some states, a special type of enabling legislation has been passed that permits two or more municipalities or other political subdivisions to establish joint park or recreation programs. Normally this is done by setting up independent districts that function in this area of government only. As in the case of regular enabling legislation, such recreation or park district laws may include provisions dealing with the power to acquire, develop, and maintain recreation areas and facilities, sponsor programs, and employ personnel.

They also usually stipulate:

1. The minimum number of legal residents required and population required within a potential district
2. Methods of annexing additional land for the park or recreation district
3. Procedures to be followed in petitioning to have a district established
4. Composition of the managing board or commission; usually, since the powers assigned to them are higher than those given to the board of a regular recreation or park department, they are required to be elected rather than appointed

Illinois is an example of a state in which the district system has been well established by state law and local practice. A number of larger districts have extremely well-developed park or recreation facilities; usually they have their own taxing power and provide services normally offered only by local government units, such as independent police forces, highway maintenance personnel, and similar services.

Home-rule legislation. Many states encourage a high level of local self-determination by permitting municipalities and counties to develop their own charters for home-rule government. If provision for recreation and parks is not made in the original charter, it may be added in the form of a charter amendment that provides general authority for this function, to be followed by later, more specific ordinances outlining the responsibilities and powers of government in this area.

Liability in recreation and parks. One other aspect of law that must be considered in administering recreation and parks is the question of liability. Obviously, in any field of activity involving sports, outdoor recreation, use of equipment of many kinds, and different age groups, there is the possibility of lawsuit. Public recreation and park departments may be held liable for personal injury, committing nuisances, infringing on property rights of others, ignoring contractual obligations, and similar actions. The most serious of these is the problem of personal injury. Although recreation and parks, like other municipal departments, would normally be covered by municipal insurance plans covering both staff and participants, it is necessary to take careful precautions to protect the public.

In general, lawsuits based on injury claims are settled on the basis of the circumstances of the actual case, such as the degree of negligence involved. However, municipal government generally is held to be liable less frequently in those states where judicial decisions have held recreation to be a governmental rather than a proprietary function. This implies that it is considered to be a legitimate and necessary service in terms of meeting important public needs. The term *proprietary* in this context implies that the function is a less significant one and is carried on in a manner isolated from the stream of normal governmental process.

Example of recreation and park legislation. A good example of local recreation and park legislation may be found in the Dallas City Charter, as adopted in 1907 and amended in 1968. In Chapter XXII of the charter, under the heading of *Park and Recreation Department*, sections appear with the following titles:

Section 1. Park and Recreation Department
Section 2. Organization of Board and Terms of Office of Members
Section 3. Board Vacancies, How Filled
Section 4. Jurisdiction of the Park and Recreation Board—Scope of Activity
Section 5. Appointment of Employees—Rules and Regulations
Section 6. Police Authority
Section 7. Conflicts between Park and Recreation Board and Other Boards to be Determined by the City Council
Section 8. Reports
Section 9. Disbursement of Funds
Section 10. Titles and Signatures

The heart of this legislation lies in Section 4, dealing with the powers and jurisdiction of the Park and Recreation Board. Specifically, and in considerable detail, the board is authorized to carry out eighteen functions, several of which are summarized here: (1) to control and manage a variety of city-owned properties; (2) to manage, maintain, and repair buildings in the park system; (3) to establish rules and regulations in park and recreation facilities and programs;

(4) to supervise and equip playgrounds and playfields and to conduct programs in them; (5) to make charges for services on park properties and grant lease or concession rights in them; (6) to be responsible for plants and trees on public properties throughout the city; (7) to maintain an animal zoo; (8) to police parks and certain other public properties; (9) to make all contracts necessary to carry out its function; (10) to enter into cooperative agreements with other public agencies for joint use of facilities; (11) to contract for the use of Fair Park, a large fairgrounds owned by the city; (12) to maintain abandoned cemeteries as park properties; (13) to conduct a variety of public events on park properties; and (14) to cooperate with civic, historical, or other appropriate non-profit organizations to promote community welfare.

MAJOR TYPES OF RECREATION AND PARK AGENCIES

There have been several distinct approaches to the problem of establishing recreation and park departments within a framework of local government. Based on such factors as the provisions found in enabling legislation or other state or provincial laws, political factors, and prevailing governmental trends, local provision for recreation and parks may take any of the following forms:

1. Separate recreation department, operating under its own board or commission, or simply as a unit of local government
2. Separate park department, operating under its own board or commission, or simply as a unit of local government
3. Separate department or simply an area of adjunctive service provided by local school board
4. Combined or merged recreation and park department, including functions of both existing agencies within a single structure
5. Assignment of responsibility for public recreation services, all or in part, to another agency of local government, such as a police department, welfare department, highway department, housing authority, or youth commission
6. Jointly operated programs, sponsored by contractual agreements, between municipal government and a school board, or as a consortium between municipal government and a voluntary agency, or by a combination of several separate units of local government

During the early decades of the recreation movement, it was a common practice to have a separate park department, established during the last years of the nineteenth century, operating side by side with a recreation department formed during the early twentieth century. In some cases there existed only a park department, which provided playgrounds and other recreation opportunities, usually of an outdoor type. In other cases, a recreation department was established that operated playgrounds, small parks, pools, and other physical facilities throughout the city, During this period, there tended to be a heated argument about which agency was best equipped to provide recreation services within the modern community.

Recreation as an independent government function. The following arguments were made for recreation as a separate responsibility of government, to be provided by an independent recreation department: (1) it was a unique function and should be given visibility by having its own department; (2) if made independent, it would receive the undivided attention it required and would not be lost in the general concerns of a larger agency; and (3) an independent recreation department would be in a better position to coordinate total community efforts in recreation and to be given an adequate budget.

On the other hand, it was argued by others that (1) having recreation as a separate agency unnecessarily creates another governmental operation whose function could be carried out by existing ones; (2) this would add to governmental overhead and the burden of administrative operations; and (3) since recreation departments must depend on park departments and school districts for the use of their facilities, it would be better to assign *them* the recreation function rather than to establish a new and unnecessary department.

Recreation as a school board function. Similarly, there were heated disagreements about the desirability of having school boards or districts assume responsibility for sponsoring public recreation programs.

Those in favor of this administrative arrangement held that schools possess the facilities, manpower, and contact with children and youth needed to operate successful recreation programs; that they already have the standing and financial resources needed to carry out this function; and that recreation and education are closely allied processes, with recreation serving to extend educational learning and achieve important educational outcomes.

On the other hand, those who have opposed the schools as community recreation sponsors have held that school facilities are limited and cannot meet the total leisure needs of the community; that school personnel, although they may possess useful skills and general preparation for working with children and youth, do *not* have a sound preparation in the area of recreation; that educational administrators generally are not convinced of the importance of recreation as a school function and fail to support it adequately; and that when financial pressures compel educational retrenchment, recreation, along with other noncurricular functions of the school, is likely to be cut sharply.

Over the last few decades, the scope of community recreation has become so broad—in terms of the kinds of population groups served and the varied program elements offered—that few school systems have been able to meet the contemporary challenge in this field. In addition, many school systems, struggling with their own philosophical, financial, and social problems, have recognized their inadequacy to do the kind of resourceful and visionary planning needed to provide a vigorous community recreation program.

Summing up, schools today have three roles with respect to recreation:

1. To sponsor community recreation directly, particularly in those states (as in California) where the state education code lends strong support to this function, including the power to tax directly for this purpose

2. To co-sponsor recreation programs with other agencies, by contractual arrangement, under which the school is responsible for specific aspects of the program that it is best equipped to handle
3. To provide facilities, such as gymnasiums, auditoriums, art and music rooms, or outdoor sports facilities that may be used by other municipal recreation agencies or community organizations.

In addition to this, schools should have the responsibility of *educating for leisure*—a function first assigned to them by the Cardinal Principles of Secondary Education published by the National Education Association in 1918.

This vital task should include not only teaching skills for the constructive and creative use of leisure in such areas as physical education, art, music, theater, and the like but also of helping to develop an understanding of the role of leisure and recreation in one's personal life and in community development. It has become an important priority, particularly in school systems that have undertaken vigorous community education programs (Chapter 9).

Consolidation of recreation and park functions. As the provision of recreation services expanded in the United States and Canada after World War II, it became clear that there was little justification for maintaining separate recreation and park departments with similar or overlapping functions in many communities. Thus there was a trend toward the consolidation of municipal recreation and park functions in local government during the 1950s and 1960s. Arnold sums up the positive arguments in favor of linking recreation and park functions in single departments.[21] It was believed that consolidation contributed to:

1. Stimulation of long-range planning and concerted effort toward the development of more adequate areas and facilities
2. A reduction in the complexities of government
3. Simplification of operating procedures
4. Closer coordination between facilities and program
5. Reduced overlapping or duplication of services

TABLE 1

Types of recreation and park agencies reported in 1961 and 1966*

	1961	1966
Combined recreation and park	466	1,304
Separate recreation	949	818
Separate park	543	428
School department	274	142
Other public agencies	530	425
Private agencies†	206	25

*From Recreation and park yearbook, 1961, New York, 1961, National Recreation Association, p. 32; and Recreation and park yearbook, 1966, Washington, D.C., 1966, National Recreation and Park Association, p. 32.
†Since these are reported in a listing of local public agencies, the assumption is that "private" agencies are voluntary agencies that receive public support and have quasi-official responsibility for meeting community recreation needs.

6. An increase in the prestige of the service and a clearer interpretation of the program for the public
7. Budget savings in some cases
8. Improved services at all levels, including equipment, personnel, and the maintenance and appearance of facilities
9. Centralization of responsibility and authority, with improved efficiency overall

Recreation and parks are now accepted as logically *combined* functions of municipal and county administration. This is illustrated by the shift of agency titles in the period between 1961 and 1966.

There is general agreement that this has been a desirable shift in administrative structure, although in many municipal departments full integration of recreation and park services has not yet been achieved. In some cities, the past loyalties of divisional administrators have kept them from working effectively together. In some cases, when recreation has been absorbed into an existing park department, program personnel have been kept subservient to maintenance or custodial personnel. Typically, a community center director may be unable to give specific directions to the building's custodian (who is technically his counterpart, within the division of maintenance) without having such directions approved by a central departmental office. In other cases, maintenance personnel still have control of major facilities, such as golf courses, swimming pools, or athletic fields, which should be operated by recreation leaders and supervisors. Such situations are found most frequently in larger and older cities.

The cities that have been most successful in overcoming such problems of divided or conflicting authority between recreation- and park-oriented personnel are those that have combined *both* functions in all key supervisory and administrative positions. Thus there is no problem of conflict of interest or divided authority, and the line personnel who actually carry out programs or maintain facilities are given clear-cut and efficiently organized responsibilities.

Other sponsorship patterns in local government. In addition to the kinds of administrative patterns just described, many American and Canadian communities have developed other types of sponsorship patterns for providing local recreation services. Several examples follow.

Specialized municipal agencies. Particularly in large cities with diverse needs, it is not uncommon for other municipal departments to assume responsibility for providing recreation programs for special populations. For example, many cities have youth boards or divisions, which meet the varied needs of adolescents, including recreation. Others have special departments that assist aging persons in the community with multiservice programs, including recreation. Large cities with many low-income housing projects may have public housing authorities that conduct their own recreation programs. In addition, departments of social services or welfare or police and fire departments may also directly provide recreation or give auxiliary services. In still other cities, museums, zoos, libraries, or tax-supported cultural agencies may have significant recreation roles.

Since such agencies exist side by side with the major public agency having a primary responsibility for recreation, it is essential that every effort be made to develop a high level of coordination and cooperative planning among them.

Joint operation by several governmental units. Not uncommonly, several governmental units that overlap geographically, such as a city, county, and school district, may develop contractual relationships for jointly sponsoring recreation programs. As an example, the City of Pasadena, California, the Los Angeles County Board of Supervisors, and the Pasadena Board of Education (which extends into two Los Angeles County districts) share responsibilities for providing recreation programs and facilities through a carefully worked-out formula. All school facilities, such as pools and gymnasiums, are made available without charge to the Pasadena Recreation Department. Conversely, all municipal facilities, including twenty-two parks, a civic auditorium, and the Rose Bowl, are made available by the city park department without charge to jointly operated programs. The director of recreation is regarded as a key school official and is directly responsible to the superintendent of schools; however, he is also considered a city department head. Such arrangements provide the maximum opportunity for intelligent planning of all facilities for public use.

A less common arrangement is one in which several different governmental units that do *not* overlap geographically agree to share responsibility for conducting a joint program. An example may be found in NOR-WEST (Regional Special Services Program), in northern Westchester County, New York. This agency was formed to meet the special recreation needs of the handicapped children and adults in four neighboring area (Town of Cortlandt, Village of Ossining, City of Peekskill, and Town of Yorktown). Although these towns and communities were not able, individually, to mount quality programs for the handicapped, they were able to do so cooperatively. With an annual budget of about $50,000 and much volunteer help, they now provide special programs for the disabled throughout the four areas. Policies are set by a board consisting of the recreational directors of the four communities, with the NOR-WEST director casting a deciding vote.

Joint operation by government and voluntary agency. Another example of joint sponsorship is found in the Village of Mt. Kisco, New York. Here the village has entered into a cooperative agreement with the Mt. Kisco Boys' Club. Both organizations share a budget of several hundred thousand dollars (about half tax funds and half raised through voluntary efforts) with a joint staff and full interchange of facilities. A large indoor center is provided by the Boys' Club, and the Recreation Commission provides chiefly outdoor facilities. Through this arrangement the jointly operated program is able to take advantage of both the strength and stability of its governmental status and the flexibility and private status of the Boys' Club.

RECREATION AND PARK BOARDS AND COMMISSIONS

A key element in the administration of recreation and parks is the role played by departmental boards and commissions. These are established to oversee and direct the work of the administrator of the department, and they have their composition and functions defined by law. They fall into three broad categories:

1. Completely *separate and independent* bodies with full authority for establishing and overseeing policy
2. *Semi-independent* bodies, with the power to make policy but dependent to some extent on a higher legislative or governmental body
3. *Advisory* boards or commissions, with powers generally limited to making recommendations

The titles of *board* and *commission* are generally used interchangeably. In some cases, the functioning organization itself may be known as the Recreation or Park Board or Commission. In other cases, it may be known as a Recreation and Park Department, operating *under* a Board or Commission.

Boards and commissions may be either elected or appointed. Appointment is generally done by the mayor, city manager, or county executive officer, sometimes with the approval of the city council or county board of supervisors. Park or recreation districts usually elect their boards, just as school districts do. Boards normally have between five and seven members, although they may have as few as three or as many as eleven members. Customarily, they serve for overlapping 3-year terms so that there are always some members with experience on the board and some new members each year. Generally, board membership should reflect various groups in the community in terms of age, socioeconomic, religious, and racial or ethnic background. They may also be selected to represent different community agencies or service organizations. In addition, a member of the city council or school board may be assigned to serve ex officio on a community's recreation and park board.

It is important that some members of the board possess clout or major influence in the community. Although intelligence and dedication are essential qualities, unless they also have personal dynamism and drive the best efforts of the board may die aborning. Bank presidents, powerful politicians, successful businessmen, or strong union officials—one or more of these can add great strength to a board or commission.

Boards or commissions often are organized into standing committees, elect officers, and meet regularly, with agendas planned as follows:

1. Call to order, roll call to determine whether a quorum is present, and review and approval of the previous meeting's minutes
2. Hearing of announcements and communications
3. Report and discussion of the department executive
4. Unfinished business, new business, and adjournment

It is *extremely* important that accurate minutes be kept of all meetings, because decisions are made that provide the basis of many department actions and policies. If such minutes are not kept and reviewed, controversy is likely to ensue.

Functions of boards and commissions

In general, recreation and park boards and commissions serve to interpret the work of their department to the community and to develop the support—

both moral and financial—of citizens and political groups. It is their task to approve all policies and to develop plans for meeting the present and future recreation needs of the community being serviced. They should consider and approve all personnel appointments or promotions and determine personnel functions and salaries, operating within a civil service structure. They must be involved in all facility planning decisions and should develop long-range planning, in cooperation with other municipal agencies, for recreational needs.

Specifically, their functions may include:

1. To define the objectives of public recreation and parks and to develop policies and plans that will realize these goals
2. To select the department executive and define his professional responsibilities
3. To interpret the role of recreation and park service to the general public and to feed back the reactions and wishes of the public to the recreation director and his staff
4. To maintain effective liaison between the recreation and park administrator and other governmental agencies or officials
5. To establish personnel and employment guidelines or standards and to be involved in the process of hiring, promotion, and firing
6. To develop an effective fiscal plan for the department and to review and give final approval to budget requests; to oversee and approve all departmental contracts, leases, or similar commitments.
7. To perform all acts necessary to acquire, develop, and maintain recreation and park facilities and to provide stability to the general operation of the department
8. To review, evaluate, and report regularly on the work of the department, in relation to its overall objectives

Some recreation and park boards or commissions are extremely vigorous, whereas others are lackadaisical in their approach. It is important to draw a sharp distinction between their role in *determining* policy and their potential role in *administering* policy. They should *not* interfere with the functions of the departmental administrator by attempting to dictate how the details of administration should be carried out and meddling with department routines or developing close relationships with his subordinates. Although a board's approval is normally required for many specific administrative acts, such as hiring and firing, the acts themselves should be clearly regarded as the domain of the administrator.

Bannon comments:

> How the relationship between a lay board and the recreation director is balanced has always been crucial; today it is even more so. . . .
> Another way of viewing director/board relationships . . . is that the board generally makes *value* decisions, and the director makes *factual* decisions formulated on these values.[3]

The tendency for a board or its members to interfere in the administration of a department often begins inadvertently and without deliberate intent. The evil effects can be devastating, however. A board member expresses interest in gaining more knowledge of the workings of the department—an innocuous request. As the executive officer provides additional reports, photographs, and plans, introduces board members to more of his staff, and takes them on tours of his operations, new relationships develop.

Board members take a liking to certain subordinate staff members and begin calling them separately, requesting information or small favors that the executive might not approve. Other members may become so familiar with certain operations of the department that they will go out individually into the community and and speak officially for the department, perhaps contradicting the executive or making seemingly official promises of service that the department is unable to deliver.

This relationship is a highly delicate and sensitive one, and it takes the utmost skill on the part of the professional executive to keep the interest, enthusiasm, and dedication of his board members high while clearly retaining direct control over the administration of his department. This is one of the most telling tests of the true professional.

As indicated, once the board or commission has defined the objectives of the department, established written policies, and hired an administrator, it must be prepared to delegate real authority to him. On the other hand, the administrator must be open with his board, provide it with all important or relevant information, seek its advice on all controversial matters, efficiently carry out its policies, and weigh its views seriously. It helps greatly for board members to be tolerant, tactful, and willing to work hard and to support the work of the administrator before the public and community groups.

In terms of community relations, Sternloff suggests that:

1. Boards or commissions should seek to truly know the community and the recreational aspirations of those being served.

2. They should establish and publicize channels of communication so that citizens can easily bring their proposals to the board.

3. They should publish agendas of their meetings in advance to inform the public of what is to be discussed, particularly when special meetings to consider new projects or community needs are being held.

4. Boards should conduct open meetings and encourage public attendance.

5. They should report all discussions and decisions to the public.

6. They should publicly recognize and encourage community residents who have made significant contributions to the recreation and park program.[4]

Recent trends in board and commission functioning. Many of the most successful recreation and park departments established in the decades before and after World War II were sharply centralized operations. They were directed by highly capable, dynamic administrators, who had the strong support of influential civic leaders and business executives on their boards. During the mid-1960s, this began to change. Increasingly, there were vigorous demands for representation by more varied groups in society—blacks, the Spanish-speaking, women, youth, the aged, environmentalists, the poor, and similar constituencies.

Many boards and commissions expanded to as many as fifteen to twenty members and became increasingly vocal in exerting pressure on their departments. Even as this cut into the administrator's capability for independent action, a second trend appeared in many large cities—decentralization. More and more, decision-making and the determination of priorities and bugetary allocations were assigned to district levels in such cities. Citizen groups had their say through Model Cities Committees, Community Planning Boards, Little City Halls, and Mayors' Task Forces.

The tendency in such communities was to undermine the authority of the legally constituted board or commission and to necessitate great numbers of hearings and planning sessions with community groups, all of which made it difficult, if not impossible, to proceed with the traditional board-director relationship. Indeed, in a number of larger cities throughout the United States, public recreation and park departments that had operated for decades under policy-making citizen commissions have repealed ordinances or changed their charters, so that their boards or commissions now have advisory functions only. Today, administrators in such cities have become directly accountable to the mayor or city manager and council rather than to citizen boards.

This trend has not affected most cities, towns, and villages with smaller populations, which continue to operate under the traditional board or commission structure.

Boards of voluntary and therapeutic agencies

[handwritten margin note: many operate under similar Advisory on policy making structures.]

Although most textbooks on recreation and park administration focus only on the role of boards and commissions in public recreation and parks, many voluntary and therapeutic agencies also operate under advisory or policy-making boards. Several illustrations will be given here of such arrangements: Boys' Clubs of America, Girl Scouts of the U.S.A., National Jewish Welfare Board, and two independent organizations, the San Francisco Recreation Center for the Handicapped, and the Northern Minnesota Therapeutic Camp.

Boys' Clubs of America. Typical of many large national organizations, the Boys' Clubs organization publishes a constitution and set of by-laws to assist local chapters or units around the country in developing their own structure and operating procedures. An individual Boys' Club may choose to be structured as a corporation, association, or administrative committee, although it is generally recommended that it be a corporation under existing state laws. This arrangement assures that there will be a large group of representative citizens closely associated with the organization and having responsibility for its development. The overall membership then is responsible for electing a board of directors, who directly oversee club operations.

The suggested Boys' Club Constitution includes name, purpose, membership rules, meetings, board of directors, officers, executive director, and similar elements. Under the by-laws, specific recommendations are made as to the appropriate officers of the board (president, vice-president, secretary, and treasurer) and needed committees for finance, program, personnel, public relations, nominating, and property management. Under this broad structure, the individual Boys' Club may operate in a highly autonomous way as it seeks to carry out the goals and objectives of the national Boys' Club movement.

Girl Scouts of the U.S.A. This extensive national youth organization has a somewhat more tightly structured system of government. Founded through congressional charter, the Girl Scouts of the U.S.A. operates under a constitution that identifies three major levels of governance: the national council, the national board of directors, and local Girl Scout councils.

The membership of the national council is constituted by the members of the Girl Scout Corporation, who are elected delegates from local councils (up to the number of 2,000), members of the national board of directors, and other elected persons. The council serves as the coordinating head of the Girl Scout movement in the United States. More specific powers are assigned to the national board of directors; this body has responsibility for establishing requirements for membership, local council charters, standards, and other major operating procedures. Finally, local Girl Scout councils directly administer and supervise programs, according to goals and policies established by the national council and board of directors (Chapter 4).

National Jewish Welfare Board. This organization, which assists and promotes the Jewish Community Center and YM-YWHA movement throughout the United States, does not dictate the precise structure or policies of local centers. However, it helps them in many ways, through program development, personnel recruitment and training, and by developing organizational guidelines. As an example, it publishes a detailed *Manual for Board Members: A Guide for Service,* which summarizes the history and philosophy of the Jewish center movement and presents useful guidelines for the development of effective boards of directors. It suggests the appropriate size and composition of boards and their recommended functions. Board members are expected to be more than figureheads; they are encouraged to play an active role as officers or committee chairmen, as members of other social agencies or councils, in building or fund-raising efforts, or as volunteers in the center program. Clearly, in this type of voluntary agency structure, the board of directors is viewed as a key factor in the center's success or failure.

San Francisco Recreation Center for the Handicapped. This unique voluntary agency serving the comprehensive recreation needs of the disabled was founded in 1952. Today it provides varied programs for all age groups in an outstanding new facility. It operates under the guidance of an active board of directors whose members are broadly representative of the health and welfare field, including doctors, educators, business executives, and recreation specialists, as well as parents of handicapped children served by the center.

The board delegates formal administrative responsibility to the center director and business manager, who in turn work closely with board members through eighteen active standing committees. These committees include, among others, budget, building construction, camping, insurance, medical and technical, parents' auxiliary, personnel, program, publicity, and transportation. For an organization chart of the Recreation Center for the Handicapped, see Fig. 3-6.

Northern Minnesota Therapeutic Camp. This organization was formed in December, 1967, by a group of Brainerd, Minnesota, businessmen, to provide a year-round camping and outdoor education facility, known as Camp Confidence, primarily for the mentally retarded residents of Brainerd State Hospital. Operated on 140 acres of wilderness with half a mile of lake frontage, it provides the only year-round camping program for the mentally retarded in the northern half of the United States. Its strength lies in the full support it has received from the officials and staff of the hospital and from a host of business concerns and other organizations that have contributed materially or provided volunteer workers.

For example, much of Camp Confidence's construction was done by a U.S. Army Corps of Engineers reserve battalion, with materials donated by railroad companies, banks, and the Brainerd Area Vocational School. Other organizations, such as Project Green Thumb, the Bush Foundation of St. Paul, the Teen Corps of America, and Foster Grandparents have also supplied invaluable help. Not surprisingly, the sixteen-member board of directors of Camp Confidence has key members representing major community organizations, including railroad and building supply executives, the state senate, bank officers, educational officials, and similar individuals. Their participation is the key to the camp's success.

INTERNAL STRUCTURE OF PUBLIC RECREATION AND PARK DEPARTMENTS

As Chapter 2 has indicated, recreation and park departments must develop a logical and workable internal structure. This is reflected in a table of organization that depicts the various divisions of responsibility of the department and the levels of responsibility, from the top administrator down to recreation attendants or park laborers. Usually, three levels of authority are shown: the *executive* or administrative level; the *supervisory* or middle management level; and the *leadership* or direct service level. In addition, such charts should show affiliated organizations or advisory groups, boards and commissions, and linkages to other branches of city government.

How are recreation and park departments broken up into functional divisions? Rodney[5] suggests that many departments have identified five major responsibilities and established a bureau or division for each. These are program, special facilities, construction and maintenance, business and finance, and public relations.

Many large recreation and park departments may also have divisions that deal with personnel, research, planning and development, or special aspects of community service, such as socially oriented programs and services. Several organization charts of municipal or county departments of various types follow.

Spokane, Washington, Park Board. Fig. 3-1 is an illustration of a fairly simple structure in which a Director of Parks and Recreation is responsible for ad-

SPOKANE PARK BOARD

REPORT OF ADMINISTRATIVE STAFF

Organization

The Spokane Park Department is administered by the Director of Parks and Recreation, appointed by the City Manager with the direction of an 11 member Park Commission. The Department is divided into two divisions, the Park and Recreation Divisions, each headed by a Superintendent reporting to the Assistant Director in charge of operations. The Arboretum is a separate function, headed by an Arboretum Director responsible to the Board and the City Manager, though the work is coordinated through the Assistant Director's position. The Park Division takes care of those things that have to do with plant material and facilities while the Recreation Division deals with what people do with these facilities. The Director's responsibilities are primarily in the area of finance, office administration, Board services and interdepartment coordination.

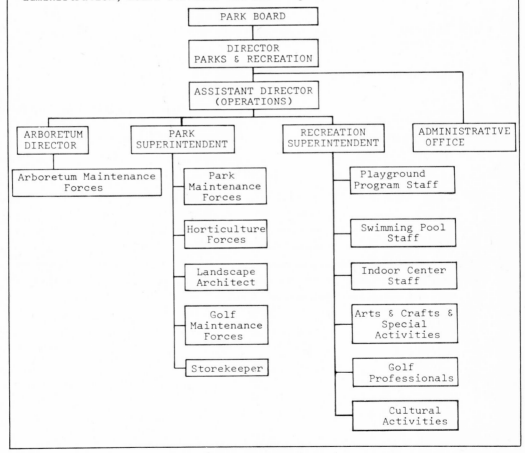

Fig. 3-1

ministering three major divisions: an arboretum division, a park division, and a recreation division. Each of these is under the control of its own director or superintendent. The park and recreation divisions are in turn divided into a number of functional units. As shown on the right side of the chart, the administrative office staff is attached directly to the central office of the director and assistant director, who is responsible for overseeing all operations.

Omaha, Nebraska, Department of Parks, Recreation, and Public Property. Like Spokane, Omaha provides both park and recreation functions under a joint department. However, as Fig. 3-2 makes clear, its department also has a major responsibility for operating municipally owned properties, including civic waterways and docks, a huge auditorium and stadium, and various other public buildings. The chart is a carefully simplified one, stressing major areas of responsibility rather than detailed functions or job levels.

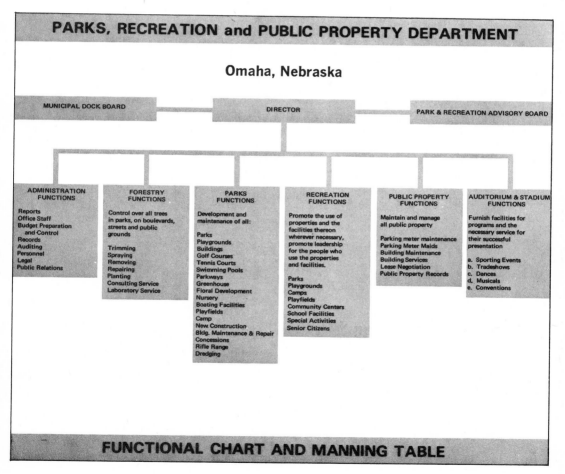

Fig. 3-2

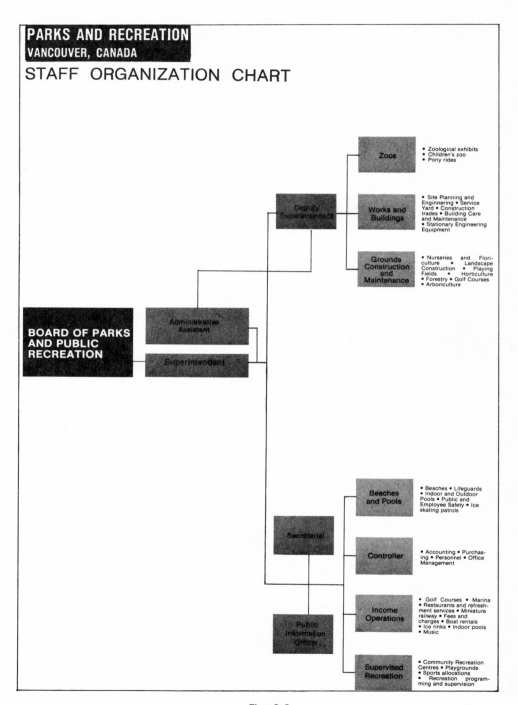

PARKS AND RECREATION
VANCOUVER, CANADA

STAFF ORGANIZATION CHART

Fig. 3-3

Vancouver, British Columbia, Board of Parks and Public Recreation. Fig. 3-3 is a highly simplified chart that divides the work of the department into several functional areas. Three of these, zoos, works and buildings, and grounds, construction, and maintenance are the responsibility of a deputy superintendent, whereas beaches and pools, administration (controller), income operations, and supervised recreation are directly under the superintendent.

Summary of organization charts. In general, these organization charts show how the major functional areas of administrative responsibility, such as fiscal management, personnel, program development and supervision, facilities planning, design and maintenance, and administrative services, are usually assigned to separate divisions. They also show how specific units of departmental responsibility, such as a zoo, golf courses, or municipal marina, may be established as a separate division. As a common practice the recreation department may house separate units, such as inner-city programs, performing arts, adult centers, golden age programs, municipal camps, summer playgrounds, aquatics, municipal athletics, and arts and crafts.

It should be stressed that basic organization charts, no matter how large the department, should be brief, clear, and indicative of the flow of action, responsibility, and authority. Auxiliary sheets, charts, or explanatory notes can carry the myriad titles and subtitles, names of individuals, or interdepartmental relationships, but the overall chart must be simple and easy to interpret.

ORGANIZATIONAL STRUCTURE IN OTHER SETTINGS

In other types of organizations, such as therapeutic settings or voluntary agencies providing recreation, the chart of organization tends to differ from those in public recreation and park departments.

Boys' Clubs of Dallas, Inc. The Boys' Clubs of Dallas, Texas, places major responsibility for administering the Boys' Club Building and its program on the agency's branch director. Other administrators, such as the director of camping and outdoor activities, are directly responsible to the executive director of the organization for the operation of city-wide services (Fig. 3-4).

Athens Mental Health Center, Athens, Ohio. Fig. 3-5 shows the somewhat more complex breakdown of an activity therapies department in a large psychiatric treatment center in Ohio. Operating in a chain of command from the Superintendent of the hospital to the clinical director to the head activity therapist, ten separate areas of activity therapy are shown. Of these, the largest in terms of staffing are recreation therapy and occupational therapy. The others, including music therapy, patients' library, education therapy, industrial therapy, art therapy, beauty shop, and physical therapy, employ fewer personnel, although the volunteer services unit coordinates the work of over 325 volunteer helpers.

Recreation Center for the Handicapped, Inc. Described earlier in this chapter, this agency has a relatively simple and functional organization chart. Program services are established as a major separate component on the chart, with direct access to the center director. Support services, such as payroll, transportation,

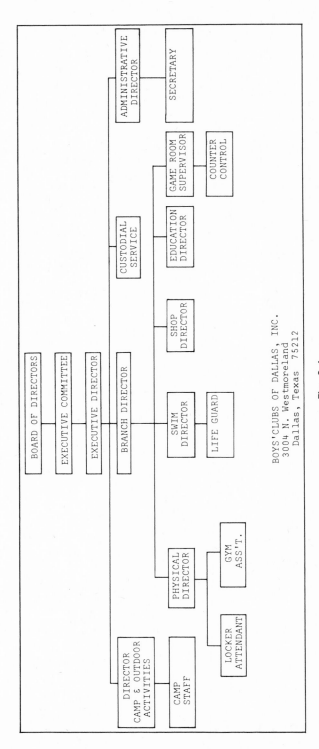

BOYS'CLUBS OF DALLAS, INC.
3004 N. Westmoreland
Dallas, Texas 75212

Fig. 3-4

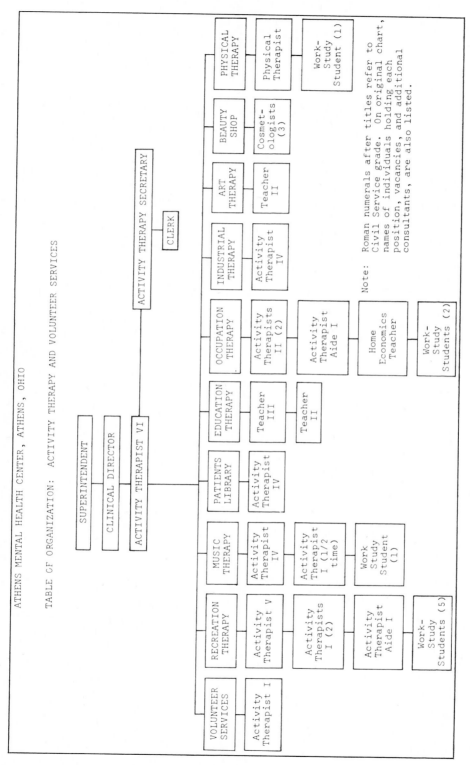

ATHENS MENTAL HEALTH CENTER, ATHENS, OHIO

TABLE OF ORGANIZATION: ACTIVITY THERAPY AND VOLUNTEER SERVICES

Note: Roman numerals after titles refer to Civil Service grade. On original chart, names of individuals holding each position, vacancies, and additional consultants, are also listed.

Fig. 3-5

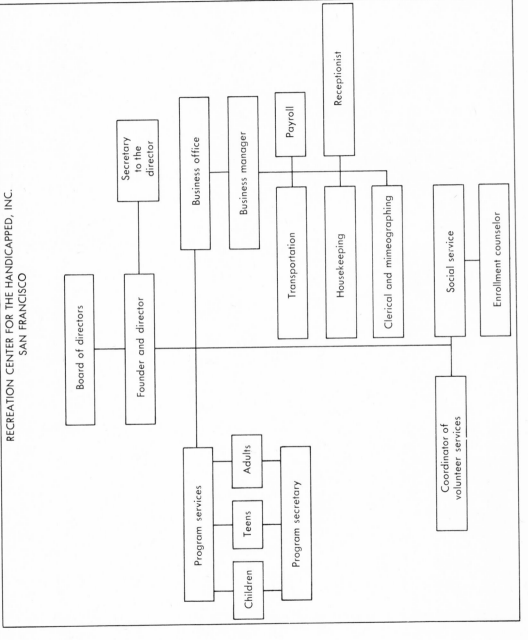

RECREATION CENTER FOR THE HANDICAPPED, INC.
SAN FRANCISCO

Fig. 3-6

housekeeping, or social service, are listed to the right, under the business manager. In terms of actual practice, it would be necessary to have a close working relationship between employees in these separate units (Fig. 3-6).

Example of commercial recreation: Disney World. In the field of commercial recreation, one of the outstanding examples is Disney World in Lake Buena Vista, Florida. This extremely successful enterprise has too complicated a structure to depict here. However, it may briefly be described as consisting of both internal divisions and external or subsidiary companies. To illustrate, it has the following major functional divisions:

Finance—handles the business side of the operation: budgets, financial planning, statistics, etc.

Food—responsible for food outlets, restaurants, and special sales

General services—provides essential services such as wardrobe, safety, warehousing, and staff development and training

Administration—coordinates, plans, and directs entire operation

Employee relations—supervises all personnel functions, such as hiring, personnel records, job assignment, compensation, benefits, relocation, and employee relations

Entertainment—produces all special live shows and provides entertainment groups

Facilities—responsible for maintaining and operating facilities with safety, efficiency, and cleanliness

Operations—supervises guest relations, security, and fire prevention; operates the actual program attractions and rides

Marketing—a communications and promotional unit that coordinates various business and industry group trips and events

Merchandising—designs and sells souvenirs and other speciality merchandise in Disney World

Hotel—operates major hotels for visitors

In addition, this huge complex has established a number of other companies to carry on specialized services, provide utilities, or meet other needs. These in-house or wholly owned subsidiaries are responsible for such functions as construction, engineering, land development and master planning, general insurance, advertising, outside merchandising, gift shops, and electric, gas, water, incinerator, and sewage facilities. Both in the complexity and range of its organization and in the sophistication of its operation, Disney World and its California counterpart, Disneyland, pose an impressive example for all leisure-service organizations.

SUMMARY

This chapter has presented an analysis of the legal basis for operating public recreation and park agencies and has described the major types of such agencies in terms of nature of sponsorship. In describing the composition and function of boards or commissions and the table of organization of public and therapeutic agencies it has concentrated on *structural* elements rather than on the *process* of administration.

In the chapters that follow, the development and carrying out of policy, as well as specific functions with respect to personnel, program, fiscal policy, and facilities development, are described in detail.

Suggested assignments for student reports or projects

1. Attend the meetings of a municipal recreation and park board or commission over a period of time (at least two or three meetings). Based on careful notes, develop a critical analysis of its operation, including: (1) relationship of the departmental administrator and the board or commission; (2) the real functions of the board or commission; (3) areas of successful performance and areas of difficulty; and (4) recommendations for improved functioning.
2. Select at least three recreation agencies of different types (such as a school board department, a separate recreation department, and a combined recreation and park department). Based on meetings with the chief executive and examinations of programs, reports, and administrative policies, compare the three agencies. This might be carried out as a group project by several students.
3. Develop a hypothetical table of organization, including board or commission, administrator, and various levels of personnel, for a munic-

ipal recreation and park department or voluntary agency. Develop a statement of responsibilities on each level and show relationships of different divisions within the organization. Base this on examples given in the text or taken from other sources.

REFERENCES

1. Butler, George D.: *Introduction to Community Recreation*, New York, 1976, McGraw-Hill Book Co., pp. 425-427.
2. Arnold, Serena, E.: *Trends in Consolidation of Parks and Recreation*, Washington, D.C., 1966, National Recreation and Park Association Management Aids Bulletin No. 41.
3. Bannon, Joseph J.: "Who Really Makes Policy?" in *Parks and Recreation*, July, 1973, pp. 31-32.
4. Sternloff, Robert E.: "Recreation and Park Boards," in *Parks and Recreation*, September, 1968, pp. 52-53.
5. Rodney, Lynn S.: *Administration of Public Recreation*, New York, 1964, The Ronald Press Co., p. 87.

CHAPTER 4

POLICY DEVELOPMENT IN RECREATION AND PARKS

A key element in recreation and park administration is the process of developing goals, formulating policies, and making decisions that govern all departmental operations. In carrying out this responsibility, administrators are influenced by five key elements: (1) the legal mandate—that is, the laws empowering them to function and setting guidelines and controls under which they must operate; (2) the political framework of service, including the governmental system, in a given community; (3) the wishes of residents, both on a community-wide basis and as representatives of different socioeconomic, ethnic, or age groupings; (4) the practical realities presented by available funds and human and material resources; and (5) the philosophical, academic, and experiential background of the department head. Beyond these factors, two elements govern a department's total operation: its overall philosophy and a set of policies that set guidelines in major administrative areas of practice.

PHILOSOPHY OF ORGANIZED RECREATION SERVICE

The goals of organized recreation service have been stated in many ways. National organizations in the field have issued documents outlining the social objectives and value systems underlying the provision of leisure services. National conferences have developed systematic statements of national priorities for leisure, recreation, and park development. Individual communities have evolved similar statements, geared to the needs of their own constituencies. Authors have written extensively in this field.

For example, two influential California writers, David Gray and Seymour Greben,[1] one an educator and the other a leading recreation and park administrator, recently developed a statement of critical priorities for the recreation and park movement in the United States. It included such needs as these:

1. To rethink the future of the movement in terms of its meaning for people in the local community, the nation, and the world
2. To adopt a humanistic ethic as the central value system of the movement; to develop and act on a social conscience that focuses on the major social issues and problems of the time
3. To reorganize and reorient agencies and the movement as a whole to make them more responsive to human need and social change

4. To establish common cause with environmentalists to work on common problems
5. To develop an effective interpretation program capable of articulating to a national and worldwide audience the meaning of park and recreation experiences in human terms
6. To organize members of the recreation and park movement as a political force capable of influencing local and national political processes

Although these are impressive and desirable objectives for the recreation and park movement as a whole and provide desirable goals for all practitioners, they are somewhat abstract and remote from the day-by-day concerns of recreation and park managers on the action level. It becomes necessary, therefore, to translate them into action-oriented priorities or steps that can and must be taken by all practitioners to strengthen the movement.

On a more concrete level, what are the specific purposes of *municipal* recreation and park departments? Many boards and commissions have outlined their objectives—some in broad philosophical statements and others in precise listings of immediate and long-range goals.

GOALS OF MUNICIPAL RECREATION AND PARK DEPARTMENTS

The Department of Recreation of the District of Columbia made the following statement of purpose in a recent annual report:

> Municipal recreation in the District of Columbia is intended to provide a comprehensive and varied program of public recreation activities, services and resources for its citizens at all age levels, from pre-school through senior citizens, in part by the department's desire to provide experiences that are designed to meet constructive and worthwhile goals of the individual participant, the group, and the community at large.

Similarly, the Recreation Division of the Milwaukee public schools stated as its basic philosophy:

> In Milwaukee, the Recreation Division seeks to promote the well-rounded development of all boys, girls, men and women, and to meet the needs and desires of all individuals it serves. By emphasizing educational as well as entertainment values of recreation, the varied activities of the different programs conducted by the Recreation Division contribute to increased learning, better social adjustment, and needed relaxation for all participants. Programs are planned by professional recreation personnel, to meet neighborhood interests and needs, providing suitable facilities, adequate equipment, and qualified leadership are available.

Some departments have created fuller and more specific statements of their philosophy and objectives than these. For example, the Board of Park Commissioners of Fort Wayne, Indiana, has approved the following statement:

GOALS OF THE BOARD OF PARK COMMISSIONERS, FORT WAYNE, INDIANA
Introduction

There are in the lives of the citizens of our community increasing opportunities to participate in leisure time activities, and in order to meet the diversity of interests and needs of all people, these patterns of recreation must be shaped into stimulating programs through effective leadership, adequate facilities, planning, and financial support. Extended periods of free time [are] one of the great challenges today, and constructive use of leisure time, in its many aspects, [is an] important function in our present society.

To meet the needs of all people, the Board of Park Commissioners through its leadership and its many beautiful parks and gardens and various organized recreation programs, dedicates itself to providing meaningful leisure for enriched living at every age, and therefore adopts the following objectives:

Program objectives

To develop an understanding and appreciation of democratic living through respect for others, cooperation with others, willingness to accept responsibility, and participation in community life.

To help develop the total health of the individual, physical, mental, and social, that will give organic power, physical vigor, motor coordination, and release from tension; emotional stability, high ideals toward health and to understanding health standards; friendship, fellowship, and acceptance of other national and religious groups; and qualities of fair play, humility, and appreciation of beauty.

To develop the individual personality to the maximum by teaching self respect, emotional control, self confidence, and poise, which will provide a sense of achievement, social approval, recognition, a sense of belonging, a new experience, and appreciation of the value of solitude.

To educate the individual in the worthy and purposeful use of leisure time through interests, skills, and knowledge in a variety of activities; understanding and ability in creative expression; and an awareness of community resources.

To develop the qualities and skills of leadership in the individual participant by appreciation of one's own capabilities; understanding the qualities and techniques of leadership; appreciation of the significance of leadership; attitudes and qualities necessary for voluntary and community services; and maintaining respect for property.

Administrative objectives

In order to best achieve the stated objectives of the Park Board the following administrative objectives are adopted through well trained, democratic, professional leadership:

To provide opportunities for recreation throughout the year which the people cannot furnish for themselves.

To provide such socially acceptable opportunities in leisure which will provide personally satisfying experiences, consistent with the varied interests, needs, and abilities of all citizens, without regard to age, sex, race, creed, or social status.

To stimulate and help the people to enjoy and conserve the natural environment, develop and protect the land and water areas in the public domain of Fort Wayne, and to encourage the full recreative use of these areas.

To provide opportunities that will enhance an appreciation of the beautiful in order to help the citizenry, young and old, strengthen their ties with nature—the land, animal, and plant life.

To help provide the opportunity for social and cultural development, for group participation, but also, whenever possible, for individual solitude.

To provide the opportunity for pleasure and comfort in urban living, by furnishing opportunities for individual creativeness, self-expression, and self-fulfillment.

To provide opportunities to promote citizenship, to develop leadership by emphasizing the privileges and obligations of democratic living.

To utilize the resources, especially in outdoor recreation areas and the natural environment, and to enrich the opportunities for the recreative use of leisure as a social, cultural, and economic asset.

To provide challenging opportunities to meet basic human desires for new experiences, sociability, recognition, participation, and beauty, which when met contribute to life fulfillment.

To provide sufficient and safe facilities, well maintained and properly managed and supervised, in order to enable communities, families, and other groups and individuals to engage in a variety of activities of their choice.

To promote and organize advisory committees at playgrounds, recreation centers, and other activity locations where the municipal park and recreation programs are in operation, in order to encourage public partnership.

To cooperate in the coordination of all community resources, and with all agencies, private, voluntary, and public, in providing the community with a functional overall park and recreation program for all citizens in our city.

To periodically review existing programs, facilities, services, operational policies, procedures, and these objectives, and to make necessary changes to better serve the citizens of an everchanging community.

Such statements of philosophy and goals are important because they express the basic conviction of each department or agency and clarify its objectives for the public at large. In addition, they provide a basis for guiding and directing an organization; objectives provide a target to aim at and help to motivate employees on all levels. It is important that any statement of goals be couched in terms that are relevant to the organization and that they are clearly stated. Beyond this, they should be realistic, in that it is possible to accomplish them, and yet at the same time should provide a significant challenge. Whenever possible, goals should be stated in concrete, measurable terms, rather than abstractions or value judgments.

As an example of concise goals that may be identified to give direction to an organization's program, the Boys' Clubs of America list and describe twelve major program objectives in their *National Program and Training Services Manual.*[2] These are (1) citizenship education, (2) leadership development, (3) skills development, (4) health and fitness, (5) preparation for leisure, (6) personal adjustment and development of individual potential, (7) educational-vocational motivation, (8) intergroup understanding, (9) value development, (10) sense of community, (11) enrichment of family life, and (12) enrichment of community life.

To realize such statements successfully, it is necessary to translate them into direct action. This can best be done by formulating policies that are much more specific in nature and that provide the basis for day-by-day decision-making.

DEVELOPMENT OF RECREATION AND PARK POLICIES

Exactly what are policies? The *Administrative Policy Manual* published by the National Recreation and Park Association describes policy as a

. . . settled or determined course of procedure adopted by a governmental body or an individual. In the light of this statement, it would seem that policies for park and recreation departments are those policies which are adopted by the department acting through its administrative board or governing body. The work of governmental bodies is given a sense of direction by the making and keeping of policies. Policies well made and well kept are the foundation and guide to the administration of a park and recreation department.[3]

Generally, *policies should be viewed as administrative guidelines that reflect major departmental principles, in the provision of service, operation of facilities, management of personnel, or similar administrative areas.* They are *not* simply procedures but outline major areas of decision-making or day-by-day action. Policies are broad in their scope and application; procedures are the specific actions or rulings that are required to carry them out. In *some* cases, a manual of departmental policies may contain even the most minute details of administrative practice. However, this is not the most common meaning of the term *policy.*

It should be understood that policies are *not* irreversible. They may be changed at any time, as either circumstances or departmental philosophy change, or when the need arises for a new or more flexible course of action. However, when such changes are carried out, *it should not be done at whim,* but only after careful deliberation.

Basis for policy making

There are several ways in which a recreation and park board or commission, in cooperation with a departmental administrator, may determine effective policies. Usually, the following factors come into play.

1. *Professional literature.* Recreation and park administrators, college educators, board members, officers of professional organizations, and other influential individuals may write articles or carry out studies published in the literature that influence the development of policies in a given department.

2. *Recommendations of professional organizations.* Frequently, professional organizations such as the National Recreation and Park Association or its branch societies, the National League of Cities, or the International City Managers' Association hold conferences or appoint task forces that lead to the recommendation of policies within key areas of administrative practice.

3. *Expectations of funding agencies.* Federal or state agencies, private foundations, or other funding organizations may establish guidelines that compel compliance by municipal departments. Frequently such guidelines deal with the need for nondiscriminatory practices or the need to serve a given population; they are becoming increasingly peremptory in such matters.

4. *Departmental factors.* More concretely, the opinions of board members, the influence of other branches of municipal government, political considerations, the judgment of legal counsel, or the overall expression of public opinion are all likely to play an important part in determining policy.

When a recreation and park board or commission determines policy in a given area, it must take all of these factors into account. The ultimate good of the community and the success of the program in meeting its stated objectives should be key factors in arriving at departmental policies.

When appropriate, other relevant city officials should be consulted. The mayor, city manager, or city council should be involved in the process. If the policy involves money, it would be wise to explore it with the municipal treasurer or comptroller. Policies affecting the use of personnel should be cleared with the municipal civil service board or personnel department. Legality should be confirmed by the city manager or attorney.

When policies are put into effect for the first time—particularly if they have a significant effect on the worklife of employees or on the way in which the public may be served—they should be appropriately publicized. It may be desirable to hold special meetings with leaders and supervisors to explain and discuss a new policy and its applications and to avoid gossip, distortion, or misunderstanding. Any new policy that affects program services should be publicized both in newspapers and in the departmental manual or brochures.

Usually it is advisable to put all policies into written form as soon as they have been formulated. These may be distributed down the chain of command in the form of bulletins, newsletters, or handbooks. Written, official policy statements are essential to ensure that they are available to all in the same form and can readily be checked for an exact interpretation of their meaning. In addition, the process of writing and approving policy statements ensures that administrators and supervisory personnel will think about them carefully and be certain of their intentions. Most efficient administrators keep records of policies, putting them into a policy book or manual, with the date when they were adopted. Usually such policy manuals are organized so that specific policies fit into a major set of categories of administrative function, all coded for easy reference. Such policy books are kept on file and in the possession of major administrative or supervisory officers.

Preparation of a policy manual

It is recommended that policy manuals be bound in loose-leaf form so that additions or revisions can easily be inserted in the appropriate locations, following a numbering system according to categories. McChesney and Tappley[4] suggest that each policy be listed on a separate page, with legal references (such as state law, city or county law or ordinance, or resolution by local managing authority) and the date of adoption of the policy listed at the bottom of the page. They suggest that a manual be divided into several basic parts, in the following manner:

1000	*Administration*	*5000*	*Participants*
2000	*Community relations*	*6000*	*Program*
3000	*Finances*	*7000*	*Maintenance*
4000	*Personnel*		

Within each section, major subclassifications would have a prefix beginning with 100, and secondary subclassifications of these would begin with 10. To illustrate, the "Personnel" section might include policies under the following numbers, covering such areas as:

4000	*Personnel*	4400	Rules of conduct
4100	Personnel organization chart	4500	In-service training
4200	Employment	4600	Travel
4300	Duties and qualifications	4700	Compensation and related benefits

To illustrate the third level of detailed policies, they list suggested headings under "Compensation and related benefits" as:

4710 Salary classification and guides
4720 Time reports and pay checks
4721 Hours of work, work schedule
4722 Overtime
4730 Insurance
4731 Automobile
4732 Health and hospital
4733 Workmen's compensation
4734 Accident and liability
4740 Sick leave
4750 Holidays
4760 Vacations
4770 Retirement compensation
4780 Absences

Such a policy manual represents an extremely detailed document, and not all departments will prepare one including such a range of subheadings. Those who wish to will find the *Administrative Policy Manual* outlined by the National Recreation and Park Association a useful guide for policy manual organization.

Examples of policy statements: public agencies

As indicated, policies may cover a wide range of administrative subjects and may include both broad matters of social priority or purpose or specific items dealing with day-by-day procedural concerns. The following examples illustrate sample policies taken from manuals of different communities. They show how policies may include precise administrative directives (Nassau County, New York), somewhat broader guidelines for administrative operations (Oak Park, Illinois), and extremely broad matters of policy (San Diego, California).

Nassau County, New York, Department of Recreation and Parks. Administrative Directive 101, *Scheduling of Personnel,* indicates the department's approach to having a uniform system for the scheduling of personnel and lists specific procedures that must be followed with respect to this process.

Oak Park, Illinois, Recreation Department. Administrative Policy No. 204.3, *Rental of Facilities,* provides a detailed outline of departmental policy with respect to renting recreation department facilities to community groups and organizations. Excerpts from it are presented here.

The remaining section of the manual dealing with rental of facilities covers the following items: schedule of rental charges, storage of equipment or materials, insurance and liability, rental procedures (reservations and cancellations), and rules for use of facilities.

San Diego, California, Mission Bay Park Commission. The Municipal Code of the City of San Diego, California, provides for a standing committee to govern the operation of Mission Bay Park, an outstanding city-owned boating, swimming, and fishing park along the Pacific coast. Excerpts from the policy manual governing the development of this park are shown in Fig. 4-1.

NASSAU COUNTY

Department of Recreation and Parks

Administrative Directive 101

SUBJECT: Scheduling of personnel

PURPOSE: To prescribe a uniform system for the scheduling of personnel to insure adequate supervision and coverage of public-use Facilities

IMPLEMENTATION

SS-1 RESPONSIBILITY FOR PERSONNEL SCHEDULING

It is the responsibility of all Division Heads to insure that work schedules are developed for all personnel assigned to public-use Facilities. It is recommended that all levels of supervision within these Facilities formulate schedules for their respective units with the understanding that they will be reviewed and approved by the next level in the chain of command within the Facility. It is recommended, but not mandatory, that personnel schedules be utilized by administrative offices and within other areas of the Department.

SS-2 SCHEDULING PROCEDURE

Personnel schedules are to be made out on Department Form PK-5027. The schedule is to be signed by the Facility Head indicating that the schedule meets the criteria established for Department personnel schedules and then forwarded to the level of supervision established by the Division Head as the Approving Authority for personnel schedules. When reviewed and signed by this individual, it then becomes an approved, official schedule.

Approved schedules are to be posted, two weeks prior to the commencement of the schedule, on Personnel Bulletin Boards in the main administrative offices of the Facilities. Additional schedules may be posted at other locations within a Facility if a sufficient number of personnel report to a location other than the main administrative office.

Form PK-5027 is to be filled in completely, indicating the name of the Facility. The schedule week will begin on Friday and end on the following Thursday. The exact dates should appear in the area on which the days of the week have been pre-printed. When listing the names of personnel on the schedule, group similar functions together and skip a line between each function; e.g., supervisory personnel, cashiers, rink guards, museum attendants, greenskeepers, etc. This will assist in the review of the schedule to determine adequate coverage.

The time that the individual is to work is to be indicated by writing in the exact hours; e.g., 9:00-4:45, 8:30-4:30, etc. If an individual is not scheduled to work due to personal entitlements, the payroll symbol for that entitlement should be entered in the scheduled hours space.

If overtime is required, the hours to be worked must also be indicated and circled in red in the scheduled hours space.

SS-3 CRITERIA FOR SCHEDULING

Every effort should be made to make the scheduling of personnel as equitable as possible. This includes dividing evening, weekend, and holiday assignments as evenly as is practical. The major portion of the staff should be scheduled during peak load periods and the appropriate skill level of staff must be available to provide the service offered.

The following guidelines should be used in developing work schedules:

a. Provide adequate staff to insure facilities are manned during the days and hours facilities are open to the public.

SS-3 CRITERIA FOR SCHEDULING—cont'd

> b. Avoid assigning personnel to positions which vary greatly from their own job descriptions.
> c. Recognize the personal needs and desires of employees for scheduling preferences.
> d. Normally, a five-day work week is to be followed.

SS-4 CHANGES TO APPROVED SCHEDULES

Personnel schedule changes must be approved by the designated Approving Authority or notification given as soon as possible after an emergency schedule change has occurred. In the former case, all copies of the schedule are to be corrected after approval is secured, and the printed initials of the Approving Authority are to be noted next to the change.

OAK PARK, ILLINOIS
Recreation Department
Manual of Policies and Procedures

Administration	June 17, 1970

Rental of Facilities	204.3

The Recreation Department facilities are available on a rental basis under the following policies:

1. Recreation Department facilities are available to resident groups and organizations for reservation from the hours of 6:00 P.M. through 11:30 P.M. when the facility is not scheduled for department supervised or sponsored programs. Facilities will normally not be available on Sunday mornings or holidays.
2. Rental Categories and Priority:

Recognizing that the Department facilities will provide only minimum space and time for the many individuals, clubs, and organizations that desire its use, the following priorities by category will be followed in scheduling a facility.

A. Recreation Department supervised programs
B. Recreation Department sponsored organizations and activities
C. Educational, cultural or civic meetings or programs of Oak Park organizations (Oak Park organizations must consist of at least 50% Oak Park residents)
D. Meetings sponsored by political or other special interest organizations in Oak Park
E. Oak Park groups and/or individuals requesting the facility for such activities as parties, teas, meetings, wedding receptions, etc. where no admission is charged
F. Groups and/or individuals renting the facilities for activities that are of a commercial nature or that require an admission fee
G. Non-resident groups in any of the above categories subject to Board approval.

```
                    CITY OF SAN DIEGO, CALIFORNIA
                         COUNCIL POLICY
┌─────────────────────────────┬──────────┬───────────┬──────┐
│ SUBJECT                     │ POLICY   │ EFFECTIVE │ PAGE │
│                             │ NUMBER   │ DATE      │      │
│       MISSION BAY PARK POLICIES │ 700-8    │ 7/29/65   │      │
└─────────────────────────────┴──────────┴───────────┴──────┘
```

PURPOSE

Over a period of several years, the Mission Bay Commission has recommended a number of policies designed to guide the orderly development of Mission Bay Park. It appears advisable to give official sanction to these policies and to list them together for the joint benefit of administrators and the general public.

POLICY

It is the policy of the Council that Mission Bay Park shall be created primarily as an aquatic recreation park for the enjoyment of all the citizens of San Diego and the visitors to this community. This policy shall encompass the following goals:

1. Every effort shall be made during the planning, design, and development stages to insure the utmost beauty, utility and year-round usage of the facility through utilization and enhancement of the natural aspects inherent in the area.

2. The total land area of all leases shall not exceed twenty-five percent of the total dedicated land area in Mission Bay Park.

3. The major emphasis in developing Mission Bay Park shall be on the creation of facilities for the use by the general public without unnecessary restrictions.

4. The development of land areas shall be designed to further the aquatic utilization of the park. Land areas within the boundaries of the park, which because of location are not suitable to aquatic recreational development, may be developed for park and recreation areas, operation centers, or secondary activities supporting the aquatic park and recreation needs.

5. Water areas shall be conserved and developed to an optimum level to provide as nearly as practical for all forms of aquatic recreation.

(Note: the remaining sections of this policy statement deal with: funding sources for development of park facilities; use of private capital to diversify park services; granting of leases, permits and concessions; policies protecting the public's right to use facilities; adherence to master plan for Mission Bay; and arrangements regarding options to be given to prospective lessees.)

Fig. 4-1

Example of policy statements: voluntary organization

Girl Scouts. Such voluntary organizations as the Girl Scouts of the USA must also formulate precise policies to govern their operations. For example, the National Board of Directors of the Girl Scouts has formulated a list of twenty-two policies, which each council, in its application for a Girl Scout Charter, must agree to accept. These policies are intended to uphold the values of the Girl Scout movement and to protect it against exploitation or misuse. They deal with such subjects as (1) admissions qualifications for membership, (2) the selection of adult members and boards of directors, (3) the place of religion in the Girl Scout movement, (4) health and safety, (5) political and legislative activity, (6) restricted use of membership and mailing lists, (7) fund-raising methods, and (8) permissions for commercial endorsements or use of Girl Scouting. Some examples of these national policies are the following:

> *Place of Religion in the Girl Scout Program.* Girls are encouraged and helped through the Girl Scout program to become better members of their own religious group, but every Girl Scout group must recognize that religious instruction is the responsibility of parents and religious leaders.
>
> *Political and Legislative Activity.* Girl Scouts of the USA and any council or other organization holding a Girl Scouts of the USA credential may not, nor may they authorize anyone on their behalf to participate or intervene directly or indirectly in any political campaign on behalf of or in opposition to any candidate for public office; or participate in any legislative activity or function which contravenes the laws governing tax exempt organizations.
>
> *Permissions for Commercial Endorsement.* Permission to endorse commercial products or services or to give endorsement of such by implication must be obtained from Girl Scouts of the United States of America and shall be granted only when such endorsement is in keeping with Girl Scout principles and activities.[5]

POLICIES AS A BASIS FOR DECISION-MAKING

In some cases, policies must be developed to deal with fluid problems and emergencies. Because of the need to keep departmental action flexible and to apply creative problem-solving approaches, such policies rarely find their way into policy manuals. This is particularly the case when recreation and park administrators must respond to sudden political emergencies, demands for action, or similar pressures.

Frequently during a political campaign, sudden demands are made on the elected chief executive of a municipality. The high-tension atmosphere of a city hall may compel sudden changes in established policies. Long-range plans, strict enforcement of procedures for locating new parks and repairing others, the equitable distribution of personnel and supplies to all parts of the city or district regardless of its voting record or potential—all these come under a hail of fire during political crises. Usually the shooting is done by lesser functionaries on the chief executive's staff, who may use his name and influence to force policy decisions. Damage in such cases is usually superficial and can be repaired by the recreation and park department after the battle is over.

During the late 1960s, upheavals within the schools, armed forces, universities, and big-city parks caused some departments to declare the firm policy statement an obsolete tool. "Wing it!" or "Play it by ear!" were common suggestions. This is a grave error. The well-thought-out and philosophically sound policy provides a solid base for departmental action; it can accommodate occasional expedient action or compromises under fire. However, if this solid base for decision-making is removed, chaos results.

A number of examples of the types of problems that call for a flexible approach to problem-solving, rather than fixed policies, follow. In each case, several typical questions are suggested.

1. Problems of fiscal management
   a. When budgetary cuts or freezes are imposed, how are they to be absorbed within a department?
   b. When it is necessary to impose or increase fees or charges, how is this to be done?
   c. What are approaches toward co-sponsoring special programs with major companies or getting special support from foundations?
2. Development of new facilities and programs
   a. What factors should be primary in determining priorities for developing new or expanded facilities or programs?
   b. Should social need, inadequate existing facilities or programs, availability of land, ability of residents to pay special fees, political power of residents, or other elements be used in determining priorities?
3. Vandalism and social control
   a. How are problems related to vandalism, crime, or domination of parks or playgrounds by antisocial groups to be handled?
   b. How effective are alternatives such as use of patrols and security forces, stricter enforcement of ordinances, new types of protective construction (alarm systems, night-lighting, fencing, elimination of windows, and so on)?
   c. What is the possible role of the department in providing special programs for deviant populations, youth gangs, hippies, and the like?
4. New approaches to community relations and local control
   a. To what extent should community residents be drawn into planning new recreation and park facilities?
   b. To what extent should they be involved in planning, or possible staffing, of new programs?
   c. What should policy of the department be with respect to decentralizing administration of programs and involving local people in the decision-making process?
5. Problems of environmental protection
   a. In what ways can a recreation and parks department effectively promote environmental and antipollution concerns?
   b. How are such recreational activities as snowmobiling or boating, which are potentially dangerous to the environment, to be controlled?
6. Coordination with other agencies
   a. What are some methods of developing effective coordination of varied recreation services within a city or large suburban area?
   b. Give examples of specific cooperative arrangements for sharing facilities, manpower, or funds between different public and voluntary agencies.
7. Subcontracting of departmental functions
   a. What are some possible uses of new approaches in subcontracting specific functions (such as maintenance, cleaning, design and construction, or recreation program development) to other voluntary or commercial organizations?
8. Determining legitimate areas of responsibility
   a. Facilities: should a municipal recreation and park department be responsible for operating major stadiums, museums, libraries, cultural centers, or other municipal properties like airports, docks, or cemeteries?
   b. Programs: should a municipal recreation and park department assume responsibility for social-work type programs in areas such as school tutoring, drug addiction services, vocational training and placement programs, and the like?

Each of these areas indicates the need to determine departmental policies that may then provide the basis for dealing with new problems, issues, or opportunities as they appear. In general, rather than develop a precise statement of its position in such areas, a recreation and park board is likely to agree on a general stance, from which it may then operate flexibly in response to problems as they appear.

A variety of groups should be regularly involved in hearings or planning sessions that lead to policymaking in key areas. These should include board or commission members, administrators and supervisors in the department itself, community residents with special interest in the problem, other government officials, representatives of other community groups, and experts in the field, who may offer technical advice or authoritative information. Although policymaking is the ultimate responsibility of recreation and park boards and commissions, it should be democratically shared with those who will be affected by it and those who must carry it out.

Political implications of policymaking

In a number of important policy-related areas, such as the hiring of personnel or the development of new facilities or special neighborhood programs, the recreation and park administrator may be subjected to strong political pressure. He or she may be expected to hire only the right summer workers or build a new playground only in the neighborhood loyal to the political party in power. This question of political loyalty and professional integrity is discussed more fully in Chapter 12. However, it should be said here that the recreation and park professional must face and live with the reality of political life in his own community.

Recognizing this, he must strive wherever possible to determine all policies on the basis of what is best for the community at large. Many administrators who have done this, rather than go down the line for the party in power, have gained such a high level of community respect and support that they have been able to survive successive turnovers in City Hall from Republican to Democratic and back again! On the other hand, the recreation and park director who is an ardent loyalist and has played the political game up to the hilt may well be fired the moment the new administration takes over.

The invisible power structure. The perceptive recreation and park administrator will recognize that goal setting and policy determination must be carried on, not only with consideration for visible political forces in the community but also the invisible power structure that exists in many cities, counties, and towns. Many organizations and special-interest groups exist that may wield a far greater influence on social and governmental affairs than elected officials and their traditional hierarchy. Examples include the following:

League of Women Voters	American Legion or V.F.W.
Bar and medical associations	Knights of Columbus
Savings and loan associations	Rotary, Kiwanis, Lions, Optimists
Women's clubs	Churches and synagogues
Police Benevolent Association	Parent-Teachers Associations
Little League or Babe Ruth League	Realty boards

Such lists can be endless when the many ethnic (Italian-American Club), regional (West Texas Cattleman's Association), and other civic or other social interest groups are added. The important thing is for the recreation professional to have a good working knowledge of the philosophy and programs of such groups and to perceive accurately the power clusters and alliances in the community. There is no substitute for regular contacts with such organizations, either as a scheduled speaker or simply an informal visitor at monthly meetings or events to obtain a gut feeling as to their attitudes with respect to recreation and parks, sports, teen centers, budget trends, and the like. Without such contact, the recreation professional may inadvertently make policy decisions that unnecessarily tread on strongly-held community opinions or undermine his support among civic groups.

One example of this took place several years ago in a Pennsylvania city of about 50,000 residents. For some time, the leadership of the local American Legion post had become increasingly resentful against several local hippie youth groups. Legion members labeled them as "un-American and disgraceful," and criticized their long hair, tattered clothing, and nomadic ways. At this moment, a not-too-perceptive director of recreation chose to open his summer concert series with a weekend of hard rock music, bringing into the city's park and surrounding residential streets over 5,000 of the very people the Legion was railing at. The confrontation and indignation were inevitable, and the director alienated the powerful Legion for years to come. Knowledge, fuller contact, and communication could have softened or prevented this abrasive situation from developing.

In conclusion, then, the task of determining goals and setting policies is a major concern of recreation and park administrators. Many such goals and policies relate directly to the task of personnel management, which is described in the following chapter.

Suggested assignments for student reports or projects

1. Prepare a detailed and well-thought-out statement of philosophy of a modern urban or suburban recreation and park department. Include at least ten specific goals related to meaningful community needs or benefits.
2. Visit at least three such departments and examine their written statements of objectives. If these are not available, determine their goals and priorities through a meeting with the administrative director. Then carry out a comparative analysis of the three sets of objectives. This might be done as a panel assignment by several students.
3. Prepare a detailed section of a policy manual dealing with a specific area of administrative function, such as the application of fees and charges, the admission of residents and nonresidents to recreation facilities, the handling of departmental funds, or the improvement of community relations. Include both broad policy positions and specific procedural or operational policies.

REFERENCES

1. Adapted from: Gray, David E., and Greben, Seymour: "Future Perspectives," *Parks and Recreation,* July, 1974, pp. 53-54.
2. "National Program and Training Services Manual," New York, 1974, Boys' Clubs of America.
3. McChesney, James C., and Tappley, Richard A.: *Administrative Policy Manual,* Washington, D.C., 1966, National Recreation and Park Association Management Aids Bulletin No. 61, p. 5.
4. *Ibid.,* pp. 8-9.
5. "Leaders' Digest of Documents, Policies and Procedures," New York, 1973, Girl Scouts of the U.S.A., pp. 8-10.

CHAPTER 5

PERSONNEL MANAGEMENT

[handwritten: CONCERN AREAS / PERS. management / Budgets / policy]

This chapter is concerned with one of the major areas of responsibility in recreation and park administration—personnel management. The task of recruiting, hiring, and supervising personnel and of maintaining a smooth-running operation on all levels of employment is crucial to achieving departmental goals.

An analysis is presented here of various job levels and descriptions, both as they are defined by professional organizations or authors and as they are formally described in municipal civil service codes. Next, the major functions of administration with respect to personnel management are presented, including (1) recruitment, selection, and hiring of personnel; (2) orientation, in-service training, and supervision; (3) personnel policies related to hours of work and leaves, health and welfare, probation and tenure, fringe benefits, promotion, or separation; (4) professional development in terms of working relationships, morale of personnel, and meaningful evaluation; and (5) the effective use of volunteers.

Strong emphasis is given in the latter part of the chapter to the goals, philosophy, and methods of effective supervision. The final two sections deal with current trends in the professional preparation of recreation and park personnel on all levels and current issues and problems related to personnel policies in public recreation and park agencies.

PERSONNEL CLASSIFICATION SYSTEMS

[handwritten: Imp. Job Cl. / Job Titles / Job Respon. / Requirements / pay / two / classes / 1) class / 2) series]

Within any area of public administration, the classification and standardization of job titles is essential to effective organization. It provides a basis for defining responsibilities clearly, having comparable salary levels for comparable qualifications or job demands, and establishing a career ladder with opportunity for promotion through the system.

Positions are frequently grouped into classes and series within a civil service structure. A *class* refers to a group of positions with roughly comparable responsibilities and qualifications, which may be stated in terms of education, experience, and specific knowledge or job skills. Positions on the same class level may be found in different departments and usually are subject to the same policies with respect to pay, fringe benefits, promotions, and similar personnel matters.

A *series* represents a form of vertical classification of employees, usually found within a particular department or specialization but with a gradation of skills and qualifications, as well as different levels of salary and status. As an example, a series of titles within a recreation department might run from Recreation Trainee or Assistant through several grades of Recreation Leader up to Recreation Supervisor or Director.

Classification systems represent a plan through which all jobs are defined and fitted onto an organizational chart and a civil service or other personnel structure. Each position is identified as to class or grade and is assigned a salary range, specific work responsibilities, required qualifications (usually stated in terms of education and experience and sometimes accompanied by an examination procedure), and other benefits (usually defined by a union contract or municipal personnel plan) in terms of holidays, vacation, leave, hospitalization, and similar personnel benefits.

In many large municipal or county structures, workers may come into the personnel system only on an entry level, such as recreation assistant or leader. Promotions are made through a system of required examinations or service ratings after set periods of employment, and only those already in the system are able to move up the career ladder—with the exception of the top administrative staff, which is usually directly appointed and not part of the civil service system.

JOB SPECIFICATIONS IN RECREATION AND PARKS

Large recreation and park departments hire an amazing variety of workers, some in specializations that would appear to have little to do with recreation as such. As an example, the civil service schedule of the Philadelphia Recreation Department lists eighty-four different positions. Of these, only about ten have titles using the term *recreation.* Other typical positions include account clerk, administrative analyst, architect, building maintenance superintendent, brick mason, camp director, carpenter, cement finisher, city planner, civil engineer, clerk stenographer, and construction project technician.

It would be a mistake to think of all these job categories as representing specialized professional employment in recreation and parks. It does not matter particularly to a cement finisher whether he is finishing the outside of a park department building or a downtown department store. The heart of the personnel department in a recreation and park agency is that group of employees directly concerned with the administration, supervision, and direct delivery of recreation services *or* with the planning and overall administration of recreation and park facilities that are *used* for leisure activities.

However, every effort should be made to imbue those workers who are not within the category of professional recreation and park employees—such as clerks, truck drivers, or switchboard operators—with a sense of the mission and purpose of the department. Through meetings, conversations, house publications, and training it is possible to develop their awareness of the department's work and to stimulate a special pride and loyalty that increases their effectiveness and pays rewards in improved public relations.

JOB TITLES AND DESCRIPTIONS

Customarily, positions in this field are assigned to one of three levels: administrative, supervisory, and leadership. Examples will be given of titles and job descriptions on each of these levels.

Administrative positions

Depending on the community, regional customs, or civil service codes, the specific title of the individual who is the chief administrative officer of a recreation and park department may be General Manager, Director, Administrator, Superintendent, or Commissioner. This position entails major responsibility for planning and implementing a recreation and park program to meet the needs and interests of the total population of a community. Specific responsibilities of the chief administrative officer include:

1. Administering the overall work of the department in accordance with the policies established by the governing authority (board, commission, city council, city manager, or other legal authority)
2. Directing the acquisition, planning, construction, improvement, equipment, and maintenance of all areas and indoor and outdoor facilities
3. Recruiting, selecting, assigning, training, supervising, and evaluating the work of all department personnel
4. Preparing a budget and directing, controlling, and accounting for all departmental expenditures, revenues, and fiscal operations
5. Organizing, directing, and controlling all recreation program activities, either as direct departmental functions or in cooperation with other organizations or citizens' groups
6. Maintaining an effective public relations program and developing constructive relationships with other municipal, voluntary, and community organizations
7. Evaluating the department's overall effectiveness in attaining its objectives through both formal and informal evaluative procedures, research studies, and reporting systems
8. Providing inspirational and creative leadership essential to the progress of the department

The qualifications of chief administrative officers usually include graduation from a recognized college or university with a bachelor's degree in recreation leadership or administration, park management, or a closely related field, and successful experience over a period of years in recreation supervision and/or administration. Customarily, commissioners or superintendents in larger cities are expected to have graduate degrees or a specified number of years of high-level experience.

In large municipal departments, there is likely to be an administrator with the title of Deputy or Assistant Administrator of Recreation and Parks. This person usually assists the executive head of the department and is responsible for the following types of functions.

1. Assisting the chief administrative officer in all responsibilities, particularly in areas of business management, such as budgeting, purchasing, or personnel management
2. Serving for the administrator in his absence or in official meetings or community hearings, as a deputy
3. Carrying out special studies and investigations and preparing annual reports and evaluations
4. Advising on technical problems and operational functions
5. Handling correspondence not requiring the administrator's direct attention
6. Conducting staff meetings and assisting in the selection, supervision, and in-service training of staff

Dependent on the organizational chart of the department, there also may be directors or superintendents of separate divisions or bureaus, such as a Director of Recreation, Superintendent of Maintenance and Operations, and similar titles. These involve more highly specialized functions but are on a high enough level of responsibility to be regarded as clearly administrative posts.

Qualifications for such positions normally reflect the specific technical skills required to carry out these functions effectively, in terms of both educational background and experience.

As indicated earlier, such positions frequently are not assigned on the basis of civil service eligibility or promotion through the ranks. Instead, they are often based on direct appointment and must therefore be politically approved by the party currently in power. Unlike lower position levels, recreation and park administrators usually do not hold tenured positions and are more affected by changes in the political climate of a community.

Although it is not possible for job descriptions or formal statements of eligibility to specify the needed personal qualities of administrators, it is clear that the most effective ones have a high degree of personal drive and command ability as well as élan—a capacity for stimulating both their staff and constituents to a high level of interest and involvement in the department's work. The chief executive in the recreation and park department of a large city should never be a mere graduate of the system he leads; he should be its soul and its generative source. If such a person can be found *within* the system, he should be moved up to head it. If not, such a person should be sought *outside* and brought directly in when a change is to be made.

Supervisory positions

Supervisory positions represent a secondary level of administration, in that supervisors normally are responsible for overseeing the overall recreation or recreation and park operations within a given geographical area or district of a city *or* within a major category of program service. Supervisors have a degree of administrative responsibility, particularly over the line personnel who work directly under their guidance. They also serve as representatives of the chief administrative officer, carrying out his directives and promoting the overall policies of the department.

Recreation Supervisor (general). The Recreation Supervisor who is in charge of a geographical area or district is responsible for all phases of the recreation program within this area and for the professional supervision of all personnel in the area. Although he may be responsible for some direct leadership, his function is primarily one of coordinating and directing the work of others, scheduling activities, and acting as a link between the chief administrative officer of the department and leaders in the field. Specific responsibilities include:

1. Serving as a deputy for the recreation director or superintendent in his district by actually administering all phases of its program
2. Determining needs within his district and planning programs to meet these needs
3. Supervising, training, and evaluating all recreation personnel assigned to his district and serving as a liaison between them and the personnel office or chief administrative officer
4. Overseeing direct maintenance and use of all facilities and areas in his district, either as a direct responsibility or in cooperation with a maintenance or parks supervisor for the district
5. Carrying out a program of local public relations, both in preparing publicity for events and activities and in maintaining effective relations with community groups
6. Participating in departmental planning, research, and evaluation and carrying out district studies
7. Assisting in the preparation of budget requests to meet district needs and supervising the expenditure of funds and the collection of fees and charges for local participation
8. Maintaining all necessary records and preparing annual and special reports for the district

The functions of a Recreation Supervisor who has more specialized responsibilities might include (1) being in charge of a large community center or other recreation complex, such as a cultural center or sportsman's center, (2) being in charge of a major area of activity, such as performing arts, athletics, aquatics, or nature and outing programs, or (3) being in charge of programs for a particular population, such as the handicapped, aging, or youth. These responsibilities would be similar to those described for the General Recreation Supervisor but would involve a heavier concentration on planning and carrying out special activities and directing and training other personnel.

There are comparable positions within the area of park maintenance and facilities construction. Thus the person who is responsible generally for the operation of physical facilities (such as playgrounds, centers, and small parks) within a major district of the city might be known as the District Parks Foreman. If he has a functional responsibility within a special area of maintenance throughout the city, he might be titled Horticultural Park Supervisor, as an example.

It was customary, in the past, to have individuals clearly assigned to *either* recreation or parks responsibilities and to have their job titles reflect this. Today, in many cities, district recreation and park supervisors may be appointed who have responsibility for both areas within a district.

The qualifications for supervisors normally include graduation from a recognized college or university with a degree in recreation, or recreation and parks, or a closely related field, plus a specified period of professional experience in recreation. In some job descriptions, a minimum number of credits in professional recreation courses (such as fifteen or eighteen) may be acceptable.

Fig. 5-1. A, Recruitment of capable young people is an important part of the administrator's role. Here, three Nassau County young people fill in for Recreation and Parks Commissioner Richard Fitch and his deputies on Career Day. **B,** As part of in-service training, Milwaukee Recreation Director George Wilson orients a new intern to the city's school-sponsored recreation and adult education program. **C,** In-service training takes many forms. Here, recreation leaders in Los Angeles' Recreation and Park Department learn arts and crafts skills.

Leadership positions

Recreation Leader. This is a full-time, professional position in which an individual is responsible for planning, organizing, and supervising recreation programs in one or more facilities or directly leading or teaching within a particular area of activity in which he is a specialist.

The Recreation Leader may be a generalist or a specialist. His functions in the first role include:

1. Assisting in administering the recreation program in an assigned area or district and taking full responsibility for it within a specific facility, such as a playground or center
2. Supervising the work of assistant recreation leaders or other subordinates
3. Working directly with groups of participants and supervising them in various activities, instructing skills, conducting trips, and the like
4. Planning daily schedules, requisitioning supplies, maintaining records and making reports, preparing local publicity, meeting and working with local groups, inspecting facilities and equipment for safety purposes, and carrying out other direct service routines in the conduct of the local program

When employed as a specialist in a given area of activity, the Recreation Leader might be responsible for promoting that activity throughout a district; arranging for special tournaments, exhibitions, clinics, or shows; assisting in the design of areas and facilities or the purchase of equipment and supplies (as in the case of an aquatic facility or an arts and crafts studio); and advising and training other leaders to conduct this activity. In some departments, specialists are assigned specific titles related to activities. Thus, in the Chicago Park District, workers are hired under the following job titles, as specialist leaders: Art-craft Instructor, Astronomer (works in a planetarium), Dramatics Instructor, Lifeguard, Music Instructor, Physical Instructor (male), Physical Instructor (female), and Zoo Leader. In a number of these areas, specialist supervisors are listed as well.

Typically, some departments may have several grades of Recreation Leader, such as Leader I, II, and III. In some cases, the levels may include a Senior Leader category as well as regular Recreation Leader. Usually, these titles represent promotional opportunities within a series and may or may not be based on the individual's meeting higher qualifications or taking a promotional examination. Job descriptions may reflect different grades. Thus, in some cities, the Senior Recreation Leader is responsible for directing activities at a large recreation center or major park or playground, and the regular Recreation Leader directs a smaller playground or center or assists at a larger one.

Civil service qualifications for the position of Recreation Leader usually specify either a college degree in recreation or a related field or a minimum of 2 years of college study. An increasing number of community colleges have begun recreation leader or technician training programs to supply needs for personnel on this level. When experience is required, it can usually be met by college field work experiences or summer or part-time employment.

Recreation Aides or Assistants Fourth Level

In all municipal recreation and park agencies and in many hospitals or similar settings, there are subprofessional positions with titles like Recreation Aide, Assistant, Attendant, or Intern. Although these titles are not used uniformly around the country, generally they are applied in the following ways:

Recreation Aide. Involves assisting a Recreation Leader in the conduct of activities under direct supervision. May assist in teaching children games, sports, arts and crafts, and so on, accompanying them on trips or similar responsibilities.

Recreation Assistant. (Term is often used interchangeably with Recreation Aide.) May be put in direct charge of small playground or after-school center.

Recreation Attendant. Does routine work of a manual, clerical, or leadership nature, under supervision. May mark or prepare courts, fields, or other facilities and perform other routine custodial or maintenance tasks. May also keep records, assist leader in maintaining order and safety or in officiating games, or serve as locker room attendant.

Recreation Intern. May refer in some cases to a college graduate who is in a special position in a department, performing a variety of administrative and supervisory tasks under close direction for a set period of time. The term also may be used to refer to a student recreation leader or trainee.

Generally, positions on subprofessional levels do not require college study; applicants may have a high school diploma or equivalency certification. Because of the increased interest over the past several years in hiring members of minority racial or ethnic groups or young people from poor neighborhoods, many departments and state hospitals or mental health systems have developed new paraprofessional job lines. It is important that such positions provide the opportunity for advancement. In some cities, work-study plans have been worked out under which Recreation Aides and Assistants may study at local community colleges or universities with a degree of released time from work to move up the career ladder in their departments.

Newer approaches to position analysis

The preceding section of this chapter has presented a traditional approach to defining job levels, titles, and functions. It applies chiefly to public recreation and park departments and less so to voluntary, therapeutic, private, or commercial agencies. With this in mind, attempts have been made to analyze positions within the broad field of leisure services in a more generic way. The New York State Recreation and Park Society, for example, has developed an alternative way of identifying job levels and responsibilities in a recent publication dealing with personnel criteria and standards.[1]

Functional classification. In a functional classification, three levels of responsibility are identified: *managerial, logistical,* and *operational.*

Managerial units include top and middle-management positions with such titles as Administrator, Commissioner, Director, Manager, Superintendent, and Assistant Superintendent.

Logistical units usually comprise *staff* personnel, with titles such as Budget Officer, Planner, Designer, Personnel Officer, or Public Relations Officer.

Operational units involve the *line* personnel directly responsible for program execution and plant operation. Titles may be classified as Generalist (Supervisor, Senior Leader, etc.), Specialist (Aquatics Director, Dramatics Instructor, etc.), or facilities-related (Caretaker, Engineer, Groundsman, etc.).

Whatever method of job classification is used, it is essential that thorough and accurate job description sheets be prepared for each position in a recreation and park department. Typically, these include *title, civil service grade* (if governmental), *listing of responsibilities and functions, required knowledge and skills, minimum acceptable education and previous experience,* and *physical or medical standards.* In some cases, desired personality characteristics may also be specified in job description sheets.

PROCESS OF PERSONNEL ADMINISTRATION

There are essentially five major phases of personnel administration. These include (1) recruitment, selection, and hiring of personnel; (2) orientation and in-service training; (3) establishing sound personnel policies; (4) effective supervision leading to positive departmental relationships and personal development of employees; and (5) use of volunteers.

Recruitment, selection, and hiring of personnel

Recruitment, selection, and hiring constitute a key element in the entire personnel process. The goal is to employ the best-qualified men and women to fill openings in the department. There are several distinct phases in this overall process.

Job description. A written job description should be prepared giving essential information about the responsibilities, salary, personnel benefits, and hiring qualifications and procedures of the position to be filled. It should be concise and attractive, completely accurate, and approved by the department's personnel office or the community's personnel director. It should include deadlines for filing applications, examination dates, and other needed information.

Publicizing the position. Announcement of the job opening should be carried out with the use of newsletters, mailing of brochures, announcements at professional meetings, direct correspondence, or placement of the opening with the personnel placement service of professional organizations. State or regional recreation and park societies frequently maintain listings of job openings.

Consideration of past employees. Frequently recruitment may be carried out directly by considering past employees for positions. Many recreation and park departments employ college students during the summer or on a part-time basis during the winter and spring. When they have graduated, they may be considered for full-time employment, with the obvious advantage of having the department familiar with their work and vice versa.

Selection procedure. Normally the selection procedure includes (1) filling out a detailed job application form, (2) a detailed consideration of the candidate's background, past performance, and references, (3) a personal interview with the candidate, (4) a written examination, usually part of a state, county, or municipal civil service series, (5) a physical examination, (6) a character investigation, and (7) in some cases, a performance test in specific skills areas.

Job application form. An example of a job application form developed by the Nassau County, New York, Department of Recreation and Parks (Fig. 5-2) includes (1) personal details about the applicant, (2) educational background, (3) employment history, (4) personal references, (5) recreational interests and involvements, and (6) listing of specific skills in administrative, supervisory, or leadership areas. This form is used as the basis for interviewers to make hiring recommendations and as a convenient reference source through which department administrators can locate a wide variety of needed skills among its staff members.

Customarily, based on the applicant's performance on examinations, he is placed on an eligibility list, with appointment to be made from the three highest-ranking candidates. Appointment may then be made when the opening occurs.

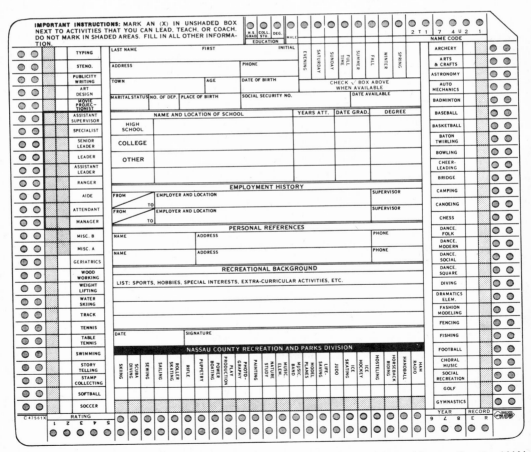

Fig. 5-2. Job application form, Nassau County, New York. (Courtesy Nassau County, N.Y.)

In some cases, a candidate may be appointed on a provisional basis, because no examination has been scheduled that applies to the position in question. At a later point, he would be required to take the examination. This process is normally carried out by a municipality's personnel department, although the actual choice of the candidate from those who have been certified as eligible for the position should be made by the departmental administrator and approved by his board or commission.

Appointment and probation. Following the actual hiring of the candidate, he would normally undergo a 3- to 6-month probationary period. He should be carefully observed and evaluated during this period. If his performance is satisfactory, he is then eligible for permanent employment and may not be discharged except for cause, according to the personnel procedures or union contract that govern such actions.

The entire process of recruitment and selection is a key one in terms of selecting the best candidates to fill open positions. Often the vigor, efficiency, and overall image of a recreation and park department are dependent on its being able to hire the best-qualified and most capable individuals for entry-level positions. In part, this is dependent on freedom from political dictation and manipulation in the hiring process—and every administrator should strive for such freedom to hire the best possible candidates, regardless of political influence.

Paradoxically, in some cities where little or no political patronage pressure exists, recreation and park administrators are surprisingly lax in their long-term recruiting and selection processes. Rarely will a department be found with carefully catalogued job and personnel needs charted over a period of time with a deliberate program of recruitment of high-quality personnel.

In the past, many recreation workers were hired who lacked formal education in this field. Because of insufficient college and university programs of professional preparation, it was necessary to accept applicants with training in allied fields. Today, with a greatly expanded number of recreation majors in higher education, it should be possible to hire only those who have had specialized recreation and park degrees.

Orientation and in-service training

It is essential that the first weeks or months of an employee's job experience include a thorough orientation. This might include such elements as a tour of the total department and exposure to its various divisions and functions, a careful outlining of all responsibilities and procedures, and a period of thorough supervision with, in some cases, the individual working directly as an assistant in a center or other facility before being given more independent responsibility.

A key element in the orientation should include the worker's being given a departmental personnel manual, which includes detailed descriptions of the legal structure and organization of the department, personnel practices and obligations, guides for leaders in various settings, and a statement of the objectives of the department.

Following the orientation period, there should be a well-organized program of in-service education that serves to heighten the employee's understanding of his work, improve his skills, and generally enhance his professional growth. In too many departments, insufficient attention is paid to this need. This is the most sensitive and impressionable period for a new employee, but often, even in apparently sophisticated departments, new workers are given only a brief orientation and left to drift for themselves. In-service education includes several key elements.

Individual conferences with supervisors. Workers should be regularly observed and should have the opportunity to meet with their supervisors to discuss their work in a nonthreatening, constructive fashion.

Staff meetings. At various levels, staff meetings contribute to in-service training. The staff of a large center or district or even the entire recreation staff of a department may meet monthly to be informed of departmental plans, policies, and similar matters and to take part in problem-solving discussions or project planning. Individual members of the staff may be requested to report on aspects of their work, or committees may be appointed to study special problems and present them to the group. Individuals who have attended professional conferences may be asked to report back to the staff on these meetings.

Special institutes. These are short-term training workshops, usually dealing with a special activity within the recreation program, such as theater, arts and crafts, sports, or camping and nature activities. They may also deal with special programs, such as activities for the mentally retarded or the development of Golden Age clubs. Institutes may last for only a day or two or may extend over a period of several days. Such institutes may be staffed by experts from the department itself or from neighboring departments or professional organizations, or they may be conducted in cooperation with nearby colleges or universities.

Preseason training institutes. Customarily, preseason institutes are held before the summer season and train seasonal employees for work on playgrounds and other special programs. In some cases, several municipal departments may join together to sponsor such a training institute. Topics assigned might include the following:

1. Goals and objectives of recreation programs
2. Orientation to the recreation and parks department in terms of major personnel, divisions, officials, and so on
3. Guidelines for scheduling activities
4. Responsibilities of playground leaders, personnel practices, rules of employment, and characteristics of effective leadership
5. Specific training sessions in program areas
6. Guidelines for maintaining safe programs, basic first aid methods, and instructions on steps to take in case of an accident

In some cities, such workshops are held not only just before the summer season but also between the fall and winter seasons or winter and spring seasons, when it is possible to bring all staff members together for intensive institutes in areas of professional concern.

In-service training courses. In-service training courses are comparable to institutes, except that they usually are extended over a period of time, with perhaps one morning or early afternoon a week devoted to attendance. In small cities, perhaps one such course might be offered during the winter season. In large cities, several such courses might be offered simultaneously in different districts of the city. The same topics might be covered in each district, but on a rotating basis. Normally, in-service training programs, when scheduled during work hours, are compulsory, although the department administrator may designate them for certain personnel only. In some departments, they may be given as week-end or evening classes and attended voluntarily. Such courses may have three types of emphasis:

1. They may deal with recreation leadership skills such as crafts, sports, or music.

2. They may deal with problems of community relations or socially oriented needs and programs. For example, a recent in-service training course in the city of Detroit included such topics as "Alcoholism," "You and Your Police Department," "The Mental Health Program," "Personnel Policies and Procedures," "Vest Pocket Parks," and "Drugs: Use and Abuse."

3. They may attempt, through rap sessions that are modeled on encounter group approaches, to change the attitudes of veteran workers and make them more sensitive to community needs. In long-established, bureaucratically organized departments, older civil service employees tend to have become complacent and have great difficulty in responding to the needs of younger people, disadvantaged groups, or representatives of racial minorities who are today making stronger demands for enriched services and facilities. Such training sessions have as their purpose helping all members of the staff understand their own attitudes better, become more receptive to innovation, improve motivation and morale, and develop more trusting and cooperative relationships among staff members on all levels.

Other in-service education methods. In addition to the preceding approaches, staff members may be encouraged, given brief leaves, and even assisted financially to attend national or regional conferences in recreation and parks.

They may be encouraged, similarly, to attend college or university courses in recreation and parks leadership and administration or to work toward appropriate degrees, with adjustments being made in their schedules to make this possible.

A library may be maintained of books and magazines in the recreation field, and staff members should be encouraged to read and make use of these.

Staff members may be encouraged to join professional organizations and take part in their activities, in part because of their value in professional development. Visits may be arranged for staff members to recreation and park departments in neighboring communities as a form of in-service education.

In any recreation department or agency, in-service training must be recognized as a key aspect of personnel administration. It is not enough to schedule several meetings and clinics throughout the year, almost at random, and then conclude that the job has been done. Instead, Dimock[2] suggests that the training program should be carefully worked out with as many staff members as possible participating in its planning. He identifies six key steps to developing in-service education programs:

1. Collecting information on staff needs and interests
2. Establishing specific objectives for training
3. Planning a training design with sequence and continuity
4. Preparing specific training activities and events
5. Conducting the training program
6. Evaluating the program

The exact nature of any staff development program will depend on the specific organization and its needs and capabilities. For example, the Boy Scouts of America operates with a relatively small core of paid professionals and many thousands of volunteer adult leaders. The national headquarters of the organization therefore develops an extensive training program for leaders with national and regional training events, clearly stated standards and goals, training manuals, and award certificates. Such programs, which are carried out by many other youth organizations, ensure a constant staff development process for both new and veteran volunteer leaders.

Many hospitals conduct extremely effective in-service education programs. However, often they provide less guidance for their regular employees than they do for college field-work students who are assigned to their recreational therapy departments. For example, the Beatty Memorial Hospital, a large psychiatric hospital in Westville, Indiana, has designed an extensive training program for field-work students to provide (1) an understanding of the causes, development, and treatment of mental illness, (2) an understanding of the role of recreation in the treatment of the mentally ill, (3) clinical experience, under close supervision, in a psychiatric treatment program, and (4) an understanding of professional ethics and responsibility.

In the Beatty Memorial Hospital, these objectives are achieved through a 480-hour training program, including the following:

1. Orientation—tour of hospital areas, facilities, and clinical and administrative staff (20 hours)
2. Clinical psychopathology—operational definitions, classification, and introduction to mental disorders (130 hours)
3. Orientation to recreation philosophy, objectives, functions, and organization (20 hours)
4. Music, occupational therapy, and volunteer services (40 hours)
5. Observation and assistance experience in recreation programs (126 hours)
6. Conducting own program (80 hours)
7. Diagnostic and disposition staffings; case histories and patient evaluation (12 hours)

8. Administrative duties, records, and reports (40 hours)
9. Supervisory conferences with director—counseling, discussion, and self-evaluation (12 hours)

In some cases, smaller community departments that are not able to mount their own in-service training programs because of limited numbers of staff and training resources have joined with other departments to establish joint in-service education programs. Several such departments may cooperate on a county-wide level to establish summer leadership training institutes. Not infrequently, state professional societies, in addition to their regular conferences, develop special courses and workshops for their members. In 1972, for example, the Connecticut Recreation and Park Society established a series of one-day institutes for all professionals in the state, dealing with such concerns as program evaluation, budgeting, leadership training, and facilities management.[3] Such efforts are extremely important in providing training opportunities for recreation and park employees on all levels.

DEPARTMENTAL PERSONNEL POLICIES

A key aspect of personnel management is the development of sound, up-to-date and attractive personnel policies. Customarily, these must be consistent with personnel policies prevailing through all municipal employment. However, in some respects, they may be adapted to the special requirements within a given field of service.

McChesney has written an excellent manual describing personnel policies in recreation and park departments, based on the practices followed in a number of outstanding departments. This manual covers the following major categories of personnel policies, including the following:

Sample manual outline

I. General regulations
    Responsibility
    Adoption
    Revision
II. Classification plan
    Contents
    Maintenance of plan
    Employee review
III. Definitions
    Full-time
    Seasonal
    Salaried
IV. Employment
    Application
    Recruitment and selection
    Appointment
    Probation
    Seasonal
    Evaluation and ratings
    Promotions
    Assignment and transfer
    Disciplinary actions
    Separation and resignation
    Reinstatement
V. Hours of work
    Work week
    Full-time salaried employees
    Full-time hourly employees
    Work schedules
VI. Compensation and related benefits
    Salary classification and guides
    Pay periods and time reports
    Deductions
    Holidays
    Overtime
    Vacations
    Insurance
    Retirement
    Credit union
VII. Absences and leaves
    Absences
    Health or hardship leave

VIII. Travel and vehicle use
   Departmental vehicles
   Private vehicles
IX. In-service training
   Purpose
   Conference attendance
   Staff meetings and conferences
X. Rules of conduct
   Dress and appearance
   Employee cooperation
   Reporting for duty
XI. Relations between employees—department—community
   Employee-administrator relations
   Employee-community relations
   Gifts
   Solicitation of funds
   Management of funds
   Publicity releases
   Employee-patron relations
   Accidents to patrons[1]

In the typical large-city personnel manual, detailed policies are stated with regard to each of these areas of practice, as well as many others not listed here. It is not possible to list such policies here in detail. However, illustrations of recommended policies are given under several major headings.

Recommended personnel policies

Hours of work and leaves. There should be a consistent schedule of work for all full-time, salaried employees, rather than a week-by-week adjusting of schedules to meet the needs of a given season or program. Although this schedule may require employees to work evening or weekend hours because of the nature of recreation programming, there should be uniform policy on the maximum number of hours a week, which is consistent with that of other public employees. If employees are required to work beyond this maximum number of hours because of special circumstances, they should be given compensatory time off.

However, a totally rigid approach to the problem of scheduling will limit a department's effectiveness. People and their time represent the most precious commodity available to the recreation and park department. Much more time and effort should be invested in the development of effective time utilization. Too often, the rigid 9-to-5, Monday-to-Friday basis for scheduling hamstrings any attempt to meet emerging community needs. Ideally, the approach should be one of plotting programs, opportunities, and schedules on a weekly chart, working backward to the covering of all commitments with adequate personnel. Despite the labor union and civil service challenges such an approach might provoke, it would be a real demonstration of the principle that service to the public is the recreation and park department's highest concern.

There should be an official policy regarding absences, vacations, and leaves, including the following elements.

1. Personal leaves of absence with compensation may be granted for such reasons as marriage, military assignment, religious holidays, jury duty, attendance at professional meetings, injuries, pregnancy or sickness. Normally, a minimum of 1 day per month is allowed for sick leave, and days not taken may be accumulated to be used later—usually with a maximum limit on the number of days.

2. Leaves of absence for travel or other personal reasons may be granted, usually without compensation. Employees absent without leave for a specified minimum period of days may be considered to have resigned.

3. Full-time employees who have worked a minimum of 1 year are usually

granted a 2-week vacation; those with longer periods of job service may be granted up to 4 weeks of vacation annually. Sabbatical leaves, with pay, may be granted to long-term workers, and special leaves for study may be given under work-study arrangements.

Health and welfare benefits. The same benefits that are available to other municipal employees should be granted to recreation and park full-time employees. These normally include health and hospitalization plans (including usually hospitalization, medical and surgical group plans, and sometimes dental and disability insurance), group life insurance, Workman's Compensation, liability insurance, and a departmental retirement plan. In some cases the employee pays the full cost of these benefits but receives a substantial deduction because of the cut rate for group plans.

Promotions, assignment, and transfer. *Promotions* or upgrading to higher classifications should have two purposes: to improve departmental performance by filling upper-level positions with capable personnel and to improve incentive and morale of employees by such rewards as higher salary, status, or job security. Promotions should be made on the basis of merit and should include consideration of service record, demonstrated performance, examination results, appraisals by supervisors, and additional training obtained by the employee. Normally procedures for promotion are spelled out carefully in civil service guidelines and job classification plans.

Assignment of personnel to specific positions of responsibilities is usually determined by the department head in the case of a small department or by a district or area supervisor in a larger one. Employees desiring new assignments or transfers should submit a written application to the department or division head. Although seniority is usually a key factor in the consideration of personnel for assignment or promotion, it should not be the sole basis of such action. All too frequently, less promising people stay around longer and pile up seniority credits. As a results, a department may become encrusted with high-seniority workers who lack imagination and initiative but hold their posts by virtue of longevity. Steps should be taken—where possible—to prevent promotion sclerosis from setting in, or all incentive will be destroyed for young and ambitious junior personnel.

Disciplinary action. Departmental personnel manuals should clearly specify the required behavior of employees in such areas as dress, smoking or drinking, persistent lateness, acts of dishonesty or pilferage, refusal to perform assigned tasks, violence or verbal abuse of patrons or co-workers, unauthorized absence, use of departmental vehicles, or general attitude. Both informal and formal disciplinary actions should be set forth in the manual. Depending on the nature and degree of the infraction, disciplinary actions should include the following procedures:

1. *Reprimands,* either verbal or formal, which are entered in the service record
2. *Suspensions,* or temporary separations without pay, for specified periods of time

3. *Demotions,* involving placing employee on a lower job classification at a a lower rate of pay

4. *Dismissals,* which are discharges or separations for cause

Usually such procedures are taken only in serious cases, in which there is clear evidence of the employee's unsatisfactory performance or violation of department requirements. The department should provide opportunity for a hearing or grievance proceedings in the case of such disciplinary actions when the demoted or discharged employee wishes to resist the departmental action. Increasingly, municipal labor unions are playing a role in such proceedings.

Personnel evaluations. The use of service ratings has already been mentioned with respect to promotion and disciplinary actions. Recreation and park departments should provide for regular and systematic evaluation of the work of *all* employees. Such evaluation may be carried out through on-the-job observations and ratings made by departmental supervisors, which may be required at stated intervals, to be placed in the employee's service record, and general appraisals of the employee's work, including elements of overall personality as well as specific performance on the job. Usually, such ratings are most efficient when they cover specific categories of performance and provide a gradation of specific descriptions of behavior, rather than a general reaction to the employee.

For example, in a Performance Evaluation form used by the Nassau County, New York, Department of Recreation and Parks, employees are rated by their supervisors under eight major headings: "knowledge of duties," "performance of duties," "effectiveness in working with others," "leadership characteristics," "judgment," "adaptability," "use of resources," and "writing ability and oral expression." Under each heading, the supervisor must check the descriptive phrase that best applies to the employee. For example, under "effectiveness in working with others," the following options are provided:

1. Ineffective in working with others; does not cooperate
2. Sometimes has difficulty in getting along with others
3. Gets along well with people under normal circumstances
4. Works in harmony with others; a very good team worker
5. Extremely effective in working with others; actively promotes harmony

The supervisor is also asked to make additional open-end comments in the Nassau County form, to provide an overall evaluation of the employee, characterizing him or her as "outstanding," "excellent," "effective," "average," "below average," or "unsatisfactory." A statement of the employee's potential for promotion in the department is also required. The entire evaluation report must be reviewed and signed by the subordinate employee and, in turn, by the general supervisor for the division.

Another systematic approach to regular employee evaluation is found in the Edmonton, Alberta, Canada Parks and Recreation Department. There, both the leader and the supervisor share in evaluation responsibilities. The *leader* is required to fill out a detailed form, which lists his job responsibilities under a number of major headings, assigning them "time percentages," and then to describe his work with respect to his relationships with others, working conditions, and similar factors. The *supervisor* then must list six of the employee's chief functions and evaluate how well he is performing these, including detailed statements of his professional knowledge, skills in planning and organizing his work, personnel management, communications, problem-solving ability, and similar concerns.

The key element in the Edmonton evaluation system is that the supervisor is required to identify at least three priority areas in which the employee must be encouraged to improve performance during the work period ahead. He then must suggest the methods he intends to use, such as "directed self-study," "formal courses," "counseling," or "outside seminars or clinics," to help bring about this improvement.

Each organization or agency is likely to identify certain key elements which are particularly important to its work, which it stresses in employee evaluations. For example, a large suburban YMCA rates its employees on the following characteristics in a Performance-Promotability Rating Form:

1. Overall performance
2. Response to community needs
3. Peer work group cooperation
4. Working relationship to superiors
5. Working relationship to subordinates
6. Use of resources
7. Working with boards and committees
8. Follow through
9. Supervisory skills
10. Emotional stability
11. Program skills
12. Racial sensitivity
13. Fund-raising ability
14. Planning ability
15. Statistical accountability
16. Building accountability
17. Initiative
18. Cooperation with community agencies
19. Involvement outside regular position
20. Innovation

Depending on the circumstances, there may be one or more performance elements that are extremely important to the employing agency. For example, in Disney World, the employee's image in meeting the public is of crucial concern; precise guidelines are established for appearance in such areas as hair grooming and coloring, sideburns, mustaches, wigs, cosmetics, perfume, fingernails, jewelry, and accessories. The employee's "presenteeism" (management's term for his or her total appearance and manner before the public) is strictly regulated, with rigid taboos governing behavior with "guests," use of narcotics or intoxicants, gambling, dishonesty, or similar matters.

EFFECTIVE SUPERVISION PRACTICES

As indicated earlier, one of the important responsibilities of district supervisors is to work with subordinate employees, to help them improve their performance and thus upgrade the entire recreation and park operation. The process of effective supervision is of special importance in recreation and parks, where many workers are assigned to locations where they are on their own—and where it becomes difficult to measure output or accomplishment in conventional terms. It therefore is all the more important that they receive careful and constructive supervision.

What are the key elements of supervision? Several can be identified:

1. To regularly observe the performance of line personnel and to:
   a. Assist them in seeing their own strengths and weaknesses
   b. Provide technical assistance in terms of helping them solve problems and operate more effectively
   c. Help to resolve conflicts that may exist among personnel
   d. Improve and maintain the morale and motivation of employees to ensure more dedicated on-the-job performance
2. To provide a basis for judging the work of employees, to be used in:
   a. Service ratings
   b. Making decisions with respect to promotions, demotions, transfers, and special assignments

Seen in another light, it is the supervisor's task to establish a constructive climate of human relationships and promote favorable work attitudes on the part of employees toward their job, each other, and the organization itself. The supervisor interprets and applies company policies and work orders, trains new employees, counsels and disciplines employees (where necessary), initiates or recommends personnel actions, and plans and puts into action time and work schedules and procedures, subject to limitations on his or her authority. Thus the supervisor may be viewed as a leader and trainer of others, an implementer of fresh ideas and approaches, a superior to lower-level employees, a co-worker with others, and subordinate to top management. He must be able to understand and effectively express the needs of those on all levels and, where necessary, help to mediate employee needs or enforce overall management policy.

Supervisors must not be regarded narrowly as overseers whose task is primarily to determine that individuals are not loafing on the job. Instead, they should be seen as helpful and sympathetic co-workers who are interested primarily in helping workers reach their full potential to make life within the organization more satisfying and the daily routine more interesting and ego-fulfilling.

Today the stress is on making work psychologically satisfying to the employee, varying it to maintain interest and challenge, and giving the worker himself the ability to make his own decisions and operate with a considerable degree of autonomy. The hoped-for outcomes of this approach are to provide intrinsic rewards, in terms of the self-respect and feeling of accomplishment and importance on the part of the employee, that will lead to greater effort and fuller accomplishment.

According to Horney,[5] five elements are essential in the process of achieving effective management through improving motivation:

1. A process of *staff development* should involve staff members in goal-setting and planning and assign them a fuller degree of responsibility, so that they feel that their work is important and significant to the entire organization.

2. Effective *channels of communication* should eliminate misinformation, rumors, mistrust, and insecurity and ensure full awareness among all staff members of what is going on in the organization. There should be honest and open communication, both written and spoken, among all levels of staff, so that employees feel that they are not simply cogs in the machine.

3. *Accountability* must ultimately reside with the head of any department, but he or she must be able to *delegate responsibility* with trust by permitting lower echelon employees to be creative in their work and using new approaches without fear of reprisal if they are not successful.

4. The *work load* and *goal-setting procedure* should be jointly developed by the administrator or supervisor and staff members, with frequent individual conferences held to provide opportunities to check progress, discuss obstacles, make plans for needed training, and revise performance expectations.

5. *Compensation*, in the form of salary increases, promotion, or recognition of superior work, *is* important and should be systematically and fairly decided on, with workers understanding the basis for decisions made regarding their advancement.

Horney sums up these guidelines by concluding:

> In the final analysis, the most effective way to motivate staff members is to assign them challenging work which gives them the responsibility to help attain department objectives and goals, and at the same time gives them a reasonable hope for success in their performance.[6]

Job enrichment

Many departments have developed deliberate programs of job enrichment, in which they have sought to use people to their maximum by restructuring and expanding work responsibilities and providing fuller opportunity for personal achievement, growth, recognition, and advancement. Edginton[7] comments that the stereotype that many recreation and park departments convey of themselves as happy, humanistic organizations "moving toward well-accepted goals in a smooth, virtually friction-free atmosphere" is questionable at best. Too often, he suggests, individual employee problems have contributed to the deterioration of organizational goals. One major technique for dealing with this problem is to enlarge the job through what Edginton calls "vertical job loading," a restructuring that builds greater satisfaction and motivation and a higher level of performance.

Often the very manner of the supervisor may determine his or her effectiveness. One's style of giving orders and instructions may illustrate this. Bittel suggests a number of dangerous pitfalls among industrial supervisors, along with suggestions for avoiding these pitfalls, such as:

An offhand manner. If you want employees to take instructions seriously, then deliver them that way.

Assuming a worker understands. Give him a chance to ask questions, raise objections. Let him tell you what you've told him.

Too many orders. Don't get order-happy . . . keep them short and specific . . . wait until one job is done before asking that another be started.

Choosing only the willing worker. Some people are naturally cooperative . . . be sure you don't overwork the willing horse and let the hard-to-handle people get out of their share of tough jobs. Employees want the work distributed fairly.

Playing the big shot. New supervisors sometimes flaunt their authority. Older supervisors know that you don't have to crack a whip to gain employee's respect and loyalty.[8]

Stroking for improved motivation

Such mistakes as those just listed should be carefully avoided by the perceptive supervisor. A positive approach to building confidence and cooperative attitudes is to use stroking. Simply described, a *stroke* is a pat on the back or word of appreciation. Clary comments that all human beings need some kind of stroking—physical or verbal—if they are to maintain positive morale and good mental health. It is a need that must not only be met but constantly repeated and reinforced. Clary writes:

As an individual grows up, he becomes more willing to take word stroking instead of the physical stroking he had when he was a baby. He still needs and wants physical stroking but often has to settle for word or symbolic stroking. Symbols of recognition become highly prized and are expected at every meeting between people. Saying "hello" and having someone reply "hello" is a form of stroke. An incentive award is a form of stroke.[9]

There are various forms of negative stroking, such as criticism or actual punishment, but it is generally recognized that these tend to have undesirable effects and are less effective in modifying behavior favorably than positive stroking. The following are stroking suggestions for supervisors:

1. Find and reward any good performance.
2. Reward or stroke frequently on a scheduled basis.
3. Try to shape or change behavior gradually, not all at once.
4. Use many nonfinancial rewards.
5. Develop the ability to give unconditional rather than conditional strokes; that is, "I like you . . ." rather than, "I like you if . . . or when . . ."

Since people tend to be subjected so often to negative criticism in their childhood or youth, by parents and teachers, often they develop negative self-images. One of the values of stroking behavior on the part of a competent supervisor is that it builds a positive, can-do attitude, which stresses the employee's confidence and eagerness to do a good job. The supervisor must not be false or insincere in his approach but must seek to be genuine and avoid manipulation of others.

Supervisory guidelines

Practical suggestions for supervision may be found in many personnel management manuals developed by municipal recreation and park departments. For example, *Springboard to Recreation—Institute Instructor's Guide*[10] has been prepared by the West Side Recreation and Park District of Taft, California. This contains a number of useful guidelines and case studies and presents eight steps that a supervisor should take to help members of his staff work together as a whole:

1. Realize the need for recognition.
2. Help each person on the staff attain recognition through:
   a. Bestowing credit
   b. Praising accomplishments
   c. Seeking opinions
   d. Showing consideration
   e. Acknowledging their share in the whole
3. Assign staff members to tasks where their various abilities are fully utilized.
4. Eliminate, as far as possible, grievance-causing factors.
5. Develop initiative by delegating responsibility.
6. Set high, but still attainable, standards.
7. Clearly define "work area" and "accountability" of personnel, with emphasis on their coming to supervisors with, not for, decisions.
8. Make as full use as possible of "status symbols," in coping with the need for personal self-esteem among staff members. Though they may seem trivial, such things as parking privileges, gasoline allowances, office accommodations and privacy, possession of sets of keys, or ready access to telephone are all important symbols to staff members.[11]

The same manual offers a number of guidelines for the actual day-by-day functioning of supervisors in working with staff members. For example, it lists responses to typical questions raised by supervisors about on-the-job problems.

What procedures may help to avoid complaints before they lead to grievances?
1. Watch for changes in attitudes, signs of dissatisfaction; associate these with causes; overcome employees' fears.
2. Discuss performance and work problems with employees frequently.
3. Inform employees of changes.
4. Get employees' suggestions for improvement.
5. Improve working conditions when feasible.
6. Listen sympathetically to employees' problems; know each employee well.

When an employee comes to you with a complaint, name the procedures which will be helpful.
1. Don't block the person in his attempt to get something off his chest.
2. Get all the facts—not just one side of the story.
3. Help employee analyze all aspects of the case; eliminate causes, if possible.
4. Weigh evidence before making a judgment.
5. When you make your decision as supervisor, be decisive; "sell" your solution to all involved; notify the employee directly of action taken.
6. Follow-up should be made to determine effects of decisions; be sure promises are kept.

What are the different types of visits a Supervisor may make to a facility or recreation area?
1. New worker—staying at a facility and helping to "break in" a new employee.
2. Observational—staying at an area for a period, and observing employees working with their groups.

3. Demonstration—going to areas and showing employees how to do something new, or something they have trouble with.
4. Delivery—brief visits while delivering supplies to facility.
5. Windshield visit—checking as supervisor drives past facility in car.[12]

It should be stressed that the preceding personnel and supervisory guidelines are geared to the needs and capabilities of larger departments with substantial numbers of full-time employees who must be recruited, selected, trained, and supervised. Realistically, there are many smaller communities, in which the public recreation and park department may have no more than two or three professional staff members, along with clerical assistance and maintenance workers. Similarly, the numbers of recreation personnel in voluntary and therapeutic agencies also vary greatly according to the size and type of the organization. For example, generally in therapeutic settings, such as hospitals, nursing homes, or special schools, staffing ratios of professional workers to patients or clients are high. As an example, at the Midwestern Regional Center at Palmerston, Ontario, Canada, a residential facility serving approximately 240 boys and girls with various types of disability (including mental retardation, physical disability, autism, or other emotional problems), there are ten full-time recreation staff members. They are responsible for all sports, crafts, music, fitness, social events, camping, and other forms of personal or social skills training and are assisted regularly by five field-work students from the University of Waterloo.

However, in many other special settings, there is a less satisfactory ratio of staff to participants. Many public recreation and park departments, as well as youth organizations or hospitals, have had to rely heavily on the use of volunteer workers. The effective direction of volunteer services is therefore an important aspect of personnel management.

Use of volunteer workers

Volunteers can assist recreation and park departments and organizations in a variety of ways, including the following:

1. Assisting in administrative, promotional, or advisory activities
2. Working with specific groups or activities, in playgrounds, community centers, and similar facilities, or providing adult direction for teen-age or Golden Age clubs
3. Mounting special community projects, particularly in areas related to the arts, ecology, or social service, where special expertise and interest are called for
4. Providing clerical assistance, helping with mailings, preparation of reports, and similar assignments
5. Offering special technical assistance (as in the case of residents who are architects, lawyers, or planners) with studies, films, or other projects designed to promote the work of the department

Of these, the largest area of use is in direct leadership of groups, or assisting professional leaders at work. Four elements are necessary for this process to be successful: recruitment, training, supervision, and recognition.

Recruitment of volunteers. It is necessary to seek out volunteers in a systematic way because they usually will not appear on their own volition. The most useful techniques for enlisting volunteers are through appeal to organizations with an interest in recreation, such as church groups, Parent-Teacher Associations, or special-interest organizations whose members are interested in promoting their hobby or interest. Hospitals frequently employ coordinators of volunteer programs, who develop contacts for reaching potential volunteers. In some cases, there may be a community council of social agencies, which serves to publicize the need for volunteers and channels volunteers to appropriate agencies for work assignments.

In general, the most effective kinds of volunteers are those with special training or interest, such as parents, school teachers, those with previous recreation leadership experience, or hobbyists who have special skills that they enjoy teaching to others. Many departments use large numbers of college students as volunteers. Often, these are students who are majoring in education or recreation, in which case the volunteer assignment may constitute a field-work course for college credit.

Training of volunteers. Volunteers should be carefully screened and trained before being assigned to specific tasks. Those who are unstable, or who have unrealistic expectations of the volunteer assignment, or who lack the potential for making a real contribution should be weeded out by the coordinator or supervisor of volunteers. Following this, there should be a series of orientation sessions or meetings designed to familiarize them with the objectives and philosophy of the department, departmental rules and policies, principles of recreation leadership, and the specific responsibilities they are expected to assume. If sufficient numbers are involved, special training institutes may be held for the orientation of volunteers.

Supervision. The function of supervising volunteers is similar to that of supervising paid personnel, except that they tend to require closer attention and more technical assistance and advice. Supervisors must help them realize that the department counts on their regular involvement just as it does that of paid employees and that their attendance must be consistent and dependable. If they are given meaningful assignments that challenge their capabilities, their involvement *will* be more consistent than if they are given trivial or mechanical jobs to perform. It must be realized that they are *not* trained professionals, and there is a limit to which any department can depend on the use of volunteers.

Recognition. Finally, it is necessary to make clear to volunteers that their work does make a major contribution to the department. This can be done through simple verbal appreciation, recognition of volunteers in reports and publicity, department meetings in which their work is singled out for praise, special dinners or meetings (sometimes on an annual basis) designed to recognize the work of volunteers and promote fuller volunteer involvement, or awards, plaques, or other tangible expressions of appreciation.

The real potential of volunteer leadership in recreation work has yet to be explored. Many recreation and park executives tend to take the position: "Volunteers are okay, but they take too much of my time, and they're not reliable." In truth, few executives give sufficient attention to the screening, training, and supervision of volunteer workers, and thus their success or failure is left largely to chance. That there are so many successes in the use of volunteers, despite this, bears out the dedication, persistence, and skill of many residents who are determined to contribute to recreation programs in their communities.

A final important value of volunteer services in many community or therapeutic agencies is the bridge that they help to build between the program and the community at large. At the Penetanguishene Mental Health Centre, Ontario, Canada, hospital authorities recognize the contribution made by volunteers not only with respect to leadership services they provide within the hospital itself but also in term of their external role. Volunteers who work in the hospital with patients are seen as an important means of educating those in the outside community as to the nature of mental illness. They help to break down the isolation that affects mental institutions, and this makes it easier for patients to enter community programs and activities either during hospitalization or after discharge. In addition, many volunteers who begin by doing hospital work later take on responsibilities with the Canadian Mental Health Association, both in its routine office operation and in promoting its programs and goals in the community.

For all these reasons, the successful conduct of volunteer services must become an increasingly important part of recreation and park administration today.

PROFESSIONAL PREPARATION OF RECREATION AND PARK PERSONNEL

Professional-level recreation and park positions normally require a bachelor's degree in recreation and/or parks or a closely related field, and upper-level supervisory or administrative positions may require graduate study in addition to experience.

Specialized academic preparation in recreation and park leadership and administration has been available in American colleges and universities since the late 1930s, with the first programs in Canada established during the 1950s. In the late 1960s and early 1970s, as a consequence of national support of open-space and outdoor recreation programs, expansion of many municipal departments, and the growth and diversification of therapeutic recreation, higher education in this field grew rapidly. By the mid-1970s, it was estimated that there were approximately 350 colleges and universities providing specialized degree programs in recreation and parks in the United States and Canada.

A major trend has been the development of 2-year community college curricula in recreation and parks. These were initiated because of the overall growth of community colleges in the United States and Canada, the perceived shortage of qualified personnel to take direct responsibility for leadership of program activities, and the need to provide career opportunities for students who, at this stage of their lives, were not ready for admission to four-year colleges. In many cases, 2-year degree programs were begun to provide new career opportunities for urban disadvantaged groups, particularly members of racial minority populations.

Students in community colleges usually have the choice between *terminal* programs, which equip them for technical or direct leadership positions in the field, and *transfer* programs, which are geared to the student's moving on to a senior college to complete work for the baccalaureate. Increased numbers of community college students have, in recent years, transferred to senior colleges and have performed well on this level.

On all three levels of higher education in recreation and parks (2-year,

Fig. 5-3. A, Another form of in-service training. Chicago Park District employees practice rescue methods for pond ice-skating emergencies. **B,** Top administrators and supervisors of Philadelphia's Recreation Department hold all-day staff conference to plan programs. **C,** Design of new facilities is a key aspect of administration. Here, Spokane, Washington, recreation planning specialists confer.

4-year, and graduate) there have been a number of major conferences and professional projects intended to identify curriculum needs and program guidelines. The National Park and Recreation Education Accreditation Project[13] established a set of Standards and Evaluative Criteria in 1972, which would be useful in developing and critically evaluating college curriculums on the baccalaureate and graduate levels. The standards include guidelines for the following curriculum elements:

1. Philosophy and purposes of curriculum
2. Recreation and park faculty
   a. Number of faculty and specialists
   b. Teaching load
   c. Personnel policies
3. Student recruitment, selection, counseling, professional participation, and placement
4. Organization and administration
5. Areas, facilities, equipment and instructional materials and resources
6. Curriculum content—undergraduate and graduate
   a. General education
   b. Professional education
   c. Professional emphasis (options)

Recent surveys have indicated that specialized options are today provided in a wide range of service fields in recreation and parks. These include such major categories as recreation and park administration, recreation resources management, and recreation programming, with dozens of sub-options in areas such as armed forces recreation, college union management, environmental education, industrial recreation, parks management, commercial recreation, religious agency recreation, school recreation or leisure education, and voluntary agency management. On 2-year and 4-year levels, the emphasis is chiefly on preparing line professionals for leadership and supervisory positions; in graduate curricula, more specialized or advanced functions, such as administration, research and planning, consultation, and professional education are stressed.

Certification and accreditation. Closely linked to the problem of professional preparation of recreation and park personnel are the joint processes of certification and accreditation.

Certification refers to the procedure by which an applicant for entry into a professional field is given approval that makes him eligible for employment. It may be based on such elements as education, job experience, results of written, oral, or performance examinations, and personal recommendations. In such professions as medicine, law, or accounting, it is usually determined by completion of an approved college or university program of study, plus taking an examination offered on a state-wide level that is framed with the assistance of professional societies, such as a state bar association.

In a number of states, formal certification procedures for recreation and park employment have been established through state legislation. The most common pattern, however, has been for state or provincial recreation and park societies to develop registration plans through which qualified professionals might have their credentials reviewed and approved. In the early 1970s, a

National Registration Board was established in the United States, and the National Therapeutic Recreation Society developed standards for several levels of therapeutic practitioners. It seems clear that there is a need to strengthen the professional standards used to screen those entering this field. Sharpless writes:

> Leaders in the park and recreation field have long considered the lack of an effective registration/certification system to be a major roadblock to the achievement of the stature and recognition to which the profession is entitled. The certification of park and recreation personnel, simply stated, is a process that guarantees that certain standards have been met by examination and/or proof of prescribed educational and and experience requirements.[14]

It must be recognized that registration or certification programs on the national or state levels are essentially voluntary in nature and do not compel compliance on the part of employing agencies, as a mandatory licensing system would. However, there is increased recognition that a widely accepted national system of registration or certification would define standards more sharply, assist public agencies in particular in hiring qualified individuals, and thus would upgrade the quality of service in recreation and parks. Some individuals have challenged this approach, claiming that certification based largely on the possession of a degree in the field would promote uniformity and crowd out people from other fields or with specialized talents. However, there is widespread agreement that an improved system of identifying and selecting qualified recreation and park professionals is absolutely essential.

At present, the majority of governmental recreation and park departments must rely on civil service procedures to screen applicants. These are based on a system of examinations and eligibility lists, which may be applied on a county or state-wide basis or through municipal civil service commissions. Although their original intention was to provide hiring procedures that ensure a merit-based system of appointments and promotions that would not be subject to political interference, there is widespread discontent with the way civil service has operated in the recreation and park field.

Cumbersome hiring procedures make it difficult to hire personnel when needed or when available. The examinations themselves are challenged in terms of their relevance. In some cases, individuals who have received provisional appointments and acquitted themselves favorably over a period of time must then take civil service examinations and may lose their positions to others who score higher on these tests. If civil service is to prove fully effective in the personnel management process, many of its bureaucratic procedures must be revised, and its approach to specialized fields like recreation and park service must be redesigned to take into account the needs of these fields. Too often, civil service officials and examiners are almost totally ignorant of the recreation and parks field and of the demands made of its practitioners; their examinations reflect this lack of understanding. Fortunately, within the past several years, a number of state recreation and park societies have succeeded in upgrading civil service requirements and providing input that has helped examinations and other hiring procedures become more relevant to actual professional needs.

Accreditation refers to the process under which college or university degree programs in specialized professional fields are formally approved. Thus far, accreditation has been under the aegis of organizations concerned primarily with physical education and has been of a limited and inconsistent nature. However, through the efforts of the National Recreation and Park Association and Society of Park and Recreation Educators, accreditation standards for college and university programs have been established, and evaluation of specific institutions was begun on an experimental basis in the mid-1970s. Ultimately, it is expected that a nationwide system of accreditation in recreation and parks will result in a higher quality of curriculum, staffing, and student services. This in turn will be invaluable in administering a more effective certification/registration system, by identifying approved institutions of professional education.

Current trends and problems in public recreation and park personnel management

We will now consider a number of major problems and trends in recreation and park personnel management, particularly in urban public agencies.

Problems of racial militance. An important aspect of urban life during the 1960s was the emergence of racial antagonism and conflict in many large American cities. This resulted in increased vandalism and crime in many parks, playgrounds, and recreation centers and frequently made it necessary to shift personnel from district to district, based on ethnic factors. The use of ethnic (defined in this sense as members of racial minority groups) personnel in this way does not represent a sound long-range personnel practice.

Regular staff members tend to be cynical about it (seeing it as a patronizing or vote-getting technique), particularly when job standards are reduced and attractive new jobs opened up for individuals who do not meet traditional qualifications. At the same time, the same staff members who criticize such tactics most vigorously are often the ones who have failed to serve minority groups or low-income neighborhoods effectively in the past. The best solution, of course, is to recruit increasing numbers of qualified minority group members on all job levels and to assign them, circumstances permitting, to appropriate centers or districts, regardless of their ethnic or racial identification.

For several years, with substantial federal funding in the United States for ghetto neighborhoods and job-related programs for black and Spanish-speaking youth and adults, many cities established special work-study programs and paraprofessional job opportunities in recreation and parks. More recently, financial support for such programs has been largely withdrawn, and little concern has been expressed regarding the recreation needs of minority groups. However, it seems clear that a fundamental concern of recreation and park administrators in large United States cities must continue to be the development of more effective programs in disadvantaged or ghetto neighborhoods, and the hiring of increased numbers of minority group personnel. This, of course, is closely tied with the need to expand higher education programs and opportunities in recreation and parks for black and other minority group students.

A new minority—women. On every level, the place of women in society has been a matter of increased public concern during the past several years. Essentially, the heart of the so-called women's lib argument is that women have historically been second-class citizens in the Western world. Subservient to men in a social, physical, and psychological sense, they have been discriminated against in the spheres of educational opportunity, community life, politics, and employment. Without discussing the total merits of this argument, it is clear that within the field of recreation and parks, women *have* been second-class citizens.

This may be demonstrated in two ways: (1) far more emphasis has been given to serving boys and men than girls and women in public recreation programs and (2) employment opportunities for women have been sharply limited compared to those for men.

With respect to the second point, a 1973 study of member organizations of the American Park and Recreation Society revealed that men dominated the recreation and park work force by a 2:1 ratio. A far greater percentage of men than women held high-level administrative positions, and job for job, women were paid an average of $1,717 a year less than their male counterparts.[15] Studies in Canada have revealed a somewhat comparable situation, with the ratio of men to women in public recreation in the Province of Ontario determined as 3:1.[16]

In the United States, discrimination for race, color, sex, or national origin in the provision of program opportunities or employment, training, and promotion was prohibited by Title VI of the 1964 Civil Rights Act. Increasingly, programs of affirmative action in public and private agencies of all kinds are removing barriers to the hiring and advancement of women. Beyond compliance with legal codes, however, many recreation and park administrators and boards have begun to reject old stereotypes of appropriate and inappropriate job assignments based on sex and have begun to recognize the capability of the individual as the only relevant concern. As a consequence, increasing numbers of women have been appointed to top-level positions in national, state, and local recreation and park departments, rather than be confined, as in the past, to largely program-oriented or specialist positions. Similarly, the effect of Title IX of the Education Amendments Act of 1972, which demands equal treatment for girls and women in educational settings, and of recent court decisions outlawing discrimination based on sex in physical education and athletic programs will be to break down patterns of inadequate or limited programming for girls and women.

Flexible use of personnel. In the past, chiefly because of the influence of the scientific management approach to personnel, which stressed the need for specialization in function, most recreation and park leaders were assigned to positions that they held on a full-time, year-round basis, in the same facility.

For a number of reasons, this approach has been shifting toward the use of personnel in more diversified ways. It has become clear that few cities have enough full-time professional leaders to be able to staff all their facilities on a permanent basis. In addition, because of the nature of recreation scheduling and program changes during the year, it is not administratively economical or logical to assign the same person rigidly to the same location throughout all seasons. Many departments are therefore changing their personnel assignment policies in the following ways:

1. They are rotating assignments at different seasons, so a given individual might work at various times in a Golden Age center, in a youth center, on a playground, or in a camp—depending on where he can be most productive at a given time.

2. In addition to their regular assignments, leaders may be assigned to other district-wide or city-wide roles, which they can carry on in slack periods during the day or week. For example, a playground director may be given responsibility for supervising a satellite after-school program during the winter season, or he may be given the job of serving as district chairman for a particular tournament or program, or member of a committee planning a city-wide special event, such as a bicycle rodeo or soap box derby. Such assignments ensure that staff members are used to their fullest potential and that adequate staffing is given to these special programs.

3. In many cases, leaders who were formerly assigned full time to face-to-face leadership in a facility have been given greater responsibility for coordinating and directing programs, with the actual leadership tasks being given to part-time workers or seasonal leaders with special skills that they can use in a rotating way in several locations.

Such varying assignments help to maximize the department's productivity and to make each individual's job assignment more challenging and interesting. Although veteran employees may resist this sort of job diversification, preferring the security blanket of a fixed, regular, familiar assignment, most younger workers welcome it. As a consequence, they also develop a broader view of the department's goals, problems, successes, and failures; often, too, they are compelled to work with a wide mix of fellow employees and residents of varying ages and ethnic backgrounds.

Another approach to job diversification lies in the structuring of actual positions to break away from the traditional mold of having a fixed number of full-time, year-round employees supplemented by a limited number of specialists throughout the year and a considerable influx of summer workers. Many commercial recreation organizations operate in a much more fluid manner, so that they can be responsive to immediate surges or slumps in program demands. Disney World, for example, has three basic types of personnel classifications:

> *Permanent:* Employment in an established job on a permanent basis for four days and at least 20 hours per week
> *Casual Regular:* Employment under which an individual is regularly scheduled at least one day but less than four days per week
> *Casual Temporary:* Employment designed to accommodate a specific period of expanded activity, such as summer or winter seasons, holiday weeks, etc.

This type of personnel plan makes it possible to tailor the supply of workers to fit the exact needs of the job situation, day by day and week by week. Although it poses a threat to the traditional job pattern found in most public agencies, it is particularly useful, given the nature of recreation and park program operations. It explains why many public departments choose to have private concessionaires operate restaurants and similar facilities in parks rather than manage them themselves. The fact is that private operators are able to run such ventures at a profit, partly because of their flexibility in personnel hiring and assignment procedures, when compared with public administrators who are constrained by civil service personnel contracts and union agreements.

District decentralization roles. A strong trend in many large-city governments over the past several years has been the attempt to decentralize operations by establishing local planning task forces, or little city halls. The purpose of these local or district offices or committees has been to bring municipal government closer to the people, to facilitate local control, or to achieve "maximum feasible participation" by neighborhood residents in the process of government.

In numerous large cities, attempts have been made to apply this approach to recreation and park administration. Increasingly, attempts have been made to form local or district recreation and park councils and to assign fuller responsibility for working with community groups and developing relevant neighborhood programs to recreation and park district supervisors. The role of such supervisors has shifted to acting as catalysts, community organizers, and coordinators.

Fuller responsibility is being given, in many cities, to district supervisors in terms of hiring and assignment of personnel, establishing local priorities with respect to programs, facilities, equipment, and supplies, and developing cooperative relationships with neighborhood organizations and residents.

Free-wheeling programs and staff generalists. Another innovation to have come out of the crisis-ridden 1960s in urban recreation and park agencies was the establishment of semi-independent, free-wheeling program units. At a time when student unrest and street riots demanded that civic officials take to the streets, tuning in on the turbulent vibrations, recreation and park departments were often called on to deliver spur-of-the-moment shows, entertainment events, and spectacles. When old-time civil service personnel argued as to neighborhood needs and priorities or complained of staff shortages or equipment inadequacies, mayors and their assistants began to turn to new delivery systems. In many cities, they established special funding sources and scheduled groups to provide mass events in sports, music, theater, and dance. These shock troops in what was often called the Mayor's Office of Cultural Affairs had talent and enthusiasm as well as a readiness to deal with street people; the more blighted and crowded the neighborhood, the more zealously they performed.

Similarly, in many cities, mayors and city managers discovered that they got better results in reaching neighborhood youth with crash summer programs by working through antipoverty organizations, indigenous leaders, or special youth divisions, than by going through traditional department channels and programs. Recreation and park executives must recognize the inevitability of such new modes and alignments, but they must also strive to improve staff attitudes and skills and keep programs flexible and fresh, so that they are able to meet such challenges themselves, rather than yield the ground to non-professionals.

A related trend has been toward the use of generalists, as opposed to trained specialists, in recreation and park administration. In many cities and counties over the past several years, a new wave of young men and women, attractive, highly intelligent and articulate, often with college backgrounds in law, economics, or political science, have become aids to political candidates for local office. After successful campaigns, the new mayor or governor has often selected such young people as staff assistants because of their ready availability, lack of commitment to the past, and capacity to address knotty problems in a fresh, even ruthless way. Frequently, such staff generalists have been assigned to key posts in recreation and park departments to shake them up, identify and solve problems, and provide new administrative insights.

Although generalists of this type have been resisted by old-line personnel because of their abrasiveness and lack of specific experience in recreation and parks, many department administrators have welcomed them because of their youth, idealism, intelligence, and knowledge of modern management practice. The alert and progressive recreation and parks manager will put such generalists to work as he grapples with such crucial problems as fiscal management and budget-stretching, vandalism, crime and public security, personnel psychology and union negotiations, and data processing and systems analysis.

Effect of municipal labor unions. A comparatively recent phenomenon that has complicated the task of personnel management in public recreation and park administration has been the emergence of powerful new public employee unions. In part, this has been a reflection of the growth of public employment in the United States. In 1959, there were 7 million public employees; 10 years later there were over 10.5 million, and it was estimated that by the mid-1970s there were 15 million workers in government. Of these, three quarters are employed on the state or local government level.

Overall, over 1 million government employees are today represented by unions with collective bargaining agreements. The largest union representing public employees is the American Federation of State, County, and Municipal Employees, AFL-CIO. According to Buechner,[17] it grew from fewer than 10,000 members at the time of inception in 1936 to over 400,000 members in 1969.

Sam Kinville, government affairs director for the Washington State Labor Council, AFL-CIO, asks: "Why are public employees on the march as far as organization is concerned?" He sees the matter as being primarily economic:

. . . wages of public employees have in recent years lagged drastically behind wages of employees in the private sector. . . .
Public workers are no longer willing to collectively beg; they are no longer

willing to accept unilateral decisions made by their employers concerning hours, wages and conditions of employment. Public workers by and large now expect true, meaningful collective bargaining. They expect written bilateral agreements signed by their representatives as well as their employers.[18]

Although laws vary considerably around the United States, today in most states public employees have the right to *organize*. Despite the fact that, in a number of states, they are specifically denied the right to *strike*, in an increasing number of cases municipal teachers' unions, firemen's and policemen's associations, sanitation worker's unions, *and* recreation and park employees' unions have called strikes, walkouts, slow-downs, job actions, and similar tactics to compel recognition by employing authorities or improved contracts.

How has the trend toward unionization affected recreation and park administrators specifically?

In 1971, respondents to a survey of recreation and park departments in cities of over 100,000 population reported that about half of their departments were unionized. Eichhold and Redmond indicate that two major conclusions emerged from the study:

> First, the typical park and recreation director is required to work with a union agreement negotiated by someone else. This may be an advantage, provided the negotiator is more skilled in this art; negotiating a union contract is not a job for an amateur. Second . . . the park and recreation director is frequently involved in at least some of the negotiating process. This is important. Just as the negotiator is likely to be more skilled in labor relations, the park and recreation director will be more knowledgeable about operating problems. . . .[19]

In general, the responding administrators reported that their relations with the public employee unions were favorable—either "congenial" or "tolerant." Only seven strikes involving recreation and park employees were reported. However, it should be made clear that when a strike of employees does occur, it can be extremely serious in its consequences. For example, in Vancouver, British Columbia, Canada, there was a 7½-week strike by all Park Board unionized employees in 1972 that continued from April 27 to June 19, with the following effects:

> . . . the parks suffered most as all maintenance of grass areas, gardens and landscaped areas ceased during our most intensive growing period. Emergency and essential work was performed by a handful of officials and union-excluded staff members who fed zoo animals. cut golf greens at six golf courses to prevent them from being put out of use for a year, and performed essential office duties including answering thousands of telephone calls by the public who were greatly inconvenienced because of the closure of most facilities, including the zoo, community centres, swimming pools, restaurants, golf courses, refreshment booths, etc. . . .[20]

Clearly, strikes and work stoppages can be highly destructive in their effects. In general, most grievances that deal with unsatisfactory working conditions, disciplinary actions, or alleged contract violations or violations of work rules can be settled without the threat of strike. However, this imposes constraints on recreation and park administrators in terms of being able to assign personnel appropriately or to change conditions of work according to the needs of a given situation. The demotion of an individual or, in some cases, failure to promote, may readily become the subject of a union grievance procedure.

This is best illustrated in the resistance some municipal recreation and park unions have shown toward attempts by department administrators to create new job functions, employ minority group members under reduced civil service requirements, decentralize supervisory functions, or in other ways respond creatively to current challenges. Because they have seen such actions as threats to the security or professional status of their members, union locals have resisted them vigorously and, in some cases, successfully. What this means, in the long run, is that recreation and park administrators who are seeking to streamline or shake up their departments or to make them more effective in meeting critical social problems, must now buck two kinds of opposition: the frozen municipal bureaucracy, which frequently resists any kind of innovative change, and the labor union, which, although professing liberal social goals, frequently acts in highly reactionary ways. In many large cities, this takes the form of the maintenance workers' union strongly resisting opening up more jobs to minority group members.

In recognizing this problem it is necessary for recreation and park administrators to work as effectively as possible in cooperation with public employees' unions. Buechner suggests that the "line official" is at the front when it comes to supervision, handling grievances and disciplinary action, and adhering to other terms of labor agreements. He offers several labor relations "rules of the game" that should be helpful to administrators in working constructively with employees:

1. Develop complete job descriptions and duties including pay grades.
2. Familiarize yourself with the collective bargaining laws of your state and local jurisdiction and keep current on new legislation.
3. Train your supervisors on how to deal with union complaints and grievances and be sure that they are familiar with the terms of the agreement.
4. Establish a grievance procedure—even if you don't have unions.
5. Employ or retain a qualified labor relations director . . .
6. Remember that unions are not the enemy. They are a group of your own employees.
7. Do not put union relationship on a once-a-year, contract-time basis. It is a full-time job.
8. If supervisors cannot be discouraged from unionizing, at least separate them from the bargaining unit of the employees that they supervise.
9. If possible, determine the bargaining unit through a secret election rather than a show of cards, or other means.
10. Do not panic or fear union leaders or concede to their every demand. When you feel you are justified, say no!
11. The union should be prohibited from conducting union activities during working hours, except for presentation of grievances—and even this should have a supervisor's approval . . .
12. Always bargain in good faith, learn to control emotions, and develop patience. Don't give the union cause or opportunity for criticism.
13. Do not underestimate union organizers. They are experts in their field, well trained and knowledgeable in labor relations matters.
14. Take disciplinary action as required and provided for under the agreement. If you let one employee off the hook others will expect the same treatment.[21]

To these guidelines one might add the following advice. It is important to keep in regular touch with the union rather than to wait for emergencies. Union members should be kept well informed about personnel plans and developments and should be involved in major policy discussions, although not in the decision-making process. In confrontations, the recreation and park administrator should insist on courtesy, comfortable surroundings, and orderly procedures. He will be wise to listen more than he speaks, to acknowledge the sound points of the union representatives, to avoid harangues or hot arguments, and, finally, to withhold *all* decisions until he has had a chance to think them over carefully after the meeting.

Probably the best advice is that of W. D. Heisel, Director of the Institute of Governmental Research of the University of Cincinnati, who comments, "You can create an atmosphere of hostility, or an atmosphere of harmony. You can deal with union leaders as interlopers, or as equals. You can make or break the labor relations directors' efforts. Unions are here to stay; I suggest that we learn to live with them in peace."[22]

As an example of the recognition of this as sound advice, the American Park and Recreation Society has sponsored Labor Relations Seminars geared to the needs of recreation and park officials. The first of these, held in 1970 at the University of Cincinnati, dealt with such topics as disciplinary procedures under formal union relations, grievance handling at the operating level, managing employee relations, arbitration of grievances, procedures for negotiation, and a mock bargaining session. Increasingly, recreation and park administrators are becoming aware of the need for such training sessions.

Suggested assignments for student reports or projects

1. Carry out an analysis of civil service procedures in recreation and parks in a municipality, township, or county system. Include such elements as job classifications and descriptions, examination and hiring practices, and promotional opportunity. Describe both the strengths and weaknesses in this system.

2. Prepare a comprehensive plan for employee orientation and in-service education for a large recreation and park system. Include such elements as initial orientation, in-service training workshops, and preseason clinics or workshops for seasonal personnel.

3. Examine at least one college program of professional preparation in recreation and parks and evaluate its effectiveness in preparing individuals for professional work in this field, based on interviews with working practitioners.

REFERENCES

1. "Guide to Personnel Criteria and Personnel Standards," Peekskill, N.Y., 1975, New York State Recreation and Park Society.
2. Dimock, Hedley G.: "How to Train Successful Camp Leaders," *Social Agency Management*, March, 1975, p. 27.
3. Ledger, Peter and Weiner, Myron B.: "In-Service Training in Connecticut," *Parks and Recreation*, November, 1972, p. 35.
4. McChesney, James C.: *Personnel Policies*, 1966, National Recreation and Park Association Management Aids Bulletin, No. 66.
5. Horney, Robert L.: "Administration by Motivation," *Parks and Recreation*, August, 1968, p. 48.
6. *Ibid.*, p. 48.
7. Edginton, Christopher: "Bring Out the Best, With Job Enrichment," *Parks and Recreation*, October, 1974, p. 40.
8. Bittel, Lester R.: *What Every Supervisor Should Know*, New York, 1974, McGraw-Hill Book Co., p. 279.
9. Clary, Thomas C.: "Motivation Through Positive Stroking," *Public Personnel Management*, March-April, 1973, p. 113.

10. MacRae, Kenneth G., and Pierce, Val I.: "Springboard to Recreation—Institute Instructor's Guide," Taft, Calif., 1967, West Side Recreation and Park District.
11. *Ibid.*, p. 8.
12. *Ibid.*, pp. 25-26.
13. "Standards and Evaluative Criteria of Recreation Education Accreditation Project," Arlington, Va., 1972, National Recreation and Park Association.
14. Sharpless, Joseph B.: "Registration/Certification: A National Program of Standards," *Parks and Recreation*, August, 1974, pp. 26-27.
15. See Kerr, Dona L.: "The Status of Women in Parks and Recreation," Parks and Recreation, April, 1975, p. 38.
16. Griffith, Charles, and Ng, David: "Recreation Personnel in Ontario Non-Tax Supported Agencies and Institutions," *Recreation Review*, February, 1972, p. 20.
17. Buechner, Robert D.: "Public Employee Unions—Organizations," Washington, D.C., 1969, National Recreation and Park Association Management Aids Bulletin, No. 81, pp. 39-40.
18. Kinville, Sam: "Why Unionization?" *Parks and Recreation*, March, 1969, p. 29.
19. Eichhold, Louis B., and Redmond, Jeffrey D.: "Labor Relations," *Parks and Recreation*, November, 1971, p. 20.
20. Annual Report, Vancouver, B. C., Park and Recreation Department, 1972, pp. 5-6.
21. Buechner, *op. cit.*: pp. 39-40.
22. For a fuller statement, see Heisel, W. D., and Hallihan, J. D.: "Questions and Answers on Public Employee Negotiation," *Public Personnel Association*, 1967.

CHAPTER 6

THE RECREATION PROGRAM

This chapter is concerned with the basic purpose of recreation and park agencies, which is the task of delivering enjoyable and varied leisure opportunities. It deals primarily with the role of public departments, although some illustrations are given of programs operated by voluntary or therapeutic organizations.

The term *program* is usually intended to mean the specific activities that a department offers to potential participants, in the form of games, sports, cultural activities, or similar events, Butler, for example, states:

> The community recreation program is the term applied to the total experiences of individuals and groups resulting from community action in providing areas, facilities, leadership, and funds. The experiences represent a wide range of activities, planned and spontaneous, organized and informal, supervised and undirected.[1]

FUNCTIONS OF THE DEPARTMENT

It should be understood that the typical recreation and park department has three distinct functions with respect to program responsibility. These include the provision of facilities, the provision of organized or supervised activities, and the coordination of community recreation and assistance to other agencies.

Provision of facilities. The recreation and parks department provides varied facilities for public use on an unscheduled, generally unsupervised basis. This includes the use of parks for walking, enjoying nature, or sunning and the provision of playgrounds, beaches, scenic areas, picnic grounds, and similar areas and facilities as described in Chapter 7.

In some cases, participation in tennis, golf, swimming, or similar activities may involve scheduling, instruction, or other forms of supervision for safety purposes. Ballfields must normally be scheduled by permit for use by community leagues. Semieducational facilities operated by recreation and park departments, such as museums, nature centers, or libraries, may involve special displays, lectures, classes, or other forms of guided activity. However, the primary emphasis in this major program function has to do with providing facilities for unscheduled and unsupervised use.

Provision of organized or supervised activities. Organized or supervised activities are conducted under direct leadership. Usually such activities require registration or formal group membership, which would not be true of free play or unsupervised use of a facility. Examples of organized activities include:

1. Summer day camp or organized playground programs
2. Teenage canteens, lounge or coffee-house programs, or work-study projects
3. Sports leagues, classes, tournaments, or instructional clinics
4. Adult social clubs or special-interest groups, such as little theater groups, choruses, or art groups
5. Senior Citizens clubs or Golden Age groups
6. Organized outings and trips
7. Community celebrations or special events
8. Mobile recreation programs, which send a portable facility to different areas of a community with program activities and equipment

Coordination of community recreation and assistance to other agencies. Although it is not as broadly recognized as the other two, coordination of community recreation and assistance to other agencies is a growing responsibility of many municipal recreation and park departments today.

Fig. 6-1. A, Performing arts are featured in many recreation programs. Here, kimono-clad Japanese dancers perform in San Francisco Cherry Blossom Festival in Golden Gate Park. **B,** Boys perform Indian songs and dances in Philadelphia recreation center. **C,** Youth theater is an important part of the Los Angeles public recreation program. Here, two teenagers perform in *The Red Shoes.* **D,** A large audience enjoys an orchestra performance in Chicago's Grant Park.

It is based on two principles: in most American communities, many different public, voluntary, private, and commercial organizations provide some form of general or specialized leisure opportunity for their members or for the public at large; and the public recreation and park department is usually the *only* agency that has a *primary* responsibility for providing or promoting *community-wide* recreation. Therefore it should promote total community leisure opportunity, by:

1. Working with other agencies to provide them with technical assistance, leadership training, the use of facilities, and sometimes equipment
2. Promoting overall coordination of community recreation activities by carrying out surveys and inventories of needs and services, developing community councils or planning committees, and encouraging joint projects
3. Assisting individuals or families with special needs or interests by publishing directories of varied opportunities within the community, making referrals to existing programs, helping neighborhood groups organize, or lending equipment
4. Acting as a strong city-wide spokesman for recreation, through the press, within municipal government, with other civic departments and agencies, with business and religious groups, and, finally, in cooperation with state or federal authorities in jointly sponsored or specially funded programs

The public recreation and park department should act as a catalyst, flag-bearer, promoter, mobilizer of public interest, research center, and in any other role that promotes leisure services or related social programs.

PROCESS OF DEVELOPING PROGRAMS   5 Processes

Exactly how does a public recreation and park department determine what program activities it should provide to the public at large? Essentially, there are five fundamental approaches to this process.

Traditional approach. In the traditional approach, the program is structured chiefly on the basis of what has been presented in the past and has proved successful. Thus, if a department has offered a network of community centers, playgrounds, or other facilities providing sports, arts and crafts, music, social, and other activities in the past, it will continue to do so in much the same fashion.

Current-practices approach. Recreation administrators are alert to what seems to be the vogue or most recent trend, either in neighboring communities or in the nation at large. Generally, such innovative activities are learned of by word of mouth, articles in professional magazines, presentations at workshops and conferences, or other contacts and observations.

Expressed-desires approach. In some communities or agencies, heavy reliance is placed on surveys or checklists to determine what members of the public would like to have offered in the program. Community committees may assist in gathering such information, which then is used as the basis for trying out new program features. In many hospitals or voluntary agencies, it is customary to have members or patients fill out checklists as a regular admission procedure to determine recreation needs and interests.

Authoritarian approach. Basically, the authoritarian approach consists of heavy reliance on the judgment of the department administrator; his is the sole responsibility for deciding exactly what program elements should be offered, in terms of what, when, where, and how.

Sociopolitical approach. In recent years, a fifth element has become a steadily stronger influence on determining program content. This is the sociopolitical approach. Increasingly, in many communities, pressure is generated within specific neighborhoods or groups of citizens for desired facilities and program services. Frequently, recreation has become a major slogan within the campaign promises of political candidates, and public hearings are held at which capital development and other plans of recreation and park departments are the subject of much controversy and pressure. Similarly, the need to have recreation meet significant social needs—especially in low-income or minority ethnic-group neighborhoods —has become an important influence on program development.

Summary. In most departments, no single approach is used. Generally, an administrator and his staff work together closely, building total program plans on the basis of all five methods; within a total framework of purpose, departmental capability, and community need. In arriving at final program plans, the administrator and his staff must obviously also consider what other agencies or organizations in the community provide and what kinds of leisure opportunities are available within close geographical proximity. The elements of staff skills and resources, financial costs of program elements, available facilities, and the possibility of co-sponsoring programs with other community organizations or departments must also play a part in selecting program elements.

Principles of program development

A convenient way to develop programs that will be conceptually sound is through the application of the four Ps formula: *philosophy, principles, policies,* and *procedures.*

Philosophy. Philosophy consists of the broad framework of goals or values that constitute the general purpose of the department itself. Essentially, this overall philosophy is one of meeting the significant human needs of residents, with respect for individual dignity and human worth, to achieve worthwhile democratic values and society goals. In addition, the philosophy should incorporate a positive view of the importance of leisure and constructive recreation in modern society.

Principles. Principles generally represent a set of fundamental beliefs, or major guidelines, for the development of programs. They spell out, in separate units, the general philosophy of the department. Typically, most textbooks on recreation and park administration include a set of guidelines, or principles for program development.

Policies. The third major step of the program-planning process is to develop a set of specific guidelines for program development, which relate directly to determining program priorities, the employment and training of personnel, the location of facilities, and similar matters. The formulation of policies is described in detail in Chapter 4. Policies represent a more detailed and specific statement of principles and are tailored to the needs of communities and to the specific characteristics of departments.

Procedures. These represent the fourth and final step of the process. Procedures are concrete statements of how policies are to be translated into action. They cover, in considerable detail, how every aspect of the program is to be carried out in bringing it effectively to the public. They may deal with such elements as responsibilities of leaders, first aid and safety regulations, maintenance procedures, publicity releases, arrangements for scheduling events, fees and charges, handling of moneys, disciplinary actions, and a host of similar processes. They govern the day-by-day conduct of the program and ensure its being a smooth, safe, and efficient operation.

Statement of program planning principles. Of the four steps just given, principles offer the best means of outlining the total direction and priorities of the effectively planned and conducted community recreation programs. A widely accepted statement of program planning principles follows:

1. *Community recreation should serve all elements in the community without discrimination on the basis of age, sex, race, religion, or social or economic class.* However, this does not mean that all must be served equally—first, because this is manifestly impossible, and second, because different groups have different needs. The principle suggests that all groups must be served but that this is carried on in highly differentiated ways.

2. *Community recreation should meet significant social needs, should be couched within a framework of democratic social values, and should provide constructive and creative leisure opportunity for all.* This is the sort of statement that tends to be taken as a platitude. It is easy to pay lip service to it and then to ignore it. If it is to be meaningful, it means that each element of program service should be carefully scrutinized and the following kinds of questions asked: "Does this promote desirable self-concepts and the constructive use of leisure—or does it build on the wrong kinds of values?" "Does this program activity contribute to the physical, social, and emotional well-being of participants?" Fun, or pleasure, is a primary goal of participants and *must* be a major element in selecting program activities, but the question of social values and purpose must also be a prime factor in program planning.

3. *Community recreation should provide a varied range of activities and provide diversity and balance.* This guideline implies that program activities should place stress not only on physical recreation but on cultural, social, and other types of participation. Similarly, activities should be presented on various levels of performance—beginner, intermediate, and advanced.

4. *Community recreation programs should involve community residents in planning and carrying on activities.* Increasingly, the principle has become ac-

cepted that community residents should have a strong voice in deciding what program elements should be provided and, when possible, should be involved in conducting programs, either as volunteers or in many cases as aides, assistants, or part-time leaders.

5. *Special groups in the community should be served by recreation programs.* Over the past two decades, community recreation departments have accepted a fuller responsibility for serving the mentally and physically handicapped (including the mentally retarded, aging, physically disabled, socially maladjusted, and similar groups). In more and more communities, this has been extended to the developing of programs for delinquent or predelinquent youth (through roving workers), drug-abuse programs, or programs linked with remedial education, tutoring, vocational counseling, or similar services.

6. *Recreation activities should be consciously selected and conducted so as to meet significant personal needs of participants.* This means that activities should be geared to meeting fundamental human needs, such as the need for social acceptance and group belonging, discovery of one's creative interests and potential, challenge and achievement, developing constructive self-concepts, the need both to compete and cooperate with others, and similar needs.

7. *Recreation programs should be flexibly scheduled so as to meet the needs of participants most effectively.* Traditionally most recreation programs have been seasonally structured, with rigid daily activity schedules. Today, there is a need to program activities more flexibly, with daytime activities for mothers with young children, aging persons, the handicapped, or night workers and with fuller provision of evening and weekend programs. Whenever special circumstances compel it, it should be possible to schedule recreation programs at unusual and different times to meet potential demand. The day of the recreation or park department that keeps its offices open only from 9 to 5 on weekdays, or the school recreation department that closes down on school holidays is past.

8. *Recreation programs should be planned to make the fullest and most imaginative use of all community facilities.* Although many municipal recreation and park departments have excellent outdoor facilities and areas, few of them have sufficient indoor facilities or specialized activity resources. Therefore the maximum use possible should be made of facilities owned by schools, colleges, churches, Ys, boys' clubs, and private or commercial organizations, to meet total community needs. This may be done on either a reduced rent or exchange-of-services basis. As an example, an industry whose employees use publicly owned athletic fields for softball leagues may be willing to let some of its specialized facilities be used by the public recreation department in exchange. Bowling alleys and similar commercial enterprises are frequently willing to make their facilities available at reduced rates to instructional classes, in off-hours, simply to build clientele interest.

9. *Recreation programs should be supervised and administered by qualified professionals.* For many years, public recreation programs were directed by individuals who were drawn from other fields and who lacked formal qualifications

for this field. Today, with an increased number of colleges and universities preparing qualified individuals for work in this field, all professional-level positions above the rank of recreation leader should be filled by properly qualified individuals. Direct leadership positions may be filled, either on a part- or full-time or seasonal basis, by those who have the needed activity and human relations skills, operating under professional supervision.

10. *Community recreation programs should be meaningfully interpreted to the public at large through effective communications media and joint planning processes.* This implies (1) that every appropriate form of communication, such as radio, television, newspapers, special announcements, fliers, magazine articles, or special reports, be used to ensure that the public be given an accurate and constructive picture of the program; and (2) that consultation with community groups be an ongoing part of the program-planning or administrative problem-solving process.

11. *Recreation program activities should be regularly and systematically evaluated to determine whether they are meeting departmental objectives and the needs of the community.* Such evaluation may be carried on in many ways: through periodic program reports, through special evaluations by department supervisors, through sampling the opinions of participants and other community groups, or by having the overall program appraised by special expert consultants.

12. *Dynamism is an essential part of programming.* An element of excitement, unpredictability, and surprise must be woven in, so that staleness, repetition, and cliché are avoided. This does not mean chaos or erratic planning. It does mean that the use of varied schedules, new locations, fresh leadership, or a change of pace is as refreshing as ice water to the thirsty and keeps interest and participation high.

Taken all together, these guidelines comprise a set of principles that may be used to spell out the overall philosophy of the department and ensure professionally sound and effective practices.

Program planning: additional guidelines. Just as it was the past practice in many communities to have standardized, uniform playground designs in all neighborhoods, regardless of local needs or interests, so it has been traditional to provide uniform programs throughout a city. Today it is recognized that, wherever possible, it is desirable to develop programs that are keyed to the specific and unique needs of individual neighborhoods, the resources available, and the wishes of local residents.

Meeting neighborhood needs. Within any community, different neighborhoods are likely to have sharply varied characteristics. For example, some communities have large groups of children and relatively few aging persons. Others have high numbers of families living on public assistance and plagued by various forms of social disorientation, as contrasted with relatively stable communities in terms of economic status and social stability. Increasingly, the factor of ethnic or racial identification has come to be recognized as a key element in determining recreation needs and interests.

Regional differences may also play a role in affecting recreation programs. Because of both climatic factors and national customs, many Canadian cities sponsor a high proportion of winter-oriented activities. In Winnipeg, Manitoba, for example, a major element of the public recreation program includes instructional and competitive hockey on various levels, ice skating in many forms, and curling clubs and leagues.

Therefore it is essential to determine the specific needs of each neighborhood or area within a community in planning recreation programs. This may be done in the following ways.

Inventories of facilities and programs. A useful starting point for such an analysis is to carry out a detailed study of all recreation facilities and services—not only those operated by the recreation and park department itself but those offered by voluntary, private, and commercial agencies. Such an inventory, which may be carried out with the help of community planning councils, should disclose both what is presently available and what is missing in terms of varied recreation opportunity. It is essential that the person or team carrying out this survey have the ability to analyze and assess facilities in terms of their full potential. It is amazing how seasoned recreation professionals can overlook or misjudge a facility that has great possibilities. For example, one observer looks at a gas station and repair garage as just that—a station and garage, a business. A second and more imaginative observer sees the station as a possible site for auto repair work to involve local teen-agers, directed by skilled mechanics for a modest fee. The most commonplace warehouse, dock, church hall, store, backyard or storage loft can become a recreational facility under the eye of the alert surveyor.

Study of needs and interests. To build an opportunity model—that is, a statement of what *should* be offered to meet varied needs within a neighborhood—it is advisable to carry out a systematic survey of the expressed wishes of residents. This may be done through public meetings or hearings, through Parent-Teacher Associations or other advisory groups, through councils or community committees, or through interest checklists or surveys involving a representative sampling of all age groups.

Capability of community. Certain basic facilities and programs are normally provided free of any sort of special fee or charge, but many others require special admissions fees, registration, or special materials charges. Particularly when activities use expensive equipment, specially designed facilities, or a high ratio of skilled personnel to participants (as an example, programs for retarded or physically disabled persons), it becomes necessary to ask how such charges will be absorbed. Will the community residents themselves be able to pay such charges, so that the programs can be relatively self-sustaining? Will skilled volunteers be available from within the community, to provide special leadership when necessary? If not, will it be necessary and advisable for programs in some areas to be subsidized more heavily by the overall departmental budget than in others? These are important questions when it is a matter of determining individualized programs for different neighborhoods.

When all the facts have been assembled, recreation administrators and their staffs are able to make major decisions regarding program activities and schedules.

Many popular activities will continue to be offered year after year, because they are tried and true, well-attended, and popular with residents in all communities. From year to year, some activities may be cut from the overall program because they are poorly attended, cause serious administrative problems, are too expensive, or have similar shortcomings. Similarly, each year some new activities may be added to the overall program, either because of community requests or simply because they have proved successful elsewhere and deserve a trial.

The entire approach to program development should be both pragmatic and flexible. Administrators must be innovative, in the sense of being willing to risk what is new and different, and realistic, in the sense that they cut out what does not work. Later in this chapter, examples are given both of the traditional program elements found in most recreation departments and of many new and different types of program features offered today in a few pioneering departments.

In providing services, administrators must be aware of the wide range of possible departmental functions with respect to each activity. In the area of sports, for example, the following are examples of the varied programs that a department may offer.

Department functions in sports activities

Free-play opportunity. This function relates to the basic responsibility of all departments to provide facilities for public use on a generally unsupervised basis. Thus golf courses, picnic facilities, softball fields, tracks, and similar areas are provided for use by the public on a generally unsupervised basis. In some cases, of course, a department must schedule the use of a facility, as in the case of a ball field. In other cases, residents simply are granted the use of a facility on a permit basis or for a small fee for a specific period of time, as in the case of a tennis court.

Basic instruction. Many departments offer specific instruction in sports activities, for children in playground programs, or for youth and adults through special classes or clinics. These may include instruction in individual sports, such as golf, archery, or swimming; in dual sports such as fencing, tennis, or combatives; or in team sports such as baseball, volleyball, or basketball.

Organizing competitive programs. A department may establish formal leagues for competition in different sports, either independently or in cooperation with Little League, American Legion, or Pony League baseball committees or similar community organizations. When the latter is done, the department generally provides assistance with publicity, facility, training of officials, scheduling, and similar matters, and the organization itself recruits the players, assigns coaches, and raises whatever funds are necessary to carry on the league.

Organizing special interest groups. Frequently, recreation departments take the responsibility for helping to establish special-interest groups. Such organizations then function on their own, although they may receive help in the use of facilities, public relations, or similar functions.

Sponsoring special events. To promote interest and performance in a given sport, recreation departments frequently sponsor special clinics and workshops, demonstrations, field days, conferences, or tournaments.

Training leadership. To promote successful sports programs, many recreation departments offer workshops or classes for officials, coaches, lifeguards, or other special personnel, who are then able to carry on the activity more successfully in the community at large. Sometimes several communities in a county or regional area may join together to sponsor such events on a larger scale. Special tournaments may also be scheduled as culminating events after competitive seasons. Awards banquets and recognition events may also be sponsored.

Within other major areas of activity, such as the cultural arts or social programs, recreation departments may have parallel areas of diversified responsibility.

CLASSIFICATION OF PROGRAM ACTIVITIES

Most recreation departments have established separate divisions or bureaus that are responsible for organizing and conducting program activities. In some communities, these are structured in terms of age levels and sex: for example, playground and after-school programs for elementary age youth, daytime programs for housewives, or evening center and weekend programs for teen-agers and adults. In some cases, these separate divisions may be structured on the basis of program activities, such as performing and creative arts, sports and games, aquatics, or programs for the handicapped. The most common categories of activities are the following.

Sports and games. Customarily, these include all the major individual, dual, and team sports that may be offered by a department. Examples include:

Active sports
Archery
Baseball
Basketball
Boxing
Football (including flag and
    touch football)
Golf
Handball
Hockey (including ice, floor,
    and roller skate hockey)
Judo
Karate
Soccer
Softball
Table tennis
Tetherball
Track and field
Volleyball
Wrestling

Active games
Dodge ball
Kick ball

Lead-up team games
Longball
Relays
Speedball
Tag games

Equipment games
Billiards
Checkers
Chess
Croquet
Darts
Horseshoes
Marbles
Nok hockey
Shuffleboard
Table games

Physical conditioning activities
Exercise classes (slimnastics)
Gymnastics
Jogging
Stunts and tumbling
Trampoline

Outdoor recreation activities. These activities place stress on recreation carried on in the outdoors and emphasize the natural environment. State, county, and large township recreation departments are most likely to offer direct participation in most of these activities. Municipal recreation departments often sponsor instruction in them, special clinics, organizations, or, sometimes, the activities themselves, if appropriate outdoor facilities are available. Such activities include:

Bird walks
Camping
Coasting
Dog obedience
Gardening
Glider soaring
Hiking
Hunting
Ice boating
Ice skating
Kite flying
Mountaineering
Nature trails and nature
  museum projects

Nature study (birds, flowers,
  animals, marine life, reptiles,
  trees, and so on)
Outdoor cooking
Picnicking
Skiing
Snow shoeing
Snow tracking
Surfing
Target shooting (rifle and pistol)
Terrarium
Trap shooting

Aquatics. Although this might legitimately be seen as both a form of sport and as an outdoor recreation activity, in many departments aquatics is organized as a separate branch of program activity. It has many forms and, of course, may be carried on in both indoor and outdoor pools, on lakes and rivers, and in the ocean. Examples include:

Bathing
Boating (power-boating, sailing,
  and canoeing)
Diving
Fishing
Life saving and water safety
Rowing regattas

Swimming
Skin and scuba diving
Surfing
Water ballet
Water polo
Water skiing

Arts and crafts. This is one of the most popular categories of recreation activities for all age groups. It might be divided into separate groups of fine arts and crafts activities. However, the distinction between the two is extremely faint, and many departments simply offer such activities under a single major heading. The most popular activities include:

Basket making
Beadwork
Carving (wood, soap, plastic foam,
  and bone)
Ceramics
Drawing and sketching
Finger painting
Furniture refinishing
Graphics (print making, etching,
  lithography, wood and linoleum
  block making)
Jewelry

Leather working
Macramé
Metalcraft
Modeling
Needlework
Origami (paper folding and cutting)
Painting (oil and watercolor)
Photography
Printing and book making
Sculpture (clay, metal, stone, wood)
Weaving
Woodworking

Performing arts. Over the past decades, with the growth of community arts centers, performing arts have become an increasingly popular form of community recreation activity. They are usually divided into three major headings: music, drama, and dance.

Music
Chamber music ensembles
Choral groups
Community singing
Creative music for children
Drum and bugle corps
Fife and drum corps
Folk singing
Glee clubs
Jazz bands
Instrumental instruction
Operetta companies
Rhythm bands
Rock-and-roll band competitions
Symphony orchestras

Drama
Adult repertory theater
Charades and dramatic games
Children's theater
Creative dramatics

Experimental theater
Mask making and marionettes
One-act plays
Play reading
Puppetry
Scenery making and stagecraft
Story telling
Theater parties
Variety shows

Dance
Ballet
Creative dance for children
Ethnic dance
Folk and square dance
Jazz dance
Modern dance
Rock-and-roll dance
Social or ballroom dance
Tap and clog dance

Hobbies. Obviously, many of the activities listed under other headings may be regarded as hobbies. However, there are many interests, such as the following, which may be the basis for special clubs in community centers or playgrounds. These include, as examples, collecting and model building.

Collecting
Autographs
Books
Clocks
Coins
Dolls
Match books
Memorabilia
Sea shells

Stamps
Toys
Weapons

Model building
Airplanes
Boats
Cars
Railroads

Special services for handicapped. These include activities specially designed for handicapped children and adults in such categories as the following:

Cerebral palsied
Blind or deaf individuals
Discharged mental patients

Homebound or dependent aging persons
Mentally retarded
Physically handicapped

In some situations, such groups may share integrated programs with non-handicapped individuals. In others, they may meet in their own special groups.

Mental and linguistic activities. This generally includes quiet activities of a mental nature, usually involving language arts. Often such activities are found in institutions, such as hospitals, where participants are not able to engage in more active pursuits. Typical examples of such pastimes include:

Book club
Creative writing club
Current events discussion group
   or forum
Foreign language study
Magic tricks
Mathematic tricks

Mental games
Paper and pencil games
Poetry club
Puzzles
Radio club or hospital radio station
Spelling bee
Writers' workshop

Social activities. Usually these are activities geared to specific age levels. A recreation department might sponsor coffeehouses, canteens, or social clubs for teen-agers, married couples' clubs, social clubs for single persons, groups for widowed persons, parents without partners, as well as senior citizens' clubs for older persons. Typical activities might include:

Banquets
Barbeques and picnics
Card parties
Carnivals
Clambakes
Father-and-son or mother-and-
   daughter parties
Fun nights

Marshmallow roasts
Masquerades
Pot-luck suppers
Progressive parties (table games
   and other contests)
Treasure hunts
Talent shows

Fig. 6-2. A, Orthopedically disabled children take part in a special field trip and park outing program sponsored by the Milwaukee School Recreation Department. **B,** The Washington, D.C., Recreation Department offers an outstanding program for mentally retarded children. **C,** Wheelchair basketball is sponsored by the Boston Park and Recreation Department.

Special events. Community recreation departments frequently sponsor special holiday celebrations to celebrate such occasions as Christmas, Halloween, Thanksgiving, Valentine's Day, or the Fourth of July. Often such events are co-sponsored with service clubs or other organizations. Similarly, patriotic holidays or civic holidays of special local interest, such as Founder's Day or Pioneer Day, are celebrated with carnivals, community-wide get-togethers, and similar programs. Some communities develop traditional programs, such as rodeos, band concerts, fireworks displays, and pageants, which are held each year to celebrate such occasions.

Trips and outings. Many departments have trips and outings to sites of historical interest, lakes and beaches, state parks, or similar locations as regular features of playground or youth center programs. Often senior citizen clubs and federations sponsor specially chartered flights or bus trips for their members.

Fig. 6-3. A, Sports of all kinds are a key element in public recreation. Here, a girl enjoys bouncing on a trampoline at San Francisco Recreation and Park Field Day. **B,** A youth boxing program is offered in many cities; here, a Boston youngster is given instruction. **C,** Less vigorous, but equally competitive! Milwaukee traveling chess instructor teaches the game to youngsters at local playgrounds. **D,** For Lincoln, Nebraska, senior citizens, pocket billiards is still popular.

In some cases, municipal recreation departments have even sponsored large-scale charter flights for vacationers across the country or to Europe.

Generally speaking, trips are not well planned by recreation and park personnel. Too-long bus rides, late pickups, overheated coaches, riding on full stomachs and poor receptions on arrival are chronic weaknesses. Surprisingly, advance personnel are rarely sent ahead to scout the route, time schedules, restrooms, or eating arrangements. A general rule is—never plan any trip casually, whether short or long. Treat a trip as a major logistic matter and scout out every detail in advance. There is no penalty for overpreparedness, and the chances for a delightful trip are greatly enhanced.

Service activities. A final important aspect of many municipal recreation programs is the provision of opportunities to volunteer in public service activities. Often this involves membership on community boards and committees or such assignments as working with youth in Big Brother programs, managing sport teams, assisting scout programs, or leading music, drama, or other program activities. Some persons with special skills may assist recreation departments in carrying on publicity programs and fund-raising or in helping with the transportation of aging or handicapped persons to program activities. Often, groups are organized to visit institutions such as hospitals, homes for the retarded, or other special schools to provide recreation events. In some cases, recreation departments have organized volunteer corps to help with community clean-up or conservation-oriented projects. Others have developed teen-age groups for work with the handicapped or in other public service projects.

In addition to such traditional forms of activities, many departments have experimented successfully with new and innovative kinds of activities. A number of such programs are described in the following section.

INNOVATIVE ACTIVITIES AND TRENDS

The majority of the cities throughout the country continue to concentrate heavily on the major traditional areas of activity, such as sports and games, arts and crafts, and social programs to provide the bulk of their program offerings. However, there are certain distinct trends in program service in urban areas today. As disclosed by a recent survey of forty-five of the largest cities in the nation,[2] current trends in urban recreation programs include the following:

1. *Ethnic programming.* Many big-city recreation programs have become more sharply attuned to the interests of different racial and ethnic groups. Festivals, music, dance, and theatre activities are now geared to black and Spanish-speaking population groups and reflect interest and pride in the cultural heritage of these groups.

2. *Portable program units.* Mobile recreation units, such as swimmobiles, playmobiles, fun wagons, naturemobiles, bandwagons, puppet-mobiles, traveling zoos, libraries, and science exhibits are being used increasingly to diversify program opportunities throughout city neighborhoods.

3. *Cosponsorship with industry.* More and more city recreation departments

are now cosponsoring special programs with business and industry groups, such as newspapers and television companies, soft-drink manufacturers, banks, and automobile distributors. The companies are assisting in the sponsorship of sports programs and tournaments, portable programming, summer shows and concerts, and similar events. In many cases, they provide substantial subsidies and offer publicity aid as well.

4. *Expansion of service to the handicapped.* There is a rapid growth of services to the handicapped, in which public recreation departments assist the mentally and physically handicapped persons directly or work in close cooperation with other community agencies that have this special interest. Chicago, Los Angeles, and Kansas City are examples of cities that are providing such services to the blind, multiply handicapped, mentally retarded, deaf, discharged mental patients, members of Alcoholics Anonymous, diabetic and cardiac patients, epileptics, brain-injured and neurologically impaired persons, and similar groups.

5. *Programs for the aging.* An area of considerable growth is in the development of programs for aging persons. Almost 90% of the large cities surveyed recently now sponsor such services. In addition to typical recreational and social activities, senior centers in such cities also offer health, legal, and housing services and sponsor seminars and other educational services designed to assist aging persons with the realistic problems they face in modern society.

6. *Work-play-study programs for youth.* Increasing numbers of cities have developed programs that have significant components of recreation, paid work, and tutorial or remedial education—particularly for low-income youth. Many of these programs are modeled after the "Workreation" approach begun in Oakland, California, in the mid-1950s and today receive federal funding. In addition, a number of larger cities have initiated roving leader programs, in which they attempt to make contact and work constructively with antisocial and alienated youth in low-income areas.

7. *Camping programs.* Many cities have expanded both day camping and overnight camping programs for children and youth. In some cases, they are operating summer camps at a distance from the cities themselves—either on properties they have purchased directly, or on sites made available by federal or state park authorities.

There are many other examples of unusual or experimental programs being developed by cities large and small, which point the way to communities that seek to develop new ways of serving residents of various ages and interests.

Flying courses. Flying has become a special recreational interest of many thousands of Americans. To meet this need, the city of White Plains, New York, initiated a pilot-orientation program, in cooperation with a Federal Aeronautics Administration–approved flight school at the nearby Westchester County Airport. This course provided both classes on various phases of general aviation and cross-country orientation flights in which students were given the opportunity to handle the controls. A considerable number of youth and adults who have taken this recreation-sponsored course have then gone on to take regular flight-school instruction.

Summer state park programs for youth. As an example of the work-play-study programs described earlier, the state of Washington's Youth Development and Conservation Corps has initiated a 6-week summer program in which twelve-boy teams live and work in parks operated by the Washington State Park and Recreation Commission. They learn to work and live together, constructing drainage systems, foot-bridges, trails, roads, and campsites. They fight fires, learn about first aid, tool safety, and basic forestry skills. They are provided room and board and $25 per week and, in addition to conservation work, engage in varied outdoor recreation activities. This program, geared especially to the needs of problem youth (many have delinquent or school-dropout records), has proved to be a sound investment—both in terms of the work accomplished for the state park system and in terms of the changed attitudes and constructive personality development of the young participants.

Fishing programs. Fishing is generally considered to be an activity carried on independently in natural settings, rather than a form of organized community activity. However, several cities have developed unique approaches to this popular outdoor recreation activity. Los Angeles, California, has initiated a large-scale ocean fishing program, partially funded by federal grants, in cooperation with the Southern California Council of Conservation Clubs. Thousands of children and youth, chiefly from disadvantaged inner-city neighborhoods, are transported by boat each week to a large barge anchored several miles out at sea. Fishing gear and bait are issued there, and the youngsters enjoy a day of exciting ocean fishing in which they often catch big-game fighting fish. Other cities, like San Diego, California, have constructed huge ocean fishing piers for use by as many as 4,000 residents a day. Other cities have stocked large municipal swimming pools with trout following the summer season and provided enjoyable recreation for hundreds of participants.

Environmental programs. More and more large cities have moved actively into ecology-oriented action programs. Park and recreation departments in cities such as Lincoln, Nebraska, Dallas, Texas, and Minneapolis, Minnesota, sponsor environmental clean-up and antipollution campaigns, recycling drives, and other conservation activities. New Haven, Connecticut, for example, operates a 40-acre nature recreation center, which sponsors guided field trips, courses, and workshops concerned with ecology for thousands of students on all grade levels in the city in a program jointly sponsored by the New Haven Park and Recreation Commission and the city's school board. Other city and county park and recreation agencies have moved into marine biology and ecology programs.

Bicycle activities. There has been a great wave of interest in bicycling in urban centers, in part because of concern about physical fitness and in part as a gesture of protest against pollution of the environment by automobile exhaust and covering of terrain by concrete and asphalt. The Department of the Interior has recommended nearly 200,000 miles of bicycle trails throughout the nation, and in 1966 federal grants for bike path construction in twelve major cities were announced. In such cities as San Francisco, Seattle, Milwaukee, and New York City, boulevards and roads have been set aside on special days for bicycle hobbyists and group riding events. Boston, Massachusetts, for example, has set aside a Greenbelt Bikeway about 7 miles long, stretching from Boston Common to Franklin Park and passing ponds, nature centers, museums, and other scenic areas en route.

Traffic schools. Many municipal departments work cooperatively with the police to reduce law-enforcement problems. As an example, some operate traffic classes for elementary-age youngsters. In Vancouver, British Columbia, the city police department assists the recreation and park staff in sponsoring a traffic school playground, where children in pedal cars learn to obey traffic signs, switch lanes, and familiarize themselves with good driving habits on a marked driving course.

Sportsmen's centers. With increasing interest in hunting and fishing, many local and county recreation and park departments have established multiple-use outdoor recreation areas for hunting and fishing enthusiasts. In some cases, these have been limited to hunting preserves and rifle and pistol ranges; in others, they have included opportunity for other forms of outdoor recreation family activity, such as archery, tennis, swimming, boating, picnicking, and hiking. One of the best examples is an outstanding sportsmen's center developed in New York's Westchester County. Sponsored by the county's recreation and park commission, this center provides archery and flycasting, in addition to a complete target shooting program, with trap and skeet fields available for shotgun shooters. Many cities are cooperating with the National Rifle Association of America in sponsoring basic marksmanship and firearm safety training programs.

Lifetime sports. In addition to heavy emphasis on competitive team sports, many municipal and suburban recreation and park departments are giving increased emphasis to the development of such lifetime sports as tennis, badminton, golf, and bowling. Typically, such cities as Richmond, Virginia, have sponsored special workshops in cooperation with the National Recreation and Park Association and the Lifetime Sports Foundation to teach basic skills in these areas, encouraging competition and continued participation, and to develop clubs, associations, and skilled leaders to promote them. It is worth noting that the greatest thrust in terms of adult sports participation in the United States has been in the area of dual or individual lifetime sports, such as golf and tennis.

The estimated number of tennis players in the United States today ranges from 14 million to twice that number; in 1975, Los Angeles County experienced a 30% growth in tennis participation, bringing the total to nearly one million players in that county alone. In 1965, there were no more than thirty indoor tennis clubs in the United States. Today, there are over 1,000 in operation, and hundreds more are on the drawing board.

Cooperative sponsorship. Many public recreation and park departments enrich their programs by affiliation with the National Public Parks Tennis Association, which sponsors tournaments for public parks players in 100 cities and provides assistance in facilities planning and tennis program development. Similarly, other major sports, such as baseball, softball, or golf, have national organizations that promote amateur participation on a number of age levels, sometimes in cooperation with other industries or trade associations. For example, the Chevrolet Dealers of America, in cooperation with the American Athletic Union, sponsor the Amateur Athletic Union Junior Olympics. This local, regional, and national competition offers youngsters a choice of eighteen sports, including basketball, bobsledding, boxing, cross country running, diving, gymnastics, judo, swimming, synchronized swimming, track and field, trampoline, water polo, weight lifting, wrestling, and volleyball. In many cities, recreation and park departments sponsor Junior Olympic programs in cooperation with this program.

New values in sports participation. As sports have grown increasingly commercialized and high-pressure on the professional and college scene, many individuals have questioned their basic value in community life. It is clear that much competitive sport is carried on today under the assumption that winning is everything and that sportsmanship and consideration for one's opponent are not really viable considerations. In junior high and high school sports and even in Little League play, intense pressure is exerted on youngsters to win at all costs. Increasingly, however, many parents and young people have been challenging the philosophy underlying such a highly competitive approach to sports. Lundquist comments:

> Almost inevitably . . . in a highly organized competitive sport, the focus is on winning and the eye is on the puck. How often does the well-intended volunteer coach really think about the total experience the boys are having, including those who have spent the greater part of the afternoon on the bench, or even worse, those who were not selected to be on the team?[3]

Another element of high-pressure team sports competition has been the aura of super-machismo that has surrounded it:

> The competitive ethic views sport as a masculinity rite from which women are excluded. The great Vince Lombardi often motivated his players by indicating very overtly that to lose a game was to lose one's manhood. Abhorred by this super-masculine, square-jawed, cold-eyed approach to sport, the counter-culture advocates more coeducational activities. Frisbee, where there is no violent body contact, has been suggested as a replacement for football . . .[4]

How should public and voluntary recreation and park agencies face this matter of the role of competition in sport? First, there must be an understanding that competition is an essential part of many forms of recreational activity and that it provides structure, a framework for organized participation, and a strong spur to motivating participants. An editorial in *Parks and Recreation* comments:

> From contact sports to Ping-Pong, from chess to wheelchair basketball, the notion that individual growth and development are enhanced by competition in recreation is rooted deeply in American culture. From dog shows to beauty contests, in crafts and the arts, the competitive model is often the only form of recreation programming for participant and spectator alike . . .[5]

The implication is that those who program recreation activities should strive to provide a reasonable balance between competitive and noncompetitive activities. The goals of winning at all costs cannot be justified in any recreation-related situation. The psychological and social effects of competitive sports programs must be carefully examined and constructive policies followed. Several examples of break-through programs with relation to competitive sports follow.

Corecreational sports. In a variety of team sports situations, including Little League baseball and college-level touch football leagues, girls and women are now competing on mixed teams with their male counterparts. Although there are obviously some sports in which this would not be feasible, it is evident that in a wide variety of activities—such as fencing, tennis, swimming, diving, golf, archery, volleyball, or softball, to name only a few—corecreational participation makes great sense. Apart from the question of women's rights, this issue has implications for the overall social development of both boys and girls:

> We expect adult men and women to be able to work and function together on a cooperative basis. Yet all their growing up years they are separated and the differences between them are pointed out. They haven't been given the chance to cooperate as children, so how can they be expected to cooperate as adults?[6]

New Games Foundation. A novel approach to sports and games is shown in the effort, in San Francisco, to develop new games based on old models, which include a wide range of individual or group activities with names such as Boffing, Gotcha, Infinity Volleyball, Earth Ball, and Tweezli-Wop.[7] The games themselves may involve such tasks as (1) players armed with pillows try to knock each other off a log; (2) presented with a huge, seven-foot ball, players rush at it, push it around, get it up into the air; (3) players engage in a mass tug-of-war, with 150 on a side; (4) players compete at tossing hay with a pitchfork over an elevated bar; and (5) players race at horizontal watermelon eating without hands. Along with computer games and theater games, such improvised contests suggest that many young people in particular are seeking new forms of humorous and creative competition rather than fitting into older, traditional molds.

Sports for seniors. In general, we have regarded sports as being geared for younger participants only in our society. However, with increasing awareness of the capability of older persons and with the breaking down of stereotypes about the aging process, more and more programs of sports for senior citizens have been introduced. One such program, sponsored by Senior Sports International in Los Angeles, stages yearly games for older amateur athletes. In it, over 2,500 participants compete in over thirty different sports. Men in their 60s throw the discus over 100 feet; 55-year-old sprinters crack the 24-second mark for 200 meters, and many other men and women set records in swimming, speed skating, and a variety of field events.[8] In another striking example, the St. Petersburg, Florida, Three-Quarter Century Softball Club, players ranging up into their 90s play three seven-inning games a week from November through March. One of them, a star outfielder and line-drive hitter, is 88 years old; another has a pacemaker in his heart; one team's catcher is 91 years old. An octogenarian athlete comments, "You lay down, you die. I believe a lot of us wouldn't be living if we weren't playing ball down here."[9]

Other sports trends. In terms of indoor sports, probably the most marked single shift has been in the growth of interest in self-defense activities. Karate and judo are now part of the offering of many colleges and voluntary agencies and are offered by increased numbers of public recreation departments. A marked influence has been the fear of danger on the streets, which impels many persons toward learning self-defense techniques. However, another influence has been the fresh interest on the part of young people (particularly of college age) in a more spiritual approach to life, which for many has led to study of Oriental philosophy and religion—including Yoga and Buddhism. As a result, such activities as judo and karate have become increasingly popular, as well as less well known systems, such as T'ai Chi Ch'uan and Aikido, especially on the West Coast.

Cultural programming. Music, drama, dance, and the fine arts have all been on the upswing in many municipal recreation and park departments.

Philadelphia, for example, sponsors major music festivals throughout the summer months, with top name stars performing. In addition, it operates a network of street theater performances, rock and jazz music jamborees in Robin Hood Dell, Mummers' Band performances, and touring performances throughout the city by Civic Ballet, Police and Firemen's Band, Lyric and Grand Opera Companies, Gilbert and Sullivan troupes, and a number of Afro-American performing companies.

Chicago sponsors outstanding dramatic performances by local community groups in its Theatre on the Lake, as well as a huge, annual Summer Youth Music Competition, which gives many hundreds of talented teen-agers the opportunity to perform before large audiences and qualified judges and ultimately before television audiences.

In many cases, the varied arts are now housed in new community arts centers. Peoria, Illinois, for example, operates a new center for the arts and sciences in one of its civic parks. This center houses twenty-nine different cultural groups and offers many programs related to the arts and nature and other science interests. Each year, these groups put on performances of Broadway plays, plan symphony orchestra series and student concerts, sponsor rock music shows, drama workshops, and children's theater classes, sponsor a fine arts week, and carry on numerous other cultural activities. Many other cities are sponsoring comparable programs.

In still other cities, the performing arts have been promoted extensively through the use of mobile recreation units. In New York City, for example, in a recent summer, musicians, dancers, puppeteers, and theater programs were brought to 175,000 children and adults in the city's recreation and park department's Mobile Recreation Program.

Youth gardens. Other cities have sponsored horticultural and nature hobby activities for youth. Washington, D. C., for example, operates an extensive Youth Gardens program on over sixty-five different sites, providing as many as 1,000 children a year with an enjoyable and enriching contact with nature, as well as an early experience that may lead to work in landscaping, nursery, or garden maintenance concerns. This project has been so successful that the American Association of Nurserymen has distributed guidelines based on Washington's program to other cities, in which similar youth garden ventures are now under way.

TREND TOWARD SOCIALLY ORIENTED PROGRAMMING

As indicated earlier, the most influential single trend over the past several years has been the effort to develop new kinds of programs that meet important social needs of residents and community groups.

As early as the mid-1960s, when the Community Action Program of the Office of Economic Opportunity was used to fund special summer youth programs, it was recognized that the traditional definition of recreation as activity carried on for its own sake, without extrinsic purpose, could no longer be valid in the typical modern community.

Specifically, it was recognized that recreation could make an important contribution to the war against poverty in the following ways:

1. It was regarded as a valuable tool in reaching and involving so-called ghetto youth, improving their self-concept, and helping them become able to take on work responsibilities and other socially constructive values.

2. In many cases, recreation became linked with remedial education, drug counseling, vocational training, and other needed program services in inner-city areas; it served both as a threshold activity that attracted participants and as a valuable educational and socializing experience in its own right.

3. Recreation served as an excellent means of getting groups of neighborhood adults and youth to organize together to develop plans for community improvement. In many cases, they formed organizations that were able to get funding for social programs or that then brought pressure to bear on city government for improved services.

4. For many young people, recreation served as a means of developing constructive relationships with adults, municipal authorities, and other community agencies. Through cultural activities and trip programs, it broadened the horizons of many who were formerly limited to their own area.

5. Finally, in an era of growing delinquency and crime, recreation provided an attractive and enjoyable alternative to antisocial gang activity for many young people.

In many cases, recreation programs were used during the 1960s as a way of buying time and cooling the city to prevent summer riots. This stop-gap approach to preventing violence generally meant that last-minute funding was provided just at the beginning of each summer and that programs were terminated at the end of the summer, when children and youth returned to school. The conviction has

Fig. 6-4. Armed forces recreation, as illustrated at the Great Lakes Naval Training Center, includes **A**, billiards, with 110,000 units of play each year, **B**, sailing, with over 400 club members in 1975. (Courtesy U.S. Navy.)

Fig. 6-4, cont'd. C, An auto mechanics hobby shop, and **D,** a day care center for children of service personnel. (Courtesy U.S. Navy.)

grown that recreation, if it is to be most valuable for ghetto youth and adults, *must* be a year-round service and must meet their fundamental social needs— along with a total approach to improving education, housing, welfare, job opportunity, legal services, and other vital social programs.

Although federal support for recreation as a special service declined in the early 1970s, many cities continued to operate special programs for inner-city residents, particularly in minority-group neighborhoods. In many cases, such programs have been sponsored by municipal recreation and park departments with federal funding. As an example, in a recent year, the Philadelphia Recreation Department sponsored nine different antipoverty programs, each with a different component of federal funding, adding up to a total of over $4 million:

1. *Project Human Renewal,* which combines health, welfare, recreation and human relations and legal aid programs for 13- to 17-year olds in poverty areas
2. *Summer Work in Recreation,* a program in which teenagers staff recreation

Fig. 6-5. Boston's Park and Recreation Department offers instructions in **A,** sailing and **B,** fishing skills. **C,** St. Petersburg, Florida, sponsors an annual "Fishathon," with thousands taking part. **D,** A water skiing demonstration at a water show sponsored by the Chicago Park District on Lake Michigan.

programs for young children, with funding from the Office of Economic Opportunity; since 1969, a year-round program

3. *New Careers in Recreation*, a training program supported by the Department of Labor, which equips candidates from disadvantaged areas to take Civil Service examinations for Recreation Aide positions

4. *Model Cities Programs*, in which the Recreation Department acts as a delegate agency in certain inner-city neighborhoods

5. *Recreation Support Program*, which provides camping and other recreation activities for youth with Labor Department funding

6. *Youth Opportunity Project*, which provides vocational and drug counseling services with funding from the Department of Housing and Urban Development and the President's Council on Youth Opportunity

7. *Neighborhood Youth Corps*, in which the Recreation Department provides employment settings for teenagers hired by the Board of Education under a federal grant

8. *Transportation* grant from the U.S. Department of Transportation, which makes possible recreational and cultural trip programs for youth

9. *Special summer food program*, in which hundreds of thousands of meals are fed to needy children at recreation centers under a grant from the U.S. Department of Agriculture

PRINCIPLES OF PLANNING PROGRAM SCHEDULES

Many factors go into selecting program activities that make up municipal recreation programs. These may be summed up under the following headings:

1. *Characteristics of participants:* their age, previous background or level of skill, size of group, sex, physical condition, educational and economic level, expressed interests, and relevant ethnic factors.

2. *Facilities required:* what facilities are available to operate programs—neighborhood playgrounds, community centers, small parks, ball fields, courts, or other specialized facilities?

3. *Personnel:* what activities are to be conducted without special leadership, simply by scheduling them and providing space? What activities require general supervision, and which others require specially skilled leadership?

4. *Funds required:* what will be the costs of specific programs, with respect to leadership, maintenance of facilities, purchase of supplies and equipment, transportation, or other factors? Can fees be charged, and if so, to what degree will they offset program costs?

5. *Scheduling:* what are the time requirements of an activity? When is the best time to offer it, to meet the needs of its participants—for how long and how often?

All of these factors must be taken into account in terms of selecting the wide network of activities and programs operated by most recreation departments. Once they have been selected, they must be organized in terms of when and how they are to be made available to the public. It is necessary to develop schedules that will serve the maximum number of people effectively within the capabilities of the staff.

These are basically organized on two levels: seasonal and weekly.

Seasonal scheduling

Most departments organize their total programs through the year into either two, three, or four major periods. This might involve a winter and summer program schedule, in which the winter involves chiefly indoor programming and the summer chiefly outdoor activities. Depending on climatic factors, it might be broken down more narrowly into four seasons: winter, spring, summer, and fall.

Typically, winter programs would tend to place heavier emphasis on instructional classes and social clubs or other group activities in community centers. They would include heavy emphasis on cultural activities, such as arts and crafts or the performing arts, and on such sports as basketball or hockey.

Summer programs, in contrast, would place stress on playground and day camping activities and on outdoor sports, aquatics, and special events. Generally, since the summer is the time when children are on vacation and many adults are also free from work for extended periods, summer program schedules are greatly expanded. However, unlike the winter when many adults sign up for courses over a period of time or for other regular commitments, the summer is a time when many families go away for family vacations. Therefore attendance is less regular and stable, and it is not possible to plan activities with full assurance of regular attendance.

Example of seasonal scheduling: Chicago, Illinois. Fig. 6-6 demonstrates in detail how program activities are organized during the winter and spring seasons in the city of Chicago. This section of the original chart shows a single area of program service, "physical activities," as carried on during the months from January through June in a recent year.

It should be noted that activities flow from competition on the local park level to area (district) competition and finally to city-wide tournaments or performances. As an example, Junior Boys Indoor Volleyball Tournaments begin on January 4 on the local park level. On March 8, those teams that have won on the local level compete in area competition. On April 17, the area winners compete on the city-wide championship level.

Detroit, Michigan, Park and Recreation Department: Wintercade. Fig. 6-7 lists the free indoor-outdoor winter program presented for Detroiters of all ages, from October through March, in 275 neighborhood locations throughout the city.

The brochure stresses special opportunities for winter sports on an individual or group basis, in such activities as ice skating, hockey, sledding, tobogganing, sleigh riding, nature trails, and winter picnics. It also stresses group activities for the physically handicapped and mentally retarded and for senior citizens in special centers around the city.

CHICAGO PARK DISTRICT
PHYSICAL ACTIVITIES SCHEDULED PROGRAM

LOCAL PARK ACTIVITIES

JANUARY

4 Junior Boys' Indoor Volleyball (January thru March).
4 Plan Pinochle Tournaments.
5 Co-Rec Volleyball R-5 Reports Due.
5 Basketball School R-65 Reports Due.
5 Boys' Basketball Free Throw Tournament, R-5 and R-46 Reports Due.
8 Junior and Intermediate Boys' Basketball Reports R-5 and R-13 Reports Due Area Chairman.

FEBRUARY

4 Senior Men's Industrial Basketball R-5 and R-13 Reports Due.
6 Ice Skating R-5 Reports Due.

MARCH

1 Plan Local Chess Tournaments, complete by March 27.
2 March thru June, Plan Community Baseball Leagues School.
2 Plan Community Marble Tournaments, (March 2 to April 14).
2 Plan Community Baseball Leagues.
30 Chess Tournaments R-5 Reports Due.
31 Two-Tap Volleyball R-5 Reports Due.
31 Community Competitive Report R-5 for Novice Wrestling Due to Chairman.

APRIL

1 Basketball Schools (April thru June).
1 Boxing Shows (April thru May).
1 Plan Boys' and Girls' Track and Field Meets (April thru May 4).
1 Plan Junior and Intermediate Boys' and Girls' Softball Program (April thru June).
2 Hula-Hoop and Frisbee Contests (April thru June).
2 Plan "Let's Play Activities" Program (April thru June).
13 Marble Tournaments R-5 Reports Due.

MAY

1 Junior Boys' Softball Starts Local League Play (May thru June).
1 Senior Men's Softball (May thru June).
1 Chicago Park District Inter-Club Tennis Association Entries Due.
1 Plan Community Education and Testing Programs (May and June).
1 Plan Boys' and Girls' Achievement Tests - Softball, Track and Field.
3 Track and Field Tournaments for the Mentally Handicapped.
10 Plan Community Handball.
10 Junior Girls' Softball R-13 Reports Due.
14 Chicago Park District Inter-Club Tennis Association Entries Due.
21 Boys' Track and Field R-5 Reports Due.
21 Junior Boys' Softball R-5 and R-13 Reports and Schedules Due.
23 Local Kite Contests.
25 Junior Boys' Softball Declare Bracket Winner or All-Star Team. Special Team Roster Form and Birth Certificates Due to your Area Chairman. Draw for Area Play.

NOVEMBER

2 Two-Tap Volleyball (November thru March).
2 Bowling Tournament for the Mentally Handicapped.
2 Junior and Intermediate Boys' Basketball (November thru January).
2 Plan Boys' and Girls' Indoor Volleyball (November thru January)
2 Women's Division One-Tap Volleyball (November thru December).
2 Synchronized Swimming, Indoor Natatoriums (November to December).
2 Wrestling Community R-5 Reports Due to Area Chairman.
3 Boys' and Girls' Checkers R-5 Reports Due.
3 Plan Local Ice Skating Meets.
13 Touch Football R-5 and R-13 Reports Due.

DECEMBER

1 Plan Community Table Tennis Tournaments (December thru February 11).
1 Football Achievement Tests R-5 Reports Due.
1 Local Ice Skating Meets (December thru January).
1 Conduct Physical Fitness Testing Programs (December thru January).

AREA ACTIVITIES

JANUARY

4 Junior and Intermediate Boys' Basketball Starts.
11 Women's One-Tap Volleyball Starts, North and South Divisions.
15 Co-Rec Volleyball Reports Due to the City-Wide Chairman.
15 Junior and Intermediate Boys' Basketball Special Community Competitive Reports Due.

FEBRUARY

4 Girls' and Women's One-Tap Volleyball Finals.
8 Area Pinochle Tournaments this Week.
9 Junior and Intermediate Boys' Basketball District Championships start all Areas (February 9, 10, 11).
15 Junior, Intermediate and Senior Area Two-Tap Indoor Volleyball Tournaments this Week.
15 Table Tennis R-5 Reports Due Area Chairman.
15 Pinochle R-4 Reports Due.
22 Table Tennis Area Tournaments this Week.

MARCH

8 Table Tennis Tournament Reports Due R-4.
8 Junior Boys' Indoor Volleyball Area Tournaments Start.

APRIL

5 Chess Area Tournaments this Week.
13 Chess R-4 Reports Due.
19 Marble Area Tournament this Week.
26 All Marble Reports Due.
26 Area Kite Contests (April 26 - 30)

CITY-WIDE ACTIVITIES

JANUARY

9 Indoor Swim Meet #1 - Ida Crown.
23 Indoor Swim Meet #2 - Ida Crown.
28 Women's Division One-Tap Volleyball Championships Start this Week.
29 Novice City-Wide Wrestling Meet (January 29 & 30).

FEBRUARY

4 Women's Division One-Tap Volleyball Final Championship Game.
6 Indoor Swim Meet #3 - Ida Crown.
8 Scuba Course Starts.
13 Open Division City-Wide Wrestling Championships.
19 Junior and Intermediate Boys' Basketball Championships.
20 Indoor Swim Meet #4 - Ida Crown.

MARCH

6 Indoor Swim Meet #5 - Ida Crown.
13 Junior Girls' Two-Tap Volleyball Preliminaries and Championship Game.
13 Indoor Archery Championship - Gage Park (March 13 & 14).
15 Intermediate and Senior Girls' Indoor Two-Tap Volleyball Championships Start.
19 G.P.R.A. Pinochle Tournament.
20 Indoor Swim Meet #6 - Ida Crown.
31 Intermediate and Senior Girls' Two-Tap Volleyball Finals.

APRIL

3 Indoor Club Meet #7 - Ida Crown.
5 City-Wide Bowling Tournament for the Mentally Handicapped.
10 G.P.R.A. Bridge Tournament.
17 Junior Boys' Indoor Volleyball Championships.
17 Indoor Swim Meet #8 - Ida Crown.

JUNE

2 G.P.R.A. Women's Industrial Volleyball Clinic (June 2 thru 4).
5 Chicago Park District Inter-Club Tennis Play Begins (June 5 & 6)
5 City-Wide Track and Field Meets for the Mentally Handicapped.
5 Midget, Juvenal and Junior Boys' Track and Field Meets.
6 Roach Junior Archery Shoot - Riis Park.
9 G.P.R.A. Girls' Industrial Softball.
10 G.P.R.A. Women's Volleyball Tournament (June 10 thru August 5).
10 Youth Week (June 10 thru 16).
13 Cloat and Team Archery Shoot - Washington Park.
14 Junior Boys' Softball Championships this Week.
19 Junior Boys' Softball City-Wide Championships.
20 Robin Hood Archery Tournament - Columbus Park.
28 Junior Tennis Instruction Center Begins C.P.D.
28 Junior Center Tournament.
29 G.P.R.A. Tennis Instruction (June 29 thru August 24).

"WINTERCADE" outdoors

keep fit through

FUN

join

"wintercade"

From October through March, Detroit Parks and Recreation offers a free indoor-outdoor recreation program of more than 50 classes, sports activities and special events at 275 neighborhood recreation locations and schools.

You can swim, play basketball, learn to box, trim and tone up with an exercise group, take a ceramics or wood-working class, join a theater company, toboggan or organize a hockey team.

And that's not all!

ICE SKATING

Artificial outdoor ice skating rinks at: Butzel Playfield, Chandler Park, Farwell Field, Gallagher Playground, Heilmann Playfield, Redford Golf Course, St. Hedwig Playfield, Clark Park, O'Shea Recreation Center, Wigle Recreation Center.

Admission charges: Children, 10 cents afternoons and 25 cents evenings. (Youngsters enjoy two afternoons of free skating at each of these rinks every week.) Adults, 50 cents at all times.

(Indoor rink in the Agricultural Building at the State Fairgrounds.)

Admission charges: (all times) Children, 25 cents. Adults, 50 cents.

Natural ice rinks with supervision at: Balduck Park, Belle Isle Park, Cannon Playfield, Lasky Playfield O'Hair Park, Palmer Park, Patton Park, Peterson Playfield, Rouge Park.

Also 100 unstaffed neighborhood locations.

HOCKEY

House leagues at Butzel Playfield, Farwell Field, Heilmann Playfield, St. Hedwig Playfield, O'Shea Recreation Center, Wigle Recreation Center. (Detroit Indoor Hockey League (DIHL) at State Fairgrounds Rink.)

SLEDDING

With supervision at Balduck Park, Dorais Playfield, Rouge Park.

TOBOGGANS

Balduck Park, Rouge Park. Toboggans are available for rent at Rouge Park. The rate is a minimum $2 for three hours and 50 cents for each additional hour. There is a deposit of $5.

SLEIGH RIDES

Pony-drawn cutters ply a snowy half-mile trail through the heart of Belle Isle weekends (weather permitting), 75 cents for two-passenger cutter. Rides start near Insulruhe and Loiterway. For current schedule information call 567-5830.

NATURE TRAILS

Groups of 10 or more are invited to tour Detroit Parks and Recreation nature trails at Belle Isle, Balduck and Rouge Parks with a department naturalist Monday through Saturday. Tours reveal how animals live during the winter months. Visitors may see Arctic birds including chickadees, nuthatches and snow buntings which winter in this area.

For reservations, call the Rouge Nature Center at 538-6088.

WINTER PICNICS

For those hardy souls who picnic in any season, Detroit Parks and Recreation provides stoves and picnic tables in Belle Isle, Chandler and Rouge Parks.

Fig. 6-7

In terms of major program opportunities, it lists the following sports, games, and social programs:

Badminton
Basketball (free time, classes, team play)
Boxing (clinics, classes, boxing shows)
Crafts (ceramics, painting, woodshop, sewing, cooking)
Dancing (ballroom, folk, modern, tap, square)
Dramatics (theatrical performances, acting classes, puppetry)
Floor hockey
Golf (indoor instruction by a professional, for a fee)
Handball (indoor)
Ice hockey
Ice skating
Model building

Physical fitness (varied gymnastic activities, slimnastics, conditioning)
Roller skating
Singing (choral, community, folk)
Sledding
Social clubs
Special interest clubs (hobbies)
Swimming (free time, lessons, team, diving, scuba, synchronized, water polo, lifesaving)
Table games and cards
Tobogganing
Trips and outings
Track
Volleyball

These activities, plus other major events, such as Halloween and Christmas parties, carnivals, flower shows, and other program features, are offered in the five major districts of the city.

Summer program: Huntington Beach, California. In contrast, many cities offer extensive activity schedules during the summer months. As an example, the city of Huntington Beach, California, offers the following in a recent "Guide for Summer Fun."

Weekly playground schedule. Play is supervised on weekdays from June 21 to August 20 at twenty-nine school playgrounds throughout the city. Hours of play are from 11 A.M. to 4:30 P.M. Activities include the use of games and equipment, arts and crafts sessions, a weekly movie, and "C" League baseball daily.

Once each week, on Friday, a different event is scheduled as a special program feature on all playgrounds. In 1971, these playground events included Bake Day, Wheels-a-Go-Go, Pet Show, Pirate Day, Junior Olympics, Horoscope Happening, Penny Carnival, Peanut Day, and Aloha Special.

In addition, once each week, a different excursion is scheduled on a fee basis. These include a Princess Paddle-Wheel cruise in Long Beach Harbor, a visit to the Knotts Berry Farm, a wiener roast at Newport Dunes, tour of Universal Studios, a visit to Sea World in San Diego, visit to Lion Country Safari, and a visit to a performance of the Ringling Brothers Circus.

Other summer events and activities are provided for older age groups.

Gymnasium activities include open gym, open volleyball, table tennis, women's volleyball, women's slim 'n' trim, girls' gymnastics, weight training and conditioning, open wrestling, junior wrestling, and high school summer basketball. Each of these is carried on at different high schools or recreation centers throughout the city.

Teenage dances are held on two evenings a week, and modern dance classes are offered for teenagers and adults one evening a week. Other special program features include a girls' drill team class, teen drawing and still life painting classes, dog obedience, cake decorating, adult oil painting, tennis, and yoga classes, preschool groups at four centers, and softball and baseball leagues on various age levels.

Aquatics is a major program feature during the summer with recreational swimming at several pools, swimming lessons, lifesaving and diving classes for all age levels, a city swimming and diving championship competition, and other features such as boys' water polo, sailing classes, fishing derby, and surfboard championship at various times throughout the summer.

Scheduling of weekly programs

Although the basic overall scheduling of most recreation and park departments is usually done on a seasonal basis with certain major program activities being offered regularly and others presented as special events, the most common type of actual schedule is done on a weekly basis.

A summer playground program would normally be planned with the following factors in mind.

Dividing day into major time blocks. Typically, the day is scheduled according to certain major time periods. In addition to at least one time block of an hour during the morning and probably two time blocks during the afternoon, other shorter time periods would be scheduled to allow for activities that take shorter periods of time, free play, setting out or collection of equipment, and similar tasks. This is demonstrated in the schedules presented later.

Selecting activities for schedule. Activities would be selected on a summer playground on the basis of type, age level, and group size and then fitted into the schedule in appropriate time blocks. For example, activities of different types (games and sports, quiet activities, folk dancing, arts and crafts) might be designated for different age levels in the playground population, such as children 6 to 8 and children 9 to 12. The size of the group would determine how much supervision and what area of the playground it would require. Some activities, such as a baseball game, would normally require at least an hour or more to play and would thus be fitted into a major time block, whereas others, such as story-telling, might be fitted into a shorter time slot.

Simultaneous scheduling. Assuming that there are enough children on the playground to justify dividing them, more than one group might be scheduled at the same time. This would have to be done so that those activities that require leadership are given it, while others are carried on under general supervision. For example, at the same time one group might take part in arts and crafts or a quiet game without direct supervision (having already learned the activity), while another is supervised, such as children using a wading pool or playground slides and swings, and while another is receiving direct leadership in an activity like folk dancing or playground music.

Use of areas. Scheduling also depends on the areas available for participation. In a typical playground, there might be an area set aside for play equipment, a wading or spray pool, tables for arts and crafts, a shaded area or pavilion for story-telling and quiet games, and a multiuse blacktop area for group games, volleyball, or tetherball. In addition, many playgrounds have an adjacent ball field for baseball, softball, or other team games. The scheduling should ensure that these facilities are used properly and safely and that activities do not interfere with each other. For example, it would not make sense to schedule a noisy volleyball game at the same time and in an area immediately next to a story-telling or singing group.

Time for playground responsibilities. In addition to setting aside time periods for activities, some time must be allowed for such routines as clean-up, staff meetings or inservice training, inspection of equipment, and similar functions.

Assigning activities to different time periods. Based on the preceding, daily and weekly playground schedules would be prepared. The most popular activities, such as ball games or swimming trips, might be scheduled each day. Others might be scheduled only once or twice a week. Strenuous activities might be placed in a morning or late afternoon time slot, when the sun is less intense, with quiet activities scheduled for the middle of the day. Special events, trips, or other program features would be assigned to certain afternoons of the week.

City of Phoenix, Arizona
Parks & Recreation Dept.

PROGRAM PLANNING

BASIC DAILY PROGRAM

A good program is based on a sound, daily plan which includes time for administrative activities, self-directed activities, leader-directed activities, and assignment of leadership to specific responsibilities.

The assignment of leadership and the number of time blocks for directed activity will depend on the number of leaders on an area.

CHART OF BASIC DAILY PROGRAM

A.M. Time Block	Activity	Person Responsible (Name)
	Open area, Inspection tour for condition of area, safety of equipment	Leader
	Get equipment out and set up (tetherball, bases, table games, etc.)	Leader, Aide or Volunteer
	Start self-directed activities for early arrivals or those not involved in sports, (Table games, 4-square, tetherball, various ladder tournaments)	Aide or Volunteer
	Active team sports or tournaments (while it's cool).	Leader or Aide
	Start or check self-directed activities for those not participating in activities below	Aide, Volunteer or Leader not involved in next activity
	One or more special Interest group activities involving direct leadership (Arts & Crafts, Music, Dance, Nature-Science, Games "Emphasis of the Week")	Leader and/or Aide or Volunteer
Pre-Lunch Lunch Hour	Self-directed activities, conversation, general supervision, meetings, lunch	All
P.M. Time Block Afternoon	Indoor Activities (hot part of day)	Person Responsible
	Start self-directed activities (table tennis, teen canteen, table games)	Leader, Aide or Volunteer
2 or more time blocks	Special interest group activities involving direct leadership (arts & crafts, music, dance, nature-science, clubs, etc.)	Leader, Aide or Volunteer
Pre-Dinner Dinner Hour	Self-directed activities, meetings, preparation of reports, general supervision, dinner	All
P.M. Time Block Evening	Indoor-Outdoor Activities	Person Responsible
	Start or check self-directed activities	Aide, Volunteer or Leader
Early Evening	Girls' program slanted toward self-directed activities. Some equipment may be reserved for them at this time -- table tennis, game courts, etc. Co-recreational activities	
	Teen Clubs	Leader or Aide
	Sports -- Leader circulating as much as possible on area with one Leader	Leader
	Check on supplies, Inspect area, lock up	Leader, Aide

Planning check list:

1. Are program activities based on interests of participants and designed to meet their needs?

2. Are boys, girls, adults served? Major age groups? Varied interests?

3. Is the work load evenly distributed?

4. Do Leader and Aide have some time to think, plan and prepare?

Fig. 6-8, A

```
City of Phoenix, Arizona
Parks and Recreation Department

                  PROGRAM PLANNING

                  BASIC WEEKLY PROGRAM

In outlining a basic weekly program, only special morning activities have been in-
cluded.  The daily routine activities of opening, closing and self-directed activi-
ties are to be found on the basic daily chart.  Some of these special activities
may be conducted afternoons or evenings.  Program will vary from area to area.
```

Day	Major Activity	Person Responsible
Monday	Workshops (In-Service Training)	Leader and/or Aide to attendd
	Introduce Programs of the Week	Leader or Aide
	Introduce Tournament of the Week	Leader or Aide
Tuesday	Teen or Sports Activity	Leader or Aide
	Tournament of the Week	Leader or Aide
	Special interest Groups under direct leadership	Leader, Aide or Volunteer
Wednesday	Team or Sports Activity	Leader or Aide
	Tournament of the Week	Leader or Aide
	Movie	Volunteer, Aide or Leader
Thursday	Finals of Tournament of the Week	Staff and Volunteers
	Special Interest Groups under direct leadersnip	Leader, Aide or Volunteer
	Meeting to plan following week's program	Staff and Volunteers or "Committees"
	Preparation and sending special program plans to Information Representative	Leader
	Visiting Specialists' Program	Specialists and area assistants as needed
Friday	Team or Sports Activity	Leader or Aide
	Special Interest Groups under direct leadership	Leader, Aide or Volunteer
	Preparation of Bulletin Board for next week, Attendance and other Reports	Leader, Aide or Volunteer

```
Note:

Special Interest Groups (Creative Dramatics, Arts & Crafts, Music, Dance, Nature,
                  Games, Etc.)

1.  The kind of activity provided will depend on skills of Leader, Aide, Volunteer
    and interests of the group.

2.  The number wishing to participate and skill levels represented will indicate
    whether division into smaller groups is desirable for maximum benefit to
    participants.

Morning Programs

The leader who is alone on an area is encouraged to secure as many Volunteers as
needed to provide an adequate level of service.

Check:  Are all major events (City-Wide, etc.) included?
        Are all ages served?  Are girls' interests served as well as boys'?
        Is program balanced (varied) for all ages?  (Music, Social, Crafts,
        Sports?)
        Is there a Special Event for some group or the whole group or is one being
        planned?
        Is weather considered?  (Active sports for cooler times.)
```

B

Fig. 6-8, B

Examples of schedules. There is no ideal program schedule that applies to all situations. However, several examples are given here to show how a community or organization structures its recreational program.

Phoenix, Arizona, basic daily playground program. Fig. 6-8, A, illustrates how major activities are assigned to certain time periods during the day. It does

FREDERICK COUNTY OUTDOOR SCHOOL .... Sample Schedule, Activities are flexible.

7:15	REVEILLE - If you get up earlier - 6:30 earliest, please be quiet so you don't disturb the deer and bird life.
7:40	K.P. and Flag Raising Bell (Four campers raise the American and Maryland Flags)
8:00	BREAKFAST - Followed by lively songs. Individuals or class groups lead them. Weather Report
8:45	CLEAN-UP - Cabin and Wash Room, Staff Meeting

MONDAY	TUESDAY	WEDNESDAY	THURSDAY	FRIDAY
Cabin Assignments 9:00 Flag Raising Camp Tour of Nature Cabin, Weather Station, Dining Hall, Rec. Hall, Nature Craft, Nurses Cabin	ALL DAY FIELD TRIP Temp. changes changes in plant growth Water's effect on rocks.	COMPASS-WATER-SHED QUEST How to spot a fire Use of compass Maps: sketch & topographic Discussion of a watershed.	MOUNTAIN VIEW ROCK FORMATION Study rocks:color, texture, hard-ness Terms: Piedmont Plateau, Fault, Inland seas Mountain form-ation: age, volcanic action.	NATURE CRAFT, SKETCHING, TOOLS Use of axes, crosscuts, sledges. Sketch with charcoal. Whittle; totem-pole, pencil-holder

12:15 LUNCH: Weather Report, Songs, K.P.'s report at 12:00 to set the tables. One K.P. per table. (Each class group has 4 or 5 meals.)
LAZY TIME: Whittle, crafts, nature cabin, rest in cabins.

| 1:30 FIELD NOTE HIKE Hike in forest. Take field notes Use five senses 3:30 NATURE HUNT Teams of 4 & 5 children | COOK-OUT Each cooks his own in a mess kit. Care of forest COMPASS HIKE Use of Compass in woods. Observation of plant and animal life. | TROUT HATCHERY See 18" trout Slides of Trout View trout ponds or Pond study, fish-ing. Life in pond temp. changes in water Dissect frog, fish. | FORESTRY-TREE PLANTING Types of trees Age of trees Interesting growth Plant Succession Plant pine tree Animal life What is a forest | BUSSES LEAVE Catoctin Furnace You may wish to visit this historic area enroute home. |

4:30	SHOWER AND FREE TIME: Nature cabin, Run on Greentop, Nature crafts, Whittle, Rest
5:15	SUPPER: Skits, stunts, or jokes from boys and girls. Weather report
6:15	FLAG LOWERING: Four boys or girls
	VESPERS: Each class group has charge of one of these "nature" inspired 10 minutes. (Poems, Readings, Songs, Original writings, Choral readings)
6:30	CLASS MEETING: Each of the class groups meet separately, the classroom teacher is in charge. They evaluate the days activities and plan for the next.
7:30	EVENING ACTIVITIES: Planned at the Outdoor School by the Council. Outdoor games, stunts, campfires, games, stories and songs, star study, night noises and beauty.
9:00	TAPS: If you have a student that can play this or any of the other Bugle calls have him, or her bring the instrument.

Fig. 6-9

not commit a playground leader to exact time periods; the program is determined flexibly.

Phoenix, Arizona, basic weekly playground program. Fig. 6-8, *B*, shows how different events may be scheduled during the week, including special interest groups, tournaments, movies, trips, or other activities. In many playgrounds a special theme is used each week, with arts and crafts, music, and dance activities all centered around this theme. Then, on Friday morning or afternoon, a special party, carnival, contest, or other culminating event is held, based on this theme.

In addition, certain major activities may be planned for the end of the season,

```
                          CITY OF DETROIT
                  DEPARTMENT OF PARKS AND RECREATION
                    PATTON PARK RECREATION CENTER
                           2301 Woodmere
                        Phone:  843-1960

            FALL-WINTER-SRING SWIMMING SCHEDULE 1970-1971
```

Monday	Tuesday	Wednesday	Thursday	Friday	Saturday	Sunday
	9:00-12:30 Mixed Adult Swim	1:00-2:00 MR's				
	2:00-3:00 D.J. HEALY Swim	2:00-3:00 Harms School	2:00-3:00 Golden Algers Swim	2:00-3:00 Bennett School		
4:00-5:30 Mixed Open Swim	3:30-5:30 Mixed Open Swim	3:30-5:30 Mixed Open Swim	3:30-5:30 Mixed Open Swim	3:30-5:30 Mixed Open Swim	1:30-3:00 Mixed Open Swim 3:30-5:00 Mixed Open Swim	1:30-3:00 Mixed Open Swim 3:30-5:00 Mixed Open Swim
5:30-7:00 Swim Team	5:30-7:00 Swim Team	5:30-7:00 Swim Team	5:30-7:00 Swim Team	5:30-7:00 Swim Team		
7:00-8:15 Mixed Teen Swim	7:00-8:15 Girls Teen Swim	7:00-8:15 Mixed Teen Swim	7:00-8:15 Family Swim and Adults	7:00-8:30 Family Swim and Adults	6:00-9:00 Handicapped Swim Night	6:00-7:30 Family Swim
8:30-10:00 Mixed Adult Swim	8:30-10:00 Ladies Swim Night	8:30-10:00 Mixed Adult Swim	8:30-10:00 Life Saving and Life Guard School	9:00-10:00 S.C.U.B.A. Diving Club		8:00-9:30 Family Swim and Adults

```
   4:30 - 5:00  Daily, MONDAY - FRIDAY Organized Games and Swim Instruction

   Suits, Soap and Towels are not supplied.    N O    C H A R G E.

              BRING YOUR SUIT, SOAP, TOWEL AND LOCK.
```

9/24/70

Fig. 6-10

such as special shows, playdays, or exhibits—usually scheduled for the late afternoon or early evening—so parents can attend.

Other examples of programs. The summer playground program is only one example of how scheduling is carried on by recreation and park agencies. Several other examples follow.

Frederick County, Maryland, outdoor school. Fig. 6-9 gives the weekly schedule of a school camping program, at which children go away with their school classes for several days of living in a natural setting and learning about nature and wildlife. The major morning and afternoon time blocks are left open, with major projects or trips briefly suggested, while the other time assignments are tightly scheduled.

Detroit, Michigan, community center. The weekly schedule of the Patton Park Recreation Center in Detroit is shown in Fig. 6-10. It shows the schedule for the center pool, which has an active program throughout the week.

Newark, New Jersey, Y.M.-Y.W.H.A. physical activity schedule. The schedule for a voluntary agency, shown in Fig. 6-11, gives an extensive weekly program of sports, games, aquatics, and conditioning activities for children, teenagers, and adults. In general, this reflects the pattern found in most community centers of serving children of elementary age on weekday or weekend afternoons and school holidays, teenagers during the later afternoon and evenings, and adults during the evening and on weekends. In addition, in many centers, special groups of older adults, housewives, those who work during the night, or

Newark, New Jersey, Y.M.H.A. and Y.W.H.A.

PHYSICAL EDUCATION SCHEDULE FOR ALL AGE GROUPS

	SUNDAY	MONDAY	TUESDAY	WEDNESDAY	THURSDAY	FRIDAY
JUNIORS	1:00 Gym, Games, Scooters, Trampoline 1-3 General Swim	3:45 Learn to Swim 4:15 Fun Swim	3:45 Gym Games & Skills 3:45 Learn to Swim 4:15 Fun Swim	3:45 Gym Games & Skills 4:15 Fun Swim	3:45 Learn to Swim 4:15 Fun Swim	To Be Announced
NUTEENS	2:00 Basketball, Trampoline 3-5 General Swim	3:45 Basketball Fun & Intramurals 3:45 Learn to Swim 4:15 Fun Swim 5:00 Varsity Basketball Practice 7-8 Fun Swim	3:45 Learn to Swim 4:15 Fun Swim 5:00 Varsity Basketball Practice	3:45 Learn to Swim 4:15 Fun Swim 5:00 Varsity Basketball Practice	3:45 Learn to Swim 3:45 Basketball Fun 5:00 Intramurals 4:15 Fun Swim 5-6 Varsity Basketball Practice 7-8 Fun Swim	To Be Announced
TEENS— COLLEGIATES	10-12:45 Coll. Men Paddleball & Basketball 11-1 Coll. Men General Swim 3-5 Teens—General Swim 3:15 Teens Basketball Fun	12-3 Gym Usage College Men 2:30 Teen Boys Basketball & Gym Skills 5-6 Varsity Basketball Practice 6:15-9:45 Teen & Coll. Men Basketball & Exercise Corner 7-10 Teen & Coll. Men—General Swim	12-3 Coll. Men—Full Gym 2:30 Teen Boys Basketball & Gym Skills 5-6 Varsity Basketball Practice 6:15-9:45 Teen Girls Gym Usage—Badminton, basketball, paddleball 8:30-10 Teen girls, general swim	12-3 Coll. Men—Gym 2:30 Teen Boys 2:30 Teen Boys Basketball & Gym Skills 5-6 Varsity Basketball Practice 6:15-9:45 Teen & Coll. Men—Full Gym Usage 8-10 Teen & Coll. Men General Swim	12-3 Coll. Men Full Gym Usage 2:30 Teen Boys Basketball & Gym Skills 5-6 Varsity Basketball Practice 8:00 Teen Girls Keep Fit Class; volleyball & coed recreation 8:30-10 Teen Girls—General Swim	12-3 Coll. Men Full Gym Usage 2:30-4 Teen Boys Full Gym
ADULTS	10-12:45 Adult Men Paddleball & Basketball 11:00 Adult Men Keep Fit Class 11-1 Adult Men General Swim 10:30-12:30 Karate	12-3 Adult Men Gym Usage 6:00 Coed Keep Fit Class 6:15-9:45 Adult Men Paddleball	10:00 Ladies Volley Ball & Paddleball 10:30 Ladies Keep Fit Class 11:10 Ladies Interviews and Measurings 11-12 Ladies Learn to Swim & Fun Swim 12-3 Adult Men Gym Usage 6:15-9:45 Coed Adult Full gym usage; badminton, basketball, paddleball 8-8:30 Coed Keep Fit Class 8-8:30 Adult Learn to Swim 8:30-10 Adult Coed General Swim 8:40 Recreation, coed	12-3 Adult Gym Usage 1:15 Adult Keep Fit Class, coed 1:45 Coed Adult General Swim	10:00 Ladies Volleyball & Paddleball 10:30 Ladies Keep Fit Class 11:10 Council Center Special Swim 11-12 Ladies Learn and Fun Swim 12-3 Adult Men Gym Usage 6:15-9:45 Coed Adult full gym usage—badminton, basketball, paddleball 8-8:30 Coed Keep Fit Class 8-8:30 Adult Learn to Swim 8:30-10 Adult Coed General Swim 8:40 Coed Volleyball and Recreation	12-3 Adult Men Gym Usage 1:00 Men Keep Trim Class

This activity schedule is subject to change on holidays and school vacations

Fig. 6-11

possibly groups of handicapped persons may be served in special programs during the morning or early afternoon.

Programs in therapeutic and voluntary agency settings

Hospital programs. The problem of scheduling recreation in hospital or other institutional settings is basically similar to that of scheduling it in public departments. It involves the definition of program goals and the selection of appropriate activities (in terms of patient needs, staff capabilities, and available facilities) and then developing a logical time framework in which to carry on these activities. In psychiatric hospitals, which comprise the largest single type of institution having recreation programs, activities are often provided on several different levels.

Hospital-wide programs. These consist of entertainment or other mass events that do not usually require prescription and that all patients may attend. Examples might be movies, concerts, spectator sports events, or bingo.

Special-interest groups. Generally, these might consist of activities in arts and crafts, hobbies, music, or dance that a patient may attend either independently or by referral of the physician or treatment team. Patients from various

Fig. 6-12. A, All ages are served by public recreation. Here, a little girl proudly shows her "sports car" in a Chicago Park District sand-modeling contest. **B,** Older children in Richmond, Virginia, prepare a nature and wildlife exhibit for a playground fair, and **C,** senior citizens enjoy an annual picnic sponsored by the Washington, D.C., Recreation Department. **D,** Nature and outing activities are sponsored by the Milwaukee school system, which operates a 30-acre demonstration farm for visits by city youngsters. **E,** Winter fun includes a family sleigh ride outing arranged by the Portland, Maine, Recreation Department.

wards of the hospital may come together and participate in such activities on a regular basis.

Unit activities. These are usually activities structured and made available for a particular section of a hospital population, such as an adolescent unit or long-term care unit. They may also provide for small living units, such as a ward or floor of patients and include varied hobby, creative, social, and gamelike activities.

Dayroom activities. These are unstructured or undirected activities, such as television watching, radio, reading, quiet games, or other pastimes that patients may carry on in free time in the dayroom or ward room attached to their hospital unit.

To illustrate the way in which program activities may be grouped in the schedule of a therapeutic agency, the schedule of Mt. Sinai Hospital in New York is given in Fig. 6-13. Under the Therapeutic Activities Division of the Department of Psychiatry, programs are classified under three main headings: *leisure time groups* (activities that are clearly recreational in nature), *pre-vocational groups* (activities that are seen as contributing to work readiness), and *rehabilitation groups* (programs intended to help a patient become ready for discharge). Fig. 6-13 shows how, in a hospital situation, the nature of the patient's attendance may be designated: voluntary, by referral, or with a designated number of times he or she must attend or with the maximum number of patients permitted per activity.

Programs for health and social needs. It must be stressed that recreation service is often provided in psychiatric institutions within the much broader framework of *activity therapy.* This term is used in many institutions to describe several related services, such as recreation therapy, occupational therapy, art, music, and dance therapy, vocational training and counseling, and similar functions. Not infrequently, it places heavy emphasis on *ADL* (Activities of Daily Living), which uses a variety of techniques for helping psychiatric patients relearn the essential skills of self-care and independent community living. An increasingly important rehabilitative function that many therapeutic recreation specialists have undertaken in psychiatric institutions is *recreation counseling.* In a recent study of thirteen Provincial Psychiatric Care Centres in Ontario, Canada, it was found that eight institutions provided recreation counseling; in the majority of these, recreation therapists were responsible for individual and group counseling programs designed to accomplish the following:

1. Help clients form new ties with other persons
2. Teach clients to make efficient use of available community resources for recreation
3. Help clients maintain and strengthen their existing affiliations with family, friends, churches, etc.
4. Mobilize community resources for fostering mental health and cooperating with psychiatric centers[10]

Increasingly, programs designed to serve special populations such as emo-

100th STREET AND FIFTH AVENUE · NEW YORK 29, N. Y.

Therapeutic Activities Division

ACTIVITIES GROUPS AVAILABLE   as of 1/1/72

LEISURE TIME GROUPS

	Notes
POETRY Fri. 12:30-1:30	No referral required, voluntary. Music Room.
CURRENT EVENTS DISCUSSION GROUP Mon. 2:00-3:30 Thurs. 2:30-4:00	Voluntary. Music Room.
MUSIC LISTENING Fri. 2:00-3:30	Voluntary. Music Room.
CRAFTS WORKSHOP Tues. thru Fri. 10:15-11:30	Maximum 4 patients per unit. Min.4 ses. By referral. Referrals start Tues. Rm.2
PAINTING 10:00-11:30 Mon. 2:00-3:30 Tues.	2 sessions a week. By referral.
CO-ED BODY MOVEMENT Wed., Thurs., Fri., 5:30-6:00	Voluntary. Gym.
MEN'S EXERCISE GROUP Tues., Fri., Sun., 7:00, 6:00, 6:00.	Voluntary. Gym.
SEWING GROUP Mon.+ Thurs. 10:15-11:15 Wed. + Fri.-2:00-4:00	4 sessions min. By referral. Room 2. Unit therapists supply wool + needles.
CLAY WORKSHOP Mon. + Thurs. 2:00-4:00	4 sessions min. By referral. Room 4.
SOCIAL DANCING Wed. 10:00-10:45	Gym. By referral.

PRE-VOCATIONAL GROUPS

FOOD A LA CARTE (COFFEE CART) Tues. + Thurs. 10:15-11:30 Fri. 2:00-3:30	Pts. attend all 3 sessions. 2 wks. min. By referral.
PRODUCTION LINES Tues. thru Fri. 10:15-11:30	2 separate groups--Tie-Dye workshop and Candle-Making workshop. By referral. Permanent assignment, until discharge. Room 4.

REHABILITATION GROUPS

PLANNING FOR LEISURE TIME Mon. 5:00 and Thurs. 12:00	2 meetings a week. By referral. Room 2.
FOOD AND NUTRITION Wed. + Fri. 10:15-11:15	4 sessions min. By referral. Room 5.
WOMEN'S DISCUSSION GROUP Thurs. 1:00	By referral. 7 South Dining Area.

Fig. 6-13

tionally disturbed, mentally retarded, physically handicapped, or dependent aging people must include not only the traditional kinds of diversional recreational activities but also activities geared toward meeting overall health-related or social needs. In many senior centers, for example, nutritional guidance and hot-lunch programs, legal aid and housing assistance, medical and dental examinations or special clinics, and other seminars or action programs, designed to improve community services for aging persons, are part of the basic program.

Another example is found in programs provided by United Cerebral Palsy for youth and adults. These include a wide range of hobby activities, such as crafts, music, dance, photography, or bowling, along with varied social programs. However, they are enriched by social clubs, residential camping services, travel programs, and other special forms of counseling. In the past, the question of sexual involvement for youth and adults with cerebral palsy tended to be ignored or repressed by serving agencies. Today, it is fully recognized that the disabled have sexual needs and are sexual beings—and that programs must serve their needs. Therefore recreation specialists working with cerebral-palsied populations today provide individual and group counseling, work with parents, and help their clients achieve a full and appropriate sexual identity. This includes the development of intelligent policies and program settings with respect to dating, courtship, and, for some, marriage and family planning.

The basic point is that, in many therapeutic settings, recreation must be perceived as far more than merely an enjoyable leisure activity. Instead, programs must often be health-related and geared to the development of constructive social attitudes and community-living skills.

YMCA and YWCA. Similarly, in such major national organizations as the YMCA and YWCA, there is a close integration between activities that are clearly recreational in nature and others that are geared to the individual's vocational development, health and fitness needs, or family and community relationships. Such programs are also closely related to the broad social goals of the organization and to critical problems affecting young people in modern society.

Many Young Men's Christian Associations today operate mobile units and vans that take Y services into communities or neighborhoods where they are needed. The YMCA has initiated family-based programs of sex education, crash pads for runaways, counseling and hot-line emergency services for individuals in distress, and a variety of constructive activities dealing with youth values, antidelinquency projects, and drug use and alcoholism prevention. Many YMCAs today sponsor youth and adult international exchange programs. Others provide day care centers with special services for handicapped and mentally retarded individuals. The Chicago YMCA is the largest provider of services for retired persons in that city, operating a fleet of twenty specially equipped vans for transporting aging persons to medical facilities and shopping centers and meeting other needs of senior citizens.

The Young Women's Christian Association also sponsors many programs promoting racial understanding and cooperation and world brotherhood, as well as social action programs on the community level. During the past several years, it has given special priority to strengthening women's roles in society. While YWCAs continue to offer the traditional arts and crafts, hobbies, sports and fitness, and other social programs, today they also stress courses, seminars, and group experiences designed to help women become more independent, confident, assertive, and economically viable members of society. The full range of program activities offered by a single large suburban YWCA (White Plains, N.Y.) is listed below.

Adult groups
Aerobic exercise in the water
Art classes
Artistic expression
Art workshop
Assertive training demonstration
  workshop
Assertive training group
Basic rescue and water safety
Basic swimming instructor
Basketball
Bicycling
Bike repair
Body conditioning
Boutelle method—fitness
Bridge and duplicate
Camping
Career counseling—Vistas
Careers—A Realistic Approach—
  Vistas series
Childbirth education
Children's activities
  Arts and crafts
  Artistic expression for little people
  Art workshop
  Cooking
  Creative movement
  Drama
  Electricity and electronics
  Eurythmics
  Gymnastics
  Music
  Painting
  Pottery
  Science
  Swim lessons
  Violin
Cooking, gourmet
Cooking workshops
Copper enameling
Crewel and embroidery workshop
Dance
Diving
Divorced and separated
  discussion group
Dollar programs
Drama

English as a second language
English conversation circle
Family camping
Fencing
Fitness day camp
Gardening
Golf
Guitar
Gymnastics team
Handicapped programs
Home repair—Survival in a
  Mechanical World
Horseback riding
House plant workshop
Ice skating
Job counseling—Vistas
Job workshop—Vistas
Knitting and crochet
Learn to swim week
Lifesaving
Macramé workshop
Music
Needlepoint
Oshibana workshop
Painting
Pottery
Preschool programs
  Arts and crafts
  Creative movement
  Gym
  Music and eurythmics
  Nursery school
  Play-care
  Plunge
  Science
  Supervised playroom
  Water babies
Pressed flower workshop
Quarter milers
Quilting workshop
Science
Sculpture
Self defense
Senior citizen swim
Singles
  Punchbowl
  Vineyard

[handwritten margin notes: New Themes, Independence, Women are more sensitive to today's Issues]

Skiing
Swimming program
Gymnastics
Synchronized swimming
Table tennis
T'ai Chi Ch'uan
Teen outreach
Tennis
Therapy, exercise
Trail riding
Travel agents training course
Violin

Vistas for women
Vocational counseling—Vistas
Volleyball
Water ballet
Water safety instructor
Weight reduction program
Wheelchair sports
Woman—a sexual being
Women and finance
World mutual service committee
Yoga
Y-Women

Many of the courses and workshops listed deal with the health needs, home management skills, job training, and other critical problems of women today. Several illustrative catalog course descriptions follow:

Assertive Training Group. Learn to be comfortable standing up for your rights in work, community, family and other interpersonal relationships. Participants will be taught to differentiate among aggressive, assertive and submissive behavior and, using situations from their own lives, will practice assertive skills. Enrollment limited to ten. Advance registration required. Eight Wednesday sessions, 9:30-11:30 A.M. Y members $60.00; non-members $70.00.

Coed Discussion Group for Divorced and Separated People. Emphasis will be on discussion of feelings about key issues; with suggestions about the practical aspects of making new social contacts and about the resources available for vocational planning. Tuesdays, 8:00-10:00 P.M. 8 weeks—$24.00.

Survival in a Mechanical World. A course for liberated and unliberated women and men trying to cope with an imperfect technological environment. Learn to use common hand tools to make simple plumbing, electrical appliance, and automotive repairs, as well as understand the maintenance performed by professional repairmen . . . Thursdays, 1:00-3:00 P.M. 8 weeks—$40.00.

Women and Finance. A course designed to help women toward an understanding of personal finance. Financial ignorance is neither safe nor advisable in today's world. Areas covered include banking, credit, mortgages, investments, insurance, wills, budgeting, and taxes . . . Mondays, 8:00 P.M. 5 weeks—$20.00

Many other voluntary organizations today provide similar types of courses, workshops, and program experiences. The administrators and program planners of such agencies must seek to understand the special needs of those they serve and to meet them through imaginative and innovative program activities.

Thus far, this chapter has dealt with the broad range of program activities that are offered by recreation and park departments and other community agencies or institutions. In this final section, it describes the third role assumed by many public departments—that of helping to promote and assist community recreation programs in general.

ROLE IN PROMOTING COMMUNITY-WIDE RECREATION

As the first section of this chapter makes clear, an important function of public recreation and park departments is to promote recreation on a community-wide basis. This includes the following types of responsibilities:

1. *Providing facilities* for other organizations is a prime responsibility. Typically, recreation and park departments provide ball fields, gymnasiums, swimming pools, or other specialized facilities that meet the needs of civic organizations, industrial recreation clubs, church youth leagues, and similar groups.

2. Recreation departments *cosponsor programs* with other organizations. Often this is done in direct cosponsorship with the public schools; in some cities, there are contractual arrangements in which the city and public school system share financial and administrative responsibility for recreation services. Also, recreation departments often work with agencies serving the handicapped in cosponsoring recreational activities. They may also operate joint programs with organizations such as Little League and Biddy Basketball.

3. In some cases, recreation departments help to *coordinate* and *schedule*

Fig. 6-14. The Vancouver, British Columbia, Department of Parks and Public Recreation sponsors many interesting instructional programs, such as **A,** a traffic safety program conducted by the city police, **B,** a painting program in the park, **C,** ski lessons, and **D,** field trips and nature education.

programs for other organizations, acting as a clearinghouse to avoid duplication, publishing a directory of community services, and assisting them in public relations.

4. Many recreation departments *make equipment available* to organized groups. This may include picnic or barbecue equipment, loudspeaker equipment, costumes, games and sports kits, and similar materials—either free or on a rental basis.

5. Recreation departments frequently take responsibility for *training leaders*. This may be done through special clinics or workshops or in preseason training programs to which various organizations send their leaders-to-be.

6. *Promoting public awareness* of recreation is a final contribution of public recreation and park departments. This may be done by sponsoring performances, shows, cultural events, banquets or conferences to gain public attention and interest. It may also be done by having the recreation and park administrator work closely with other organizations (such as service clubs, major business and industry leaders, religious bodies, and educational institutions) to gain their support in promoting recreation as an important public concern.

The final program function—that of providing a network of parks, playgrounds, and other facilities for diversified public use—is described in Chapter 7.

Suggested topics for class presentations or examination questions

1. Outline a set of guidelines that should serve as the basis for developing a comprehensive recreation program in a city or suburban community. Then organize the major divisions or elements of activity, including illustrations of each type of service, to serve a population varied as to age and socio-economic level.
2. Develop an effective recreation program for a hypothetical voluntary agency, hospital, armed forces base, or similar organization. Indicate program goals, facilities, and staff first, and then outline a weekly or seasonal program in chart or other graphic form.
3. Select a single major category of activity, such as sports and games, nature and outing activities, or performing arts. Develop guidelines and a detailed statement of program services within this area of activity to serve a total community.

REFERENCES

1. Butler, George D.: *Introduction to Community Recreation*, New York, 1976, McGraw-Hill Book Co., p. 231.
2. Kraus, Richard: *Urban Parks and Recreation: Challenge of the 1970's*, New York, 1972, Community Council of Greater New York.
3. Lundquist, Al: "Is It Just the Winning That Counts?" *Recreation Canada*, April, 1973, p. 38.
4. *Ibid.*: p. 42.
5. "The Competitive Question," *Parks and Recreation*, August, 1975, p. 15.
6. Wenning, Judy, quoted in "Girls Make a Hit at Bat in Debut in Little League," *New York Times*, March 25, 1974.
7. Anderson, Walt: "Don't Just Sit There—Play," *Human Behavior*, January, 1974, p. 56.
8. Yasgur, Stevan: "The Senior Olympics: Games for Adults Who Won't Quit," *Geriatrics*, January, 1975, p. 120.
9. "Taking Part is Everything," *Sports Illustrated*, March 4, 1975, p. 51.
10. Gordon, Bill: "An Examination of Recreation Counseling in Provincial Psychiatric Care Centres in Ontario," Master's Thesis, University of Waterloo, Ontario, Canada, 1974.

CHAPTER 7

RECREATION AND PARK AREAS AND FACILITIES

Planning and design

This chapter is concerned with a key aspect of recreation and park administration—the planning, design, construction, and maintenance of recreation and park facilities.

The modern community, large or small, is characterized by certain basic types of facilities: schools, roads, hospitals, post offices, and other areas or buildings for specialized needs. Typically, most cities, towns, and villages operate extensive numbers of recreation and park facilities. As an example, the Department of Sports and Recreation in the city of Montreal, Canada, operates the following special facilities: twenty-two indoor swimming pools, twelve ice arenas, twenty outdoor swimming pools, sixty wading pools, 107 tennis courts, a thirty-six-hole golf course, 160 fully equipped playgrounds, six athletic fields and tracks, thirteen multiple games areas, 150 softball diamonds, twenty-seven baseball diamonds, forty football-soccer fields, one archery range, and 260 outdoor ice rinks and nine ski slopes for winter use. It also is responsible for 380 parks, including six large metropolitan parks, twelve district parks, ninety-one neighborhood parks, sixty small neighborhood playgrounds, and various ornamental parks, squares, and landscaped boulevards. Its total park area is about 4,000 acres.

APPROACHES TO PLANNING

How does the modern community meet the needs of its citizenry for park and recreation facilities through systematic, comprehensive planning? Several approaches have been used: (1) planning based on concepts of the neighborhood and community; (2) guidelines or standards for open space and facilities based on population, service radius, or percentage of total acreage; and (3) current urban planning methods that are based on land-use principles, analysis of community needs, and related economic and social factors.

Neighborhood and community planning approach

This basic planning approach identifies two key units of local government and residential living patterns as the basis for providing recreation and park facilities.

Neighborhoods are generally regarded as residential sections of a larger city or town, usually about three-quarters to a mile square, including about 6,000 residents overall. Neighborhoods are described in the traditional planning literature as being fairly homogenous with respect to social class, economic status, and ethnic or racial background. They provide a close-to-home social and political environment in which families may satisfy their basic needs for schools, shopping, churches, and similar services.

The term *community* is usually applied to larger residential areas, comparable in size to high school districts, just as neighborhoods are comparable to elementary school districts. Typically, a community might be described as including about three to five different neighborhoods, with an overall population of 20,000 to 40,000 residents. Although each such neighborhood may have a somewhat different character, the overall community is generally perceived as a recognized area of the city. Often, communities are set apart from each other by natural boundaries, such as major highways, waterways, or railroad lines.

Most basic recreation and park facilities are developed to meet neighborhood and community needs. Several illustrations follow.

Neighborhood play-lots. Sometimes referred to as *tot-lots*, these are small areas set aside chiefly for use by preschool children. They may be as small as 2,500 to 5,000 square feet and are often placed in open areas in the center of large housing projects or fenced off as part of larger playgrounds or parks. Usually they include such play equipment as swings, slides, seesaws, or spray pools. During the 1960s, vacant lots in many disadvantaged urban neighborhoods were converted to play-lots. Sometimes they were called *vest-pocket parks* and designed for use by adults and senior citizens as well as children.

Neighborhood playgrounds. These are usually designed to serve children between the ages of 6 and 15, although in some cases they provide recreation opportunities for older youth and adults. Guidelines suggest that neighborhood playgrounds be provided within a quarter-mile radius of all residents in crowded urban neighborhoods and a half-mile radius of all homes in less crowded areas.

It is usually recommended that playgrounds be between 3 and 7 acres in size, although they are frequently smaller in densely populated neighborhoods. They usually include the following equipment: shaded quiet areas with benches and a sandbox, play apparatus area (swings, slides, and the like), a multiple-use paved area for games, and a small building with storage space, lavatories, and an office for the playground director. Some playgrounds also have ball fields for team sports and a somewhat larger building for limited indoor activities.

Community playfields. These offer opportunity for varied sports, such as softball, baseball, football, or soccer, and often have a limited number of tennis courts and a multiple-use paved area for such sports as basketball and volleyball. According to planning guides, there should be a community playfield within a half mile to a mile of each home, depending on the population density. It has been generally recommended that playfields should be between 12 and 30 acres in size. When possible, community playfields should be located adjacent to junior or senior high schools to permit maximum use during the day as well as in the later afternoon and evening.

Community parks. Planning guides suggest that there should be at least one large community park with a minimum size of 100 acres for each 40,000 to 50,000 persons in a city. Such parks should include considerable open space and provide facilities for as many as possible of the following: day camping, horseback riding, boating, swimming, fishing, picnicking, and winter sports. Often, athletic facilities, zoos, museums, and stadiums may be part of or adjacent to large community parks.

Other major facilities that are recommended in planning guides by planning associations, recreation and park organizations, or leagues of city officials include community center buildings for varied indoor programs, golf courses, swimming pools, stadiums, botanical gardens, fairgrounds, and similar facilities.

Open space and facility standards

Almost from the beginning of the organized recreation and park movement, space and facility standards have been proposed as guidelines for the acquisition and development of parks and other specialized facilities. At the first meeting of the Playground Association of America in April, 1906, a report outlining the recommended space requirements for playgrounds and other recreation facilities was unanimously adopted. Since then, leading organizations such as the American Society of Planning Officials, the International City Managers Association, and the National Recreation Association have developed specific guidelines for planning recreation and park areas and facilities.

Usually these have been expressed in terms of the ratio of needed recreation and park acreage to the total population. The most common figure cited has been 10 acres of recreation space per 1,000 population. It has been recognized that this figure needs to be treated flexibly, depending on the population density and available park and recreation areas provided by other than municipal agencies.

In the mid-1960s, the National Recreation Association presented a revised formula of acreage standards, which included property owned both by local authorities and by nearby counties, park districts, and state agencies. It recommended that a minimum of 25 acres per 1,000 residents be provided by local government authorities and that 65 acres be provided by state government—a total of 90 acres in all. In a national forum on recreation and park standards in 1969, the National Recreation and Park Association determined that their principal purposes were to accomplish the following:

1. To assist in the development of a comprehensive plan of park and recreation areas and a systematic approach to land acquisition
2. To help determine what and how many recreation facilities are needed to best serve the people and where they should be provided
3. To justify to political bodies proposals for the acquisition and development of park and recreation lands and facilities and to determine priorities
4. To provide an objective measure against which the effectiveness of the park and recreation system can be evaluated[1]

Despite the recommendation of this forum that space standards must reflect the needs of people in the specific areas being served and must be reasonably or substantially attainable, the fact is that comparatively few communities have been able to meet recommended standards in the past. For example, a 1955 study of almost 200 cities throughout the United States indicated that only 27% were living up to the basic standard of one acre of recreation space per 100 population.

In addition to the space standards approach a variety of other guidelines have been formulated. Standards for special facilities have been developed, which indicate what types of facilities should be provided according to population totals in the community being served (Table 2). Another approach is to determine needs on the basis of percentage of land area devoted to recreation and park uses or remaining as undeveloped open land. The most commonly applied guideline has been that 10% of the total area of a city should be devoted to recreation and open space available to the general public. Still another approach has been to identify a maximum service radius for each type of recreation facility; for example, there should be a neighborhood playground within a quarter mile of each elementary school child's home, or there should be a neighborhood center within a half mile of each high-school–age youth's home.

It must be recognized that because cities differ so widely in terms of their population density, residential housing patterns, industrial character, socioeconomic level of residents, financial capability, and recreation needs and interests, it is not possible to propose any single set of standards that can apply equally to all cities. Despite the traditional concepts of the neighborhood and the community as the basis for facilities planning, it also seems clear that many residen-

TABLE 2
Standards for special facilities*

Type of facility	Recommended standard
Baseball diamonds	1 per 6,000
Softball diamonds (and/or youth diamonds)	1 per 3,000
Tennis courts	1 per 2,000
Basketball courts	1 per 500
Swimming pools—25 meter	1 per 10,000
Swimming pools—50 meter	1 per 20,000
Skating rinks (artificial)	1 per 30,000
Neighborhood centers	1 per 10,000
Community centers	1 per 25,000
Outdoor theaters (noncommercial)	1 per 20,000
Shooting ranges	1 per 50,000
Golf courses (18 hole)	1 per 25,000

*Drawn from Rodney, Lynn S.: Administration of public recreation, New York, 1964, The Ronald Press Company, p. 313; Meyer, H., and Brightbill, C.: Community recreation: a guide to its organization, Englewood Cliffs, N. J., 1964, Prentice-Hall, Inc., p. 404; and Buechner, R. D., editor: National park recreation and open space standards, Washington, D.C., 1969, National Recreation and Park Association.

Fig. 7-1. Parks may offer elaborate and expensive facilities. Here, in St. Petersburg, Florida, is **A**, an outstanding swimming pool, part of the Municipal North Shore Beach and Pool complex, which includes putting greens, tennis courts, softball field, and other areas; **B**, a huge municipal pier and marina for boating, fishing, and other water sports; **C**, a back-to-back baseball field complex; and **D**, an outstanding civic auditorium, the Bayfront Center, which houses such events as the Ringling Brothers Barnum and Bailey Circus.

tial areas are so mixed in terms of racial or ethnic background, age, and socio-economic class that the assumption that each neighborhood should be provided with a uniform set of playgrounds, small parks, or community centers is no longer valid.

Although traditional space standards continue to be used by many planners, it should be recognized that they represent only one type of input in modern recreation and park planning.

Current urban planning methods

There are essentially three levels of planning that relate to recreation and park facilities and services. These are (1) total master planning that considers all aspects of municipal growth, including industrial and residential development, transportation, education, housing, health, and other major aspects of community life; (2) planning that focuses solely on recreation and park development within a total community, sometimes as a separate portion of a total master plan; and (3) planning that is concerned with the development of a particular facility, or the needs of a single neighborhood.

Master planning to meet community recreation and park needs usually includes a complete inventory and analysis of existing facilities and areas, carried on in conjunction with the city's comprehensive land-use plan. It involves a projection of future recreation needs based on population and income factors and taking into consideration the geophysical factors and other conditions affecting the recreation potential of the area. Usually such planning results in recommendations for immediate, short-range, and long-range acquisition of sites, development of facilities, and financial programs to support these recommendations. Such plans should be officially adopted by the city council or other governing authority and used in all subsequent consideration of zoning, housing, transportation, school construction, and similar needs.

Planning may be carried on by specialists who have been trained in a variety of disciplines. Some are drawn from the field of public administration and others from landscape architecture or civil engineering. Still others may have been trained in economics, sociology, or law. Increasingly, urban planning has become recognized as a special discipline, although there is obviously no single philosophy or set of principles that governs the recommendations of planners.

Some planners, particularly those with a background in economics, tend to see leisure activity as a marketing system in which the laws of supply and demand operate and in which the recreation planner must view the provision of facilities and services as a product manufactured and paid for by consumers like any other product.[2] Planners with a primary orientation in architecture or landscape architecture place major emphasis on the visual and environmental aspects of land development. The need to create open space and attractive vistas and structures within the urban setting transcends other concerns in their eyes. Closely related to this approach is that of the conservation-oriented planner, who seeks to protect open spaces and natural areas at all costs, rather than permit them to be used for purposes such as schools, recreation, or other public uses.

It is essential that recreation and park administrators be given a significant voice in the total planning process. Gold writes:

> The expertise of the park administrator can play a primary role in open-space preservation, urban beautification, historic preservation, recreation program, and pedestrian or bicycle circulation. He can also assume a significant role in the review of proposed housing, commercial, or industrial development for leisure-use potentials.[2]

In the past, urban planners developed ideal models of what the good community should be like. They assumed that each type of land use (such as heavy industry, shopping areas, residential areas, or public service facilities) could be placed in a logical juxtaposition to the others. Thus it would be in the most convenient location in terms of efficient operation (heavy industry, for example, would be close to major highways or railroad lines for convenient transportation) and at the same time would be so located that residential housing would be screened from unattractive or unpleasant land uses—in terms of traffic, noise, smell, or other problems. Certain models have been developed in the past by land-use planners to show what such idealized communities were like.

One such approach consists of a concentric-circle pattern, with heavy industry in the innermost sector of the city, surrounded by light industry, lower-class housing, shopping, business districts, and finally middle- and upper-class housing, protected by rings of green space from the less desirable parts of the city.

The model of the idealized city tends to have little relation to many of the newer suburbs around large cities, which consist of large residential areas often lacking central services and in which school, police, and fire districts, post offices, sewer, sanitation, and highway services tend to be offered by different jurisdictions. Such communities are unlike the traditional view of the city or town as a self-contained unit, with a core of central services and a constituency that guides the development of its own public services.

Gans[3] comments that a basic flaw of traditional urban planning has been its assumption that ideal cities can be developed by providing the ideal physical environment. As a consequence, he writes, it has permitted architects and engineers to dominate the planning process and has assigned little importance to the social, economic, and political processes that influence human behavior.

As an alternative to traditional planning, Gans suggests an approach that he calls "goal-oriented planning." This method takes the position that planning must begin with the goals of the community and its citizens and then develop those programs that constitute the best means of achieving these goals without undesirable behavioral or cost consequences.

Recreation and park planning should, in Gans' view, become *user-oriented*, with a serious effort to find out what residents want in the present and what they are likely to accept in terms of as yet untried facilities. He suggests that public priority determinations ought to be compensatory wherever possible, so that members of society who receive the most limited resources from the private sector of society ought to obtain the most from the public sector.

He concludes that metropolitan areas should place stress on parks that provide many of the conveniences usually associated with resorts or vacation areas. Ideally, they should offer a variety of outdoor recreation, commercial entertainment, restaurants, cafes, museums, and zoo facilities, as well as the other features usually found in a park. Low-income urban neighborhoods should be supplied with small parks, playgrounds, and swimming pools for people who do not have cars and do not have either the time or money for trips and vacations.

A number of city planners have proposed the criterion of social need as the basis for planning recreation and park facilities and programs in American communities. For example, the Community Council of Greater New York carried out a thorough analysis of recreation facilities, agencies, and leadership in New York's seventy-four officially designated neighborhoods in the early 1960s.[4] It found that nine of the seventy-four neighborhoods contained over 53% of the total park land and outdoor recreation space in the city. In contrast, 45% of the neighborhoods, particularly those in disadvantaged, older areas, had only 10% of the park and recreation acreage. It was found that the sixteen neighborhoods in the city with the highest rate of socioeconomic need and community disorganization rated well below the average of all neighborhoods in terms of available public and voluntary agency group work and recreation services.

Recognizing that this disparity meant that compensatory efforts to provide improved facilities and services to disadvantaged neighborhoods were needed, the New York Planning Commission carried out a detailed study that identified areas of the city where social pathology was highest and assigned these a top level of priority for park and recreation development.

This was done by dividing the city into three types of areas: *major action areas*, where poverty, poor housing, disease, and crime were at their worst and where facilities and programs were inadequate; *preventive renewal areas*, which were densely populated areas located in the path of outward migration from major action areas; and *sound areas*, in which social problems were minimal and recreation and park opportunities adequate.

It then recommended budgetary allocations aimed at bringing major action areas up to the city-wide average for facilities and programs by assigning them the highest priority. Secondary priority was given to preventive renewal areas, and the lowest allocation of resources was assigned to sound areas.

Other cities, particularly Los Angeles, have developed similar systems of measuring the available recreation resources and degree of social need of each neighborhood, relating them to a city-wide index, or standard, and using this information as a basis for planning recommendations.

Recreation and park studies. Any planning study that seeks to develop meaningful recommendations for recreation and park space and facility planning in a community must take into account the following:

1. Quantity and quality of existing public, private, commercial, and voluntary-agency lands and recreation resources
2. Demographic and socioeconomic profiles of those to be served (age, sex, family size, income, education, cultural and ethnic characteristics)
3. Geographic location, climate, and special topographical conditions
4. Local traditions and customs or regional trends or patterns in recreation
5. Expressed desires and leisure needs of the citizenry

Based on a combination of all these factors, planning studies are carried out; their reports usually include the following elements or sections:

1. Inventory of existing areas and facilities (indoor and outdoor)
2. Inventory of potential resources
3. Identification of specific sites available for acquisition
4. Population projections and profiles (age, sex, income, and the like)
5. Transportation and other growth patterns
6. Systematic assessment of citizen views and suggestions
7. Review of current program and administrative structure in recreation and parks

8. Review and application of standards, taking other factors into account

9. Financial resources of community

10. Statement of priorities and plan of action; summary of recommendations

Planning studies usually include a general statement of the present status of the community's recreation and park resources and a statement of what those resources should consist of by a given date to serve the anticipated population satisfactorily. This requires an estimate of *demand projections*, which would be arrived at by measuring the present and anticipated uses of various types of facilities and by calculating projected population trends, developing forecasts of ultimate use when population has reached its maximum density in a given area.

Normally, three types of recommendations may be presented: (1) a *long-term* statement of needs and recommended acquisition (this might outline a total program of development for a 15-year period); (2) a *short-term* plan, covering action to be taken over the next 3 to 5 years; and (3) *immediate* recommendations for land acquisition and development.

Guidelines for urban recreation and park planning

In conclusion, a number of basic guidelines for urban recreation and park planning have been identified in the literature. These include the following:

Planning guidelines

1. Recreation and park systems should be established to meet total community leisure needs and should provide equal recreational opportunity to all, as far as possible.

2. Planning should be based on a comprehensive and thorough inventory and evaluation of existing public, private and commercial facilities and programs, including the public schools.

3. Planning should reflect the needs and wishes of all citizens and should involve them in data-gathering and decision-making processes.

4. Each recreation center or park should be centrally located within the area it is planned to serve and should provide safe and convenient access for all residents. Insofar as possible, facilities should be equally distributed throughout the major areas of the city.

5. Design of each park or recreation facility should be done individually to ensure that it is adapted to the needs of the specific population it is to serve.

6. Beauty and functional efficiency are major goals of planning, with convenience and economy of maintenance important added considerations.

7. Communities should have a long-range plan for site acquisition, with a total master plan to ensure that properties are acquired while still available.

8. Every effort should be made to achieve space standards through acquisition in advance of anticipated needs, even if limited financial resources delay actual development of facilities.

9. Properties acquired should be held in perpetuity (protected by law from encroachment, or diversion to non-park and recreation uses).

10. Recreation properties should be designed and developed to permit the fullest possible use by different groups at different times, on a year-round and around-the-clock basis.

11. Public school buildings should be designed for the fullest possible community use, through reciprocal agreements and operational coordination between school and park and recreation authorities.

12. It is the function of the recreation and park board to meet the needs of the city for wholesome recreation, rather than to act primarily as a land acquisition agency; thus planning should not be restricted to physical elements but must be on a programmatic and operational basis.

For truly effective planning today, the following elements should also be considered, in addition to the preceding guidelines.

Fig. 7-2. Parks have many uses. They offer a chance **A,** for quiet contemplation on a park bench, **B,** for mothers to enjoy an outing in the sun with their babies, or **C,** for a dad and his son to get together on a park swing. **D,** Families enjoy picnics casually in Montreal's Mount Royal Park.

Planning as total community concern. Any planning study that examines *only* the facilities operated by a public recreation and park department today and ignores the facilities and programs of other public, voluntary, private, or commercial agencies is doomed to failure. Planning *must* examine all potential resources and must place recreation and parks within the total spectrum of social, educational, health, environmental, and transportation concerns.

Emphasis on operational effectiveness. In many cities, playgrounds, community centers in housing projects, and other recreation facilities are either understaffed or not staffed at all. A continued emphasis on developing facilities for their own sake, without serious preliminary consideration of how they are to be operated, results in ineffective planning recommendations. Recommendations for the acquisition and development of recreation and park facilities must take into account those who will use them, at what times of the day, week, or year, what the costs of operation will be and how they will be met, and similar concerns.

Predetermination of program priorities. Any program of land acquisition and facilities development based on the standard listing of needed facilities, without regard to the particular priorities and needs of a given neighborhood or community, is poorly based. Instead, by examining currently available facilities and the nature of the present and anticipated population, it is possible to project recreation needs in specific detail, geared to the unique needs of the people to be served.

Intergovernmental planning. It is no longer feasible for a single department to move ahead unilaterally in planning its own facilities. Recreation and park departments may receive financial support from the federal government's Land and Water Conservation Fund or from state open-space subsidy programs. Certainly, close coordination with these larger units of government is essential. In addition, many smaller communities coordinate their efforts with neighboring communities, townships or county departments to avoid overlap of facilities. In many cases, cooperative planning and operation of facilities has been successfully undertaken by neighboring governmental units.

Similarly, it is essential to plan closely with other departments, such as school boards, highway departments, health departments, or police departments, in developing facilities.

Community representation in planning. Today it has become accepted that individuals and groups within the community should become fully involved in the planning process. In some cities today it is required that when an architectural firm is given the assignment of preparing plans for a facility, they must consult directly with community groups, hold hearings, and submit their proposed designs at various stages for their approval. Such involvement in the planning process may include various techniques: use of interest inventories, fuller involvement of local people on advisory committees, public hearings, and formal presentations before civic organizations.

Assuming that the planning process has been effective, the next step involves following up on planning recommendations by acquiring needed recreation and park areas for facilities development.

ACQUISITION OF PROPERTIES

The selection of sites to be acquired for recreation and park use must be carried out in a systematic way. The size and exact location of each area should be part of an overall community plan that provides balanced opportunity to all neighborhoods within a city. In cities that have already been heavily developed, with a minimum of available open space, it is difficult to accomplish this goal. Often, in such circumstances, it is necessary to *create* open space through urban renewal programs that involve the demolition of blighted tenement areas or razing of old factory or railroad yard areas. In many cities, parks, playgrounds, plazas, and other recreation areas have been created in this way.

In general, the methods through which municipalities may acquire land for recreation and parks are the following.

Purchase. Direct purchase of property from its owner is the most common method of land acquisition. Through the right of eminent domain, government may acquire property by means of condemnation, with the court fixing a fair purchase price, if the owner is unwilling to sell his land directly.

Transfer. Recreation lands may be acquired by transferring or exchanging properties from one government department to another. As suggested earlier, dumps, warehouses, river frontage properties, and even tax-delinquent lands may become available. Although such land may appear inappropriate for recreation development, through landfill and other engineering methods it often can be converted to outstanding recreation and park use.

The Bureau of Outdoor Recreation suggests a variety of possibilities for acquiring marginal properties that may be available: (1) railroad rights-of-way, for hiking trails; (2) utility rights-of-way, for hiking, biking, or horseback riding; (3) flood plains for seasonal use as linear parks, with picnic areas and trials; (4) properties surrounding water supply reservoirs; (5) airport buffer lands; (6) power generation sites, which may provide useful boating, swimming, and fishing close to hydroelectric plants; or (7) atop municipal underground parking facilities. The Bureau of Outdoor Recreation gives numerous illustrations of such uses and provides technical assistance on acquiring and developing such multiple-use areas.[5]

Leasing. Long-term leasing arrangements are sometimes used to make land available for park use. These are best applied between government agencies or departments. If the intention is to use the property for recreation on a permanent basis, the temporary nature of the lease poses a special risk when the arrangement is with a private owner.

Gifts. Many cities and counties have been able to acquire substantial park properties through gifts and bequests from public spirited citizens. Although this is obviously the cheapest form of land acquisition, such properties should only be accepted when free from narrow use restrictions and suitable in location and topography for recreation use.

Dedication by subdividers. A growing practice in many suburban communities is to require a land developer or subdivider to set aside a certain percentage of his property for recreation and park use. In some cases this land may be deeded to an organization of home owners who have bought houses in his development. In others, the land may be given directly to the town or other government in which the land has been developed. In some cases, subdividers have been permitted to pay a sum of money, instead of land, to be used for purchasing and developing nearby property for parks and recreation.

As an example of such mandatory dedication, Anne Arundel County, Maryland, has an ordinance that states, "The developer of a single family or duplex subdivision . . . shall provide 1,000 square feet of recreational land per each or every lot or dwelling unit . . . within the proposed subdivision." For multifamily subdivision areas, a scale of percentage of property that must be given has been developed. The greater the number of dwelling units per acre, the higher the percentage of the total area that must be given for recreational use. In addition, it is stipulated that the property given must be desirable land, reasonably accessible, flat, and dry.

Easements. In some cases, land may be made available for recreation without direct acquisition. This may involve an agreement between government and private property owners that permits specified recreation use of the land. In some cases, flood-control lands or property adjoining highways or airports are made available for recreation on this basis, without the land being transferred to the public recreation and park department. In others, owners of undeveloped land are given a reduced tax rate as compensation for keeping the land as open space, rather than developing it.

Kershaw points out that many special kinds of arrangements have been worked out involving exchange of properties, or permitting people to retain a portion of their land, or use it during their lifetimes, with major tax advantages. He concludes:

> It is the obligation of every parks and recreation director who has the responsibility of acquiring parkland to explore and become fully knowledgeable about the broad implications of tax loopholes, negotiations procedures, and other incentives that will expedite or enhance his jurisdiction's ability to efficiently acquire park property.[6]

Once land has been acquired for recreation and park use—through any of the methods described—it is necessary to determine exactly how it is to be developed and to have designs prepared.

Much of this should have been accomplished through the planning study. A sound planning report will have analyzed community needs and interests, identified appropriate sites for acquisition, and indicated the best uses to which these properties might be put. The planning report should also suggest a financial program for developing the property itself. The next step is that of preparing a design for the facility.

DESIGNING AREAS AND FACILITIES

Although minor facilities are sometimes developed without employing professional architects, it is today considered essential that not only buildings but land areas be designed by individuals who are professionally qualified in this field.

A few picnic tables scattered here and there and a swing set and teeter-totter do not make a park. Such poorly designed facilities hardly meet a community's needs, usually receive little or no maintenance, and quickly become the targets of vandalism. To prevent this happening, it is necessary to invest in a comprehensive, well-thought-out plan that can be executed over a period of time as funds become available. This does not mean that a great deal of money need be spent on expensive reconstruction of an area or on special facilities. Intelligent design avoids overplanning and excessive equipment. Splenda writes:

> Good design is space, simplicity, consistency, useability, scale, and dominance. Good design is the direct result of the existing physical site feature analysis. Most sites cannot satisfactorily support every recreation need or piece of equipment. Overuse of the land through excessive programming is counterproductive and results in poor design and use.[7]

Selecting and employing the architect

Parks, playgrounds, or other outdoor areas should be assigned to architects or architectural firms who have had past experience in planning recreation areas and facilities; have original ideas about design and do not simply copy past designs; have adequate staff resources to carry out the assignment; and are ready to work with various levels of government, community groups, and recreation personnel in developing the plan.

Too often, architects selected for important recreation and park assignments have lacked experience in this field, although they may have designed homes, schools, hospitals, or other institutions. An examination of their past work and a thorough discussion of their philosophy of park development will be helpful in selecting the best individual or firm.

When the architect has been selected, a contract should be drawn up by the community's legal counsel. This should include all details relating to the architect's role in carrying out preliminary investigation, surveys, and the like; meeting with recreation staff, community groups, or other parties; preparing preliminary drawings; reviewing and revising plans; preparing final working drawings and detailed specifications; putting the construction contract out for bids and preparing the contract with the developer; and performing general supervision of construction.

In some cases, a city may go to a large recreation equipment company that provides a free planning and design service. As an example, the Miracle Recreation Equipment Company of Grinnell, Iowa, may develop a total design of a park or recreation complex for a community, with color layouts, models, and expanded versions of separate sections. It then supplies needed equipment for the plan, either for full immediate development or in installments over a period of time, as the city is able to pay for their purchase. Other companies supply similar services.

Fig. 7-3. Unusual facilities operated by the Montreal, Canada, Department of Sports and Recreation include a Garden of Wonder with old-world charm and many interesting displays such as a trick-seal act.

In some cases, the design function is assumed by an architect or civil engineer who is a regular employee of the recreation and park department or the municipality. The Chicago Park District, for example, has a large engineering and design staff. However, in most cases outside personnel are employed.

Process of design

Preliminary investigation. In addition to information that may have been developed in the planning report, the architect should gather additional information about a facility's potential use *before* going into the actual design process. He should understand clearly what specific program elements are planned for it, what service radius it is to have, and what population will

Fig. 7-4. Other Montreal park facilities include **A**, a delightful Winter Wonderland with **B**, unusual lighting and **C**, a fine new aquarium. **D**, In another city, Richmond, Virginia, outstanding foliage displays are offered in the Bryan Park Azalea Garden.

be using it. He should examine the surrounding area to ensure that his plans make the facility compatible with the neighborhood, climatic factors, and problems of access that may affect his plans.

As part of his preparation, the designer should have a detailed map of the area, including a topographical survey giving such elements as trees, rock outcroppings, water or swampy areas, and similar information. He should have full information on soil and drainage conditions and on availability of water mains, sewers, or other utility lines.

The designer should become aware of any legislation affecting the site and facility to be built, including municipal ordinances, building codes, and zoning laws or restrictions. In addition, he should get full input from appropriate citizen groups or representatives and from staff members of the recreation and park department as to their views of how the facility should be designed.

He should also understand thoroughly the financial program for the facility—in terms of both the amount of money that can be spent to develop it in the present and what might be spent in later construction. He should also know, as far as it is possible to be specific on this, what kinds of staffing assignments will be made, so that his plans provide for the most efficient use of leaders or supervisors and for effective control, in terms of the layout of areas and facilities.

Finally, if there is specific expertise needed to design an appropriate kind of facility, the architect or engineer should make sure to get this. If he is planning an artificial skating rink, he should explore similar facilities in the same climate belt to determine the relative value of different types of construction, freezing systems, and design layouts. No designer is likely to be an expert in all phases of construction, but when he undertakes a specialized project of this kind, he must become—for a time at least—an authority on its special problems and needs.

An interesting example of the factors to be considered in planning and designing an urban ski facility is provided by Branch and Rowan.[8] The key factors at the outset are terrain, climate, and temperature, as well as good access and a water supply adequate for snowmaking. Beyond this, the task of designing a trail and slope system with appropriate drainage, protection from wind and erosion, uphill transportation (such as surface cable lifts, chair lifts, tows, and gondola or tramways), snowmaking equipment, lighting, and buildings, is a highly technical one. Often it makes sense to involve an engineering firm that specializes in the design of such facilities as a paid consultant from the very outset.

Preparation of preliminary drawings. The architect prepares a set of preliminary plans or sketches based on information gathered to date and his analysis of the most efficient and imaginative uses to which the property may be put. He might prepare several alternative plans for the site, giving different locations for certain facilities, different kinds of access, or even ranging from a heavily developed plan to a much more natural plan.

Review of preliminary drawings. At this point, the tentative plans are examined by all who have a stake in them, including the recreation administrator and his staff, other city officials, the recreation and park board, and involved community groups. Not infrequently, public hearings are scheduled to review the plans and make suggestions about them.

Some of the criteria that should be applied to both preliminary drawings and final working drawings are the following:

1. *Esthetic quality.* Is the facility or area attractively designed? Although this may represent a subjective judgment, the element of beauty is an important factor in the architectural design.

2. *Utility.* Does the proposed layout provide adequately for needed play spaces as planned in the initial proposal for the facility? Are the various areas and structures laid out so they can be used with convenience?

3. *Ease of supervision.* Does the layout lend itself to easy supervision by staff —particularly of those program areas that require observation?

4. *Safety.* Are playground apparatus, games courts, roads, and paths all laid out to provide maximum safety? Are children's play or sitting areas separated to provide protection from active games or car traffic?

5. *Effective use of full site.* Does the layout ensure that every part of the site will provide either beauty or functional use? Has an effort been made to provide multiple-use areas to meet needs of different activities, age groups, or seasons of the year?

6. *Adaptability.* Will the proposed structures or areas lend themselves to remodeling or expansion to meet changing needs with a minimum of cost?

7. *Suitability for site.* Does the layout, including both areas and structures, lend itself to the natural topography of the original site? Does it make use of natural features, such as flat areas, trees, natural slopes, or similar elements in a logical way to meet program needs?

8. *Economy.* Has the layout been planned to be both as inexpensive as possible in construction, by avoiding unnecessary grading, draining, or blasting operations, and economical in continued maintenance and operation?

9. *Access.* Will it be convenient for younger children and older adults to reach the areas designed for them? Is circulation within the area or facility designed for easy movement from spot to spot?

10. *Conveniences.* Has adequate provision been made for parking, restrooms, drinking fountains, seating, and similar needs of participants?

11. *Awareness of neighborhood residents.* Has the site been planned to cause minimum annoyance to its neighbors? Have activity areas that are likely to cause noise or draw crowds been placed as far as possible from adjoining homes? Has night lighting been located so that it will not bother residents?

12. *Harmony of layout.* Do the various elements in the plan fit together in a logical coordination for both ease of supervision and convenience of use?

13. *Use by handicapped.* Will residents with physical disability, using crutches, walkers, or wheelchairs, be able to use the facility safely and conveniently?

14. *Energy economy.* Has the facility been designed so that it can be operated with the maximum economy in terms of use of electricity and other fuel-consumption systems for heating, cooling, or lighting?

Many other technical elements must be considered in reviewing the preliminary plans. For example, the use of lighting, fencing, paths and roads, water sites, construction materials, and sanitation should all be considered and at least tentative indications given of how they will be handled.

As an example of how architectural firms work with municipal recreation and park departments, the City of Philadelphia Department of Recreation has prepared a printed statement, "Standard Specifications for Architectural Services." In the first section, the following responsibilities are listed:

Preliminary work

1. *Studies.* The Architect shall attend all required meetings with members of the Recreation Department staff and other interested parties. He shall make a detailed study of the site to determine program and budget feasibility.

2. *Preliminary plans.* The Architect shall prepare preliminary plans. They shall include site plan; building floor plans, elevations and sections; and all major engineering systems as required by the Department of Recreation.

3. *Outline specifications.* The Architect shall prepare outline specifications using the CSI Format for division classifications. They shall include a brief description of work to be done and materials to be used.

4. *Rendering.* The Architect shall prepare a rendered presentation drawing to be used at a public meeting in a large auditorium for the purpose of describing the work to be done. The rendered presentation shall be on hard back material, the size and medium to be determined by the Department of Recreation.

5. *Cost analysis.* The Architect shall analyze the costs for the possible schemes, and make recommendations to the Department of Recreation. A preliminary estimate along with the preliminary plans and outline specifications must be submitted to the Department of Recreation before preliminary approval will be given.

Preparation of working drawings. When preliminary plans have been thoroughly reviewed and revised, the architect is normally authorized to proceed with working drawings and specifications. In most cases, this will require formal approval by the recreation and park board or by the municipal department that is responsible for designing and carrying out *all* construction. It is *essential* that recreation personnel who will have responsibility for operating the facility play a meaningful role in the process to avoid having facilities reach the final stages of planning and even construction with serious errors that might easily have been avoided.

Working drawings normally include detailed plot plans, landscape design (including plantings, ground surfaces, and the like), floor plans of all structures, elevations, and full specifications of all utility lines, such as plumbing, heating, electricity, and ventilation, and required engineering sections and details. The section of the Philadelphia Recreation Department guide for architects dealing with this phase lists the following requirements:

Detailed design

1. *Working drawings.* The Architect shall prepare working drawings of sufficient detail for bidding and construction. All structural, plumbing, mechanical and electrical engineering design shall be performed by registered engineers. All drawings shall be prepared on 4 Mil Mylar Tracing Paper of overall dimensions 30″ × 42″. The Department of Recreation standard title block shall be located in the lower right hand corner.

2. *Working specifications.* The Architect shall prepare project specifications using the CSI Format for Division Classification. They shall include a detailed description of work to be done, and methods and materials to be used. The Architect shall submit 60 bound specification books to the Department of Recreation.

3. *Final cost estimates.* The Architect shall prepare a detailed cost estimate based on unit costs using the CSI Format for Division Classifications. The costs shall be totalled for each prime contract and each of the alternate bids. The Architect shall be responsible for keeping the cost of the work within the designated budget. If bids exceed the allocated budget, the Architect shall perform whatever redesign is necessary at no additional cost to the City.

Bidding and construction. When final plans have been approved, they are normally opened to bids by qualified construction firms. Actually, construction may be handled in two ways. *Minor* remodeling or construction is usually done by regular employees of the recreation and park departments. *Major* construction practices vary. Some large city departments have their own architectural, engineering, and construction staffs and do all of their own work except such major projects as a large building or stadium. In some cases, plans may be designed by the department itself, with the construction work done by private contractors. In others, private architects may be employed to design the facility, which is then constructed by the personnel of the public department. In a few cases, cities employ firms that are responsible for both the designing and the construction of facilities as a package arrangement. This is not a common practice, because the architect is usually relied on to supervise and ensure the quality of the work done by the contractor.

When plans are let out for bids, this must normally be done by public advertisement or announcement. Bidders must familiarize themselves with the contract requirements, the specifications, and the plans, and they should examine in detail the site of the work to be done and all conditions affecting the project. Normally, when they submit bids for the assignment, they are required to show that they are responsible and capable of performing the work to be done under the contract, that they have successfully completed equivalent contracts, and that they have the financial resources needed to perform the task within the time required.

Bids from qualified builders are submitted in a sealed envelope, and the public agency is normally required by law to accept the lowest responsible bidder. The contract is normally based on a fixed sum for the total job, although alternative costs or conditions that might affect the cost of the job may be stipulated. In some cases, contracts may be handled on a cost-plus basis, in which the job is done at cost, with the contractor then receiving a specified percentage of this amount as his fee.

The architect's role in supervising construction is detailed in the Philadelphia Recreation Department guide.

Construction administration

1. *Approvals.* The Architect shall review all cost breakdowns, subcontractors, shop drawings, catalog cuts, payment requisitions and change orders. He shall indicate his approval on each of these documents, and forward them to the Department of Recreation.

2. *Job meetings.* The Architect shall conduct a conference of all the prime contractors once each week at the site of the work. He shall prepare and distribute the minutes of the meetings.

3. *Modifications.* The Architect shall investigate all modifications suggested, make plans and cost estimates, review the contractors' proposals and recommend the course of action to the Department of Recreation.

4. *Inspections.* The Architect shall be present at the semifinal and final inspections, and he shall prepare and distribute the required punch lists.

5. *As-built changes.* The Architect shall be responsible for keeping accurate records of all changes in location, types, sizes, etc., of all the facets of the project. At the completion of the project, he shall revise the tracings to reflect all of these changes.

Frequently, recreation and park departments will have detailed checklists applying to different types of facilities, which are used in reviewing design plans in supervising construction and approving the final job.

Role of administrator in design and construction. As this chapter has made clear, in most situations an outside architectural or engineering firm is employed to design new recreation and park projects. In some cases, it is done by qualified engineers who are regular employees of city government, often in a department of public works. What is the role of the recreation and park administrator in this process?

In smaller communities, he is often likely to be intimately involved. In some situations, he works closely with the designer; during the actual construction process, he may participate in laying out excavation lines, making decisions as to materials, and even instituting change-orders directly at the construction site.

In larger cities, however, the recreation and park administrator tends not to be involved as fully—either because his own responsibilities are too demanding or because departmental lines are more sharply drawn. Instead, the major responsibility for selecting the architectural firm, approving the design, and following up on the construction process falls to the city or town engineer. There are certain advantages to this. The municipal engineer, who is usually a well-qualified professional, may regard the recreation facility as one of his own projects and give it his full attention and support. On the other hand, many municipal engineers tend to be narrow in their thinking and fail to understand recreation and park needs, particularly in terms of programs and people-oriented factors.

For this reason, recreation and park administrators should seek to become as fully involved as possible in each construction project, according to the following guidelines.

1. The recreation and park director should familiarize himself with all background information related to the facility plan and should be actively involved in all public hearings and planning sessions about it.

2. He should meet and discuss the project with all public officials or civic leaders—such as city councilmen, members of planning boards or school administrators—who have a stake in it. He should be thoroughly familiar with their views and wishes and consider their suggestions seriously.

3. He should insist on being involved in the selection of the architectural or engineering firm that is to do the plan. Although the choice may not be his to make, he should press strongly for the selection of a designer who is highly qualified by experience and performance, rather than the lowest bidder or the firm with political connections.

4. He should strive to be present at all design and modification conferences to present his department's point of view and make sure that programmatic needs are considered.

5. When construction begins, he should visit the site regularly, either with members of his department or with the architect on his inspection visits. He should study the construction process carefully and note all problems. It is important to follow up on these immediately to correct errors that might be much more expensive and difficult to remedy at a later point.

6. He should insist, through channels if necessary, that all construction details or standards be carried out exactly as specified. He should not approve any facility or authorize payment at any stage unless fully assured that the job is being done as specified.

If the recreation and park administrator follows these guidelines, not only

Fig. 7-5. All facilities must be maintained under steady use. **A,** Here, Chicago Park District workmen repair swings while, **B,** others remove a dead tree that has been cut down. **C,** One of the key problems of building maintenance has been the spreading practice of scrawling obscenities and slogans on buildings and walls. Here, the Boston Parks and Recreation Department offers citizens their own graffiti board.

will the construction project itself be more successful, but his own role with respect to facilities design and construction will become more fully accepted.

Maintenance and operation. Once the facility has been completed, it is ready for operation. At this point, the maintenance function becomes all-important in promoting full and effective utilization of a facility by the public.

Fig. 7-6. The task is never ending, and the equipment used ranges from, **A**, this huge earth-drilling machine used in Spokane to, **B**, this cherry-picker used to reach George Washington's head in Boston and, **C**, finally, hands, backs, and, most important, tender loving care.

An indoor facility should be kept bright, clean, and cheerful; an outdoor facility should be carefully and regularly cleaned, watered, weeded, or fed, according to its special needs. Good maintenance will earn citizen respect for a recreation and park facility and will encourage participation as well as lengthen the life of a facility and the equipment in it. Poor maintenance practices will do just the opposite. In addition, through regular inspections and prompt repair of broken equipment or dangerous conditions, accidents will be prevented and lawsuits avoided (Fig. 7-5, A).

Normally, a maintenance schedule is developed by a parks foreman or building custodian. It identifies each specific task and indicates when it is to be carried out.

In some large recreation and park systems, instead of following the traditional procedure of having a custodian in charge of a building or one or two maintenance men in charge of a playground or small park, there has been a trend toward developing mobile maintenance teams. In such cities, the most economical and efficient way to carry out outdoor maintenance is to develop highly mechanized approaches to watering, cleaning, weeding, feeding, and trimming lawns, trees, and shrubs and developing regular schedules of painting and rehabilitation of equipment or buildings (Figs. 7-5, B, and 7-6). Since tasks vary according to the season of the year (for example, grass watering and cutting might be a major problem in the summer, whereas snow clearance and maintaining heating systems would be wintertime responsibilities), there is a rotation of job assignments for all personnel.

Some departments have carried out time-and-motion studies in which each job function is clearly described, with standards developed, work assignments specified as to frequency and duration, and the entire assignment carefully systematized. Functions are grouped together and instruments and methods carefully developed to measure the cost of job performance and assist in evaluating employee work output and assigning tasks or planning budgets.

In Chapter 11, guidelines for the maintenance of certain types of recreation areas and facilities and sample maintenance schedules are provided.

Challenges to traditional playground design

Probably in no area of facilities design has there been more serious questioning of traditional approaches than in the area of playground design. Every large city in the country and most smaller city, village, or township programs maintain a network of playgrounds designed for use by younger children. There is increasing evidence that these facilities are *not* serving the purposes for which they were intended. Any casual observer of neighborhood playgrounds in large cities will note a great variation in amount of use. He is likely to see many playgrounds that are comparatively deserted and in which the city's capital investment and assignment of personnel seem to be comparatively wasted.

Often this is true even during the height of the good weather season and at hours at which one would expect playground attendance to be strong. Diana

Dunn, who visited twenty of the United States' largest cities in a study for the Department of Housing and Urban Development, found that "Many urban parks and recreation areas were empty much of the summer, particularly small ones without fountains or swimming facilities. Mornings, afternoons, evenings, weekends—isolated areas made a mockery of minimum open space and park standards. . . ."[9] Another investigator, Nanine Clay, writes:

> Something has gone wrong. After visiting over 200 small neighborhood parks, we were constantly struck with how empty they were even on warm days and evenings when we expected them to be teeming. . . . In some places, neighbors complain the minipark causes increasing vandalism to nearby homes, brings "winos, peeping toms, drug users, and lovers" and "ruins" the neighborhood. . . . Recently, neighborhood groups in a large Eastern city turned down eight out of 12 proposed vest-pocket parks as being irrelevant to the needs of the people. . . .[10]

In many cases, facilities are built to serve children alone and ignore the needs of adults, aging persons, teen-agers, and family groups. Often those facilities that *are* designed for children apparently do not appeal to them as much as other environments—such as streets, sidewalks, roofs, and backyards—do.

Many critics have concluded that the play equipment and designs of most playgrounds fail to attract children because they are fixed, static, and allow no opportunity for creative exploration. Dattner describes the typical large-city playground:

> Characteristically, it is an unbroken expanse of concrete or asphalt pavement, punctuated by the forlorn presence of metal swings, a slide, and some see-saws. Not only does this design lack any possibility for real play; the most interesting activities are prohibited anyway by signs saying "No" in huge letters, followed by a list of all things children like to do. . . .[11]

He comments that the basic fault of typical playgrounds is that they lack anything to inspire interest and curiosity. After a little swinging, sliding, and see-sawing, the built-in opportunities for play are exhausted. Often children then become inspired to use equipment in ways beyond the "designer's wildest imaginings":

> Swings become hanging battering rams for an exciting and noisy battle; children with nerves of steel play swing-the-swing-around-the-top-in-a-full-circle. See-saws make excellent catapults and are great for the jump-off-while-your-partner-is-in-the-air game. And after these limited and perilous options are used up, there are the games of destruction, in which children pit their ingenuity . . . against the designers of these play facilities. . . . The final expression of the frustration of the otherwise powerless children is the scrawling of obscene remarks on the unyielding and inhospitable asphalt.[12]

Commonly, city children seem to prefer playing in neighborhood streets to being in their local playgrounds. Cohen[13] suggests that it is the very excitement and danger offered by the city street that attracts the child; indeed, the pattern of children playing ball games, tag, hitching rides on trucks, dodging in and out behind parked cars, racing in and out of alleyways and on tenement roofs in city slums is obviously far more challenging and creative an experience than the traditional playground can ever offer.

Fig. 7-7. A, St. Petersburg provides land on which semi-private organizations, such as the Skyway Rod and Gun Club, may operate their own programs. **B,** A similar facility is operated by the St. Petersburg Lawn Bowling Club, the largest in the world with twenty-three links. Most cities today provide new and exciting forms of playground equipment. Here are examples, **C,** in the Chicago Park District and **D,** in Philadelphia.

What innovative solutions have designers found to meet this need? For two examples, see Fig. 7-7, *C* and *D*.

Theme playgrounds. In many cases, designers have developed new kinds of play equipment designed to challenge the child's imagination and foster creative play. Typically, such creative playgrounds offer huge animals made out of concrete or metal, new kinds of climbing apparatus or slides, brightly colored and designed in contemporary style. In some cases, entire playgrounds have been developed to embody a *theme* of interest to children.

For example, in Oakland, California, a three-masted 65-foot-long Chinese junk, a Chinese wall maze, and a play area carrying out Chinese design motifs were conceived and built by Chinese residents to provide a stimulating environment in terms of Chinese culture for their children. Elsewhere in Oakland, a "Death Valley Mining Town" has been constructed to five-eighths scale, including a hotel, blacksmith shop, mule barn, livery stable, jail, sheriff's office, and other stores and buildings typical of pioneer days.

Sunnyvale, California, has four such facilities: a *space age* playground, with "craters of the moon," space ships, rockets, and satellites; a *prehistoric park,* with dinosaur climbers, a Stone Age spray pool, and a cave in a sandbox; a *southwestern* playground boasting a Spanish galleon and Spanish-style fort, and a *Mississippi River* park, complete with riverboat, riverside "town," and even a muddy flowing stream. Other communities have developed playgrounds based on comic characters, such as "Dennis the Menace," other themes of children's fiction, or world history and travel.

Adventure playgrounds. Adventure playgrounds represent an attempt to develop play areas providing creative possibilities for play, at the same time maintaining an adequate level of safety and control. Adventure playgrounds provide a variety of challenges ranging from activities that young children can master to problems that require the skill and agility of older children. Often, they involve little more than an empty lot, a pile of scrap lumber, tools, a few sheets or pieces of canvas, and other waste materials.

Lady Allen of Hurtwood, a distinguished British designer of innovative play areas, writes of adventure playgrounds as

> . . . places where children of all ages can develop their own ideas of play. Most young people, at one time or another, have a deep urge to experiment with earth, fire, water, and timber, to work with real tools without fear of undue criticism or censure. In these playgrounds their love of freedom to take calculated risks is recognized and can be enjoyed under tolerant and sympathetic guidelines.[14]

Adventure playgrounds are not limited to construction or do-it-yourself projects. Increasingly, designers are making use of new kinds of equipment for experimental and exploratory play by young children—free-form playgrounds, animals, earth or stone mounds, tunnels, pyramids, and climbing areas. Walls and area separators are used that become play equipment in themselves as children climb or walk along them and that create separate sitting areas. In some cases, movable pieces of modular playground are provided that children can use to build play environments that change from day to day.

Child guidance experts generally are enthusiastic about this type of play environment. They see it offering a learning experience in which children invent novel uses for ordinary objects and are free to engage in make-believe and symbolic play, to discover their own resources and creative abilities, and to transform their world—which they cannot do with conventional fixed equipment. Dattner writes:

> A playground should be like a small-scale replica of the world, with as many as possible of the sensory experiences to be found in the world included in it. . . . Once we have provided a place overflowing with things to see, touch, smell, hear, and taste, we must encourage the interaction of the child with them. The materials must be able to "respond": things that can be burrowed in, piled in heaps, thrown, carried, sifted, eaten, pounded, pushed, slapped, dammed, collected in vessels, spilled, floated on, drunk, and splashed.[15]

Innovative design for fixed equipment. Probably the most widespread trend in playground design has been the development of new kinds of fixed equipment that offer imaginative and creative variations of such traditional pieces as slides or jungle gyms. Designers have developed forms that are irregular in their proportions, that provide children with the opportunity to jump, climb, crawl, and hide, and that stimulate imaginative play. Cohen cites as an example:

> A tower combining a spiral slide, staircase, ladder, sandbox and lookout post allows children to play more than one-at-a-time with many different perceptions in their minds. This type of arrangement multiplies the number of different activities by the creative ability of the group as a whole.[16]

In such play environments, the function of any piece of equipment may be determined by the child's imagination. A well-designed playground rewards children by developing their balance, agility, strength, initiative, and self-confidence. Form, color, and texture help to stimulate creative and sustained play activity.

Other trends in playground design. Designers have developed new approaches to the use of levels in playgrounds. Conventionally, steep or sloping surfaces were bulldozed flat to provide a single level play area. Increasingly, architects are laying out areas that have steep grades and contrasts in levels. These provide the opportunity for coasting, hiding, pretending to defend or attack a fort, using rope swings or pulley rides, climbing along monkey bridges, or rolling down slopes. In some cities, granite boulders are being left in their natural position to serve as climbing areas. Today, many designers are building hills on playgrounds where none existed before or deliberately planning large mounds and pyramids of dirt or stone.

Swedish playground designers have promoted the elevated play street concept, based on the natural instinct of children to try to travel distances without touching the ground. Such streets are designed to offer challenging pathways so that children must step, swing, jump, or climb from structure to structure, using horizontal bars, teetertotters, ropes, aerial walkways, and similar equipment. So-called traffic playgrounds have been developed by Swiss and French designers to teach children about road safety while they enjoy pedaling miniature automobiles around facsimile streets, complete with traffic signals, stop signs, and crosswalks.

Increasingly, wood is being used instead of iron for outdoor play equipment and climbing or building forms. Although it is esthetically more attractive than steel, some authorities have found that it tends to deteriorate in damp climates, to be slippery and dangerous when wet, and to injure children with splinters.

In general, it must be recognized that equipment by itself cannot ensure the success of any playground. Friedberg writes:

> Benches, tables, and play apparatus by themselves cannot create a fulfilling experience. The total of the environment is important. The play of spaces, relationship of forms, intricacy of patterns, tactual quality of textures: all these and more come together to produce a world of experiences necessary for a successful recreation area.[17]

What evidence is there that adventure or other types of innovative playgrounds are more effective than traditionally designed facilities? Rutledge suggests that they are more successful in meeting the "arousal-seeking" needs that psychologists have recently identified as underlying much play behavior. He describes a careful study of playground effectiveness, carried out at the University of Illinois:

> Scores of third graders were taken to two playgrounds, both similar in size and number of structures, yet differing in that one was a "complex" system and the other a "simple" assortment of typical swings, slides, spring horses, and roundabouts. The kids were asked to express their preferences on the entire site, individual structures, and the kinds of play allowed. The results were compared against time-lapse movie coverage of the play. Preference expressions and actual usage coincided—the complex playground was overwhelmingly favored.[18]

Modern approaches to facilities design

One of the key elements in contemporary recreation and park facilities design is the imaginative use of space.

New uses of space. A number of large-city school systems have experimented with new ways of using space in heavily built-up urban districts. For example, several years ago, a high school was built in New York City atop stilts to provide playground areas and more convenient access. In another crowded neighborhood of the same city, a junior high school was built above subway yards, with facilities for community recreation.

In other large cities, housing, recreation, and school authorities are planning new building codes that will transform their communities' roofs into neighborhood oases of greenery and play areas. In many urban areas there are thousands of tar and gravel rooftops that are essentially unused and that might provide many acres of safe recreation space.

One good example of such imaginative use of space is the Nashville, Tennessee, YMCA, which has constructed a highly successful rooftop running track, eighteen laps to the mile, above its Physical Fitness Center. Although the building also has an indoor track, the rooftop facility, surfaced by a Chevron asphalt compound, which provides a comfortable and resilient surface with good drainage, has been heavily utilized (Fig. 7-8).

Other cities are exploring ways of using available open space for badly needed community recreation. One of the most obvious—yet usually overlooked—potential sources of space is the parking lot. Customarily, public, private, and commercial parking lots are closed to other uses when not filled with cars. In areas where lots are normally filled only 8 or 10 hours a day, such blacktop sites are thus wasted for at least 14 hours each weekday and 24 hours on weekends. Hogan[19] suggests that combined efforts by neighborhood residents, lot owners, and municipal governments might transform their "asphalt deserts" into recreation spaces during the late afternoon and evening and on week-ends. Other site possibilities include garage roofs, space over railroad tracks, piers, and highways, under municipal building complexes, and in vacant lots in disadvantaged areas with extreme shortages of play space. Frequently, portable playground equipment is used, including basketball and volleyball standards and nets, to provide temporary play areas.

Fig. 7-8. Many YMCAs have superior sports and fitness-oriented facilities. The Nashville YMCA operates, **A**, a rooftop running track, and, **B**, a rooftop swimming pool. (Courtesy Nashville YMCA.)

Fig. 7-8, cont'd. C, It also has well-equipped exercise rooms for adult fitness programs. **D,** It pays to present an attractive image. (Courtesy Nashville YMCA.)

Mobile recreation facilities. Many communities are making increased use of mobile recreation units to enrich program opportunities on play streets, in vacant lots, and in other improvised settings. Although they are not a new form of service, mobile units have expanded greatly in recent years. Many cities and towns in the United States and Canada have developed new mobile recreation units of the following types:

> *Cultural units:* Band show-wagons, portable stages and platforms, portable shells, puppet theaters, craftmobiles, bookmobiles, filmmobiles, historymobiles, and other units used for the performing arts and creative programs
> *Sports and games:* Units with playground equipment, skatemobiles, boxingmobiles, circusmobiles, physical fitness trailers, portable swimming pools, and other sportsmobiles
> *Nature and science units:* Naturemobiles, zoomobiles, sciencemobiles, starmobiles, etc.

A number of manufacturing companies sell mobile recreation units, either as standard items or as specially designed equipment. In an extensive study of mobile units, Frieswyck also gave a number of examples of recreation departments that had built their own units. More and more cities are experimenting with unique mobile program ventures. As a single example, the city of San Pablo, California, has developed a mobile Senior Citizens Center. This 35-foot converted school bus, called Omnibus II, was built with the assistance of a state grant. It contains built-in lounges and tables, a phonograph and movie projector, and is well stocked with board games and craft supplies. Carrying its own power sources, it makes scheduled, well-publicized 3-hour stops at various locations throughout the community as determined by a survey of senior citizens' needs.

Ecological recovery and recreation. Many recreation and park planners are working closely with environmental groups to halt the unbridled spread of industrial and residential building that threatens our nation's land and water resources. Of the original 127 million acres of wetlands and marshlands in the United States, over 45 million have been ruined by unrestricted draining, filling, and dredging. The natural resources of recreation are being steadily diminished. Great rivers and lakes are polluted by industrial and human waste. Forests are leveled by lumbering interests and wildlife slain by uncontrolled chemical poisons, hunting, and the destruction of breeding and feeding grounds.

More and more, recreation and park authorities are playing a leading role in national and state open-space programs. In many cities and counties, they are leading antipollution campaigns, conducting recycling and litter collection programs, and promoting the cause of ecology.

In addition, imaginative planners are actually using waste materials or the damaged environment to develop exciting new facilities. For example, one solution to a growing problem of urban ecologists—garbage disposal—has been found by the recreation and parks department of the Borough of Etobicoke, near Toronto. Instead of burying the town's refuse or dumping it in a river, it is being used to build a large ski hill. The hill is constructed by piling sanitary industrial wastes, covering it with additional fill, and planting trees to anchor it. Charges for dumping privileges ordinarily are higher than the cost of building the hill, so it is anticipated that a fine new winter sports facility will be made possible for Etobicoke without extra cost to the municipality.

A similar facility, aptly called Mount Trashmore, has been developed over a period of several years by Virginia Beach, Virginia (Fig. 7-9, *B*). In the mid-1960s, the problem of solid waste disposal was seen as an increasingly critical problem for the city. With the assistance of substantial federal grants, between 300 and 1,200 tons of waste were compacted daily for five years and deposited on the chosen site with alternating shallow layers of clean soil. Today, Mount Trashmore is 65 feet high and extends 900 × 300 feet. It stands between two man-made lakes and is becoming the key feature of a major recreational complex, including a hilltop garden, picnic areas, a 10,000-seat waterfront amphitheater, soap-box derby ramp, and docks for unmotorized boats on the lakes, which have already been stocked with fish. Particularly in flat regions, where hills may provide the opportunity for new forms of recreation—skiing, sledding, and tobogganing among others—an increasing number of cities are likely to experiment with similar plans.[20]

In some cases, sites that have been used for mining, leaving ugly scars in the land, are now being converted to recreation use. For example, in Polk County, Florida, the American Cyanamid Company mined over 700 acres of swampland for underlying phosphate rock deposits. After the excavation, the area was contoured, filled and graded to provide a recreation area for the benefit of thousands of residents in the area. When the mining process was completed, the land was donated to Polk County, which proceeded to develop a major park facility on the site.

Similarly, Lackawanna County in Pennsylvania purchased a substantial mining property to develop a recreation and tourist center. Picnicking, camping, nature study, fishing, ice skating, and other recreational facilities are being developed, along with a $1.5 million Anthracite Mining Museum as a major tourist attraction.

In some cases, recreation sites are being developed on what was formerly simply rundown property. In Santa Barbara, California, where an 81-acre section of dumping ground and hobo shacks had long been an irritant, the voluntary contributions of local residents and businessmen succeeded in turning a community eyesore into a beautiful oceanfront area including a half-million-dollar community park and zoo.

More and more cities are developing nature centers—in part to conserve existing natural areas and in part to ensure that future generations will learn the elements crucial to maintaining the environment. Several hundred such nature centers have been established in the United States and Canada over the past 10 years, and new ones are being added each year.

According to Shomon, every community of 25,000 needs a nature center, and cities over 25,000 should have additional ones. Every major county park system should have at least one, and others should be provided in state and national parks, forests, and refuges.

Fig. 7-9. A, Innovative recreation facilities include a new Sport Court for practicing or playing sports adapted to a small closed area. Other examples are **B,** Mt. Trashmore, at Virginia Beach, Virginia, and **C** and **D,** the unusual Big Surf facility at Tempe, Arizona. (**A** courtesy Sportatron Co., Salem, Conn.; **C** and **D** courtesy Big Surf, Tempe, Ariz.)

C

D

Fig. 7-9, cont'd. For legend see opposite page.

A nature center is a specially planned and developed land area in or near a city which has the support facilities and personnel to promote a "land for learning" program. These elements are essential: at least 50 acres of suitable land, an interpretive building as a focal point, trails and interesting outdoor interpretive features to show that the outdoor world is exciting and alive, and a dedicated staff of highly specialized teacher-naturalists.[21]

In some cases, cities are developing new natural sites by ingenious methods. For example, in Foothills Park in Palo Alto, California, spring water seepage was dammed up to create a natural-looking marsh with a variety of wildlife and plants in an area where most of the natural terrain had been drained, filled, and reclaimed for housing and other commercial development. A marsh area of sizable dimensions was created through the work of youth crews and volunteer local residents. Plants were transplanted into the marsh, and Scout troops donated frogs, toads, salamanders, and turtles gathered on trips. Inevitably, other forms of wildlife began to appear, ranging from microscopic life and insects to varied birds and mammals. Park visitors today delight in observing the unusual setting and ecological lessons displayed in this seemingly natural marsh.

Air-supported structures. Air-supported structures are being used today to cover both large and small areas, such as tennis courts, swimming pools, track and field sites, and ice rinks. An air-supported structure, which consists basically of a skin that serves as walls and roof, can be anchored in place, blown up, and made ready for use within a day. It can be deflated, untied, folded like a tent, and stored in even less time. Air-supported structures are comfortable and safe and are easily maintained; however, they have a life expectancy of only 5 to 7 years and are easily susceptible to vandalism. In many neighborhoods, zoning laws must be changed to permit their construction. Such bubbles provide great flexibility in that the same area may be kept open during the warm months of the year and then quickly enclosed during the colder weather.

Swimming facilities. Swimming pools have undergone a variety of innovations in recent years. In Houston, Texas, a fenceless pool area has been constructed, replacing the typical wire fence with a 40-foot-wide, 4-foot-deep moat, featuring moving water. A commercial company has designed a four-seasons pool, which can easily be converted to a basketball and volleyball court in the fall and spring and a skating rink in the winter. The city of Decatur, Alabama, now operates a three-pool swimming complex. It consists of an aquadome (an indoor-outdoor pool used in all seasons), a wave-activated pool, and an Olympic-size pool.

Technological advances have made new forms of recreation, such as surfing, available to areas of the country that would not normally have had them. The world's first inland surfing facility has been built in the middle of a *desert,* in Tempe, Arizona, by a privately operated recreation complex (Fig. 7-9, *C* and *D*). This cleverly engineered facility features a 2.5-acre lagoon, 9 feet at its deepest point. It is 400 feet long, 300 feet wide, and contains four million gallons of recirculating treated water. Big Surf's waves are made by a custom hydraulic system housed in a 160-foot long reservoir at the base of a keyhole-shaped lagoon. Waves are made by pumping water to a prearranged height in the reservoir and releasing it suddenly through underwater gates. The volume of released water breaks over the baffle (artificial reef) adjacent to the gates, forming breakers of up to 5 feet, which sweep down into the lagoon. Participants may swim, sun bathe, ride surfboards or rubber rafts, or enjoy other sports in this unique recreation complex, which is designed in Polynesian style and fully illuminated for night operations.

As another example of facilities design in water sports, in the Susquehanna Valley, near Sunbury, Pennsylvania, a 3,000-acre pool has been created by the use of an oversize tube of rubberized nylon that is stretched across the Susquehanna River. The Fabridam, as it is called, provides a barrier that pools water to a depth of 9 feet; it has made possible a recreation lake extending 8 miles up the river, providing recreation facilities for swimming, fishing, boating, and other forms of water play. In some cases, sizable lakes have been developed in desert areas with the use of plastic undercoating that prevents water drainage into the subsoil.

Even water skiing is now available in a newly engineered, boatless form. Through a privately developed and marketed device called *Skinautika,* which employs a patented moving dual overhead cable system to supply towing power, from ten to twenty skiers can ski simultaneously. This ingenious system can be used in relatively shallow water and is particularly appropriate in small private lakes; it avoids noise, water pollution, and the wake generated by power boats.

Winter sports facilities. Technology has enabled many municipal or county recreation and park departments to develop winter sports facilities in climates where it formerly would have been impossible to maintain them. Both commercial and public agencies have constructed ski slopes, with artificial snow-making machines and chair-lifts or tows, in areas of the country where skiing had never before been possible. Artificial ice rinks, refrigerated toboggan chutes, and similar inventions have created many new winter sports opportunities.

An outstanding example is the Hillend Ski Centre, operated by the Edinburgh, Scotland, Parks Department. This is the largest artificial ski slope in Europe; it is 400 yards long and offers a choice of two runs from the top station, which is served by a chair lift. The Hillend Ski Centre is used primarily on weekdays for ski instruction classes of public school children; at other times, it is used by the public for recreational skiing, skiing courses, racing events, instructor training, and similar events. The surface itself is Dendix matting, which has proved to be a highly acceptable substitute for snow, laid in six-by-four-foot mats. As an example of the popularity of such facilities, during the first four months of 1973, 114,940 skiers went down the Hillend slope.

Recently a new plastic ice-skating surface that may be used indoors has been developed. The plastic surface is easy to maintain and provides an adequate surface for skating for beginners, youngsters, and figure skating, although not for speed skating. Many marinas in northern climates are now equipped with automatic bubbling mechanisms that prevent freezing, so that boats may remain safely in the water throughout the winter months. In northern Illinois, an inland lake that would normally be frozen solid during the winter is now kept unfrozen

Fig. 7-10. The Eugene, Oregon, Department of Parks and Recreation provides **A**, neighborhood playfields for such sports as flag football for adults, and **B**, craft centers, housing such activities as ceramics. Recreation facilities in Detroit include **C**, this beautifully designed small park and a fleet of small Swimobiles—**D**, filled and **E**, empty.

all year round with such an electrically powered mechanism. It has become a winter haven for 1,200 wild ducks, geese, swans, and loons and has turned the lake into a fascinating area for naturalists and others.

Zoo design. Many cities are developing exciting new zoo facilities. The city of Los Angeles, for example, has built a modern, multilevel zoo in which moats and natural barriers are used instead of fences and cages. This permits a close view of all specimens from safe positions; bridge spans provide exciting panoramas from above. So natural is the environment that a number of types of animals that have become increasingly scarce are now breeding successfully in this setting. Animals from a particular continent are in areas with settings depicting their typical native environment; each continental area is in effect a complete zoo in itself.

The Philadelphia Zoo, the nation's oldest zoological garden, has continued to develop innovations; it has now constructed a monorail. Monorail riders enjoy a mile-long, 20-minute tour through the most interesting parts of the zoo, during which they listen to a taped commentary describing the animals and birds 15 feet beneath them.

Another unusual facility is the new Tropical Rain Forest at the Topeka, Kansas, Zoological Park. This is housed in a circular building topped by aluminum-framed clear acrylic panels, forming a high dome, which permits a great variety of colorful tropical birds to swoop about in free flight. Moist air is circulated at a high volume throughout the structure. Many types of lush vegetation and exotic animals coexist in an authentically planned and delicately balanced environment; the careful planning of the Tropical Rain Forest included a data-gathering trip to the Amazon River Basin in South America.

New sports facilities design. Many communities have developed innovative approaches to the design and use of sports and fitness-oriented facilities. For example, a number of cities have developed fitness parks for adults modelled after the *vita parcours*, which were built originally along autobahns in Switzerland to reduce accidents because of driver fatigue. These are made available for free public use in a University of Montana housing area and in a similar facility in Vancouver, British Columbia. The Montana fitness park features a ⅛ mile jogging track and nine exercise stations—including leap-frog, hurdles, stride jumping, chin-ups, stair-running, bench sit-ups, and push-ups—all fitted into a site 100 yards long and a maximum of 40 yards wide.

Another unique approach to facilities design is found at the University of Idaho, which has recently designed a portable football field within a large enclosed structure for year-round use. This installation makes use of a 74,000-square-foot Tartan Turf surface, providing a field for football, soccer, golf instruction, baseball, and other sports normally played on grass. The surface is brought into the stadium in six 35-foot sections and bolted together; it can then be rolled up with electric winches and stored in about an hour. The area can then be used for sports requiring a hard surface, such as basketball, volleyball, tennis, badminton, or other team or dual sports.

In many cases, colleges and universities have developed their own recreation or sports facilities, which have then been made available for community recreation use. An example is Grinnell College, Iowa, which built an outstanding physical education complex in 1972. This huge plant provides 87,000 square feet of floor space with double courts for basketball and special courts for tennis, volleyball, handball, paddleball, and squash, as well as multipurpose areas for archery, dance, and gymnastics, a 220-yard track, and a large swimming pool with separate bays for instruction, diving, lifesaving courses, and small-boat handling lessons. Grinnell College has fully accepted the principle of a private college's responsibility for sharing its resources with the surrounding community in a constructive town and gown relationship. Believing deeply in education for leisure as well, it has made the physical education complex available for community use through a series of organized programs: early morning exercise (beginning at 6:30 A.M.), noontime recreation, Sunday family recreation, open swimming periods, and extended use of the whole facility during college vacation or recess periods. The director of the Grinnell public recreation and park department administers all community programs, using paid college students as leaders and supervisors. The public pays a modest individual-visit or annual family fee to support the expenses of this program.

In many other ways, community sports facilities have been expanded and enriched. One of the key ways is through night lighting, which has lengthened the hours of use of many sports programs. For example, the city of Huntington Beach, California, recently installed an extensive new lighting system in Murdy Park, a 17-acre year-round sports complex, with football and softball fields, basketball and tennis courts, and a community center. In addition, pier and beach areas have also been lit to levels that now permit nighttime fishing, swimming, and even surfing. The volume of participation has increased greatly because of Huntington Beach's new capability for extending play well into the evening hours. In addition, the city recognizes several other values of night lighting: (1) it is a major deterrent to personal crime, vandalism, and theft; (2) it serves to distinguish various activities in the park, with various sports areas easily recognized by their unique lighting systems; and (3) it beautifies the appearance of the park by enhancing plants, trees, and architectural features and helps to integrate the park into a unified complex.

Communities that are considering installing night lighting in recreation and park areas have basically three alternatives: fluorescent, incandescent, and high-intensity discharge systems. The appropriate choice depends on cost factors, specific use needs, and such concerns as efficiency, lamp life, and maintenance; careful engineering consideration must be given to the design of lighting systems.

Biking facilities. It is estimated that more than 57 million American children and adults today ride bicycles; 5 million bikes are sold in the United States each year. The interest in bicycling has grown markedly, both because of the concern about physical fitness and the need for exercise and because of the need to reduce air pollution and automobile traffic in urban settings. As a result, communities all over the country have expanded special facilities for biking.

Many cities have developed and marked extensive systems of bikeways, usually consisting of secondary routes parallel to main streets, leading from commercial or residential areas to schools, shopping centers, parks, playgrounds, and recreational and cultural centers. Bikeways are marked with easy-to-read signs, are safer for cyclists because fewer vehicles use them, and are easily and inexpensively maintained. One of the most ambitious plans for public biking has been developed in Fremont, California, providing a network of interconnecting paths covering a 90-mile square area. These paths connect the central city with five satellite or suburban communities and have subnetworks of paths connecting schools, parks, playgrounds, and other facilities.

Other special biking facilities being developed today include bicycle rodeo areas (with a maze of paths, intersections, and obstacles), velodromes (bicycle racetracks), special park drives or roads, bike racks or stands, and youth hostels providing low-cost accommodations primarily for young people traveling in groups.

Many other types of special facilities are being developed by recreation and park departments throughout the country. In some cases, these are being planned and constructed in cooperation with school departments and other municipal agencies.

Facilities designed to minimize vandalism. The problem of preventing vandalism and crime has become an increasingly serious matter for recreation and park departments throughout the United States. Almost three fourths of the large cities in this country now have a serious problem with break-in and damage of indoor facilities. In some cities, hundreds of thousands of dollars each year are spent to repair buildings and equipment damaged by vandals.

One approach to minimizing vandalism has been an increased reliance on supervision in the form of building watchmen, police patrols, and park guards or rangers. Improved and extended programming also helps reduce vandalism, since children and youth—who are the chief vandals—are not as ready to damage a facility that they use regularly and for which they have some respect. However, a key point at which vandalism can be forestalled is in the design process.

Architects are avoiding the use of ordinary glass windows in many recreation buildings. Instead, they are substituting Plexiglas, wiremesh glass, or solid glass panels or glass brick panes. Other fixtures, ranging from toilet seats to water fountains, are designed to be as vandal-proof as possible.

Typically, most buildings today are designed without low walls or roofs that potential vandals might climb upon or hide behind. Indentations in buildings or low shrubbery that might hide prowlers or muggers are now avoided. Fuller use is being made of night lighting around centers, often turned on and off by special timing systems. New burglar-proof locks and alarm systems are being used to prevent vandals from breaking into buildings. In some cases where vandals have deliberately poured gasoline under entrance doors and then set fire to it, sending buildings up in flames, new sliding steel doors have been installed, with overlapping sills that catch the gasoline and prevent it from flowing into the building.

In many other ways, facilities are today being designed with architectural features intended to make them resistant to vandalism and as inexpensively maintained as possible. Graffiti boards, as in Fig. 7-5, *C*, allow individual expression and offer an alternative to defacing walls.

Access for the physically handicapped. Another important trend in designing recreation and park facilities is the increased recognition of the need to make them accessible for physically handicapped children and adults. It is estimated that in the United States today, there are 6.2 million people who use orthopedic aids such as wheelchairs, crutches, or walkers. Millions of others have limited mobility because of blindness or impaired vision, artificial limbs, or similar disabilities. In the past, little effort was made to consider the needs of physically handicapped persons in designing recreational facilities; often, therefore, it was either impossible or extremely difficult for them to gain access to such leisure areas. Organizations concerned with the needs of the handicapped have made the following case:

> Today, thanks to modern medical treatment and prosthetic appliances, ingenious self-help devices and expanded means of rehabilitation therapy, a growing number of people with physical limitations are able to live productive and meaningful lives. When a disabled person has worked hard to gain sufficient mobility and confidence to attempt recreation in a public park, it is important that his experience be a successful one.[22]

Today, almost all federal, state, or provincial governments require that public facilities be made fully accessible to the physically handicapped. The National Society for Park Resources, the National Research Council, and numerous organizations concerned with architectural standards have developed guidelines for facilitating access to recreation and park facilities and improving opportunities for successful participation. These include:

1. Logical design of walks and trails, with minimum widths and grades, appropriate surfaces for wheelchair use, elimination of expansion joints, and appropriate resting and pick-up places for the handicapped and elderly
2. Picnic tables, fishing areas, specially designed nature trails, golf putting areas, and similar facilities which permit use by the blind, or those in wheelchairs
3. Redesign of ramps, doors, vestibules, dressing rooms, swimming pools, toilets, drinking fountains, showers, and similar areas to facilitate use by the disabled

Specific technical recommendations are provided in a number of publications that have been issued in recent years by architectural design organizations or government agencies. They include both general guidelines and suggested designs for various types of facilities. Among the widely accepted recommendations are the following[23]:

> One primary entrance in every building should have at least a 32-inch opening, lightweight doors, and level thresholds. This entrance should provide access in multifloor buildings to elevators large enough to allow a wheelchair to turn around.
> Floors should have sufficient texture to allow wheelchairs to move without slipping and people with canes and crutches to navigate with ease.

Restrooms should have at least one stall wide enough for a person in a wheelchair. This stall should also have grab bars, as should urinals.

Ramps to entrances above ground should have a gradient of not more than 1 foot for every 12 feet. A ramp should have 32-inch-high handrails on at least one side.

Ground surrounding a building should be graded to provide at least one primary entrance accessible to handicapped individuals.

Parking lots should have several larger spaces reserved for the handicapped.

Outdoor theaters should have some removable seats to accommodate wheelchairs.

Smooth-surfaced (not slick) walks should be installed across soft sanded areas, such as beaches, to bath houses, rest rooms, swimming, fishing, and boating areas.

Warning signals should be both visual and audible for the deaf and blind; safety devices which depend on sound, such as a lifeguard's whistle, should be augmented by visual warning flags.

Any department that undertakes the design of new facilities or the redesign and rehabilitation of older areas or buildings should become thoroughly familiar with such guidelines and recommendations and should make certain that they are incorporated in the final plan.

Energy conservation and facilities planning. The need to conserve energy in recreation and park operations first was recognized as a critical emergency during the gasoline and heating oil shortages of 1973-1974. Although the situation is not now as critical in terms of immediate supply of fuels, both the high cost of all energy sources and the recognition that we must conserve fuels as part of a long-term survival approach make it essential that recreation and park administrations assign energy conservation a high priority in their overall planning. The measures to be taken are of two types: (1) policies designed to curb operational uses of energy through direct program or travel restrictions; and (2) incorporation of energy-saving principles in the design and construction of new facilities.

Under the first heading, the following kinds of measures have been instituted:

- Creating car pools for travel
- Reducing car speed, weight, or horsepower
- Not using air conditioning in vehicles
- Eliminating excessive travel
- Reducing excessive playing of radios, television sets, or stereo equipment
- Lowering building thermostats and using draperies or other means to conserve heat
- Not heating empty rooms and using air conditioning in buildings only when necessary
- Shortening building hours
- Cutting field trips or special events
- Reducing water temperature in pools
- Eliminating night programs involving night lighting

The second approach involves a total analytical study of the design, construction, and use of recreation and park facilities to reduce energy consumption. Elements of heating, cooling, providing hot water, or lighting should be investigated so that through intelligent layouts, placement, use of materials, insulation, and construction, energy consumption can be controlled. Every design factor must be considered to eliminate present and future waste. Beyond this, recreation and park planners are exploring new and more imaginative ways of saving energy. For example, a number of pool-heating systems employing solar energy are now on the market—a point of special interest in states such as California, which have banned future use of water heaters in private pools.

A leading recreation and park planner, Arthur Mittelstaedt, asks:

Why can't we incorporate solar systems into the roof systems of rinks, indoor pools, community centers and even park comfort stations? Why can't we use wind-mills in parks as an energy source and learning resource? Why can't we introduce bio-systems and cycle waste into heat sources? There are many other suggestions for introducing energy consumption reduction, and the lack of technology is not the excuse. . . .[24]

SUMMARY

This chapter has dealt at length with the planning, design, and development of recreation and park facilities. This area of administrative responsibility is heav-ily dependent on financial resources that make it possible to acquire and develop such facilities. Chapter 8 deals with this broad area, outlining the principles of budget development and financial management in recreation and park adminis-tration.

Suggested topics for class presentations or student reports or projects

1. Discuss the major types of facilities stan-dards today, including their value and lim-itations. Indicate which of these you would make use of in carrying out a planning study of recreation and park facilities in a modern community.
2. Describe contemporary and innovative new approaches to facilities design with respect to a specific category of recreation and park facility, such as a playground or sports complex.
3. Visit, examine, and systematically analyze the network of areas and facilities in a specific community. Evaluate it in terms of the diversity of facilities, the availability of needed areas in different sections of the community, and the extent to which future needs are being anticipated.

REFERENCES

1. For full description of standards developed by National Recreation and Park Associa-tion, see Buechner, R. D., editor: *National Park, Recreation and Open Space Stan-dards*, Washington, D.C., 1969, National Recreation and Park Association.
2. Gold, Seymour M.: "Environmental Plan-ning: A Professional Challenge," *Parks and Recreation*, June, 1972, p. 23.
3. Gans, Herbert J.: *People and Plans*, New York, 1968, Basic Books, Inc., p. 122.
4. "Comparative Recreation Needs and Ser-vices in New York Neighborhoods," New York, 1963, Research Department, Com-munity Council of Greater New York.
5. "Question—Have You Taken Advantage of . . . Corridors, Flood Plains, etc.? Washington, D.C., 1975, Bureau of Out-door Recreation.
6. Kershow, Warren M.: *Land Acquisition*, Arlington, Va., 1975, National Recreation and Park Association, p. 25.
7. Splenda, Richard: "Park Design: Unclutter and Uncomplicate," *Parks and Recreation*, March, 1974, p. 29.
8. Branch, James, and Rowan, David: "De-veloping an Urban Ski Facility," *Parks and Recreation*, September, 1975, p. 20.
9. Dunn, Diana, in *Modernizing Urban Park and Recreation Systems: National Forum Proceedings*, 1972, National Recreation and Park Association, p. 9.
10. Clay, Nanine: "Miniparks—Diminishing Re-turns," *Parks and Recreation*, January, 1971, p. 23.
11. From *Design for Play* by Richard Dattner. Copyright 1969 by Litton Educational Pub-lishing, Inc. Reprinted by Permission of Van Nostrand Reinhold Co.
12. *Ibid.*
13. Cohen, Ira: "City Streets as Play Areas," *Parks and Recreation*, September, 1968, p. 46.
14. From Lady Allen of Hurtwood: *Planning for Play*, Cambridge, Mass., 1968, M.I.T. Press, p. 55.
15. Dattner, *op. cit.*, pp. 44-45.
16. Cohen, *op. cit.*, p. 46.
17. Friedberg, M. Paul: "Super-Block Play Areas," *Recreation*, April, 1965, p. 65.
18. Rutledge, Albert, J.: "Playground Design

With a Motive in Mind," *Parks and Recreation,* February, 1975, p. 43.

19. Hogan, Paul: "Double-Duty for Parking Lots," *Parks and Recreation,* May, 1970, p. 68.

20. Houston, Jourdan: "The Rise of Mt. Trashmore," *Parks and Recreation,* January, 1973, p. 28.

21. Shomon, Joseph J.: "No Time to Talk," *Parks and Recreation,* September, 1970, pp. 37, 82.

22. "A Handbook of Design Standards: Outdoor Recreation for the Physically Handicapped," New York State Council of Parks and Outdoor Recreation, 1967, p. 3.

23. "Trends for the Handicapped," "Washington, D.C., 1974, National Society for Park Resources and National Service, p. 8.

24. Mittelstaedt, Arthur H., Jr.: "Implications of the Energy Crisis," New York State Recreation and Park Society Conference, May, 1975.

CHAPTER 8

BUDGETS AND FISCAL MANAGEMENT

President Calvin Coolidge once said, "The business of America is business." Certainly it is true that support for every form of public service—including recreation and parks—*must* come from adequate financial backing and intelligent fiscal management. Yet it is a curious commentary that the area of administration in which many recreation and park executives feel least competent is that of budget-making and fiscal operations.

The setting of departmental goals and the design of a budget intended to achieve these goals, the process of budget review and approval, and the actual administration of a fiscal program through the year constitute a major responsibility of recreation and park administrators. It represents a cycle that never ends, usually recommencing with new goals and preliminary plans before the previous year's budget has been evaluated. It can be an extremely complicated process, involving expertise in the realm of bonds and indebtedness, credit management, working with private funds and foundations, expenditure and control systems, pension plans, and similar concerns. Typically, many recreation and park executives approach this responsibility with a mixture of fear and ignorance.

Yet it should not represent such a difficult hurdle. It is not necessary for administrators to become financial wizards. Provided that they have a basic understanding of the elements of budget-making and fiscal management and that they continue to learn and grow in this field, they can operate effectively. In most cities, finance commissioners or comptrollers, city managers, budget analysts, or lay finance chairmen have helped recreation and park executives develop the competence needed to function intelligently and effectively in this area.

It is a testimonial to this competence that the gross value of publicly owned recreation and park resources—including ice rinks, marinas, parks, tennis courts, golf courses, sportsmen's centers, swimming pools, and other facilities—has swollen to many billions of dollars. However, by the mid-1970s in both the United States and Canada, increased costs of municipal, county, and state or provincial government imposed a new need for austerity on all forms of public service. It is essential, therefore, that recreation and park administrators become doubly competent in the day-by-day fiscal management of their departments, in the most imaginative and creative approaches to the use of available financial resources, and in the gathering of *new* forms of budgetary support.

This chapter seeks to provide basic information regarding the function and types of budgets, fiscal controls, and sources of recreation and park funding. It also presents guidelines for enhancing productivity and for developing new budgetary sources and concludes with a number of suggestions intended to strengthen the administrator's general capability in this field. Throughout, it is concerned not only with policies and procedures but with *strategies* for effective fiscal management.

THE BUDGET PROCESS

The major financial instrument used—or misused—by administrators is the budget. The term itself comes from the French word *bougette*, meaning bag or wallet. This would suggest that many persons think primarily of their budgets as bags full, or partly full, of money, to which they turn to purchase equipment, hire personnel, or pay administrative charges.

However, the word has a broader meaning. The budget should be thought of as a management plan through which a work program or project is outlined, including the financial details and schedules necessary to achieve certain predetermined goals. Butler has written:

> The term "budget" in governmental practice is used to denote a plan prepared by an executive or board for financing the work of a department or other public enterprise for a given period. Until it receives the approval of the appropriating body, usually the city council, the budget is merely a proposal. After approval it becomes a controlling financial plan for carrying out a program of operations and services and for raising the necessary resources for it.[1]

The well-conceived and effectively presented budget should accomplish the following:

1. Provide a general statement of the financial needs, resources, and plans of the department, including an outline of all program elements and their costs and allocations for facilities and personnel
2. Inform taxpayers and government officials of the amounts of money spent, the sources of revenue, and the costs of achieving departmental goals
3. Help in promoting standardized and simplified operational procedures by classifying all expenditures and requiring systematic procedures for approving them
4. Serve as a means of evaluating the success of the program and ensuring that its objectives are met

To illustrate, within the voluntary service field, the United Community Funds and Councils of America provides a sample budget form for all member agencies, which includes (1) a detailed set of questions regarding sources of all funds, such as fees and charges, grants, United Funds, program income, and investment income; (2) a section that analyzes expenditures in such categories as national dues or support, supporting services such as management or fund-raising, or direct program services; and (3) a program cost analysis section, which requires precise analysis of costs of various program elements, service volume, number of units of service, and direct cost per unit. This approach is linked to the program budgeting method (p. 204). Through it, one is able to gain an overall view of each member agency's operation.

Types of budgets

In the past, budgets tended to be identified according to the following major types: object classification, function classification, performance budget, or organizational unit classification.

Object classification. This type of budget classifies all proposed expenditures according to a systematic breakdown or classification by type. Typically, categories would include such elements as personal services, purchase of supplies and equipment, or contractual services. The major object groups in a widely used object classification system are as follows[2]:

1000 Services—personal: involves salaries and wages
2000 Services—contractual: involves work performed or services rendered, or materials supplied on a contractual basis
3000 Commodities: supplies and materials
4000 Current charges: includes rent, insurance, licenses, etc.
5000 Current obligations: fixed expenses such as interest, taxes, loans, etc.
6000 Properties: cost of equipment, buildings, or land
7000 Debt payment

A more detailed explanation of the terms used in this system would include the following:

Services—personal. Personal services involve salaries and wages paid to persons employed by the government body.

Services—contractual. Contractual services involve work performed for the government through agreement or contract by other than employees, as well as the provision of equipment and furnishing of commodities under agreement.

Communication and transportation. These expenses include the cost of telephone, postage, freight, express, and drayage, and the cost of traveling expenses for transporting persons.

Printing, binding, and advertising. These expenses include all charges for printing, including advertising and publication of notices, and expenditures for mimeographing, photography, blueprinting, and binding.

Supplies. A supply is a commodity that is consumed, impaired, or worn out in a reasonably short period of time. For example, stationery, food, fuel, ice, clothing, cleaning, and motor items are supplies.

Materials. Materials are items of a more permanent nature that may be combined or converted to other uses. Here would be included lumber, paints, iron, or other building materials, masonry and road materials, fiber products, leather, and repair parts.

An illustration of a line-item budget using the object classification system is found in Fig. 8-1, the Annual Budget of the City of Huntington Beach, California (including the current year's budget and the proposed budget). Here proposed expenditures are listed under three main categories: personal services, operating expenses, and capital outlays.

RECENT ANNUAL BUDGET
CITY OF HUNTINGTON BEACH

FUNCTION: Recreation/Parks

DEPARTMENT: Recreation/Parks Administration and Recreation Operation

FUND: Recreation & Parks Facilities

DEPARTMENT HEAD: Norman L. Worthy

Account No. 790

	Personal Services		Current year's budget	Proposed budget
110	Salaries, Permanent	$	149,289	$169,272
120	Salaries, Temporary		200,000	260,000
130	Salaries, Overtime		1,596	2,960
	Total Personal Services	$	350,885	$432,232

Operating Expenses

201	Utilities, Water	$	100	$ —0—
203	Utilities, Gas		—0—	300
204	Utilities, Electricity		5,000	6,000
210	Communications, Telephone		3,000	3,000
211	Communications, Postage		200	200
220	Supplies, Office		3,500	4,500
221	Supplies, Special Dept.		22,000	26,000
224	Supplies, Awards		4,300	4,300
225	Supplies, Reimbursable		13,000	13,000
247	Gasoline		—0—	1,000
380	Rentals, Land (Edison Co., U. S. Navy)		2,250	2,250
396	Contractual, Park Appraisals		1,000	1,000
400	Printing		—0—	300
431	Maintenance, Office Equipment		100	100
432	Maintenance, Vehicle		1,500	1,500
440	Maintenance, Building & Grounds		10,100	11,800
462	Conferences & Meetings—Dept. Head		300	150
463	Conferences & Meetings—Staff		500	150
464	Meetings—Commission		1,980	2,280
500	Memberships, Dues, Other		200	200
509	Memberships, Periodicals		275	150
540	Training & Schools		150	150
596	Property Taxes (H.B. Co. Lease)		700	700
	Total Operating Expenses	$	70,655	$ 78,730

Capital Outlay

611	Land Acquisition—Parks	$	974,372	$836,554
638	Improvements—Parks		188,164	79,770
640	Vehicles, Automobiles		2,000	—
641	Vehicles, Pick-ups		4,400	—
647	Vehicles, Jeep		4,760	—
650	Equipment, Office		2,790	—
659	Equipment, General		57,064	—
	Total Capital Expenditures		$1,233,550	$916,324

Fig. 8-1

Although object classification budgets offer a convenient means of looking at the major categories in which money is spent, they do not relate expenditures meaningfully enough to programs. Therefore, some departments use budget classification systems that attempt to relate expenditures to the actual function being carried out.

Classification by function. In one system, proposed expenditures are assigned to the specific departmental *function* they will serve, such as playground operations, indoor centers, or Senior Citizens' program. Although there is no single widely used classification system that illustrates this method, one common approach is to divide the budget into three major functional areas: administration, facilities, and special services.

Classification by organizational units. In another approach, expenditures are classified according to the *organizational unit* of the department that is responsible for them, such as Division of Recreation, Personnel Department, Maintenance Bureau, and so on. Thus the relative cost of each section of the department is illustrated, rather than the item being purchased.

Classification by fund. Some departments that draw their revenues from several different sources classify all expenditures against the different *funds* that support them. This approach is particularly useful when funds are restricted to special uses, but it does not otherwise give a useful picture of how monies are to be spent.

Performance budget. Performance budgeting is a combination of object and function classification. Expenditures are classified by listing the main expenditures by object or categories of object to be purchased (including services, materials, charges) in the left-hand vertical column and by listing the functions of the departmental operation horizontally across the top of the page. By examining such a budget, it is possible to tell more clearly just *how* money is to be spent. For example, the budget will show exactly what amounts are allocated for such items as staff salaries, rentals, supplies and equipment, and printing and postage, for a specific aspect of the program, such as Senior Citizens' centers.

Program budgeting. Each of the types of budgets just described is essentially a *line item* budget. This type of financial plan shows, line by line, specific amounts earmarked for specific items. The annual cost of each staff member, the amounts to be spent on charges for utilities, and so on are all clearly laid out. Such instruments are easy to prepare and appear to be businesslike, orderly, and logical. Their major shortcoming, however, is that they do not really explain the program they are intended to finance and do not carry a meaningful message for the reader.

For this reason, many business organizations and government departments have moved in the direction of program budgeting. In this approach, budgets are designed in such a way that large units of work, or special programs, are isolated, identified, and clearly presented.

For example, the boys' baseball program of a given community might be identified and described in terms of its past development, number of boys involved, nature of staffing, number of games played, community support, and recognition system. Costs of the program would be identified, usually under an object classification system, and totaled. The concluding statement would indicate the overall cost and relate it to a participation figure. If this section of the budget is placed completely on one page, it provides a graphic reference that assists the mayor, city councilman, or civic association president in determining exactly how the department is operating in each area of activity—and what the unit cost of each program is.

If the program budget demonstrates that the cost of serving a single individual in ceramics for the course of a season is $15, compared to the cost of serving an individual in modern dance at $30, it becomes possible to provide a basic financial measure by which the two programs may be compared.

Much more work and detailed preparation go into assembling a program budget than a conventional line item budget. For this reason, the majority still rely on line item budgets. However, the trend is toward program budgeting, and it may be expected that more and more municipalities will move toward a modified program budgeting technique. This trend is being facilitated by the rapid development of computer services, since program budgeting and unit cost analysis rely heavily on computer analysis.

In many business and governmental agencies, there is increased interest in benefit-cost evaluation as a valuable tool in decision making. To use it, it is necessary to gather detailed and precise information as to attendance and participation, length of participation, and both direct and indirect program costs. In addition, cost efficiency is not the *only* criterion through which program success or value should be measured. Meserow, Pompel, and Reich point out that a more costly program for disabled or culturally deprived individuals may be of far greater value to society than a less expensive community center program. Nevertheless, they conclude:

> . . . a cost-efficiency evaluation system is a tool which can be used in a variety of ways by park and recreation administrators. With benefit-cost analysis figures at their disposal to defend judicious and beneficial programs, administrators will have more freedom to innovate, to expand, and to attempt establishing new areas of service for their communities.[3]

Operating budget versus capital budget. A final distinction that should be made is between *operating* and *capital* budgets. The operating budget is the document that contains detailed statements of all administrative costs in the form of personnel salaries, office rentals, gasoline, typing paper, baseballs, or paint brushes required to *operate* the department for the course of 1 year. In many cities, the fiscal year is identified as July 1 to June 30, although it may be identical to the calendar year or any other legally authorized 1-year period. In a few cases, budgets may be set up for a 2-year period. Normally, a municipality assembles and reviews its entire budget, consisting of the separate budgets of each of its departments, such as police, fire, schools, and the like, at one time.

The capital budget is a separate document that includes plans and proposed

expenditures for carrying out major purchases and construction projects of a substantial and long-term nature. These would include the purchase of heavy snow
removal trucks whose cost might be over $20,000 each and that might be ex-
pected to serve for over 20 years, *or* the purchase of parkland, *or* the construction
of new golf courses, ice rinks, or recreation buildings. They might include major
renovation projects but would not include routine maintenance charges.

Capital budget costs are substantial and are normally paid for through the
sale of bonds. Often they require special approval by the citizens of a community for this reason.

Legal aspects of a budget

Unlike certain other elements of recreation and park administration, in which
there is no legal compulsion to operate in a certain way, fiscal management is
usually a carefully defined process. The principle has long been accepted that
the most appropriate method of financing recreation and park needs is through
tax funds. State enabling laws and city charters usually assign this power to
municipalities and specify regulations governing all public budget procedures.

Normally, these broad regulations are supplemented by local ordinances or
administrative procedures that require that an itemized budget of appropriations
be placed before the city council and that may also define the method of presentation, the calendar of presentation, required public hearings, the officials
who must be consulted, or similar details. The budget process varies considerably
among cities.

In the mayor-council form of municipal government, the mayor is usually
designated as responsible; in other structures, the city manager or a member of
a city commission may be assigned the budget-making responsibility. In larger
communities, special budget officers and staff are employed for this purpose.
Normally, they would work closely with the recreation and park administrator in
preparing his department's annual budget. In extremely large cities, special
financial analysts or budget experts would be assigned directly to the staff of the
recreation and park department and would serve as liaisons with the city comptroller or financial officer on budget matters.

Normally, the budget process is divided into three stages: preparation,
authorization or approval, and execution. This process is a continuous one and
usually is in motion, at one stage or another, throughout the year.

Budget preparation

The preparation of the budget is a job for the chief executive and his key
staff members, and it must involve much more than merely making routine adjustments in the previous year's budget. A long-term and carefully thought-out
program of budget development is essential unless the administrator enjoys
chaos, confusion, and fiscal defeat. This implies the need for careful advance
preparation of all program elements and costs and for a logical short-, medium-,
and long-term construction program, tied to an intelligent plan for financial
support.

The stages of budget development are usually fixed to a calendar that indicates when certain actions are necessary and which individual or office is responsible for providing information or proposed plans. For example, the budget timetable for an eastern city is outlined as follows:

Budget

> The Department of Recreation & Parks will submit its annual Budget request to the Commissioner of Finance not later than January 15th. Funds for the recreation program, administration and maintenance are appropriated annually by the Common Council. Fiscal period is July 1st to June 30th.

Budget Timetable

(a) Staff members will submit budget requests to Commissioner by December 15th.

(b) Commissioner will submit 10 copies of proposed budget to Commissioner of Finance by January 15th.

(c) Commissioner of Finance will meet with Commissioner of Recreation & Parks to review proposed budget by February 1st.

(d) Commissioner of Finance will submit proposed budget to Common Council by first Council meeting in March.

(e) Commissioner of Recreation & Parks will review proposed budget with Recreation Committee of Common Council at earliest convenience.

(f) Public Hearing is customarily held on total proposed budget at first April meeting of Common Council.

(g) Budget will be officially adopted on or before May 1st.

(h) Allotments—Immediately before the beginning of the budget year, Commissioner of Recreation & Parks will submit to Commissioner of Finance a work program for that year, to include all appropriations for program maintenance, and acquisition of property, and it shall show the requested allotments of said appropriations for the Recreation & Parks Department by quarters for the entire year.

Note—The Commissioner of Recreation & Parks may submit a revised allotment program to the Cimmissioner of Finance at the beginning of any quarter during the fiscal year, with a request for a revision of the allotments for the remaining quarters of the fiscal year not to exceed the unexpended appropriation balance.

In essence, the budget process may be divided into eight stages. These are:

1. Establish a time schedule that will deliver a final budget to the budget officer at an appointed time. Ideally this schedule should begin immediately after the previous year's budget has officially gone into effect.

2. Study the budget and departmental performance record of the past 5 years.

3. Interview all staff personnel within the department who play a significant role in program development and allocating and spending funds.

4. Arrange a series of community meetings with a wide range of residents and invite their proposals, suggestions, and criticisms for the coming year, in terms of program needs and budget priorities.

5. Assemble the varied suggestions and program changes into a proposal for the coming year; on the basis of this, prepare a rough budget draft.

6. Submit this draft to an informal budget committee of responsible personnel in the department for an objective review.

7. Submit this draft also to representatives of local organizations who have a

stake in recreation and park programs, pointing out the items that have been included, based on their requests, and those that it has not been possible to include. Ask them to submit fresh comments and suggestions.

8. Develop a final statement of the budget that reflects as fully as possible the overall development plan and goals of the department, expressed community needs, and the capability of the department.

This process does not assume that there is a ceiling figure imposed by the city-wide administration that sets limits for the budget of the recreation and park department. Nor are internal divisions of the department asked to frame their requests within specific budget limits. Such cautions or devices to prevent overspending prevent the development of an honest and meaningful budget. This does not imply that municipal funds are unlimited. However, it makes clear that a budget should reflect the legitimate needs of the constituency to be served and the justified program of the department, rather than merely a listing of items that can be afforded under an arbitrary budget ceiling.

On the other hand, it is a mistake to inflate a budget request deliberately, in the expectation that it will be cut down by a certain percentage, to come out with a reasonable budget total. During the course of review by the city's financial analysts, hearings, and other means of examining budgets, each item will be carefully scrutinized and *must* be strongly justified.

Items must not be included simply because they were in earlier budgets. Pet projects, holdovers, and similar program features must be examined ruthlessly and with total objectivity. Every item should be examined as though it were being considered for the first time. If it is weak, wishy-washy, without clear goals or a reasonable promise of being productive, it should be rooted out. The budget must be lean, rugged, and as tight as possible. Legislators, city councilmen, mayors, and budget officials develop an uncanny ability to perceive the bloated budget. Like one's reputation for honesty, budget credibility can never be recovered by the recreation and parks executive once he has been exposed as a budget fraud.

For this reason, budgets must be developed through a year-round process of analysis, planning, and discussion of all relevant parties. Regular staff meetings devoted to budget planning, meetings with the municipality's corporation counsel, city council, or recreation and park board should be carried on throughout the year.

The municipal council or other county or town legislative body will usually schedule a series of public hearings on all of its proposed budget sections, to provide the general public with an opportunity to voice pros and cons. Such hearings should be well announced and attended.

Public hearings. Public hearings represent a crucial stage if the budget that has taken so much effort in preparation is to be carefully considered and fairly evaluated. Public hearings, whether on a village, town, county, or large city level, can be tense and sometimes extremely difficult situations. The introduction of pressure groups and political lobbying, the presence of committee chairmen from the city's legislative body, the presence of reporters and sometimes television cameramen make it essential that the departmental administrator conduct himself with maximum coolness and efficiency. The following guidelines will help ensure success during this stage of budget considerations.

Careful preparation. The recreation and park executive must be thoroughly familiar with his proposed budget, including each item and the justification for it. It can be extremely embarrassing for him to fail to locate needed budget materials or the documentation for items under sharp questioning by an appropriations committee chairman. Statements like "I'm sorry, I can't seem to locate it" make him appear weak, confused, and ineffective.

Opening statement. The administrator should briefly make an opening statement that describes the prime thrust of the department, its goals, and a brief mention of some past successes. It should clarify the new directions and priorities found in the budget and should present a positive and optimistic picture of the work of the department. This statement should be delivered semi-extemporaneously, rather than ponderously read. Ideally, a relaxed conversational manner should be used.

Response to questions. Responses to questions raised at the hearing should be short and informative. Just as in a courtroom, it is a mistake to answer more than is asked and to wander off into dangerous territory that may open up discussion points not within the area under questioning. Responses should be precise and factual, not philosophical.

Demeanor of administrator. At all times, the administrator should strive to be affirmative and confident. He should not back-pedal or vacillate under fire. If he has done his homework well and prepared the budget to the best of his ability, it is a serious mistake to reply to challenges with such comments as, "Well, I didn't really expect you would pass that item" or "I don't feel I can fight for this program." Such expressions of weakness may imperil the entire budget presentation.

The administrator must also strive to remain controlled and confident at all times and not permit himself to be drawn into angry exchanges under sarcastic questioning or critical jibes frequently heard at public hearings. Instead, he must rely on facts and documentation to support his case. If questioning becomes illogical or wandering, it is best for him to remain silent; after a particularly unjustified tirade or attack, the executive may return with such a statement as: "Now, if we may return to the subject of the budget, sir, . . . "

After the series of budget hearings and behind-the-scenes meetings, it is likely that additional changes may be made in the budget. In some cases, these may be the inevitable result of overall financial problems or policies of the municipal government with respect to the coming year. However, assuming that the budget is a sound one, it should be substantially accepted and authorized for the coming year.

Budget execution

Once the budget has been finally modified and adopted, it is in effect for the following fiscal year. However, it is essential then that it be carefully followed as a fiscal plan and as a guide to attaining the goals and objectives of the department.

Budgetary controls have a reputation for being relatively loose in the field of recreation and park administration. It is essential, therefore, that the departmental executive take every possible step to ensure responsible practice beyond the routine requirements placed on him by his city government. This means careful advance planning and estimates of costs of new programs, search for the best buys in products and services, and training and supervision of departmental personnel who have financial responsibilities.

Perhaps the most flagrant and persistent violation in recreation circles is the emergency or last-minute purchase or other expenditure. The flexible nature of the work surely justifies some emergencies, but many recreation and park administrators are notorious for blaming all unplanned purchases, deficits, and unscheduled costs on these emergencies. The vast majority of these could be avoided by sound professional planning, by calculating all contingencies in advance, and by a systematized approach to year-round activity programming. In the absence of such planning, the recreation and parks operation may become viewed by budget officials as erratic and frivolous.

The successful administration and execution of recreation and park budgets involve establishing a system of effective budgetary controls, an adequate financial accounting system that provides regular reports on department expenditures, and a thorough and prompt audit of work programs or capital projects throughout the year.

Effective budgetary controls. An essential element in executing an annual budget is a work program, which outlines tasks to be performed, standards of service and efficiency, and methods to be used. Such a program defines each task, how often it is to be carried out, how long it should take, and what manpower it requires. It thus breaks all departmental functions down into measurable units. Since overall costs have already been calculated in the budget, it is possible to measure the cost of each unit of service or activity and thus to control the amount of expenditure within each area of maintenance or program leadership.

Using such a work program, an allotment system may be set up to schedule expenditures on a monthly or quarterly basis. This provides a means of control through which all funds are spaced out properly through the year and in which normally it should not be necessary for any expenses to go beyond the allotted amount. When it *is* necessary to transfer funds from one budget line to another, normally this may be done if the change is within a specific category, such as personnel services or supplies or equipment. If the change is between separate categories, then it is usually necessary to receive approval for the transfer from a municipal financial officer.

There are several procedures that ensure efficient and honest performance with respect to expenditure of funds. These include:

1. Procedures for *purchase* of supplies or equipment. Customarily, items that

cost less than a given amount such as $50 or $100 may be purchased directly, without special approval being sought. Items or materials costing more than this, but less than $1,000, for example, may be purchased from an approved supplier. Items costing over this amount may only be purchased from an approved supplier *after* the materials to be purchased are advertised and bids received from at least three suppliers. While procedures in this area vary from department to department, normally there are controls to ensure that materials are purchased at the lowest possible cost from responsible suppliers.

2. Procedures for *receipt of direct funds.* In many areas of program service, personnel collect registration fees, admission fees, charges for supplies, permit fees, and similar items. It is essential that rules regarding the collection of money and turning it over to a central departmental office are precisely defined and exactly followed.

3. Procedures for making *contractual agreements.* When individuals or outside firms are hired on a contractual basis to carry out specific responsibilities for the department, again there must be clearly outlined procedures for selecting them and precise contractual agreement to define their task, the basis for payment, and the like.

The most important aspect of maintaining financial controls, however, is that of keeping adequate financial records and preparing and submitting monthly reports relating expenditures to the appropriate categories in the annual budget. It is essential, therefore, that there be an efficient accounting system that monitors every aspect of financial management.

Financial accounting system. Hines defines accounting as follows:

> Accounting is concerned with recording information relative to the financial operation of the department of parks and recreation. Accounting is also involved with the collection of monies, interpretation of the source and use of monies, and finally attesting to the transactions that have happened.[4]

A related process is auditing, which describes those procedures concerned with verifying and confirming the validity of fiscal transactions. Both accounting and auditing are essential in the carrying out of recreation and park budgets, for the following reasons:

1. Records of financial transactions and expenditures are normally required by law.

2. It is essential to guarantee that public funds are being used as authorized.

3. The responsibility for expending funds must be assigned to authorized individuals or administrative units; the accounting process guarantees this.

4. They help to prevent carelessness, graft, or the misuse of funds and help to facilitate the overall efficiency of the budgetary process.

Accounting and auditing are important to maintaining internal control of funds within a department. Normally, countercheck procedures must be used, so that more than one employee must verify information, sign checks, approve expenditures, or do similar tasks to prevent dishonesty.

There are a number of special methods or procedures used to guarantee effective accounting systems. These include cost accounting, accrual accounting, the use of balance sheets, and concurrent auditing.

Cost accounting. This represents a form of recording financial expenditures so that they are keyed to work performed or services rendered. In essence, it is a way of following up on program budgets or performance budgets. It involves keeping separate accounts for each function within a department, such as administration, facilities, or special services. Hjelte and Shivers[4a] point out that cost accounting is useful in the following ways:

1. It facilitates and promotes evaluation of departmental efficiency.

2. It can be used to evaluate individual personnel performance.

3. It is valuable in determining the feasibility of constructing facilities with either the agency's own labor force or on a contractual basis, using outside firms.

4. It is helpful in determining the proper balance between different phases of departmental operation.

Accrual accounting. This is a widely used accounting system under which all encumbrances, or charges, against specified accounts are shown on reports of expenditures that are kept regularly up-to-date. In most large municipalities today, computerized systems are used that feed out monthly reports showing total amounts authorized in each section of a budget, the amounts spent to date, and the balance remaining. This system is essential to efficient fiscal administration, in that it gives an instant, up-to-date picture of all disbursements and obligations and the current status of each section of the budget.

Balance sheets. These represent a form of bookkeeping report showing the assets and liabilities in a given fund or budget. They illustrate the financial status of a department and its ability to finance future expenditures, particularly with respect to capital development or major rehabilitation or refurbishment projects. Balance sheets may be used to show the actual cost of programs by indicating the initial investment in a facility as well as the annual costs of operating the activities carried on in it. The information provided in the balance sheet is particularly useful in long-range planning of areas and facilities.

Concurrent auditing. Customarily audits show expenditures only after they have been authorized and carried out. However, the procedure of concurrent auditing or control auditing takes place either before or during the expenditure of public funds. It represents a preaudit of expected income or disbursements and assists in preventing improper or inappropriate expenditures.

Customarily, municipal departments must issue financial statements or reports at stated intervals during the year, as well as in year-end financial reports. Typically, such reports describe the overall operations and revenue of a department. They usually present both operational costs and revenues in columnar form. Items presented under *operations* include the appropriation for each object, expenditures to date, outstanding encumbrances, the unencumbered balance, and the percentage of appropriations not yet spent or committed.

The items usually found in a statement of revenues include the following:

1. A statement of estimated monthly and annual estimated revenues

2. Actual monthly revenues and monthly profit or loss (based on anticipated revenues)
3. Total estimated income to date, actual income to date, and profit or loss (based on anticipated revenues)
4. Balance required to meet annual estimate, based on above

Auditors usually provide such financial statements at the end of each month and at the end of the fiscal year. They are obviously helpful in allowing administrators to adjust the operation of the program to the level of expenditures and revenues at any given time or throughout a given period.

Audit of work programs. A final form of financial control is exerted through a formal check, or audit, of specific administration or program divisions of a department or of construction or maintenance projects. Here, instead of an overall balance sheet or accrual accounting system, the emphasis is on checking to ensure that the work plan is up-to-date, that items paid for (in the form of materials or services) have actually been delivered, and that all projects are being carried on as efficiently as possible.

SOURCES OF INCOME FOR RECREATION AND PARKS

The basic sources of funding to support both operating and capital budgets are taxes, bonds, fees and charges, income from concessions, government grants, and other gifts or bequests.

Taxes

It has been estimated that over 90% of the funding of municipal and county recreation and park departments is derived directly from local tax revenues. Although initially private organizations contributed heavily to the support of community recreation, since the beginning of the twentieth century, recreation and parks have been viewed as legitimate responsibilities of local government and thus as functions to be supported by taxes. Taxes used to support recreation and parks fall into four major categories: general, special, millage, and special assessment.

General taxes. These represent the most common form of tax revenues used to support recreation and parks. They consist of the local real estate or property taxes, which are the chief source of municipal funds or of local school district financing. These are derived by assessing industrial or residential property within the borders of the municipality at a given rate; usually this is expressed as a percentage ranging from 20% to 50% of market value. A tax rate is established by the municipality for a given fiscal year. When the assessed value of the property is multiplied by the tax rate, the resulting figure is the tax that must be paid by the property owner. The tax rate may be expressed in terms of mills (tenths of a cent) on the dollar, cents on the hundred dollar unit, or dollars on the thousand dollar unit of assessed value. Thus, if a property has been assessed at $20,000 and if the tax rate is $35 per $1,000, the annual real estate tax will be $700.

The general real estate tax normally provides support for such services as police, highways, health, sanitation, recreation and parks, and similar services. Not infrequently, in suburban areas individuals must pay separate taxes to the county, township, or village for different services provided by each of these units of government. Normally, however, real estate taxes are all paid into the general fund of a single municipality, and it is from this source that budget allocations are made to support municipal services.

In a growing number of cities, income taxes are being imposed on residents and nonresidents who work within municipal borders. However, this does not yet comprise a major form of revenue on the local level; it *does* represent a major source of income for the state and federal levels of government. The general real estate tax has been under considerable pressure in recent years because of rapidly growing costs of municipal government. Although the obvious solution to raising more general tax funds is to increase either the assessment rate or the tax rate, this approach reaches a point of diminishing returns when residents or industrial firms begin to leave a city because of oppressive taxes.

Special taxes. In some cities and, more commonly, in areas that are served by a special park or recreation and park district, special taxes may be used to support public recreation. Thus, taxes on liquor, amusement admissions, or items such as motorboat fuel may be assigned directly to the support of municipal recreation and park services.

Millage taxes. A millage tax represents a specific tax (usually low and therefore expressed in mills) leveled against the assessed value of residential or industrial property. Here, too, the amount derived is assigned directly to a recreation and park fund and used exclusively for that purpose. In some states, such as California, millage taxes are authorized in the state education code and assigned directly to the support of school recreation and other community-related programs. The advantage of special taxes of this type is that residents are taxed directly for the support of parks and recreation; if they value this service, they will normally support the tax, which is not lost within a total general fund appropriation.

Special assessment taxes. In some municipalities there is the custom of taxing only those residents who stand to benefit from a particular service for the support of that service. Special assessment taxes are frequently used to support highway and sewer construction programs; in some cases they are also used to support recreation and park developments for residents in separate districts of a community.

Bonds

Bonds represent a second major support of municipal recreation and park programs. Normally they are applied only to the financial support of major capital development programs. With respect to recreation and park departments, they are used chiefly for the acquisition of land and the development of such major facilities as large parks, swimming pools, stadiums, ice rinks, sportsmen's centers, or golf courses. In some cases, a municipality or large recreation and park district may float a substantial bond issue that includes a number of separate recreation and park development projects; in other cases, a bond issue may be intended to support the development of a single major project.

Bonds represent a form of deferred payment by which the cost of any government enterprise can be spread over a period of years rather than applied to a single year's budget. In addition to recreation and park facilities, they also are used to pay for the development of schools, highways, sewer systems, and similar projects. They are sold to both corporations and individuals and pay an interest rate over the life of the bond, which makes them more attractive than simply investing money in a bank would be. Bonds normally are to be repaid within a 10- to 30-year period and thus ensure that those who will be using facilities over this period will be paying for them at a reasonable rate during the period.

Types of bonds. There are several types of bonds, which vary according to their method of retirement: term bonds, callable bonds, and serial bonds.

Term bonds. In this type of bond, the government agency promises to pay off the entire principal at the end of a given period of time. Normally, it would use the *sinking fund* method, under which an annual sum is put aside each year, with the amount accumulating each year until the full principal has been set aside at the end of the term of the bond.

Callable bonds. This is a special type of bond in which the government has the option of calling in bond issues for payment at a specified time before the end of its term, or at any time it chooses. Since bond interest rates tend to fluctuate, it is thus possible for the issuer to call in a bond and reissue it at lower interest rates, depending on market conditions.

Serial bonds. Under this method of financing capital outlays, the government pays the bond purchaser a specified portion of the principal, plus interest, each year that the bond issue is in effect. Thus a percentage of the bond is reduced each year through payments of approximately equal sums. This is similar to the way in which homeowners normally pay off mortgage indebtedness over a period of years.

Other types of bonds. Bonds may also be classified according to their method of gathering funds for debt service. *General-obligation bonds* are those in which the payment on interest and principal is drawn from the general tax revenues of the municipality. *Assessment bonds* are those in which the money is derived from special assessments on residents benefiting from the improvement. *Revenue bonds* are issues in which the money used to pay off the bond is derived specifically from the facility that has been built, such as a golf course, marina, or cultural center.

Although it is not essential for recreation and park administrators to be highly sophisticated about the different types of bond issues, it is helpful for them to know the fundamental features of each type. If a recreation and park bond issue is to be presented to the public for approval, the recreation and park administrator must build a strong case and gather all the documentation possible to convince the public that this is a desirable project for the municipality to undertake.

The preparation of a major bond issue for a large land acquisition or facility construction project can be a most challenging and demanding exercise. Included are planning, engineering, architectural, financial, public relations, publicity, political, and merchandising responsibilities; the total effort can be one of the surest tests of the effective recreation and parks executive at work.

Selling the bond issue. Pezoldt[5] points out several different approaches that may be taken by recreation and park administrators in developing public understanding and support for a bond issue:

> *Maximum effort.* The administrator wants to reach all voters for a large referendum turnout; he pulls all stops and mounts a total barrage of public information using all media.
>
> *Minimum effort.* Little effort is made, either because the administrator is too lazy or does not have the needed know-how. This usually results in failure of the referendum.
>
> *Controlled-effort approach.* This is particularly useful in bad economic times with a difficult tax climate. The administrator concentrates efforts in precincts with a history of high voting turnouts and favorable votes on past recreation and park bond issues.
>
> *Tax-stretching approach.* The administrator emphasizes that passage of the referendum will make possible full use of the facility by all agencies (city, school, park district) resulting in tax saving for community.
>
> *Split-ballot approach.* Rather than have one huge, expensive bond proposal, split it into several separate items and sell each on its own merits.

Fees and charges

Fees and charges represent a new and increasingly important source of income for public recreation and park departments. For several decades there was a widespread acceptance of the view that public recreation and park services and facilities should be free or almost free to all potential users. However, as the facilities provided have grown more elaborate and expensive and as the types of programs offered have become more diversified, it is clear that some system of imposing charges to support programs is increasingly necessary.

Types of fees and charges. Hines has categorized the most common types of fees and charges as follows:

1. *Entrance fees.* Charges made to enter large parks, botanical gardens, zoos, or other developed recreational areas, such as fairgrounds, game preserves, or historical sites.

2. *Admission fees.* Charges for entering buildings offering exhibits or performances, such as grandstands or museums.

3. *Rental fees.* Charges for the exclusive use of property that is not consumed or destroyed and that is returned, such as boats, cabins, canoes, checking facilities, skis, archery equipment, or parking.

4. *User fees.* Charges made for the use of facilities or participation in activities usually carried on simultaneously with others, such as artificial ice rinks, ski lifts, driving ranges, swimming pools, or golf courses.

5. *License and permit fees.* Charges for the right to carry out certain activities, such as hunting, fishing, or camping; vending or exhibition permits.

6. *Special service fees.* Charges for special or unusual services, such as entry fees for team competition, instruction in organized classes, summer camp enrollment, and workshops or clinics.

Arguments for and against fees and charges. Serious arguments have been raised against the continued expansion of fees and charges as a means of supporting public recreation and park programs. The most common objections are the following: those who need municipal recreation service the most are generally those who are least able to pay fees and charges; recreation constitutes a basic human need and should be provided without extra charge, just as education, sanitation, or police services are; when fees and charges begin to provide a substantial part of the income of recreation and park departments, only those facilities and services that can generate income are promoted, and it becomes more difficult to obtain general tax support for recreation; special fees constitute a form of double taxation, under which residents are compelled to pay for developing and operating facilities *and* for using them; programs tend to be judged solely by their income-raising potential; and with increased fees and charges, municipal agencies tend to be viewed as proprietary institutions and to become more vulnerable to lawsuit.

On the other hand, those in favor of increased fees and charges argue the following: the public tends to appreciate more fully those facilities or programs for which they are required to pay; well-administered fees and charges make it easier to control recreation operations and to maintain discipline among participants; fees and charges represent a means of having people who *use* programs pay for them, rather than spread the cost equally among all residents; without additional funds from fees and charges, recreation and park programs will necessarily be extremely limited; the willingness of the public to pay for certain activities is a useful guide for the planning of resources and programs; and in a period of financial stringency and great demand for the tax dollar, the only way in which public recreation and park agencies can expand is through the use of fees and charges.

The latter argument is clearly the strongest one motivating most recreation and park administrators today. McCormack puts the economic case for fees and charges strongly:

> Meeting the demands of the public for parks and recreation has become so costly that existing tax moneys have become inadequate. The tax dollar has reached its stretching point. . . . There is a tremendous competition among . . . governmental functions. Parks and recreation often occupies the low position on the totem pole at appropriation time.
>
> The attitudes of the people today, the problems of balancing tax apportionments, and a severe shortage of money for parks and recreation are all factors trending toward the development of revenue-producing facilities and the charging of fees to fill the gap between supply and demand. Revenue facilities and fees and charges are the only remaining hope to many departments to enable them to provide quality programs and facilities.[6]

TYPE OF MEMBERSHIP	ANNUAL FEE
A. GOLF MEMBERSHIPS: 1. COMPREHENSIVE	$450.00
2. HUSBAND AND WIFE GOLF	400.00
3. INDIVIDUAL GOLF	310.00
4. INDIVIDUAL WEEK - DAY GOLF	200.00
5. INTERMEDIATE GOLF Birth Date / /	175.00
6. JUNIOR GOLF	115.00
B. POOL MEMBERSHIP 1. FAMILY POOL	165.00
2. HUSBAND AND WIFE PÓOL	150.00
3. INDIVIDUAL POOL	125.00
C. DAILY FEE MEMBERSHIP (Must be paid in full)	115.00
Club House Locker: Male ( ) Female (N/C)	20.00 each
Pool House Locker: Male ( ) Female ( )	10.00 each

Fig. 8-2. Charges for resident membership, Rye Golf Club, 1975. (Courtesy Rye, N.Y., Recreation Department.)

Hines agrees, pointing out that continued growth in recreation and park expenditures in years to come will have to be paid by property or other general taxes unless an increased effort is made to recover from the users of recreation services a portion of their costs. He concludes that we must

> ...take a realistic look at all operating programs to determine the extent to which the users of facilities and services are to pay for them and the extent to which the general public is to subsidize them.[7]

Income. It seems clear that in an increasingly credit-minded society, and with the kinds of financial pressures today operating on federal, state, and local government, the expanded use of fees and charges is inevitable. This is part of a long-term trend. In 1930, 11% of all operating costs of public recreation agencies came from fees and charges. In 1955, it was estimated at about 12.5%. A random examination of recent annual financial reports by major cities' recreation and park departments indicates that for many the figure is much higher.

For example, the income from fees and charges, concessions, and similar revenue sources for the city of Omaha, Nebraska, in 1968 was approximately 31% of the total departmental budget. For Spokane, Washington, in 1970, it was 26.5%. For Los Angeles, California, in 1971-1972, it was 24.7%. In many smaller cities or wealthy suburban areas, the percentage is even higher. As an example of the kinds of fees that may be charged for certain facilities, Fig. 8-2 shows the fees charged for different types of memberships in the Rye Golf Club, a publicly owned facility in the City of Rye, New York. These are charges for *residents;* business and nonresident charges run as high as $750 and $1,000 per year.

Considerations in establishing fees and charges. The trend is established, and fees and charges have not damaged the image of public recreation and park departments. However, this does not mean that revenue sources should be used indiscriminately. Rodney[5] suggests a series of useful guidelines:

1. All fees and charges for recreation services should be in conformity with the long-term program policy of the recreation system and should be consistent with the legal authorization governing such practices.

2. Fees and charges should be viewed as a supplemental sources of recreation and park funds and not as the primary source. Therefore the value of any proposed activity or facility should be judged with respect to its meeting public needs rather than its income-producing potential.

3. All services entailing fees or charges should be periodically reviewed by the department, and those facilities or programs meeting general and basic community recreation needs should not have fees imposed on them.

4. Sound business procedures and administrative controls should be used in the collection and disbursement of special revenues.

5. Policies regarding concession operations or the lease of departmental facilities should be determined as part of the general administrative responsibility with respect to fees and charges.

6. In general, recreation facilities, when not being used for departmental programs, should be made available free or at minimal cost to nonprofit and nonrestricted community organizations, particularly character-building organizations serving school-age children.

Rodney stresses also the circumstances under which imposing fees and charges may be seen as most justifiable. These include the following and tend to reflect practices in most communities around the country today: (1) programs making use of expendable materials, such as craft supplies; (2) programs using consumable materials, such as food or fuel; (3) programs requiring specialized instruction, such as golf or modern dance classes; (4) facilities requiring a high cost of construction or maintenance; (5) rental of special equipment, such as instruments, costumes, or game equipment; (6) protection of property, such as checking, parking, or police surveillance fees; (7) exclusive occupancy of a facility; (8) admissions to special departmental events; and (9) use of facilities, services, or programs by nonresidents.

The major problem connected with fees and charges is that they tend to exclude the poor, the handicapped, and other special groups. Even when charges are moderate, they tend to be too high for families on welfare, particularly when the cost of transportation is added to them.

What solutions are there for this problem? Provision must be made for serving the poor, the retired older persons on a pension, and other groups in special need. Facilities that normally have an admission charge may be opened for certain sessions during the week without charge. Facilities in poorer neighborhoods may operate without fees, while those in more affluent areas impose a charge. Sliding scales may be established or other special arrangements made to permit the disadvantaged to participate in classes or other activities requiring registration, without cost.

Fee-charging policies vary considerably, according to the type of community involved. In most affluent suburban areas or moderately well-to-do cities and towns, it is taken for granted that fees will be charged for all special-facility programs, adult classes, or youth programs in which registration is charged or instruction provided. By contrast, in larger cities with substantial numbers of low-income residents, fee-charging policies and programs themselves are often much more limited.

It seems probable that as the use of fees and charges grows more widespread, recreation and park administrators will grow more sophisticated in their application. For example, the determination of the appropriate range of admissions or other fees is far more complex than simply asking what the traffic will bear. In a discussion of fees and charges in public zoos, Gobar points out that as admissions charges are raised, per capita revenue is increased, but attendance may decrease. There is, therefore, a price that would maximize revenue, beyond which all higher prices would reduce attendance so much that total revenues would be less. Gobar concludes that to determine an optimum admissions charge policy for a particular market area (referring to density of population) that will result in the attainment of defined financial and attendance-level goals, it is necessary to

> . . . have a proper understanding of the relationship between zoo size, admissions policy, attendance, revenues and costs, to make the most efficient use of public resources to attain the objectives sought . . . whether financial . . . or public service . . . [9]

Such calculations can be extremely complex, making use of multiple regression analysis techniques. They should also take into account the effects of reduced attendance levels on other forms of income, such as concessions volume. The issue is not solely a financial or technical one. Greben writes:

> A potentially dangerous question with which administrators must deal is, "Can the desire to produce more revenue destroy, or perhaps inhibit, the quality of parks and recreation services?" This can become a real danger because administrators direct much of their thinking toward raising money and are prone to accepting "get rich quick" ideas and schemes which may actually be contrary to what they are trying to accomplish. That will not happen if administrators remember that there is a basic standard that must be met.[10]

Ticketron system. As fees and charges increase, many recreation and park departments are using individual or family identification cards, season passes or permits, and electronic Ticketron types of reservation systems to facilitate operations.

The Ticketron system is one under which such items as theater tickets, seats at sports events, and a variety of other scheduled activities are sold through a network of direct outlets located in banks, supermarkets, theaters, and restaurants, each manned by a single operator and a console hooked up to a central computer. It enables the leisure consumer to visit a location close to his home or business, discuss preferred dates and times, and purchase desired reservations immediately from the clerk, after it has been cleared through the master computer. The system is accurate, reliable, immensely convenient for the con-

ANNUAL INCOME FROM RECREATION AND PARK FEES AND CHARGES
CITY OF OMAHA, NEBRASKA

Source		Receipts
Boat Slips		$ 135
Boat Stalls		2,340
Concessions		1,700
Craft Materials		13,286
Day Camp Reservations		21,839
Golf Courses		262,459
Learn-To-Swim Program		7,340
Pavilion Permits		4,493
Rifle Range Permits		232
Swimming Pools		73,186
Tennis Permits		39,473
Miscellaneous Revenue		96
Total Park & Recreation Receipts		$426,579
Auditorium	$274,063	
Stadium	38,241	
Total Auditorium & Stadium		302,304
Grand total all receipts		$728,883

Fig. 8-3

sumer, and involves only a small extra charge. The State of California has instituted a Ticketron system for reserving public campsites; other states and municipalities have adapted it to reservations for golf, tennis, swimming, picnic sites, and similar facilities.

Example of revenue sources. As an example of income from fees and charges in a single city, in a recent year, the City of Omaha, Nebraska, obtained $728,883 from various departmental programs and facilities (Fig. 8-3). This sum was over 30% of the total recreation and park budget of $2,322,013.

Uses of income. Funds derived from fees and charges normally go into the general funds of a municipality, but in some exceptional cases may be put into revolving funds (funds that are continually being replenished and drawn from, maintaining a minimum balance) that are used to support recreation and park operations. In still other cases, they may be specifically assigned to recreation-related programs. For example, in the city of Los Angeles, under a special arrangement, 50 cents from every round of golf on a public course goes into a Golf Development Fund, amounting to a total annual rate of $325,000. Of all income from concessions in Los Angeles, 20% goes into a Concessions Development Fund, at an annual rate of $130,000, and *all* income from camp operations, $200,000 a year, goes into camp development. Other special funding sources have been developed in Los Angeles; through legal enactment, several million dollars a year from tidelands oil drilling fees goes into a major public beach development program.

Expansion of popular sports. Such sports as golf and tennis are being expanded in many municipal recreation and park programs, on a pay-as-you-go basis. According to the National Golf Foundation, there are about 12.5 million golf players in the United States, with the rate growing at almost 5% per year. Although constructing a golf course is a sizable expenditure, ranging roughly between $650,000 and $1.3 million, Fream points out that the profit potential for publicly owned courses is substantial and may be used to support other non–revenue-producing public recreation facilities.[11] In addition, the municipal golf course need not be a single-use facility. Instead, it may be the center of a recreation complex that includes swimming pools, tennis, team sports, boating, hiking, and skiing. A clubhouse may be constructed that serves a variety of community needs, rather than simply providing lockers and a pro shop. In addition to the main course, some golf courses have practice range facilities that can be used by high school or golf teams or for instructional purposes; others provide a nine-hole pitch-and-putt course as a learning ground for young golfers. With proper physical and financial planning, the municipal golf course represents an excellent example of fees and charges in action.

Similarly, with the tremendous growth of interest in tennis, many public recreation and park departments have developed tennis complexes on a self-supporting basis. One of the most successful of these is in Fort Lauderdale, Florida, where, under the direction of Jimmy Evert, an outstanding professional, the municipal tennis program now operates fifty courts within the city limits.[12] An active Fort Lauderdale Tennis Association promotes clinics and group instruction programs with many junior players, women, and seniors taking part. A major tennis complex, Holiday Park Tennis Center, was built with city funds in 1973. By 1975, 260 players per day were using the nineteen courts available for public play (one court is reserved for instruction). In a single year, the complex had over 75,000 patrons, with an income in excess of $60,000 in membership and daily play revenue. When such details as court schedule, fees, methods of reservations, balance between junior and senior players on weekends, and the role of the tennis manager or pro are properly worked out, tennis can provide an extremely popular, income-producing activity.

Concessions

Concessions represent an arrangement common in many public recreation and park departments under which public officials authorize private individuals or organizations to sell merchandise or services in parks, stadiums, or other recreation-owned properties. They are generally granted when the department is unable to provide a service efficiently or economically in comparison to the commercial organization. Some of the areas of service in which concessions are commonly granted are boat rentals, refreshment stands, equipment shops, and instructional services. For example, the city of Detroit, Michigan, has had agreements with concessionaires permitting them to operate saddle ponies, pony carts, and sleighs, to rent bicycles, and to operate a giant slide adjacent to the

Children's Zoo, a carousel, professional golf services and shops, and vending machines located in community centers, skating rinks, and other departmental locations.

The use of concessionaires permits a recreation and park department to provide services, equipment, or refreshments that it might otherwise not be able to offer because of limited manpower. Since concessionaires are private businessmen or companies, they are not restricted by civil service personnel requirements or other municipal bureaucratic regulations. They are therefore able to provide the service while charging a reasonable fee and, at the same time, make a profit on the operation. Customarily, concessionaires pay a percentage of their gross revenue to the department and might also pay an annual fee for the concession privilege.

In Canada, for example, with the exception of Vancouver and Montreal, all major cities have made leasing arrangements for food service facilities with private concessionaires. Leasing agreements are usually for 5 years and provide a percentage of gross income payment to the municipality, which ranges between 10% and 18%. Cities such as Toronto make careful checks on the quality of concessionaires' performance and derive substantial income from leasing arrangements. In Montreal, where the city parks department used self-operated vending machines as an alternative, it was found that there was heavy vandalism in unguarded refreshment facilities. Even Vancouver, which has derived income of as high as $1.5 million per year from food services, has begun to lease some facilities to concessionaires on a guaranteed-fee or percentage-of-gross basis.[13]

Gifts and bequests

Traditionally, many public recreation and park departments have benefited substantially from gifts and bequests from private sources, such as individual donors, foundations, or business contributors.

Typically, many large city parks have come from the personal gift of a public-spirited individual or family. Often larger estates as well as smaller properties have been bequeathed to municipalities, with the understanding that the land would be used solely for recreation and park purposes. Foundations have often contributed either to support a specific program element or project or, more commonly, to assist in developing a recreation facility to meet community needs. Just as wealthy philanthropists contribute money to private schools and colleges or to hospitals, so they may give funds to build a center, park, or other facility.

Finally, many cities are assisted by major industries or other business firms in sponsoring recreation events and programs. For example, in Washington, D.C., such companies as McDonald Hamburgers, Schaefer Beer, Coca Cola, and the Washington Gas and Light Company have contributed to the sponsorship of sports tournaments and cultural events. In Detroit, various sports tournaments and mobile recreation programs have been sponsored by television companies, newspapers, banks, and automobile dealers associations. In New York City, both popular and classical concerts in the city's major parks have been subsidized by companies, and many special summer programs for the disadvantaged have been funded by industry. One unique example was a recreation trip program in which thousands of inner-city children were given short sight-seeing flights by American Airlines.

In recent years, with sharp fiscal cutbacks in many communities, it has become necessary to vigorously seek out all such sources of special income and to pursue innovative fiscal policies to sustain healthy recreation and park programs.

Fiscal management in a period of austerity

Since the late 1960s, many state and municipal governments have undergone a period of severe financial stress. Because of increased costs of welfare, sharply escalated salary scales of civil service employees, and other effects of inflation, as well as problems related to crime and environmental protection, the costs of government have risen steadily. At the same time, the tax base in many cities has been undercut by the flight of middle-class residents and industry to surrounding suburban areas.

The U.S. Census Bureau reported in September, 1971, that city expenses were rising faster than municipal revenues throughout the United States. In 1970, municipalities spent $1.5 billion more than they took in; revenues were $32.7 billion, whereas outlays totaled $34.2 billion. As a result, many cities found it necessary to cut back budgets sharply and to put job freezes or even layoffs into effect. All departments, but particularly recreation and park departments, have suffered from such cutbacks, particularly in cities like Detroit, Cleveland, and New York, where problems of urban blight, crime, and welfare are most severe.

What are the positive and constructive ways in which recreation and park administrators can meet this pressing problem? It is necessary to (1) identify and seek assistance from all possible sources, such as federal and state government funding programs or foundations, (2) develop new forms of community support and cooperation, and (3) maximize productivity within the department and exercise all possible economies. The remaining section of this chapter will examine these approaches.

Federal and state support programs. During the past decade in the United States, a variety of federal agencies have provided special assistance to recreation and park agencies. Several examples of such programs follow.

Land and Water Conservation Fund. Administered by the Bureau of Outdoor Recreation, this fund assists states and municipalities in acquiring and developing open space and outdoor recreation projects. From 1965 to 1970, the Land and Water Conservation Fund provided a total of $243.3 million to the fifty states; a substantial portion of this money was used to assist local municipalities and county recreation and park departments in developing recreation facilities. Funds have customarily been provided on a matching basis. Artz and

Bermont offer the following guidelines for municipal departments seeking such grants:

1. High quality, well-documented projects are most likely to be funded quickly.
2. Basic, rather than elaborate projects or facilities, are most likely to receive support.
3. Those projects which serve the public's best interests most economically, and by providing the most extensive leisure opportunities, receive highest priority.
4. Assistance is given only after the funding agency is assured that all other types of possible financial aid have been sought.[14]

Housing and Urban Development grants. This federal program has provided grants to local public agencies or governmental units to help establish multipurpose neighborhood centers. Such centers had to be integral parts of community comprehensive planning efforts, designed to meet the varied social needs of primarily low- or moderate-income people. Similar federal grants have been made available for urban beautification and planning projects under the Model Cities Programs. The 1966 Demonstration Cities and Metropolitan Development Act has provided up to 80% of the cost of projects improving the physical environment of cities—preserving historical structures and acquiring and developing parks, playgrounds, community centers, and related facilities. In general, such grants did not provide funding for personnel or ongoing program expenses. On the other hand, a number of antipoverty programs did provide funding for such purposes.

Antipoverty programs. The Economic Opportunity Act of 1964 created the Office of Economic Opportunity to coordinate all antipoverty programs sponsored by the federal government. Among the major programs sponsored by OEO with relevance for recreation were the Job Corps, VISTA, the Neighborhood Youth Corps, and a variety of special projects known as Community Action Programs. Particularly in special summer youth programs designed to meet the needs of inner-city neighborhoods, thousands of special recreation, daycamping, and cultural projects have been funded in American cities.

A number of large city recreation and park departments have been successful in obtaining substantial grants from the Office of Economic Opportunity, the Department of Labor, Model Cities, the Department of Transportation, and the Department of Agriculture. However, antipoverty programs in general have been cut back in the United States, and few municipalities receive direct subsidies from them for recreation today. So-called categorical grants, in which departments or municipalities submitted applications for federal funding under specific pieces of legislation, have for the most part been phased out. Instead, the new federal approach in the United States has been to provide assistance through revenue sharing, in which the individual states or municipalities may share more fully in funding decisions. Revenue sharing is of two types—*general,* in which funds are automatically allotted to states based on a formula that includes population, income, and tax-effort figures, and *special,* in which specific areas of service, such as community development, education, manpower training, or law enforcement may be designated.[15]

Examples of present funding. One example of federal legislation with potential for recreation funding was the Juvenile Justice and Delinquency Prevention Act, which authorized a comprehensive program under the Law Enforcement Assistance Administration (LEAA) that would provide $350 million on a matching-grant basis to state and local governments to develop innovative projects to prevent and treat juvenile delinquency. Recreation has been identified as one of the appropriate techniques for such projects, and a number of community projects have received funding for antidelinquency projects under this act. Similarly, Title III of the Older Americans Act of 1965, as amended in 1973, supports a wide variety of services on the state and local level for senior citizens. Along with counseling, health-related and outreach services, referral, and legal and employment assistance, recreation has been designated an appropriate service for funding. Hundreds of municipalities have received federal funding through this program for services for aging persons. A final example of federal funding in the United States that has been made available to hundreds of recreation and park departments in the mid-1970s has been the Comprehensive Employment and Training Act (CETA), which has made possible the hiring of many thousands of workers in those cities which have been forced to freeze jobs or lay off workers because of fiscal cuts.

Since such funding programs change from year to year, it is essential that the alert recreation and park administrator keep his finger on the pulse of potential funding. This may be done by obtaining the *Catalogue of Federal Domestic Assistance*, published by the U.S. Government Printing Office annually, which contains descriptions of funding programs, deadlines, available literature, and lists of contacts. Other catalogues of federal funding programs are published either by individual government agencies or by commercial publishing houses.

State programs. Many communities receive funds from state governments with which to support recreation programs or to acquire open space and develop outdoor recreation facilities.

For example, state commissions on aging frequently provide local governments with grants-in-aid that assist them in providing senior center programs for aging persons. State youth commissions in many cases provide funding to local government, on a per capita basis, to assist them in developing youth services. Other states have provided subsidies to local government agencies that have established recreation programs for the physically or mentally handicapped. Often these grants represent funding programs that have come down from the federal government, in which the state has been assigned responsibility for carrying on statewide planning to assess needs and for making local grants.

Many states provide special funding to localities or separate park districts to acquire land or develop outdoor recreation resources. Frequently, money to support these grants is derived from outdoor recreation activities; several examples follow:

Arizona has a State Lake Improvement Fund derived from the registration and licensing of boats and a tax on motorboat fuel. Part of this fund is available to political subdivisions for the development of lakes or development and improvement of recreation boating facilities.

Maine has a boating facilities fund financed by a tax on gasoline for acquisition and development of public boat access facilities. There is no specific ratio of cost sharing, but usually advantage is taken of federal programs to arrive at a 25% local, 25% state, and 50% federal cost sharing.

New Jersey has a matching fund program to help municipalities protect their oceanfront beaches from erosion. A municipality can have this work done using 75% state funds and 25% local funds.

Delaware provides up to 75% matching grants to each county and to the City of Wilmington for the acquisition of open spaces. If federal funds are used, the local share cannot be less than 25%.[16]

As in the case of potential federal funding, local recreation and park administrators should be as knowledgeable as possible about current state funding programs and vigorous in pursuing those which have real potential for their departments.

Foundations. A number of municipal governments have obtained assistance for special projects through foundations, and clearly others should explore this avenue of auxiliary funding. Joyce defines the term *foundation* as:

> A nongovernmental, nonprofit organization having a principal fund of its own, managed by its own trustees or directors and established to maintain or aid social, educational, charitable, religious, or other activities serving the common welfare. It enjoys privileges with respect to taxation and continuity of existence not accorded to "noncharitable" trust funds.[17]

There are several different types of foundations: (1) *special-purpose foundations,* created by will or trust instrument to meet a special charitable purpose; (2) *company-sponsored foundations,* tax-exempt nonprofit bodies legally separate from the donor company but with trustee boards that facilitate corporation giving; (3) *community foundations,* composite foundations usually set up as trusts, functioning under some form of community control to serve a given community or area; and (4) *family foundations,* usually established by a living person or family, rather than by bequest, to serve as a continuing vehicle for gift-giving and as a means of reducing taxes. The Foundation Directory lists over 5,400 specific foundations, but there are an estimated 30,000 in the United States today. Most are small family foundations, but between 100 and 200 of the largest ones control the bulk of foundation assets and provide a major portion of the grants given annually.

During the early and mid-1970s, it became increasingly difficult to obtain foundation grants, compared to previous decades, when they were readily available. Therefore, the recreation and park department that seeks this type of special funding must approach the task in an intelligent and well-organized way. It is important to develop proposals that will clearly fit the general purpose of a foundation, that they will regard as significant and needed, that will be economical in terms of expected outcomes, and that do not represent already-available services. Joyce stresses two key factors in gaining foundation approval. The first is the preparation and presentation, through appropriate channels, of a grants appeal specifically designed to meet the interests of a foundation. The second is to make appropriate personal contacts with the key people in the foundation to ensure a careful and fair consideration of the proposal.

Grantsmanship approaches. The following strategies are suggested for recreation and park agencies that seek to develop grant proposals for foundations but may also readily be adapted to other types of fund-raising efforts. They involve several steps:

1. *Establish a foundations committee.* The department should develop an ongoing, capable group of staff members and interested outside citizens—including businessmen, professionals and other individuals—who are willing to assist in this task. The committee must have a competent chairman to lead its efforts.

2. *Prepare lists of foundations.* There are several excellent sources available in public libraries. These should be carefully analyzed to identify those foundations whose purposes and past pattern of giving seem appropriate to the needs of the recreation and park department.

3. *Develop proposal concept.* Foundations committee members consider possible approaches or concepts and select those with greatest potential value that might have specific appeal for appropriate foundations. At this point, there may be a preliminary sounding out of the foundation to determine its possible interest in the subject of the appeal, if personal contacts are feasible at this stage.

4. *Prepare formal grant proposal.* Develop, in written form, the grant proposal. It should be as brief and convincing as possible, stressing the significance of the project or study to be funded. Elements that make a proposal effective are: (a) demonstration of critical need; (b) innovative quality of the proposal; (c) availability of matching funds within department or from other sources; (d) social value to come from proposal, including possible generalizability (findings or outcomes can be used elsewhere); (e) a precise statement of the budget; (f) identification of the personnel to be involved; and (g) a time frame or proposed schedule for the project.

5. *Presentation of proposal.* The grant proposal should be neatly packaged and sent by mail with an accompanying letter or delivered personally if personal contact has been developed.

6. *Follow-through.* Shortly after the proposal has been sent—usually within 2 to 3 weeks— a meeting should be requested to discuss it. At this point, it is possible to present arguments supporting the proposal, to indicate a willingness to modify it or to accept other suggestions of the foundation, and, generally, to work together mutually to bring the proposal to the point of approval.

Developing acceptable proposals for foundations or government grants-in-aid programs is not a matter of impulsive, scatter-gun action. The process must be carefully thought out and systematically pursued. In general, recreation is not a high-priority concern in itself for most funding agencies. Therefore it is necessary to link it, logically and strongly, to other high-priority needs or programmatic goals. For example, many funding programs for aging persons or youth offer an opportunity to link recreation with social, medical, legal, housing, counseling, or other forms of personal assistance. A unique advantage enjoyed by recreation in such areas is that it often represents an ongoing agency with a facility, staff, and built-in appeal for participants. It is therefore able to mount new programs under special funding without having to develop a whole new structure and operation.

The value of personal contacts in developing and submitting grant proposals cannot be overestimated. As suggested earlier, it is a good idea to schedule preliminary meetings to determine a foundation's potential interest or to gain an interpretation of their procedures or guidelines. Similarly, personal contacts should be made with appropriate funding agencies in government to go over legislation and grant guidelines with them and to discuss possible research or demonstration project proposals *before* writing them. Effective proposal-writing requires special experience and know-how. Often, in large departments or agencies, or in city government generally, there are grants officers who can assist in preparing proposals who know individuals in funding organizations, and who are in a position to help guide a proposal along the track to serious consideration.

New forms of community support. In addition to seeking special grants, many municipal recreation and park departments have developed major programs of community support by mobilizing a wide range of private citizens, service organizations, business concerns, and other groups in a coordinated and continuing effort. San Francisco provides an interesting example. It became apparent in that city several years ago that the public's need for adequate recreation and park opportunities could *not* be met by taxes alone. It was necessary to develop a major support group that would bring together and channel a wide variety of agencies in the city to obtain financial assistance and other important forms of backing for recreation.

To accomplish this, a tax-exempt organization known as Friends of Recreation and Parks was incorporated in 1971 in San Francisco. By 1973, after intensive membership drives, over 350 individuals and companies had joined it, with annual dues ranging from $5.00 to over $1,000. Caverly writes:

> Every major city has its neighborhood associations, citizens' groups, conservation clubs, and a myriad of hobby, craft, and cultural organizations. Most communities are blessed, too, with public-spirited citizens whose generosity makes possible additional beautiful parks and serviceable playgrounds. San Francisco is not unique in this respect. . . . What *is* unique is the collective backing of these groups and the coordination of their efforts. An important objective of the Friends is to obtain financial assistance from the business community, citizens, and organizations for worthy programs (and) to contribute to the burgeoning cultural and recreation climate of the city by sponsoring events such as opera concerts and field days. . . .[18]

Since its formation, the Friends of Recreation and Parks have raised substantial sums to support special recreation projects, have developed an Adopt-a-Park program (based on the gift in 1970 of $30,000 to redesign and rehabilitate the Chinese Playground in San Francisco), and have aroused widespread civic interest and support for the city's recreation and park system.

Another example of the mobilization of citywide groups to meet fiscal problems vigorously was found in Boston, where a new program titled *Converge* was initiated to bring together all existing resources for leisure service in the city. It involved seeing the total recreation complex of the city as a joint effort; the public recreation and park department sought to bring together the Y.M.C.A. and Y.W.C.A., Boys' Clubs, Girls' Clubs, housing agencies, settlement houses, Boy and Girl Scouts, and a host of similar agencies to coordinate planning, share the use of facilities, personnel, and funding, and eliminate the overlap and duplication that exist in all large cities today.

A second phase of Converge involved bringing the problem of recreation and parks, as a total community concern, to civic leaders, business executives, religious authorities, college administrators, and other key individuals in the Boston metropolitan area.

This plan was buttressed by efforts to bring the public recreation and parks department greater visibility in the eyes of the public and to make it a high-priority concern for all citizens. Under an austerity plan that threatened to cut hundreds of municipal employees from the city's payroll, the Boston recreation and park department cut every nonessential activity and personnel item from an already slashed budget. To balance this loss, a variety of devices and techniques were used to ensure maximum involvement and participation by the public. The department, under a program entitled *Boston 1971*, developed the following emphases:

1. Programming around neighborhood resources, including neighborhood athletic clubs, men's groups, church clubs, veterans' halls, and similar facilities or organizations. Such resources were able to provide volunteers, costumes, musical instruments, meeting rooms, and other forms of assistance in joint efforts with the public department.

2. Liaison with commercial recreation, including both popular tourist attractions and commercial recreation facilities, such as bowling alleys and ice-skating rinks. Joint ventures were developed with such elements at little or no cost to the department.

3. Reallocation of funds, personnel, equipment, and vehicles. Financial stringency made it necessary to eliminate functions and responsibilities that were peripheral to the department's major goals and to make the most strategic use possible of existing resources. The relatively small force of skilled regular workers were to be used as pivots or catalysts around which volunteer or part-time personnel could be assembled.

4. Team efforts with local colleges and universities became a new priority. The use of public recreation and park facilities by these institutions was expanded, and the availability of college-owned track and field facilities, swimming pools, fieldhouses, and other recreation resources was explored. The use of faculty and students alike as volunteers and the development of joint projects involving personnel from various disciplines within the universities were key elements of this new thrust.

5. In keeping with the expanded public concern about the environment, thirty-five major clean-up projects of park and other outdoor recreation resources were undertaken—using an estimated 25,000 volunteers from every segment of the community.

Other elements in Boston's austerity program included developing closer liaison with other city departments, such as Public Works, Police, Public Facilities, and Traffic and Parking. Through the exchange of personnel and equipment, their aid in helping to run winter sports events, summer carnivals, bicycle programs, parades, and similar special projects was sought. Industrial groups and commercial organizations were involved in the sponsorship of such programs as marathon races, camping clinics, kite festivals, fishing rodeos, and other mass-participation events. New liaison arrangements were made with Boston's museums and quasi-public cultural institutions to promote participation by youth and adults in new forms of leisure involvement—such as marine biology, natural history, astronomy, and similar activities. Varied military and naval facilities in the city, such as National Guard, Navy Yard, and Coast Guard installations, were explored as possible sites for public recreation programs. Closer ties were developed with temples, Protestant churches, Catholic parishes, and youth organizations to meet public recreation needs.

Productivity and cost-cutting as a top priority. In addition to such efforts, it is necessary to give highest priority to improving a department's productivity and cutting costs wherever possible. To some employees, productivity is a suspect word, implying pressure tactics by supervisors, shortened lunch periods and elimination of relief or refreshment breaks, rigid conformity to time schedules, suspension of safety procedures, reduced overtime and, generally, more work for less pay.

Viewed more positively—as it must be—increased productivity means better work attitudes, more careful handling of materials and equipment, punctual arrival and departure of personnel, and a fuller effort to provide stronger levels of attendance and participation in all program events than in the past. Increased productivity is an essential if recreation administrators are to meet the alarming rise in inflation compounded by frozen budgets and yet continue to provide high-level leisure facilities and services. The key to productivity lies in personnel attitudes and behavior. A number of suggestions for strengthening these include the following:

1. Include budget and cost discussions at regular staff meetings. Point out specific examples of how leadership and maintenance supervisory personnel can effect small but significant regular savings.

2. Establish a budget committee made up of several top management personnel in the department. Plan all budget planning through this committee to develop greater awareness of the problem and commitment to economy.

3. Train all key personnel to do program planning on a unit-cost basis, with emphasis on making program choices on the basis of objective measures of attendance and desirable outcomes, rather than subjective judgments.

4. Recognize outstanding examples of time and money-saving techniques by department personnel.

5. Request periodic reviews of department productivity by outside firms, agencies, or individuals to ensure that the public is getting maximum value for every dollar spent.

6. On a cyclical basis, evaluate each bureau, division, or section of the department at least once a year, by closely studying its operations for waste, time loss, public relations, and efficient storage, maintenance, transportation, etc.

It is crucial that cost-cutting, like budget planning, be a year-round concern. There is nothing harsh, unethical, or antisocial about reducing costs and raising productivity in recreation administration. Some specific examples of cost-cutting practices that have been instituted by municipal departments follow:

> In Chicago, a small indoor swimming pool required the regular services of a lifeguard and a locker room attendant to assure security in the lockers. By removing and glassing a panel of the locker room wall, the lifeguard was able to view the locker room from his station, and the attendant position was eliminated.
>
> Installation of inexpensive beepers in park vehicles and limited use of the police department radio system enabled one city in Indiana to develop a more efficient and less costly truck dispatch system. Radio messages simply directed drivers to call their office for instructions.
>
> Despite the high cost of sign-painting, many departments still have hundreds of signs painted each year by hand-lettered methods. A number of excellent sign-making machines are on the market that can reduce the per-unit cost of signs by as much as 50%.

Zero-budgeting. A phrase that has become increasingly popular in many municipal and county governmental operations is *zero-budgeting.* It is a euphemism for "You're not getting a cent more in your budget than last year." In a period of severe inflation, it actually means zero-minus budgeting. Under this system, every item of expenditure must be carefully scrutinized and convincingly supported. No program element is automatically approved because it was part of previous years' budgets. Instead, it must be thoroughly justified in terms of current needs. Some administrators view the imposition of zero-budgeting as an excuse to freeze their programs, repeating the previous year's format without change. This approach can be deadly in an area of service that needs to be dynamic, people-oriented, and responsive to community needs.

An alternative approach is W.A.R. (Withdraw-Appraise-Reallocate). Under this system, recreation executives must take a hard and objective look at their programs, spotting those events or services which are out-of-date, lacking in appeal, low in attendance, or inordinately high in cost. They must feel free to withdraw such programs and substitute new, innovative elements.

Administrative know-how. Particularly in a period of fiscal austerity, it is essential that recreation and park administrators become as knowledgeable and competent as possible in the area of budget management. In general, this implies making a deliberate effort to become familiar with financial practices and business trends. Some specific methods are: (1) developing the ability to make quick rule-of-thumb estimates of construction, installation, shipping, maintenance, and similar costs to use in appropriate circumstances; (2) taking full advantage of newsletters, conferences, institutes, and other learning opportunities provided by professional organizations; (3) developing cooperative relationships with bankers and other financial experts in the community by assisting them with recreation programs for their personnel and using them as informal fiscal consultants; and (4) reading appropriate financial journals and taking part-time courses in schools of business and finance. Over a period of time, the highly motivated administrator will gain a surprising degree of financial know-how through such efforts.

Suggested assignments for student reports or projects

1. Based on interviews with recreation and park administrators, develop a set of guidelines for the effective development and presentation of an annual department budget *or* a bond issue for land acquisition or facilities development.

2. Do a comparative study of at least three recreation and park departments with respect to fees and charges. Compare their overall policies in this area, including specific charges for various types of services or admissions, waivers made for special groups, money-handling procedures, and effects of fees and charges.

3. Develop a manual or set of guidelines dealing with various forms of supplementary funding to be used in communities undergoing a period of financial austerity in governmental expenditure.

REFERENCES

1. Butler, George: *Introduction to Community Recreation*, New York, 1976, McGraw-Hill Book Co., p. 475.
2. Original classification developed by A. E. Buck; see Rodney, Lynn S.: *Administration of Public Recreation*, New York, 1964, The Ronald Press Co., pp. 256-258.
3. Meserow, L. Hale, Pompel, David T., and Reich, Charles M.: "Benefit-Cost Evaluation," *Parks and Recreation*, February, 1975, p. 29.
4. Hines, Thomas I.: *Budgeting for Public Parks and Recreation*, Washington, D.C., 1968, National Recreation and Park Association Management Aids Bulletin No. 46, p. 23.
4a. Hjelte, George, and Shivers, Jay S.: *Public Administration of Recreational Services*, Philadelphia, 1972, Lea & Febiger, p. 331.
5. Pezoldt, Charles W.: "Getting the Yes Vote on Bond Referenda," *Parks and Recreation*, February, 1975, p. 23.
6. McCormack, John R.: "History, Principles and Objectives of Fees and Charges," Report given at Revenue Sources Management Institute, 1967 Congress for Parks and Recreation, p. 4.
7. Hines, Thomas I.: *Fees and Charges*, Arlington, Virginia, 1974, National Recreation and Park Association Management Aids Bulletin, No. 59.
8. Rodney, *op. cit.:* pp. 281-282.
9. Gobar, Alfred J.: "Understanding the Zoo," *Parks and Recreation*, October, 1973, p. 32.
10. Greben, Seymour, in Harris, Richard W.: "Keys to Successful Revenue Management," *Parks and Recreation*, November, 1973, p. 15.
11. Fream, Ronald: "Tee Off With Creative Planning," *Parks and Recreation*, August, 1975, p. 20.
12. Jarrell, Temple R.: "Jimmy Evert: A Pro Off the Court and On," *Parks and Recreation*, May, 1975, p. 19.
13. Drysdale, Art C.: "Food Service—The Trend is to Leasing," *Recreation Canada*, April, 1973, p. 18.
14. Artz, Robert M., and Bermont, Hubert: *Guides to New Approaches to Financing Parks and Recreation*, Washington, D.C., 1970, National Recreation and Park Association.
15. See Dunn, Diana R., and Lee, Linda K.: "Urban Parks and Recreation Under the New Federalism," *Parks and Recreation*, May, 1973, p. 23.
16. Hoffman, Joseph E.: "Where the Money Is," *Parks and Recreation*, November, 1972, p. 24.
17. Joyce, Donald V.: "Foundation Funding . . . Where to Look," *Parks and Recreation*, February, 1974, p. 24.
18. Caverly, Joseph, "Friends of Recreation and Parks," *Parks and Recreation*, January, 1973, p. 77.

CHAPTER 9

PUBLIC AND COMMUNITY RELATIONS

Public relations represents one of the most important areas of concern for today's recreation and park administrator. No matter how attractive a program he offers, unless he can get his message across to the public at large, his efforts will be wasted. It is not just a matter of selling a program or of planting publicity in a traditional press-agentry sense. The task of public relations today is more broadly concerned with achieving public understanding and confidence.

One authority has identified three major purposes of public relations: (1) to disseminate information to the public; (2) to alter the public's belief and actions through persuasion; and (3) to attempt to coordinate the actions and attitudes of the public and the organization that is serving the public.

Why is there a need for public relations in recreation and parks? Certain prevalent attitudes enforce this need.

First, many individuals feel that public recreation is not really a necessity—that the public is able to meet its leisure needs independently. Attached to this is the view that public funds should not be spent on an amenity such as recreation.

Second, many persons have limited knowledge of the department's work and do not know of the wide range of services and programs it offers.

Third, by the very nature of recreation and park operations, there are frequent occasions on which individual citizens tend to be irritated, frustrated, or disappointed—sometimes to the point of generating an army of critics who speak out against recreational goals and programs. The father of the unsuccessful Little Leaguer, the mother of the youthful ice skater not included in the recreation department ice show, the resident whose house is damaged by a branch from a city-owned tree, or the patron who finds the door of a park toilet locked—all are potentially vociferous critics of the local recreation and parks operation.

Therefore it is essential that administrators seek to reach the public at large with a continuing and comprehensive program of public information that will bring about public understanding and good will and ensure support in terms of votes, legislative action, contributions, support on annual budgets, participation in activities, and volunteer service. The specific goals of such a public relations program may be listed as follows:

1. To provide accurate information regarding the overall program and offering of the department to the general public to overcome misunderstandings, false impressions, or lack of information about organized recreation

2. To inform the general public specifically about the services, facilities, and programs offered by the department and to encourage their attendance and involvement

3. To specifically impress the public with the values and benefits achieved by the department and to bring about a sense of satisfaction that the tax dollar is being well spent in this area

4. To keep the public fully informed of all major plans or policies of the department (this may refer to special new programs, the acquisition or development of facilities, the imposition of fees, or the scheduling of seasonal programs)

5. To bring public attention to a specific project or program at a key time (this may involve a crash effort to publicize a new program or mass event and encourage large-scale participation, or it may consist of a press campaign to give out facts regarding a proposed bond issue for land acquisition)

6. To encourage public involvement in the program in the form of volunteer leadership, serving on councils or advisory groups, or making other contributions

7. To develop a fuller public understanding of the role of recreation and leisure in the lives of individuals and in terms of community well-being: inevitably, the department is the major spokesman for this area of service and social concern

8. To help promote other forms of community involvement in recreation by encouraging the development of hobbies or the formation of new neighborhood clubs or interest groups

9. To develop channels for two-way communication with the public at large in terms of meaningful dialogues on community leisure interests and needs, problems and complaints, new proposals, and new forms of cooperative action between the department and community residents[1]

A final purpose is to demonstrate to the public that its recreation and park department is dynamic and future-oriented and that its methods include a constant search for new programs, techniques, vehicles, and concepts of recreation and leisure that will enrich community life.

To achieve these goals, it is necessary for the recreation and park administrator to determine exactly which audiences he is trying to reach or involve in his public relations program. Generally, public relations may involve either a shotgun or a rifle approach. The shotgun sprays its message over a wide range, without trying to identify any single group or tailor a specialized message. The rifle, by contrast, is aimed at a specific audience with a message that is uniquely designed for it.

There may be several audiences or publics for the recreation and park department's public relations efforts. These include the public at large; specific segments of the public by age category, such as children, youth, or the aging; groups with special characteristics, such as the handicapped; civic, religious, political, industrial, labor, fraternal, and similar organizations in the community; and the mayor, municipal council, and other agencies in municipal government.

CHANNELS FOR PUBLIC RELATIONS

The specific means of reaching these various publics include the following:

1. *Informational media* include such direct media for publicity as newspapers, magazines, newsletters and brochures, television and radio, annual reports, exhibits and displays, motion pictures, slide talks, and open houses and tours.

2. *Advisory groups* include committees or councils that provide useful links with the community at large or particular neighborhoods or populations, such as community recreation and park councils, committees and task forces, or councils of social agencies.

In planning the use of informational media, certain factors need to be taken into consideration. The type and length of the message to be delivered, the purpose of the message, the specific audience to be reached, the time available to prepare and disseminate the message, and the funds available are all important elements. It is advisable to have both regularly scheduled outlets for public information and special types of releases or media to publicize events or programs that require separate, intensive coverage.

Use of printed media. Despite the popularity of television and radio, the simplest and most effective means of reaching large numbers of people is through printed media, such as newspapers, brochures, and reports. Newspapers in particular are an inexpensive outlet for public relations, can provide sustained coverage of a program or activity, and can provide immediate and timely means of transmitting information from day to day. In addition, newspaper editors are usually receptive to printing news of popular interest, particularly when it contains elements of human interest.

The process of press relations is a key aspect of effective public relations, since public attitudes regarding any department or program are formed, for most people, by reading newspapers, watching television, or listening to radio news. Scherer writes:

> Public relations has sometimes been called "press agentry" with a conscience. For example, publicity that makes false or misleading claims obviously does an organization more harm than good. Conscientious public relations, on the other hand, is introspective before it rushes into print. It has been proven many times that some of the most beneficial press releases are those that are never issued—because someone thought a second time. Conversely, a dramatic, thoughtfully-planned, well-timed, accurate and targeted press release can clarify the position, plans or programs of an organization and win it friends. By running it, a newspaper editor has given his tacit stamp of approval and its believability is heightened in the minds of readers.[2]

When an administrator has news of interest to the local newspaper, he should inform the editor, using one of these basic approaches:

1. Prepare a news release and mail or deliver it to the editor. If possible, address the release to him by name.

2. Call the newspaper and talk to the appropriate editor. Give him the information briefly. He will indicate whether he wishes to have a release prepared

or whether he will take the details and have the story written himself. He may decide to send a reporter out to conduct an interview.

3. Arrange a news conference and invite interested reporters and editors. This device should be used sparingly; it is best to save it for really important stories that justify calling such a meeting at a time and place of your own choosing.

Guidelines for preparing newspaper releases. There are several sections of most newspapers that can be used for printing recreation and park releases. These might include general news sections, editorial pages, letters to the editor sections, columns, calendars of public events, or special departments such as sports or women's activities.

Newspaper stories should be prepared with the following guidelines in mind:

1. Newspaper copy should be kept simple, factual, and straightforward in style and should avoid editorializing. It should consist of short, easy-to-read paragraphs, with the first paragraph (the lead) including all relevant information, such as who, what, when, where, and how.

2. Whenever possible, the release should be limited to one page, with the most important information covered in the early sections and the least important in the later copy, since it is usual editing practice to cut copy, or type, at the end of a story.

3. In preparing stories, an attempt should be made to feature a prominent or interesting individual or group of people, since readers are generally interested in reading names with whom they may identify or who lend importance to an article. However, news releases should not be used simply as vehicles for political flattery or publicity.

4. Material should be neatly typed, with adequate margins, headings, and sources given, where necessary. The name of the department and the name, address, and telephone number of the person responsible for issuing the release should be printed at the top of the sheet.

5. Copy should be submitted with plenty of lead time, to be easily edited and prepared for the printer. It is important to know the deadline of the newspaper you are submitting copy for and to meet it with a comfortable margin.

In general, the key factor in obtaining newspaper coverage of departmental events or news is maintaining a positive and cooperative relationship with the newspaper editor and staff. This means that whenever news breaks occur or interviews are held, information should be given fully and honestly, and newspapermen should be treated with respect and consideration. Information should never be distorted or exaggerated. When newspapermen cover stories or events, they should be assisted with transportation, special briefings, or facilities to make their job easier. Photographers in particular should be assisted in posing subjects or groups.

It is helpful to have contacts and to cultivate useful outlets for news publicity, but it is also essential to be able to produce newsworthy copy. This means that, whenever possible, events should be produced or scheduled that *are* interesting, colorful, of human interest, and worthy of newspaper space.

Magazines. Many of the same guidelines apply to the preparation and placing of articles in magazines. Although it is not usually possible to place articles or releases in national publications unless the story is a particularly exciting or unusual one, it *is* often possible to have material accepted by local, regional, or state publications.

There are special publications that reach municipal officials, recreation and park professionals, planners, or personnel specialists. Other publications are geared to reach those concerned with rehabilitation, aging, or different population groups. Some magazines are geared to promoting tourism and accept articles on interesting events or facilities. Others may be concerned with specific interests, such as sports, hobbies, cultural activities, or travel. Generally, magazine articles must be longer and written with greater style or flair than newspaper stories. Not infrequently, a department may team up with a popular freelance writer, who undertakes to write articles on interesting subjects assigned to him on an exclusive basis. He then may undertake to place the article himself.

Picture stories tend to find a market more easily than written articles without illustrations. It is often helpful to query the editor of a magazine first about his interest in a particular story before writing and sending it to him.

This valuable medium is seriously underused because administrators expect good magazine articles to just happen. Experience indicates that the vast majority of talented recreation and park staff personnel have little awareness of, or inclination toward, the specialized field of magazine writing. One or more individuals should be designated as article writers and given full support and encouragement if articles are to be produced and marketed. A good article appearing in *American City, Nation's Cities, Parks and Recreation,* or the *Journal of Physical Education and Recreation* may represent 3 to 6 months of research, planning, writing, and marketing, but the resultant publicity is well worth the effort.

Newsletters and brochures. These are prepared by most departments on an annual or seasonal basis to present attactive description of their programs. They may range from simple mimeographed or photo-offset handouts of a page or two to elaborate four-color brochures. Generally, such brochures include a description of all major locations where programs will be held and a listing of program activities to be offered during a given season.

Usually they should include the following:

1. The name of the sponsoring department and its administrator or key staff, the names of board members, and the names of key municipal officials
2. The major city-wide office and telephone numbers and other district or area offices where information may be gotten or permits obtained
3. A listing and brief description, with map, of all major park centers, pools, and similar facilities; in a large community with many facilities, this may appear in a separate directory or guide map
4. A listing of major activities offered on a city-wide basis; this might include separate groups for each age level, special events, leagues and tournaments, courses, or other services

5. A listing of fees or charges attached to each activity, where these apply

6. A brief statement of the philosophy or purpose of the department

Such brochures may be distributed in mailings to organizations, officials, members of committees, or citizens; by house-to-house delivery; by having them available at all offices and centers; by distribution through Parent-Teacher Associations, churches, civic clubs, or similar groups; and by mailings to a special list of those who have indicated interest or been involved in previous programs.

Since such newsletters or brochures represent a major way in which most individuals come in contact with the department and gain an impression of it, they should be colorful, crisp, and attractive. At the same time, having them too thick and elaborate may give the impression of being overly lavish and cause taxpayer criticism.

Television and radio. These popular media provide an important means of reaching the public directly with spur-of-the-moment news and with direct coverage of actual recreation events. They are useful in reaching all age groups and making a strong public relations impact. Television time, in particular, is often difficult to obtain. Therefore it is necessary to identify the types of programs that may be likely to use recreation announcements or do coverage of important or interesting citywide events. These include:

1. News programs. These may provide direct coverage of events, interviews with personalities, or similar features.

2. Commentator programs. These may occasionally deal with recreation topics as entertaining human-interest features.

3. Spot announcements, to be used during programs that list community events. All stations and channels are required to carry a specified amount of public-service programming, and this may be used for recreation announcements.

4. Interviews and talks by members of the department or participants or interesting leaders.

5. Regular departmental programs. In some cities, special time is set aside one or more times a week for news of the department to be given. Just as there is a sports broadcast or a weather forecast, so there may be a recreation broadcast.

6. Panel discussions. These may be scheduled on topics of general concern, such as new and interesting kinds of programs, the leisure needs of different groups in the community, or environmental problems relating to recreation and parks.

The key factor in getting effective television and radio coverage is the ability to provide timely, interesting, and professionally prepared program materials. If the department prepares its own scripts, they must be done expertly and up to the standard of the network or station. In general, radio time is more available than television time. In attempting to get coverage on the picture medium, it is important to ask such questions as:

Is television the *right medium* for your message?

Do you have something to *show* as well as *hear?*

Can you reach the right *audience* at the right *time?*

Can you properly use *expensive* television time?

Can you *entertain* as you *inform?*

Do you have *time* to spend on a *good* production?

Usually it is not too difficult to get spot announcements used on television and radio. However, more extended coverage will require developing a contact with the local station director. Artz[1] suggests the following steps:

1. Find out local station policies on free time.
2. Determine the type of program needed.
3. Contact the program director at the station.
4. Have some definite ideas on paper.
5. Gear your program message to the audience who will be watching or listening at the time of your presentation.
6. Plan your programs with the producer.

Motion pictures. Many municipal and county recreation departments have prepared their own audiovisual materials as means of reaching community groups, professional associations, or other special audiences with information about their department. Generally, a motion picture may simply be sent to a requesting group for a specified showing date and thus may reach many civic groups, service clubs, schools, or other organizations during the course of a year. A slide talk must normally be accompanied by a speaker, who gives a prepared talk as slides are shown.

Usually a motion picture is fairly expensive to make; a professionally filmed and edited color 16-millimeter film is likely to cost several thousand dollars or more. Therefore it is important to get volunteer assistance or the help of community groups, wherever possible, in making a motion picture about the recreation and park department. Frequently, a professional cameraman or editor will be willing to lend his services as a contribution to the community.

Before investing a considerable amount of time and effort in the creation of a short motion picture, a careful study of its potential use should be made. A skillfully prepared film can have high impact but is limited by the following:

1. From the moment of decision, 3 to 6 months may elapse before the film is ready for public showing.
2. If subject matter is too specialized in interest, its audience may be too limited to justify making it.
3. If the film is highly stylized in technique, treatment, or subject matter, it may be outdated within 2 or 3 years; films are difficult to edit or change.
4. If it is too sophisticated or slick, it may be seen as overcommercial or highbrow in approach; if it is too simple or crude, audiences may be repelled or bored by it.

For these reasons, use of the movie medium demands careful planning and a high level of skill in execution.

Local colleges often have courses in filmmaking and will assist in actual coverage, editing, and providing the use of equipment, which would be extremely expensive if rented. It is important to map out the script carefully in advance and to have a thorough review of all plans for the film—although it is possible simply to shoot a random selection of footage over a period of several months and then simply edit it into an interesting, colorful, and lively film.

As in the case of a brochure, a film that sells the message of a municipal recreation and park department should include coverage of the governing structure and organization and goals of the department. However, it should be visually oriented and should give major emphasis to action and interesting events. The film that consists primarily of the departmental administrator standing deadpan before the camera making a speech is not likely to be asked back for a reshowing. Instead, the following kinds of scenes or events are likely to make good subjects:

1. Sports tournaments and action close-ups in a variety of activities
2. Performing arts, including music, drama, and dance
3. Interesting or unusual facilities, including parks, playgrounds, or other facilities under construction, with people and machines at work; rehabilitation or vandalism prevention projects
4. The recreation and park board or council, both meeting and touring or observing programs
5. People taking part in enjoyable activities

If part of the film shows the department's administrator or supervisor making a presentation about the department, this should be kept brief and lively—using visual aids, such as charts, pictures, maps, and similar materials.

A film should attempt to give a professional, colorful, and positive picture of the department, including its major features and special events, its rationale and contribution to the community, and the new directions it is pursuing. It should *not* show weaknesses or deal with controversial issues. As much as possible, it should avoid events or other elements that might tend to *date* it in the viewer's eyes; clothing and hair styles are likely to do that in any case.

Slide talks. Slide talks represent a less expensive but effective means of reaching an audience with colorful and convincing pictures and accompanying descriptions of a recreation and park department's program. It is a good idea to have a department photographer or a skilled volunteer regularly shoot pictures of special events, facilities, and other features that make good presentations. These may then be assembled easily into an effective slide presentation. If the speaker is thoroughly familiar with the material shown, he need only put the slides into the correct order and then can speak extemporaneously about them. If several speakers are to use the slides, it is a good idea to prepare a script in which each slide is numbered and the accompanying text typed out.

Artz[1] suggests the following guidelines in preparing slide talks:

1. Determine the series objective. What story do you wish to tell?
2. Prepare an outline script, and, after necessary revision, follow up by writing a shooting script.
3. Always keep in mind *continuity* in preparing the outline and the shooting script.

4. In preparing final script and selection of slides, keep the talk to a maximum of between 80 and 100 slides, or no more than 20 minutes. The reading script should be geared to no more than 120 words per minute, and, where possible, slides should be allowed to speak for themselves.

Slides offer a lively, interesting, and flexible way of entertaining an audience with a recreation and park department presentation. Despite the reputation that family slide showings may have gained, they are *not* necessarily dull if the picture and accompanying talk are good.

Since slides are much less expensive as a publicity medium than films, they may be designed to meet special purposes, such as showing to parents' groups to promote a summer camp program and encourage recruitment; promoting interest in doing volunteer work in the department; gaining support for a proposed new facility or bond referendum for land acquisition; or encouraging job applications for summer positions among high school or college students.

Speakers. It is also possible for a department to assign its supervisors or leaders to making presentations to community groups, clubs, leagues, or other organizations. In some cases, a department actually maintains a speakers' bureau, although this is not common. When it *is* done, it is crucial that the speaker have a fresh and interesting message to deliver, rather than overfamiliar, tired material.

Exhibits and displays. This provides an excellent means of informing the public about the work of a department. Since recreation itself is composed of so many varied kinds of hobbies and activities, it is possible to develop extremely interesting and unusual kinds of exhibits and displays to entertain and inform the public. These might include:

1. Art shows, science displays or fairs, photography exhibits, craft exhibits and sales, hobby shows, nature exhibits, and similar presentations that show the products of recreational programs carried on in the department. They may also include illustrated talks or demonstrations of skills, such as glass-blowing or work at the potter's wheel.

2. Special events, such as play-days, drama festivals, dance performances, aquacades, or similar showings. The purpose of these is not so much to entertain an audience as to give a *picture* of the work of the department.

3. Displays or demonstrations. These may be given in varied settings. Central points in shopping malls may be used for demonstrations when large crowds will be there. Schools, libraries, municipal buildings, and hotel or theater lobbies are all places where recreation exhibits or displays may reach large numbers of viewers.

4. Action demonstrations. Demonstrations should be well publicized and given in central locations to draw substantial numbers of viewers. In some cities, a large plaza in the downtown business district or in front of the city hall may be used to show interesting activities during lunch hours, when crowds of employees throng the streets. In the city of Philadelphia, for example, each weekday during the summer a different program is presented in the city hall square

at lunchtime; this may include sports demonstrations, hobby activities, music or dancing, or similar activities. This educates the public about different activities that are available throughout the city and gives them a positive image of the recreation department. It also gives participants themselves a chance to show off and to gain pride in their accomplishments and skills.

Tours and open houses. The open house or tour represents an excellent way of showing officials, parents, local residents, service clubs, PTA members, newspaper reporters, state or county authorities, or other interested groups exactly what is going on in a department.

Guided tours or open houses are usually scheduled at the time of dedication of a new facility, the beginning of a seasonal program, or other occasion that shows the department in a favorable light. They should be carefully planned, with attention given to the following elements:

1. Preliminary planning of the area or activity to be shown, with a schedule showing what points are to be visited at various times throughout the event
2. Arrangements for guides, organizing the visitors into groups, rest stops, seating arrangements, briefing sessions, and transportation
3. Preparation of a mailing list and invitations, mailing, and, if advisable, direct follow-up by television
4. Preparation of a tour outline, including the itinerary, program, list of those making the tour, schedule, and similar details
5. Last-minute check of all elements involved in the tour or open house and reminder of all invited participants; pretour publicity in newspapers or other media
6. After the event, thank-you notes to all involved and follow-up publicity

Annual reports. This final type of departmental publication consists of a comprehensive report published each year by the department and officially submitted to the mayor or city manager, the city council, the recreation and park board, and other municipal authorities.

Annual reports may be addressed solely to such individuals or *may* be designed to reach the public at large. In the latter case, they are likely to be less detailed and more like a brochure in appearance, with photographs and illustrations, colorful layouts, and informal style. Prepared in this way, annual reports may serve as useful public relations tools and should be widely distributed. Normally, annual reports include the following elements:

1. Departmental address and board and staff roster—with or without photographs of key individuals
2. Opening messages, which may be from the mayor, chairman of the recreation and park board, or administrator of the department
3. Table of contents and acknowledgements of appreciation to those individuals or organizations that served the department during the year
4. Organization chart
5. Financial report, consisting of a simple statement of the authorized budget

and sums actually spent. This may include summaries of past and future or predicted budgets

6. A report of physical resource development—the major facilities operated by the department, as well as acquisition, maintenance, or refurbishment projects carried out during the course of the year

7. Report of attendance and participation in programs, usually done by major department divisions or types of activities

Annual reports may deal with a specific theme or have a feature story describing some of the outstanding accomplishments of the department during the course of the year. In general, they should be professionally laid out, with contrast, balance, and interest, and should make generous use of visual devices to explain the material and attract the eye.

Annual reports are usually positive in their tone and seek to present the department in a constructive and favorable light. However, if there *are* serious problems because of lack of cooperation of other agencies or budget cuts, it may make sense to present these as fairly and openly as possible. Similarly, although most open houses or guided tours are intended to show what is favorable to the department and will create a positive impression, they may also be used to show negative aspects of a situation. Thus a department might deliberately schedule a tour of the most run-down areas of an inner-city neighborhood to show graphically the *lack* of adequate recreation resources and the *need* for a park, playground, or community center.

Creating other public relations opportunities. The alert recreation and park administrator will seek out a number of special opportunities throughout the year to provide helpful information or services that contribute to the public relations impact of his department. Examples of such opportunities include:

1. Carry out a special beautification project at several key entrances to the city with a clear identification of the department of recreation and parks as the city agency responsible for the effort.
2. Make special awards, with newspaper or other media coverage, to:
   a. Most attractive gas stations
   b. Greatest number of new trees planted (on church sites, hospital grounds, etc.)
   c. Outstanding Boy or Girl Scout troop for urban beautification projects
   d. Volunteer leaders with outstanding records
   e. Winners of window box or front-lawn garden competitions
3. Sponsor special Family Day once a year, when any family group may enter all recreation facilities or programs without charge.
4. Use press or television to issue important statements (warnings, suggestions, offers of help, etc.) to public, such as:
   a. Danger of mushy ice on ponds and lakes in spring
   b. Urging homeowners to reforest their city by tree planting
   c. Encouraging family recreation activities
   d. Suggesting and assisting neighborhood recreation events and forming of neighborhood associations
   e. Providing advice, clinics, or contests on home and community gardens
   f. Condemning vandalism as waste of taxpayer's money
   g. Providing warnings against July Fourth fireworks accidents or Halloween excesses; sponsoring safe holiday activities
   h. Urging public to use care and caution in swimming, boating, and fishing

5. In the event of local disasters, such as floods, fires, minor earthquakes, or power failures, when families may be dispossessed and temporarily housed in armories, churches, or other civic facilities, the recreation and park department may assist in mobilizing community groups to provide bedding, food, or even games, books, or other recreation activities to help lift the morale of displaced residents.
6. Promote volunteer services in community, not only for recreation and park programs but for hospitals and other social service programs as well.
7. Initiate a youth job program, which coordinates part-time and summer employment but for hospital and other social service programs as well.
8. Select a Junior Commissioner of Recreation and Parks for a day or a week. Put him or her in the Commissioner's place to tour facilities, run meetings, deal with real problems—with the press close at hand.

Such special services or projects will do much to keep the public aware of the recreation and park department's contribution to community life and promote their interest and support. Often, municipal departments may use novel ways of sending out messages to the public or sponsor unique events as a way of attracting public interest. For example:

The Raleigh, North Carolina, Department of Recreation and Parks issues regular, detailed reports to the public on the progress of major capital projects, such as golf courses, swimming pools, or skating rinks. They find the public tends to be more supportive when it is kept in close contact with each such project.

The Boston Recreation and Park Department enlisted the entire city in an urban reforestation program by calling it *Plantree* and pointing out that the city was "going bald." More than $100,000 was raised from private industry to plant thousands of new trees in parks and on school and hospital grounds.

In Atlanta, one full evening at the new Omni Stadium was used to display the talents of participants in Atlanta Recreation and Park Department programs before a live audience of 50,000 and a regional television audience of several million.

A successful rock-fest was held in an Arizona city, with the price of admission identified as one clean, usable red brick. Over 5,000 bricks were collected, and these were used in the construction of a nearby park shelter building.

The Philadelphia Recreation Department offers a unique community service by compiling and publishing a fully detailed directory of recreational activities and agencies in the Philadelphia metropolitan area. It lists major areas of activity, such as art, dance, drama, music, outdoor recreation, sports, games, flying, gliding, gardening, and motorcycling, among many others, and gives the names, addresses, and telephone numbers of all organizations that provide clubs, classes, or other events connected with these activities in the area.

Suggested public relations kit. Particularly for the small recreation and park department, it is extremely helpful to have at least one staff member who has a public relations knack. Such an individual constantly sees and uses public relations opportunities and is always working at picture-taking and mounting, tape recording, assembling window displays, writing releases, and printing, lettering, or painting publicity posters. To help such an individual use his or her bag of special skills, the department should have a kit of suggested equipment and supplies readily available for public relations purposes. Such a kit might include:

1. *Public address system.* A portable amplifier and speakers (at least 30-watt output) and light enough to be handled by one person—man or woman; phonograph turntable or tape deck

2. *Cameras.* Three different kinds are useful: (a) a 35 mm still camera; (b) a press-type Graflex, which produces an excellent glossy print for newspaper or display use; and (c) a 16 mm movie camera for making department films of events
3. *Poster materials.* Colored ink markers, pens, rulers, and plastic letter stencils and guides; a good supply of mimeograph and construction paper; drawing boards and tag boards; and a uniform poster, made in quantity, with about a fifth of its space devoted to a colorful heading identifying the department and the rest open for special announcements, photographs, or other use
4. *Display complex.* A home-made or purchased portable display complex, consisting of combinations of folding tables, hanging panels, and lights, which may easily be disassembled, moved, and set up for display purposes in City Hall, banks, restaurants, shopping malls, or conferences and training meetings
5. *Work table and hardware.* A sturdy work table, at least 4 × 6 ft, with needed scissors, paper cutting blade, staplers, and similar office tools, along with an adjacent steel filing cabinet offering organized storage of papers, booklets, and department public relations materials

OTHER APPROACHES TO PUBLIC RELATIONS

The previous section of this chapter has dealt with various types of media used to reach the public with special messages. Equally important are the direct ways in which a recreation and park department has daily contact with individuals.

For example, all individuals visiting a department office or telephoning should be treated with promptness, courtesy, and efficiency. Complaints regarding programs or facilities—from whatever source—should be received with serious attention and should be processed through appropriate channels without delay. The suggestions of participants or other residents should be solicited at all times.

Whenever assistance of any kind is given to the department by an individual or organization, this should be promptly acknowledged. All members of the department should conduct themselves with appropriate deportment, dress, and general appearance in their contacts with the public.

Buildings, offices, facilities, equipment, and vehicles should all be carefully and attractively maintained and, when it is suitable, should have departmental insignia or other identification signs to promote public awareness of the department.

Recreation administrators and supervisors, in particular, should seek to become widely acquainted in the community; it is desirable to become active in civic groups, service clubs, and similar organizations.

By the same token, they should learn as much as they can about the history of the community—its traditions, customs, famous names, and similar information. Frequently these can be useful in planning press releases or events that arouse public interest and support.

The administrator should visit and chat with the heads of major business firms, colleges, hospitals, and other organizations in the area about the philosophy and program of the recreation and park department, the needs of the city, and other relevant concerns. He or she should *not* ask for direct support at early meetings but should attempt to build a cooperative relationship first before developing the possibility of such ventures. The administrator may offer to assist the company or other institution in improving its own recreation or sports program, including assistance with facilities planning or renovation, advice on activities and special interest groups, or even the loan of films, books, equipment, or special facilities. Such tangible help is a sound public relations step and frequently makes the business firm or agency a permanent and enthusiastic ally.

The administrator should be prepared to accept speaking and panel assignments frequently and willingly at civic or religious organization meetings in the community and should present a clear and positive picture of the recreation and park department and its program.

The department should prepare and distribute pamplets giving details of seasonal programs (activities, schedules, dates of registration, locations, and fees) in as thorough, timely, and attractive a form as possible. Many parents hang or tack such brochures next to their telephones for ready references. Some communities use such brochures to include general information about public offices and services, including the names and telephone numbers of city officials and departments, special services (such as senior center clubs, health services, or suburban mini-bus program schedule), and similar materials.

The department's office should be bright, cheery, and businesslike, with colorful decorations, neat housekeeping, and a ready and responsive receptionist. Dreary surroundings or a rude, uncommunicative staff person can seriously damage citizen goodwill. In general, all recreation and park personnel must stress the department's role of assisting, guiding, and helping people find and enjoy their own recreation rather than seek to structure all program opportunities. It should constantly stress positive, constructive human relations, healthy and enriching leisure experiences, and the building of close ties with the community. There is no place in the department's fabric for jealously, spite, vindictiveness, or arrogance—these are anti–public relations elements!

Finally, the most professionally produced newspaper releases, films, or guided tours will accomplish little if the program they represent is not an effective one. The best public relations medium is the satisfied user. Actions speak louder than words, and the ultimate basis for an effective public relations program is a varied, imaginative, well-attended, and successful variety of activities enjoyed by all age groups and citizens of all backgrounds throughout the year.

Evaluating the public relations program

Given all of this, it becomes appropriate to take a hard look at the specific elements in the public relations program to make sure that they are doing the best possible job of promoting the favorable image of the department and gaining community support and involvement. The following questions may be raised in carrying out such an evaluation:

Are there effective and well-produced brochures and pamphlets to inform the public of the program during the course of the year?

Is maximum possible use being made of the public media, such as newspapers, television, and radio?

Is information regarding the program disseminated both regularly and on special occasions to promote or publicize unique situations or events?

Has consideration been given to the use of films, slide talks, speakers, or open houses or tours?

Has the responsibility for public relations been assigned to a competent individual or office within the department, or is it everybody's business?

Are adequate funds provided to carry out this function?

A departmental committee may be established to examine the overall problem of public relations and to determine exactly what views the public holds of the recreation and park department. It should make proposals for improving the public relations efforts of the department and should be made responsible for following through on them.

Public relations efforts must be aimed at various levels of public sophistication and interest. Fliers and posters about Halloween Carnivals or Little League registration featured in departmental offices only reach a small segment of potential consumers. Instead, a full variety of media, which aim at such specialized audiences as teenagers, young adults, childless couples, the elderly, and other identifiable groups of residents and which take into account their concerns and levels of sophistication, will result in a more effective public relations program.

Finally, it is essential that public relations be viewed as a two-way street. It does not just consist of passing out information. It is also a matter of listening to what the community has to say about its offerings and re-designing its program on the basis of this information. Ultimately, the total problem of maintaining an effective community relations program becomes a vital aspect of public relations.

THE COMMUNITY RELATIONS PROGRAM

One of the most important administrative considerations in recreation and parks has traditionally been to involve residents in meaningful ways, both to get citizen input and advice and to assure the public that its wishes are taken seriously.

The various types of citizen groups concerned with parks and recreation in this way have included the following.

Neighborhood or community center recreation council. A neighborhood or community center recreation council is usually formed on a local neighborhood basis to support the efforts of a large community center and athletic complex. Usually it consists primarily of members of the center, parents, local businessmen, and similar individuals. Its function is usually twofold: to assist in planning programs or schedules, usually on an advisory basis, and to help in actually carrying them on by providing volunteer assistance, raising funds, or providing supplies and equipment.

District recreation and park council or committee. A district recreation and park council or committee is a somewhat comparable type of organization intended to assist in the operation of recreation and park programs within a larger area of the city. Normally it is concerned with total needs and programs in the district. It is composed of representatives of major community organizations, such as Parent-Teacher Associations, Boy and Girl Scouts, churches, service clubs, labor organizations, and businessmen's and homeowners' associations. It is concerned with assisting and guiding overall program and facility development. It may help to raise special funds, promote special programs, or provide political support for the department when needed.

City-wide council or committee. In addition to recreation and park boards or commissions, which are usually based on legal authority and have a formal status within the governmental structure, there are a number of different types of citizen groups that promote park and recreation programs on the city-wide level. These include recreation councils, councils of social agencies, recreation and park associations, conservation clubs, or special committees and task forces.

Whenever possible, each of these types of organizations should be broadly diverse in its representation. All age groups should be represented, including youth and the aged. Various racial, ethnic, and religious groups should be well represented, and other municipal agencies, such as the schools, youth services or commissions, or police department, should also be represented.

Examples of recreation councils

In most American cities, such councils or committees are organized informally and make only limited contributions to the work of the recreation and park department. In some cities, however, a major effort is made to develop them systematically and to use them to assist programs in a meaningful way.

Outstanding examples of community councils and sponsoring groups may be found in Minneapolis, Minnesota, Vancouver, Canada, and Oakland, California.

Recreation Activities Councils in Minneapolis. The highest administrative level in the Minneapolis Recreation Department is the Park and Recreation Board, consisting of nine elected commissioners. One of the four major programs under this board is directed by a Program Supervisor for Community Centers and Playgrounds. He is administratively responsible for several District Supervisors, who, in turn, direct Recreation Supervisors, who conduct programs in each of the approximately thirty neighborhood recreation centers scattered throughout the city.

Recreation Activity Councils are directly attached to each of these neighborhood centers. These councils are composed of interested adults and parents from a common geographic area adjacent to a particular park who see the need to join forces to form a common organization to develop the greatest potential use of the recreation facilities through purposeful recreation activities. They work hand in hand with the Recreation Supervisor of the center they are attached to and also with the District Supervisor in the area.

After an initial general meeting, members of the council elect a Board of Directors, consisting of a President, Vice President, Secretary, and Treasurer, to conduct its work. Bylaws are established, although, in general, rules of operation for the council are kept fairly flexible. Each board member customarily serves as chairman of at least one committee of the council. Most recreation councils contain the following standing committees: Program Committee, Athletic Committee, Social Activities Committee, Football Committee, Girls' Sports Committee, Athletic Equipment Committee, Newsletter Committee, and Budget and Finance Committee.

The Minneapolis Park and Recreation Board relies heavily on the Recreation Activity Councils in each neighborhood to guide the development of self-directed programs, although it sees their function as being advisory and consultative, rather than one of policy-making power:

> The Neighborhood Recreation Activity Council is recognized as an advisory arm of the park system in the various sections of Minneapolis and an integral part of the overall recreation program. This type of organization advises the park system on recreation programs, and the park staff works in close cooperation with these groups.[3]

In addition to this advisory function, however, the Councils contribute directly to the operation of many programs. They carry on intensive fund-raising campaigns, effectively organize different programs (typically, they will operate various sports leagues, providing the bulk of needed manpower in terms of officials, coaches, and so on), and are responsible for many needed recreation projects related to their centers. In many cases, they own extensive equipment used in the program, publish newsletters promoting center activities, and generally contribute to the overall municipal recreation program.

Park Area Recreation Councils. The work of local Councils is promoted by Park Area Recreation Councils (PARC), a city-wide organization consisting of representatives of the local councils.

PARC's function is primarily to deal with recreation problems and needs on a broader geographical level than that dealt with by the local Councils. It strengthens their work through district and city-wide meetings. By discussing mutual problems, objectives, and proposed programs, PARC strives to develop a unity of purpose among the various councils and between the councils and the Minneapolis Park and Recreation Board.

Community Centre Associations in Vancouver. A unique example of effective community relations on the part of a public recreation and parks department may be found in Vancouver, British Columbia, Canada, where major Community Centres and recreation projects throughout the city are jointly administered by the municipal Parks Board and local Community Centre Associations.

A formal agreement signed by the Board and Association outlines their respective duties and responsibilities in the operation of Centre buildings and programs. The Parks Board is responsible for the control, care, and maintenance of the Centre building and appoints Centre directors and staff members, with the concurrence of the Association. The operating budget is determined jointly by the Parks Board and Association, with about 75% of the annual cost of running the Centre provided by the public authority, and the remainder raised by the Association. The Association, which is composed of local citizens (Fig. 9-1), is responsible for programming the Centre, furnishing the building, and providing recreational equipment and sponsorship fees in sports events, janitorial expenses, and its own office expenses.

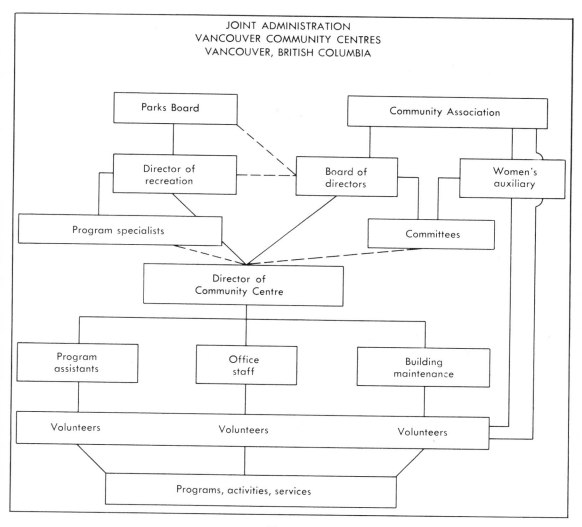

Fig. 9-1

The Association is authorized to rent the building to other community groups; it uses funds gained in this way for equipment, furnishings, and miscellaneous program expenses. Associations also secure revenues through membership fees, fund-raising activities, and through direct provincial recreational or senior citizen grants. Recreation projects are administered in much the same way but consist of decentralized programs that are usually conducted in space rented from schools, churches, or halls in the area, rather than in separate Community Centre buildings. Community Centre Associations serve to mobilize neighborhood support and interest and account for a high level of citizen participation on a volunteer basis throughout the City of Vancouver's recreation and park program.

Many other cities sponsor such councils, usually on a somewhat less fully organized basis. One such example may be found in Oakland, California.

Advisory Councils in Oakland. In Oakland the primary functions of advisory councils are to serve as a liaison between the department and various community groups and to provide support for department programs on a local level. In a manual for center directors, the Oakland Recreation Department describes the functions of such councils:

> The Superintendent and other Department Officials should be consulted in connection with the Council's consideration of proposals affecting areas in which they have jurisdiction, so that their knowledge and experience can be made available to the membership. . . . Keep in mind at all times that the Advisory Council is created to assist the Superintendent of Recreation and the Recreation Commission in developing and carrying out a recreation program for the neighborhood. It cannot pre-empt their legal responsibilities.[4]

Suggested projects for local Advisory Councils, as outlined in departmental guidelines, include the following: holding fund-raising events, promoting publicity for events and activities, providing transportation for children participating in activities, recruiting volunteers from the community, or conducting surveys to determine community interests and needs.

NEW ROLES FOR COMMUNITY ORGANIZATIONS

Traditionally in American society, all socioeconomic groups have had the right to contribute to the decision-making process and to make their needs known with respect to all areas of community need. Realistically, however, it has been the middle and upper socioeconomic classes that have been able to influence policy. In part, this has been because the middle and upper classes have had channels for wielding influence—the well-to-do simply by virtue of the posts of power they held and the middle classes through their organizations: service clubs, professional associations, civic and religious affiliations. In contrast, the poor have generally been fragmented and powerless. This point was substantiated by Clawson and Knetsch, who wrote:

> In a great many American cities, park and playground acreage is more unevenly distributed than is personal income. The lowest income areas of the city have an even smaller share of recreation area than they have of personal income, while the highest income sections have relatively generous parks and recreation areas. . . . This situation is made still worse by the racial pattern of urban living. The low-income central city areas so deficient in recreation space are likely to be Negro; the suburban and outer city ring areas, generously supplied with recreation, are likely to be white. One of the great myths of the outdoor recreation field is that free public parks are a boon to "poor" people; actually, it is the poor who frequently lack them.[5]

Participation by residents

It was in an attempt to remedy such imbalances that the antipoverty programs of the 1960s gave emphasis to maximum feasible participation by the poor in decision-making and to the expansion of varied social programs in inner-city areas. Many of these programs, especially those funded by the Community

Action Programs of the Office of Economic Opportunities, required that poor people—especially those representing racial minority groups—be involved in the decision-making or administrative process. In many cases it was stipulated that they be employed to operate their own programs. In still other cases, federal subsidies to the development of inner-city recreation facilities made it possible for organizations composed of low-income minority-group residents to build or operate their own facilities.

In a number of American cities in the late 1960s, recreation and park authorities experienced strong demands from socially disadvantaged and minority-group residents. Blacks and Spanish-speaking residents in particular confronted official agencies in their cities, demanding fuller participation in policy development, improved facilities and programs in their neighborhoods, and expanded hiring of local people.

In response to such pressures, a number of major cities took strong steps to promote participation by local residents in the planning and conduct of municipal services. Examples of three such cities follow.

Philadelphia. In Philadelphia the practice for the past two decades has been to require recreation center directors to develop advisory councils of interested neighborhood residents. These councils vote for representatives to district-wide councils, and these in turn send delegates to a city-wide council. The experience in Philadelphia has been that the most meaningful level of organization is on the local level, where the needs and problems are most immediate, and the most difficult level to organize is the district. The Philadelphia Recreation Department takes the position that such councils should not be organized formally. Quorums, by-laws, and strict voting procedures are generally too cumbersome to carry out. Instead, representation comes about through invitation or through the resident's strong interest in recreation programs.

On another level, antipoverty programs in Philadelphia were coordinated through twelve Community Action Councils and sixteen Model Cities neighborhood councils. Since recreation has received a substantial portion of federal funding in Philadelphia, such councils have played a strong role in determining where funds should be allocated and recreation programs established throughout the city.

Washington, D.C. Here, an Office of Community Services has been established that reports directly to the mayor and that works through nine major service areas in the city. In each of these areas, all forms of public service (including police, highways, education, sanitation, welfare, and recreation) are officially represented. Area planning groups meet weekly or biweekly, with considerable community participation in each of the nine service areas. In addition, the recreation department's supervisor must work closely with Parent-Teacher Associations, civic groups, service clubs, and similar organizations and encourage the development of recreation councils.

Boston. In Boston the mayor established fourteen local city halls in districts throughout the city. In each a manager was appointed, as representative of the mayor, to work with elected or voluntary local councils on problems related to all forms of public service. The chief responsibility for community relations in the recreation and park department is assigned to fourteen district supervisors, who are assigned to each of Boston's districts. These supervisors are responsible for coordinating all public and voluntary programs within their districts and providing meaningful input for all community groups.

Problems with district recreation administration

In these ways, large city recreation and park departments have made innovative attempts to develop meaningful community relations processes more fully than in the past. Such plans usually call for creating essentially new types of district recreation supervisors who will act much as if they were superintendents of smaller cities. They usually require additional funds to permit these individuals to function more effectively. Because of fiscal restraints, it has been difficult to obtain the funds needed to strengthen district recreation operations. Further, the civil service structure in a number of cities has placed roadblocks in the way of creating new positions or radically upgrading job descriptions of existing positions. Labor union resistance to decentralization (it is widely viewed as a threat to the security of civil employees) has also made it difficult to bring about personnel changes needed to further such plans.

A second difficulty that has hampered most park and recreation departments in their efforts to achieve greater local involvement has been the multiplicity of groups and organizations that claim to represent the community. Often it is almost impossible to identify those who *do* speak authoritatively for the bulk of citizens in any area of a city.

A third problem in this area is that district supervisors (even in those cities where administrators have indicated an eagerness to shift decision-making to lower echelons of personnel) are frequently saddled by a host of routine, bookkeeping, and busywork responsibilities. Although they are supposed to be community organizers, coordinators, catalysts, and idea-generators, in reality their time is taken up with reports, scheduling, requisitioning supplies, filling out personnel forms, and the like. It is a common complaint among district and area supervisors in such cities that they are given few real decision-making powers; these are retained at central administrative headquarters.

With the decline in federal antipoverty funding for urban centers since the early 1970s, less emphasis is being given today to developing mechanisms for community participation in decision-making in disadvantaged neighborhoods. Godbey points out, in this connection, that even when efforts were made to develop such participation, recreation advisory councils in low socioeconomic areas appear to be markedly less effective than in upper-income neighborhoods.[6] Poor people lack knowledge of local government, have fewer personal contacts in key agencies, and generally continue to suffer from apathy, especially in crime or gang-dominated neighborhoods. It is clear that although strong efforts have been made to involve citizen groups in urban ghettoes, our successes are outweighed by our failures.

Coordination of community agencies

Another important trend with respect to community relations has been the effort to coordinate all community agencies providing recreation facilities and programs. In the majority of American cities, as pointed out earlier, school boards either provide facilities for use by the public recreation and park department or offer programs of their own. Other agencies providing recreation include libraries and museums, police departments, housing authorities, and youth boards or commissions. In addition, voluntary agencies, service clubs, colleges and universities, religious organizations, and antipoverty councils provide extensive programs in many cities. In other cities, there is a considerable duplication and overlap of services in some neighborhoods, while there are marked shortages of programs and facilities in others.

The obvious solution is to develop joint planning and co-sponsorship arrangements among all agencies to ensure adequate coverage of the community's needs. This may involve an ambitious plan to draw all organizations together in joint programs, as in Converge in Boston (pp. 229-231). More commonly, it involves cooperation between the recreation and park department and the schools.

In Washington, D.C., for example, the city recreation department not only operates extensive programs using public school facilities but is also responsible for coordinating the use of such facilities by other community groups through a permit system. Instead of resisting such uses, the school system encourages them; many principals believe that neighborhood attitudes are more favorable toward schools that offer recreation programs and that problems of security are thereby minimized.

In Boston, a similar situation prevails, with the recreation department providing programs in school buildings. The Detroit recreation and park department also controls all community uses of school building facilities such as gymnasiums and pools through a contractual agreement with the board of education. In Los Angeles, the park and recreation department uses schools' indoor facilities, and the schools operate programs in outdoor areas belonging to them, such as tennis courts, ball fields, and tracks.

However, there continue to be numerous problems with respect to interagency cooperation. Park and recreation administrators complain that custodial charges for using school buildings are frequently extremely high. Policies regarding such arrangements vary from school to school, often depending on the attitudes of individual principals. In some cities, park and recreation administrators report that, although they are generally able to make use of schools, high school gynasiums are often not available because of varsity sports programs during the afternoon. In some cases, school principals preempt facilities that have been assigned to recreation programs without warning, thus disrupting their schedules.

Cooperation between recreation departments and schools. Since such problems exist, it is helpful to examine in detail certain communities where cooperation between recreation and park departments and school systems has been fully developed. Two examples are Spokane, Washington, and San Diego, California.

In Spokane, a Coordinating Committee was formed consisting of two members of the school board, two members of the park board, the superintendent of schools, and the park director. The primary purpose of this committee is to coordinate the use of park and school facilities by the community and to work together on planning, with the interests of both school and park departments fully considered.

School facilities are planned with the cooperation of the Park Department to provide adequate community centers for recreational use in nonschool hours. Playgrounds are planned in locations immediately adjacent to schools whenever feasible. There is a systematic interchange of facilities between the two agencies to ensure maximum public use at all times. Each department provides its own program leadership, with janitorial service, general maintenance, and utilities being provided by the host department. Parks that are adjacent to schools and that are too small for recreation programming are transferred to the school district in some cases, and school grounds are normally made fully available to the park board for summer programming.

In San Diego, the City and School District have entered into a contractual agreement for the joint operation of school facilities. School facilities serve as community centers. According to the terms of the contract, the school district makes all playgrounds, classrooms, auditoriums, cafeterias, gymnasiums, storage rooms, and other special facilities available to the municipal recreation department as needed, and recreation facilities are made equally available to the schools.

In a number of Canadian cities, similar policies prevail. The Vancouver, British Columbia, Board of Parks and Recreation, for example, has developed a number of year-round, full-utilization complexes built adjacent to secondary and elementary schools. These include such facilities as indoor swimming pools, community meeting rooms, health and welfare centers, playing fields, teenage lounges, and similar areas.

Hafen[7] points out that many problems may occur when two different agencies attempt to use the same facility. When verbal agreements are relied on, what happens when there are later misunderstandings? Who should cover expenses of utilities, custodial expenses, or breakage? What happens when school facilities are not in proper order when classes begin the next morning? He suggests a number of guidelines to prevent such problems from developing:

> There should be written policies that clearly indicate the responsibilities and rights of each agency. These should be signed by key officials representing both the recreation and park department and the school board.
> It is advisable to hold periodic conferences of school officials, recreation administrators and interested cities to assist in maintaining a cooperative relationship. A joint committee should be established as a steering body to regulate, evaluate, and establish policies and to assist in the planning of new facilities.

Community use of school facilities must not interfere with the ongoing school program.

When policies and standards are established, both school and community officials must abide by them. No individual may enforce his own policies in opposition to official agreements.

The process of making facilities available to community groups (public or voluntary) should be as simple as possible and based on a clear order of priority.

Rental fees should be established and publicized, along with other policies dealing with hours that school facilities are available, what types of activities may or may not be conducted in school facilities, regulations regarding smoking and drinking, and assignment of costs of heating, lighting, and maintenance during community use.

Policies should clearly outline the community group's responsibility with respect to cleaning up after use or payment when damage is done to facilities or equipment.

These and similar joint-use policies are often spelled out in precise detail in contracts in force between public recreation and park departments and school boards or in policy manuals of school districts.

Community schools. As an extension of such cooperation, an increasing number of cities have embarked on the development of community schools. The community-school or park-school concept embodies the basic concept of providing educational, recreational, and other social services within a single major facility. Programs are jointly planned and operated, with facilities being designed and built for this purpose from the very outset.

Since the late 1950s, more than 500 cities across the nation have experimented with community education centers. These community schools are open 12 months of the year, 7 days a week in many cases, 14 hours or more a day, if needed. They are designed to blend community life with the academic function and environment of the school. They extend the school's task, around the calendar, to areas such as youth enrichment, recreation, adult education, and the solving of community problems.

Even today, the summertime phenomenon of school buildings and adjacent play areas remaining locked and unused while children are playing dangerously in nearby streets is not uncommon. School gymnasiums are locked, playgrounds fenced, and equipment dismantled.

There is a growing conviction among educators, urbanologists, recreation authorities, and other civic leaders that schools cannot remain merely centers of academic instruction. Instead, they must become centers of community life, with a meaningful impact on social problems. By deliberate design, they should deal effectively with such issues as delinquency, illiteracy, school dropouts, poverty, poor health, unemployment, civil rights, neighborhood strife, and family disintegration. In addition to the daytime academic programs, community schools should provide social, cultural, recreational, and vocational experiences for all neighborhood residents.

Former President Lyndon Johnson stated:

Tomorrow's school will be the center of community life, for grown-ups as well as children, a shopping center of human services. It might have a community health clinic, or a public library, a theatre, and recreation facilities. It will provide formal education for all citizens—and it will not close its doors anymore at three o'clock. It will employ its buildings around the clock and its teachers around the year. We just cannot afford to have an $85 billion plant in this country open less than 30 percent of the time.[8]

In some cases, departments of education themselves have taken a major responsibility for conducting large-scale programs of recreation and allied social services. Los Angeles, Milwaukee, and Flint, Michigan, are among the cities that have taken such a responsibility. A number of major regional centers have been established around the United States with the assistance of the Charles Stewart Mott Foundation to promote the establishment of effective community school programs.

In some cases, state or provincial education authorities have taken the lead in promoting public concern with leisure needs and in stimulating community recreation programs. For example, in Canada, in 1968, the Department of Education in the Province of Ontario created a Youth and Recreation Branch to promote the community development role of school in the province. The first of the projects of this new department was to form a Youth-in-Action Program, which employed university, college, and older high school students to work in selected municipalities in Ontario on community betterment programs under school auspices. The Youth and Recreation Branch brings guidance and special resources to municipal councils, school authorities, and private agencies that supervise recreation and adult education programs in Ontario's communities. It carries out the following functions:

1. It has studied and made significant recommendations for amateur sports in the province.

2. It administers the Leadership Development program that provides teacher and adult education leaders for programs throughout Ontario.

3. It offers consultation services and active assistance to all municipal and private recreation agencies and certifies municipal recreation personnel and arena managers.

4. It provides assistance to professional preparation curricula in colleges and universities throughout the Province.

5. It offers conferences, seminars, and sensitivity-training laboratories at many levels.

6. It provides advisory services to organization and communities in developing services for the ill, aging, and handicapped.

7. It provides resource materials, such as books, manuals, and films, on such subjects as community leadership, municipal recreation programs, playground activities, and similar functions.

Another example of the community school approach may be found in Minneapolis, where a number of small neighborhood centers are being built in conjunction with elementary schools. These centers serve local residents of all ages with recreation, casework, and group-work services, as well as with small health and dental clinics. They also serve as meeting places for neighborhood organizations to use for their own functions.

Large community centers are being planned for junior or senior high schools to serve total community needs, with specialized services for adolescents, young adults, parents, and families. Supplementary services provided in such centers include employment, welfare, legal aid, and family counseling services, as well as general adult education and vocational courses. Three such centers have been built and put into operation in Minneapolis. Joint use of facilities and the effective coordination of programs are the basis of these centers.

Schools are designed so that all common-use space, such as gymnasiums, multipurpose rooms, kitchens, and libraries may be reached directly through the neighborhood center and do not require access through other parts of the school. At the end of the school day, neighborhood center staff members use varied school facilities for their programs. Conversely, during the school day, the school staff may make scheduled uses of neighborhood center facilities, when needed. The sharing of all facilities is specifically spelled out in contractual agreement between all parties involved—usually consisting of the school, the recreation and park department, and at least one other social agency.

A similar system of community-school sponsorship has been developed in New Haven, Connecticut, where there are seven such schools, each serving a different inner-city neighborhood. The concept that was officially adopted by the New Haven Board of Education in 1962 defines the community school as:

1. An educational center—a place where children and adults have opportunities for study and learning
2. A neighborhood community center—a place where citizens of all ages may take part in such things as sports, physical fitness programs, informal recreation, arts and crafts classes, civic meetings, and other leisure-time activities
3. A center for community services, where individuals and families may obtain health services, counseling, legal aid, and employment assistance
4. A center for community development, with the school taking part in the study and solution of significant neighborhood problems

Some of the services offered by community schools in New Haven include informal recreation, physical fitness, sports, civic meetings, health, legal aid, counseling, and employment services. Emphasis is placed on serving families, older persons, the handicapped, and similar groups. Courses offered include tutorial programs in reading and mathematics, electronics, Americanization classes, and a wide variety of hobby, craft, and similar activities.

The community schools are directed by their own administrators, with each principal having two assistants, one working primarily with classroom programs and the other responsible for school-community relations. Programs are planned jointly by people of the neighborhood and a Staff Planning Team, which includes the assistant principal in charge of community activities, a Neighborhood Coordinator representing Community Progress, Inc. (New Haven's anti-poverty organization), a Park and Recreation Department recreation supervisor, and other representatives from private agencies, such as neighborhood settlement houses and the Y.M.C.A. This team endeavors to coordinate the various community resources and programs with the regular educational program.

Probably the leading example of a school system assuming major responsibility for providing an extensive recreation program is Milwaukee, Wisconsin. Widely known as the City of the Lighted Schoolhouse, Milwaukee has since 1911 accepted the principle that recreation is an educational process and a strong force in human development. Under Wisconsin state law, which authorizes a mill tax levy to support school recreation, the Recreation Division of the Milwaukee Public Schools operates recreation and adult education programs in 128 of 158 present school buildings. In addition, however, it provides programs in supervised playgrounds, ice rinks, recreation centers, and some 251 different facilities located throughout the city. The schools provide over 200 different program activities, including (1) creative experiences, such as arts, crafts, drama, and music; (2) contemporary interests, such as family living, investment planning, languages for travel, and driver education; (3) personal health and fitness activities; and (4) sports activities, such as a full range of instruction and competition in varied sports interests, as well as mountaineering, gun safety, watercraft safety, and similar programs. In recent years, the Recreation Division has moved into other programs, such as outdoor environmental interpretive activities, roving playleaders and mobile playgrounds, preschool activities for handicapped children, and a Family Camping Association. Evidence of this program's success is that each year, the total annual participation count in Recreation Division activities has been almost *five times greater* than the present population of Milwaukee.

Although chief emphasis in this chapter has been on community school programs in large cities, many smaller school districts provide outstanding programs of this type. As a single example, the Hewlett-Woodmere, New York, School District's Department of Community Services coordinates a variety of important social programs. In addition to a full range of recreation activities, these include a responsibility for continuing and adult education, and drug use prevention. In an increasing number of municipal recreation and park departments, as well as school-sponsored programs, such services are being joined with recreation functions.

SUMMARY

These illustrations demonstrate how the community relations aspect of recreation and park administration has grown from a fairly simple operation involving neighborhood or district advisory councils to a much more complex task involving cooperative relationships with the public schools and other agencies.

If public recreation and park departments are to be fully successful, they must strengthen their overall community relations programs. The decentralization of program supervision in large cities, the coordination of all community agencies in the recreation or social service field, and the close cooperation between recreation and schools in community-school projects represent a key aspect of recreation administration today.

Suggested assignments for student reports or projects

1. Plan, in a fully detailed outline, a film, a television program, or a slide show to be used as part of a department's public relations program.
2. Write a series of newspaper releases for a major departmental program, such as an arts festival, major sports tournament, or other large-scale event. Include preliminary announcements, feature stories while event is being carried on, and follow-up releases.
3. Within a specific community with its own newspaper, gather and critically analyze all newspaper accounts dealing with public recreation and park activities over a period of several weeks. As an alternative, analyze the total public relations effort of a recreation and park department for a given season. Present innovative ideas for its improvement.

REFERENCES

1. Summarized from Artz, Robert M., Jarrell, Temple R., and Parker, Adah: *Publicity Handbook,* Washington, D.C., 1968, National Recreation and Park Association Management Aids Bulletin No. 79.
2. Scherer, Daniel J.: "Establishing Local Press Relations," *Parks and Recreation,* October, 1967, p. 36.
3. From: *Recommended Procedures for Park Area Recreation Councils,* Manual of Minneapolis Park and Recreation Board, 1971, p. 26.
4. From: *Guidelines for Head Directors Working with Advisory Councils,* Manual of Oakland, California, Recreation Department, p. 10.
5. Clawson, Marion, and Knetsch, Jack L.: *Economics of Outdoor Recreation,* Baltimore, 1960, The Johns Hopkins University Press, p. 151.
6. Godbey, Geoffrey: "The Poor—A Second Look," *Parks and Recreation,* November, 1972, p. 28.
7. Hafen, William J.: "Written Guidelines to Clarify a Dual Role," in *Leisure Today: Selected Readings,* Washington, D.C., 1975, American Association for Leisure and Recreation.
8. Lyndon Johnson, quoted in *The Community School,* Brigham Young Regional Center for Community School Development, Provo, Utah.

CHAPTER 10

PLANNING, EVALUATION, AND RESEARCH

This chapter is concerned with the three processes of *planning, evaluation,* and *research,* chiefly as they relate to such major aspects of recreation and park administration as facilities, personnel, program, and budget.

The key emphasis is on the use of planning in the development of a recreation and park system to meet comprehensive community needs and on the role of evaluation and research in improving program services.

These processes constitute a sector of recreation and parks administration that is badly neglected. In part, this is because many administrators gained their early experience in the field at a time when planning and research were comparatively primitive services in municipal administration. Probably the most neglected of the three is evaluation. After most programs, events, or projects are carried out, there is little inclination to look back and carefully assess their effectiveness and determine how they might be accomplished more successfully another time. The rapid tempo of seasonal programming dictates that the administrator slam shut the file, stuff it away, and move on to the next project, leaving errors, omissions, and recommendations to molder unseen—only to be repeated the next time around.

DEFINITION OF TERMS

The terms *planning, research,* and *evaluation* frequently are used somewhat interchangeably. Indeed, they often encompass similar processes. However, they represent three distinct aspects of administrative concern. Essentially, they are concerned with *intelligence.* They are all rooted in the need to gather information objectively and systematically, to provide a basis for the most intelligent organization and administration of programs, budgets, facilities, or personnel.

Planning. Planning is the process of determining needs, priorities, and available resources and programs and then developing short- or long-term recommendations to improve program services or develop physical resources for recreation and parks. It may be related to a single facility, neighborhood, district, or community, or more broadly to an entire region or state. It may deal with a single function or problem, such as the use of personnel or vandalism prevention, or it may be comprehensive in its approach.

Research. Essentially, research represents an organized search for knowledge.

It may be highly abstract and of a conceptual nature, or it may be directly linked to the improvement of program services. It may involve action in the form of a demonstration project, the testing of hypotheses in an experimental study, the review of the past in a historical study, or the analysis of the present in a descriptive or normative survey study.

Evaluation. Evaluation is concerned with determining the worth, effectiveness, or outcomes of a program, facility, or administrative structure. In recreation and parks, one might evaluate personnel, program elements, a community center, an in-service training experience, or almost any other aspect of service. One might also use a systematic set of standards to evaluate a total community recreation and park department.

Often it is difficult to separate these three processes.

Planning must have elements of evaluation in it and must rely on research techniques to gather data to serve as the basis for recommendations.

Research is frequently carried out in order to come to evaluative conclusions.

Evaluation often leads to conclusions or recommendations that might then serve as planning guidelines.

Within this chapter, however, the three processes are dealt with separately as elements of administrative concern. In each case, the goals, methods, and typical examples of planning studies, research projects, and evaluative reports are presented.

COMPREHENSIVE COMMUNITY PLANNING FOR RECREATION

In Chapter 7, planning was described with particular reference to the acquisition and development of recreation and park facilities. This is only one aspect of the planning function, but it is a major one. For example, the International City Managers Association states:

> A comprehensive plan is an official public document adopted by a local government as a policy guide to decisions about the physical development of the community. It indicates in a general way how the leaders of the government want the community to develop in the next 20 to 30 years.[1]

Many community master plans deal more broadly with all elements of community development, such as the total physical development of the community (including highways and industrial and residential development), education, health and welfare services, and other relevant concerns. Within such planning, recreation and park development is usually a major concern, and separate planning studies may be carried out in this area, as part of a larger planning process.

Who carries out the comprehensive planning process? It may be any of the following:

1. A planning unit or office in municipal government. Large cities frequently employ planning experts to conduct surveys, analyze operations, and assist in carrying out comprehensive planning studies.

2. A professional planning firm. A number of major firms throughout the country specialize in conducting master-planning studies. In some cases, they

also carry out architectural assignments, developing actual building or facility designs or detailed proposals for urban renewal.

3. A citizens' planning committee. Frequently a group of interested citizens representing various organizations, professions, or areas of social concern may be formed to carry out planning studies. They may employ technical assistants as needed, but essentially they are responsible for the project themselves.

Generally, there is agreement that, whatever agency is responsible for carrying out the study, citizens of the community themselves should be deeply involved in the process. Schatz writes:

> What is basic to this whole plan is the fact that comprehensive planning is an on-going process of people, organizations, and government working together. It is not simply the adoption by a City Council of a "Master Plan." It is the bringing together of representatives of organizations and consumer groups to bring new and needed services and facilities to communities having the greatest need, and very basic to this entire concept is the involvement of citizens and consumers for which new pro-grams and facilities are being developed. If there is one message (to deliver) it is the need to involve citizen participation in a meaningful way, in all phases of planning, from the work on separate components and surveys to the more complex job of developing necessary budgets and then overseeing expenditures.[2]

The process of comprehensive community planning usually includes the following steps:

1. Statement of goals and objectives

2. Basic studies—development of a base map, land-use map and analysis, inventory of available recreation facilities, business and residential trends, and population projections

3. Reevaluation of goals and objectives, based on new information, establishment of new priorities, or statements of need

4. Development of master plan dealing with land use, transportation, location of community facilities, open space, highways, and broad definition of industrial- and residential-use areas

5. Implementation studies resulting in specific proposals for capital improvement programs or detailed development plans

6. Recommended implementation devices, such as proposed zoning ordinances and maps, subdivision regulations, and building and housing codes

7. Development of urban renewal plan, where appropriate

8. Community action, which involves actual proposals being put before the municipal government, or voted on by the constituency, or submitted as plans requiring special funding to the federal government

Goals and objectives of planning

Goals and objectives may vary from city to city, but in general, they stress the overall goal of improving the physical environment and the social and economic structure of the community to make possible a better life for all. For example, the Chicago Department of City Planning[3] developed the following set of purposes for a major planning study in 1964:

1. To improve the residential environment by eliminating substandard housing, increasing the variety of housing choice, expanding recreation space, improving schools and other community facilities, relocating industrial plants scattered in residential areas, and reducing traffic volume on residential streets.

2. To strengthen and diversify the economy by renewing and expanding industrial areas, improving transportation facilities, strengthening the central business district, renewing outlying business areas, supporting the expansion needs of institutions for research, higher education, and medical care, and by improving facilities for education.

3. To enlarge human opportunities by improving public education facilities, supporting educational and medical institutions, increasing employment opportunities, improving public services, supporting freedom of housing choice throughout the city, and increasing the variety of housing choice within communities.

Planning methods

The traditional approach to recreation and park planning was described in Chapter 7. This approach places major reliance on the use of open space and facility standards in planning the development of parks, playgrounds, community centers, pools, golf courses, beaches, and similar facilities. A number of other techniques are used in urban recreation and park planning today, including community surveys, constituency studies, overall agency evaluation, program and participant evaluation, studies based on needs projections, needs index studies, systems analysis, feasibility studies, facilities evaluation, and simulation planning methods.

Each of these approaches will be briefly described, with examples given in a number of cases.

Community surveys. These represent one of the most familiar and useful ways of determining community needs and developing recommendations for recreation and park development.

Community surveys may range from relatively inexpensive projects to studies that cost hundreds of thousands of dollars and more. They usually involve developing a total inventory of available facilities and programs; analyzing population statistics and projections, social factors, economic and tax-base projections, residential trends, measures of social stability, climatic and regional factors, and similar forms of data to determine community needs; and developing a short- and long-range set of priorities and specific recommendations for the recreation and park development.

Surveys that are specifically concerned with recreation and park development usually include a history of the development of this form of service in the community and a description of the current administration and program structure. They may provide a neighborhood-by-neighborhood analysis of available facilities and services and may also evaluate what is offered. Normally, they would identify areas of greatest need in the community and would suggest specific sites for park or other recreation facility development. As a rule, recreation and park surveys do not go deeply into the programs provided by other than public agencies and do not explore the way in which the recreation systems operate.

Constituency studies. The constituency study is one that focuses on the mem-

---

1973 PARK VISITOR SURVEY HANDBACK QUESTIONNAIRE

JOB NO. 0 4 8

Parks Canada   Parcs Canada

KEJIMKUJIK NATIONAL PARK

№ 03262

PLEASE ANSWER ALL OF THE FOLLOWING QUESTIONS

1. How long do you plan to be away from home on your trip?
   |___| Number of nights

2. How long did your party stay in this Park on this trip?
   |___| Number of hours (If you did not stay overnight) OR |___| Number of nights

3. If you stayed <u>overnight</u> away from home on this trip, please indicate the <u>number of nights</u> spent in each of the following types of accommodation.

INSIDE THE PARK		REST OF TRIP TO DATE		
|___| Tent	|___| Tent trailer	|___| Tent	|___| Tent trailer	|___| Rented cabin
|___| Self-contained (camper truck)	|___| Other	|___| Self-contained (camper truck)	|___| Commercial house-keeping cottage	|___| Private home or cottage
|___| Cabin trailer		|___| Cabin trailer	|___| Hotel or motel	|___| Other

4. Where is your present home located?

_____ AND _____ OR _____
Town or city   Province or state   Country other than Canada/U.S.A.

5. Which one type of overnight accommodation would you prefer to use in or near this National Park?   (Check one only)

1 ☐ Privately operated campground <u>fully serviced</u> (Sewer connections, toilets, showers, food concession, etc.)

2 ☐ Privately operated campground <u>semi-serviced</u> (Toilets, small food concessions, etc.)

3 ☐ National Park campground <u>fully serviced</u>) (Sewer connections, toilets, showers, food)

4 ☐ National Park campground <u>semi-serviced</u> (Toilets, firewood)

5 ☐ National Park campground unserviced or primitive

6 ☐ Rented Cabin – no housekeeping

7 ☐ Commercial cabin – housekeeping

8 ☐ Hotel or motel

9 ☐ Private home or cottage

10 ☐ Other (please name) _____

6. Did you experience any difficulty in finding campground accommodation within the Park?   (Please check all that apply)

1 ☐ No difficulty   2 ☐ Forced to arrive early (before 3 p.m.)   3 ☐ Campgrounds Full - Camped in Park's overflow accommodation   4 ☐ Campgrounds Full - Will look for accommodation outside the Park   5 ☐ Other _____

7. How many times did your party use each of the following Park facilities on this visit to the Park?

|___| Picnic area	|___| Day use area	|___| Exhibit	|___| Unguided hiking trails
|___| Viewpoints	|___| Campgrounds	|___| Personal contacts with naturalist	|___| Guided walks
|___| Serviced Beach	|___| Wilderness campground area	|___| Exhibit trailer	|___| Self-guided interpretive trails
|___| Unserviced beach	|___| Outdoor theatre	|___| Information bureau	|___| Canoe routes
|___| Boat launching, mooring or docking site			|___| Fishing areas

8. Which, if any, would you have used if they had been available in this Park?

☐ Boat Tours   ☐ "Bike-Only" access campgrounds   ☐ Motor Boating

☐ "Boat-Only" access campgrounds   ☐ Cycle Trails   ☐ Other (name) _____

9. If you have any comments you would like to make on your visit to this National Park, please make them below:

_____

_____

AS YOU LEAVE THE PARK, PLEASE DEPOSIT THIS CARD IN THE BOX LOCATED AT THE PARK EXIT. THANK YOU.

If you are unable to deposit this card, please mail to: Chief, Planning Division, National Parks Service, 400 Laurier Ave. West, Ottawa, K1A 0H4

OFFICIAL USE ONLY

☐☐ DEPOSIT BOX   ☐☐ DAY   0 MONTH   1   ☐ MAIL-BACK   *FRANCAIS AU VERSO*

NPC 518K (4-73)

Fig. 10-1. Visitor survey form, Kejimkujik National Park.

bership of a particular organization, or those who use or *might* use the services of a municipal department or other public or voluntary agency. Schatz writes that the primary purposes of a constituency study are:

1. To provide data to the agencies participating on the distribution of their members and registrants.

2. To provide information for the general community about geographical location of persons served by the agencies which would be meaningful in identifying population groups with unmet needs.[4]

To determine the residential location of individuals using a particular agency or community service, some departments have moved into computer analysis.

They have developed electronic monitoring systems under which each participant who uses a major park or other facility has a plastic registration card that he must slip into a sensing device at the entrance to the facility. His residence and other relevant information are electronically recorded; by this device it is possible to tell at any time *how* facilities are used (in terms of the age, neighborhood, or other characteristics of users) or *what* use is made of recreation resources by people from any particular neighborhood.

As an example of such data-gathering procedures, the Town of Ramapo, New York, uses a plastic photo-identification card for admission to certain facilities. It has Hollerith coding to facilitate computer analysis of attendance data, and provides information on sex, age group, geographical residential area, type of membership (seasonal or daily), and similar information. When the card is put into the sensor, the correct fee is indicated to the gate official. As a planning mechanism used during a recent summer, this device gathered evidence that the major users of the town's swimming pool were mothers and preschool children. There were few male adults, except on weekends, and few teenagers. Based on data gathered, the Ramapo Recreation and Park Commission was able to justify a strong need for a second pool and to develop precise guidelines for its construction: a larger deck area, a women's bathhouse, and a kiddie pool.

A somewhat similar approach is used in many large outdoor recreation facilities by state and federal agencies. In the National Parks of Canada, visitor survey forms and checklists have been used to determine the volume and type of traffic, the place of origin, the location of accommodation, and the length of stay in the region. For example, the Park Visitor Survey Questionnaire used in Kejimkujik National Park in Nova Scotia (Fig. 10-1) gathers comprehensive information regarding visitors' trip plans, nature of vehicle or shelter, preferred facilities or accommodations, and similar data. Because of the bilingual nature of the Canadian population, it is printed on one side in English and the other in French.

Lane County, Oregon, carried out an in-depth study of its residents' recreational interests and participation. Using a detailed map (Fig. 10-2) of Lane County, the City of Eugene, Oregon, and adjacent park and recreation districts, participants in the study were asked to provide specific information about their schooling, work responsibilities, club memberships, use of recreational vehicles, and similar matters (Fig. 10-3). They were then provided with a list of eighty recreational pursuits, covering all the major hobbies, sports, creative activities, and similar categories. In response to this, they were asked to indicate their three favorite choices in each category of play, the activities in which they had participated regularly during the past 3 years, and the reasons why they do *not* participate in certain activities.

Some communities have carried out extensive analyses of their residents' recreational attitudes and interests. For example, the City of Wooster, Ohio, conducted a major study of the leisure behavior, attitudes, and opinions of various age groups and both sexes. In the Female Adult Questionnaire, fifty-two questions were asked (many with extensive subquestions) dealing with such

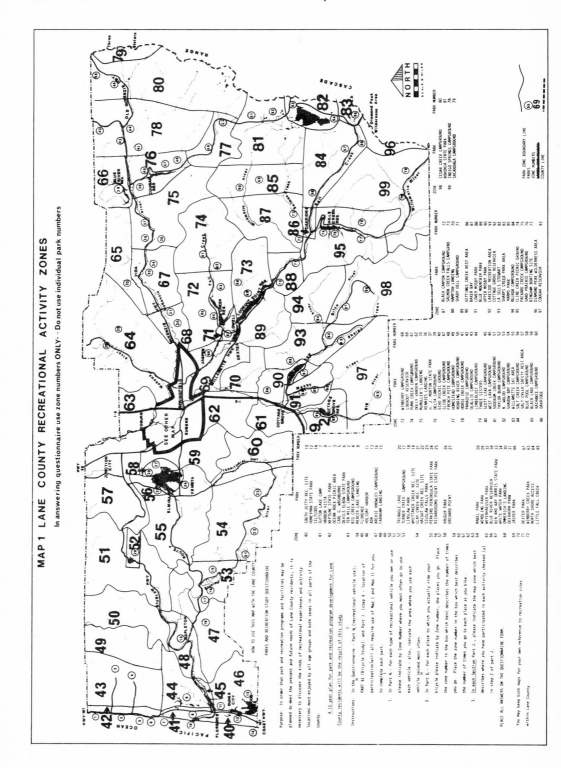

№ 15516

LANE COUNTY PARKS and RECREATION STUDY

Conducted by Lane Council of Governments with the kind co-operation of your School District.

Sponsored by: Lane County Park Department; River Road Park and Recreation District; Willamalane Park and Recreation District; City of Eugene Parks and Recreation Department

INSTRUCTIONS:
1, Please read the accompanying letter before starting to answer this confidential questionnaire.
2. Independently of each other, each member of your family age 10 years and over, is requested to fill out this questionnaire in spite of any seeming repetition that may be involved. You and your family have been especially selected to answer this questionnaire and therefore, completed forms from each member of your family are needed in order that we may plan for your family's park and recreation needs with the best information possible.

Note: All information which you provide will be confidential.

PART A – FAMILY INFORMATION

NOTE: (1) Parts A and I will be the same for all members of your family. Parents may wish to complete these parts on all forms for their children age 10 and over in order to insure their being correct and complete on all forms.
(2) All other questions are to be answered independently by each family member.

Family Member	Age in Years	Living at home? Yes	No
Man of the house			
Lady of the house			
Child One			
Child Two			
Child Three			
Child Four			
Child Five			
Child Six			
Other			

PART B – What is the age and sex of the family member whose form this will be?
(1) MY PRESENT AGE IS: (Check one only)
(1) 10 - 12 ☐ (4) 20 - 30 ☐ (7) 63 - 70 ☐
(2) 13 - 15 ☐ (5) 31 - 45 ☐ 8) 71 and over ☐
(3) 16 - 19 ☐ (6) 46 - 62 ☐
(2) SEX: Male ☐ Female ☐ (Check one)

PART C – My Address is:
House Number ____ Street ____ City/Town/R.R. ____
What is the name of the public school nearest your home?
____ School District

T / B / S

PART D – EDUCATIONAL BACKGROUND
How many years of schooling have you completed? (Check highest one only)

Grade 0-8 ☐ (1)
Grade 9-11 ☐ (2)
Grade 12 ☐ (3)
Vocational Training ☐ (4)
Some College ☐ (5)
College Graduate ☐ (6)
Post Graduate (college) ☐ (7)

Please name college from which you received your highest degree, if any
____ College
____ Degree
Are you now a college Studer.t? Yes ☐ No ☐
Name of college if "yes"
____

PART E – OCCUPATION
(1) Occupation of major wage earner in your family (If you are a farmer indicate crop, acreage) ____
(2) What does this person do on his/her job? ____
(3) If you are not the major earner what is your occupation? ____
(4) If you are retired or unemployed what was your last main job? ____

PART F – USUAL WORKING TIME
This question is included in order that we may find out when and how long you work each day of the week. Indicate the number of hours you work each day – PLACE THE HOURS YOU WORK IN THE CORRECT SHIFT POSITION FOR EACH DAY YOU WORK.

DAY	SHIFT: Day Shift	Evening Shift	Night Shift	Rotating
Monday				
Tuesday				
Wednesday				
Thursday				
Friday				
Saturday				
Sunday				

PART G – CLUB MEMBERSHIP
Are you a member of any clubs or organizations within Lane County? Yes ☐ No ☐. If "yes," please name and indicate the place (City, town, etc.) where you usually attend meetings.

Organization	Place

PART H - BICYCLE STUDY
This section is designed to find out how you personally use any bicycle you may own so that bicycling opportunities may be improved for you.
(1) Do you ever ride a bicycle? Yes____ No____. If "No", go on to Part I (Recreational Vehicle Use). If "Yes", please continue below.
(2) (A) In the column marked "Check" please check (✓) the places to which you ride your bike.
(B) Refer to the maps which we delivered to you with this questionnaire and find out which map zone you ride to for each place you go on your bicycle.
(C) Put the zone number in the "Number of Times" column which best describes how often each year you go to each place. Use one zone number only for each place you go to on your bike.

PLACE	Check ✓	0-10 Times	11-20 Times	21-50 Times	Almost Daily Allowing for Weather	Almost Daily Regardless of Weather
		NUMBER OF TIMES TO EACH PLACE WITHIN LAST YEAR				
01 School						
02 Friends House						
03 Swimming						
04 Picnic Area						
05 Other Rec. Centers						
06 Downtown						
07 Grocery Store						
08 Bicycle Hiking						
09 Shopping Centers						
10 To Work						
11 Other (Specify)						

(3) In which season do you most often ride your bicycle? (Indicate per cent for each season.)
(1) Summer ____% (2) Fall ____% (3) Winter ____%
Spring ____%
(4) With 100% as a total, what % of your bicycle riding is done in the:
(1) Morning (6:00 a.m. to Noon) ____%
(2) Afternoon (Noon to 6:00 p.m.) ____%
(3) Evening (6:00 p.m. to Midnight) ____%
(4) Night (Midnight to 6:00 a.m.) ____%
(5) With 100% as a total indicate the purposes for which you use your bicycle:
(1) Recreation ____% (pleasure, exercise, touring, racing)
(2) Transportation ____% (work, school, shopping).
(6) Using 100% as a total, what % of your bicycle riding is done on:
(1) Week days? ____%
(2) Week ends? ____%

PART I – RECREATIONAL VEHICLE USE
(By Map I or Map II Zone Numbers)

You and your family received two maps with this questionnaire. Each map is divided into numbered zones containing parks or other activity places with which you may be familiar.

We would like to know where you go for recreational purposes **within Lane County** with each type of vehicle you own.

For each type of vehicle you use please indicate where you go by **Zone Number** when you use each vehicle within Lane County.

In column one please indicate the zone number of the place you most often go for each vehicle you use.

In column two please indicate the zone number of the places you go to second most often to use each vehicle.

Please indicate only the two most often visited recreation places by zone number for each vehicle used.

TYPE OF VEHICLE	Number of Each Owned by Family	(1) Used by Zone Number	(2) Often Used by Zone Number
01 Passenger Car			
02 Truck			
03 Pick-up Camper			
04 4-Wheel Dr. Vehicles			
05 All-Terrain Vehicle			
06 Dune Buggy			
07 Antique Car			
08 Car Camper			
09 Tent Trailer			
10 House Trailer			
11 Motor Home			
12 Motorcycle			
13 Trail/Mini Bike			
14 Horse/Other Animal			
15 Bicycle			
16 Snowmobile			
17 Sail Boat			
18 Motor Boat			
19 Row Boat			
20 Canoe			
21 Kayak			
22 House Boat			
23 Go-Cart			
24 Sports Car			
25 Other (Specify)			

Fig. 10-3

elements as work schedules, TV watching, vacation patterns, outdoor recreation interests, need for children's play opportunities, suggestions for park development, use of community recreation facilities, present hobby, creative, or social interests, family's possession of musical, sports, or other recreational equipment, and similar matters. A final section, samples of which are shown in Fig. 10-4, dealt with respondents' views of the Wooster Park and Recreation Department's operation.

In some cases, constituency studies may deal with participation patterns or needs within a specific area of activity. For example, the Council for the Arts in Westchester County, New York, recently conducted a comprehensive study of cultural life and activities at the request of the County Executive Officer. It asked residents such questions as:

> How many cultural events did any adult member of your family attend last month? In Westchester ________ In NYC ________ In environs (Rockland, Putnam, Conn.) ________

CITY OF WOOSTER, OHIO
Department of Parks and Recreation

	Completely disagree	Partially disagree	Partially agree	Completely agree
I am satisfied with the Parks and Recreation facilities in Wooster	————	————	————	————
The quality of leadership provided by the Department of Parks and Recreation is good	————	————	————	————
There is a need to coordinate the existing Recreation Programs being offered by various organizations in Wooster	————	————	————	————
The City of Wooster should acquire additional open space for Park and Recreation purposes	————	————	————	————
The City of Wooster should update and install imaginative new playground equipment in neighborhood parks	————	————	————	————
I would be willing to pay additional taxes to provide more park and recreation services	————	————	————	————
More competitive athletics for females should be offered by the Department of Parks and Recreation	————	————	————	————
I would be willing to volunteer my time to help supervise recreation programs	————	————	————	————

Fig. 10-4

Have you ever subscribed to a performing arts series in Westchester? _____ Which ones? _____ Do you currently subscribe? _____ If not, why did you drop it? _____

Have you attended concerts, lectures, films, exhibits related to the arts at Westchester colleges, clubs, libraries, churches? _____ Which ones? _____

How would you rate the arts opportunities in your own community? Outstanding _____, Very good _____, Good _____, Average _____, Poor _____

Other questions ask specifically about the kinds of attractions or events respondents would like to attend, the most appropriate locations, the admissions charges they would be willing to pay, the most suitable times of the week, and the types of facilities, such as arts centers or auditoriums, that are most needed in the county. In designing and carrying out such constituency studies, it is essential to develop questions with extreme care, to ensure that they cover the key issues or problem areas. They should be simple enough to encourage a high rate of response and should permit graded choices of responses, rather than simple yes-or-no answers. Finally, careful sampling procedures must be followed to ensure that the people being surveyed are reasonably representative of the population of the community.

Overall agency evaluations. Evaluative studies may be carried on as part of the community planning process, or they may be done as part of a periodic process of self-study to assist a department in upgrading its entire operation or separate program elements. The most effective means of evaluating a municipal recreation and park department is through the use of nationally-accepted standards and criteria.

The National Recreation and Park Association has published a useful manual, *Evaluation and Self-Study of Recreation and Park Agencies: A Guide with Standards and Evaluative Criteria.* This document, which is an improved version of an instrument originally developed by the Great Lakes Standards Committee, includes thirty-five standards (major guidelines for effective practice) and 140 criteria (substatements that provide a basis for judging performance on each of these standards). These are used in measuring the effectiveness of a department under six major categories: (1) philosophy and goals, (2) administration, (3) programing, (4) personnel, (5) areas, facilities, and equipment, and (6) evaluation.

To use this manual, a study team must systematically observe a municipal recreation and park department in action, holding interviews and gathering varied forms of data to determine whether the agency is living up to recommended practices. In scoring the final report, it is possible to obtain figures through which a given department may be compared to other agencies. However, this is not the major purpose of the evaluation; rather, it is chiefly used to provide a profile of strengths and weaknesses within each administrative category and thus to indicate the need for improvement where it exists.

The Bureau of Outdoor Recreation has also published a manual, *How Effective Are Your Community Recreation Services?*[5] This document suggests major goals for the evaluation of local recreation and park agencies and presents a number of useful guidelines for measuring effective performance and for involving citizen groups in the evaluation process. It outlines a number of specific areas that should be studied, such as (1) ratings by users, (2) degree of crowdedness, (3) upkeep of facilities, (4) helpfulness of staff members, (5) hours of operation, (6) safety practices, (7) hours of attendance, (8) physical accessibility of facilities, and (9) variety of leisure opportunities offered. Many of its suggestions for successful citizen involvement in evaluation were derived from two pilot studies carried out in Rockford, Illinois, and Washington, D.C.

Evaluation of voluntary agencies. In addition to public departments, many voluntary agencies carry out a process of self-evaluation. The Boys' Clubs of America publishes several manuals to assist its local club organizations in carefully reviewing their administration, program, camping, and day camping processes. Stressing the need for rigorous and regular self-study, the national organization states:

> Evaluation is a regular, integral part of Boys' Club operation, not just a procedure which is done because of pressure from an outside group or because of some crisis. The really helpful evaluation is the result of an honest desire on the part of the Board, the Executive and the Staff to determine how well the Club is doing and what can be done to improve itself . . .
>
> Although an evaluation may be highly organized and formalized and include all aspects of program, it may also be limited to one particular phase. . . . It may also be used as a guide to the establishment of programs in new Boys' Clubs or for expanding and improving the operation of existing ones.[6]

Guidelines are presented in the Boys' Clubs evaluation manuals that outline desirable practices actually found in many clubs, as well as the opinions of many administrators and board members. In the Program Evaluation Manual, for example, as many as fifty or more recommended practices are suggested for each of the following program categories: (1) arts and crafts, (2) citizenship education, (3) cultural programs, (4) game rooms, (5) guidance program, (6) health program, (7) organized small groups, (8) physical program, and (9) special events.

In addition to rating the club's performance of each practice, the study team (which may include board, administration and staff members, as well as outside consultants, past and present members, and community representatives) is also encouraged to make suggestions for recommended changes. Although individual Boys' Clubs are not expected to live up to a national model, this evaluative process should help each individual center develop to its own fullest potential.

Many agencies carry out self-studies on a case analysis basis without using special manuals or guidelines of any type. For example, in a large Eastern city, a Young Men's Christian Association located in the downtown area of the city had for a number of years been suffering from declining attendance and community support. A new director determined to analyze the causes of this problem and to develop a number of recommended solutions. With the assistance of staff and board members, he identified the following conclusions.

The Y's problems stemmed from the following causes: (1) it was in an area that had increasingly been characterized by run-down housing, poverty, and a welfare population with a high crime rate, thus discouraging many former members who now lived in other parts of the city from continuing to be active in it; (2) the facility itself was deteriorating, and the building was not as attractive or functional as it should have been; and (3) there was a high rate of staff turnover, with inexperienced personnel in key positions.

The recommended solutions were the following: (1) to improve personnel practices through more careful hiring procedures and better communication and training programs to upgrade the motivation of all workers; (2) to carry out certain cosmetic changes in the building, through better maintenance, regular painting, and the relocation of areas, as well as to make a major investment in a badly needed new heating system; (3) to carry out intensive membership drives under a new 3-month membership option (as opposed to the past daily or annual policy); (4) to make the membership coeducational and to make a strong push for women as staff members and program participants; (5) to strengthen the program by providing courses for all age groups, an enriched cardiovascular fitness program, and a number of innovative activities and trip features that had not been tried before; and, finally, (6) better public relations, including both external and internal media.

Program and participant evaluation. In addition to such overall agency evaluations, many departments carry out separate analyses of individual program activities or seasonal efforts or reviews of participant involvement.

Typically, a municipal recreation and park department might require systematic evaluations of all major program elements. To illustrate, the Williamsport, Pennsylvania, Recreation Commission has each summer playground director fill out a detailed analysis sheet reviewing his program, at summer's end. This form asks such questions as:

Was your facility adequate as a playground site? _____ What could have been added or changed? _____

Was the equipment issued adequate for your program? _____ What other equipment would have been helpful? _____

Was there theft or vandalism on your playground? _____ What actions did you take to prevent this from happening? _____

Was the mobile games unit well-received on your playground? _____ Which games were used the most? _____

Would you recommend more citywide events to supplement your program? _____ Suggestions: _____

No standard program evaluation form would be useful in all agencies and situations. Instead, most departments develop their own forms, including the questions and areas that seem most crucial and that deal with their own local circumstances.

In addition to studying programs, some departments, particularly therapeutic agencies, carry out systematic evaluation of participant behavior. Forms such as the Record of Patient Involvement (Fig. 10-5) are used in team evaluation meetings for patient assessment.

Studies based on projections of needs. Many planning studies carried out by public recreation and park departments are aimed at meeting needs that are anticipated by a given date. Usually these involve developing population projections as well as anticipated rates of growth for industry, residential housing, and other elements of community life. Based on these background figures, planning reports identify probable needs as of a certain date and make specific recommendations for land acquisition and the development of parks and other recreation facilities.

Almost invariably, such planning studies concentrate solely on the development of facilities and make specific proposals for the development of parks, land acquisition, and raising the per capita acreage of open space and recreation re-

RECORD OF PATIENT INVOLVEMENT

Date _____ Weekly session no. _____ Participant's name _____

Activity or program session _____ Group leader _____

Categories of observable participation	Level of performance				Comments*
	Never	Occasionally	Often	Most of the time	
Appears idle and alone in the midst of the group					
Listens passively					
Shows interest but comments only when called upon					
Speaks to others but without reference to self					
Reports personal experiences with insight					
Seeks information					
Speaks with support of others' feelings					
Establishes relation- ships with others					
Expresses courage, ambition, personal aspirations					

*Focus comments on evidence of change or no change in behavior, efforts to reach out, and examples of progress.

Fig. 10-5

sources. They may also identify goals and priorities of the system, but normally they do not deal with operational concerns, staffing, or the involvement of other types of recreational agencies—voluntary, private, or commercial.

Needs index approach to planning. Simply described, the needs index planning method consists of carrying out a total *inventory* of all recreation and park resources and programs within each neighborhood or district of a city. A second study is made of all *demographic* and *socioeconomic factors* within each area that might indicate total social need. This might include percentage of families on welfare, frequency of juvenile delinquency, incidence of broken families, deteriorated housing health statistics, and similar figures—all of which, taken together, support a high level of need for social services.

By combining the two elements, it is possible to determine which areas within a city should have the highest priority for new recreation and park facilities and programs. For example, the district with the lowest amount of existing facilities and the highest statistics of delinquency, welfare, and other social problems would be given a high priority; the district with strong existing facilities and with a low level of social need would be given a low priority.

Systems analysis approach to planning. The general theory of systems analysis and planning is presented in Chapter 2, along with summaries of such special approaches as PERT-TIME, the Critical Path Method, and PPBS (Planning-Program-Budgeting Systems). As indicated there, most recreation and park departments are not extensive enough and have too many human variables in their operation to make efficient use of these approaches.

However, in the planning and ongoing administration of large-scale networks of outdoor recreation resources, such as the operations of the National Park Service, National Forest Service, or large state park agencies, systems analysis may readily be used. Such elements as the numbers of summer visitors, types of appropriate land uses, environmental effects of use, operational costs, income from fees, special problems of control, and similar matters are considered in a systems approach to decision-making. In this way, policies regarding the opening or development of new parks or recreation area, policing methods, admissions and fee structures, or environmental controls may be determined.

Similarly, systems analysis has been applied to the field of therapeutic recreation service. Peterson has defined the purpose of a therapeutic recreation service system as:

> . . . to provide opportunities for individuals with limitations to gain leisure skills and attitudes, and/or to exercise recreative abilities within a framework of preventative, sustaining, or remedial services in order to enable or encourage recreative experience.[7]

Seen as a flow pattern, therapeutic recreation consists of three elements: input, transformation, and output. *Input* consists of patients or clients who are served, and the equipment, facilities, or leadership that provide service. *Transformation* involves the actual provision of activities, counseling, or other services. *Output* is the resulting recreative behavior of the patient or client. In analyzing this process, one must take into account the elements of administration, supervision, leadership, and education or counseling, as well as the specific goals of service.

Based on this background, Peterson[8] has built an eight-stage model for program planning in therapeutic recreation:

1. *Conceptualization.* This involves an examination of the sponsoring agency and an identification of its goals for the target population.
2. *Investigation.* Alternative ways of achieving each of the stated objectives are developed.
3. *Analysis.* The various program possibilities listed in Stage 2 are analyzed in terms of their possible strengths and weaknesses; at this stage, they may be redefined or placed in different combinations.
4. *Determination.* At this point, a selection of service components is made, based on those which appear to have the greatest potential for meeting program goals.
5. *Design.* The planning group develops a fuller statement of behavioral objectives for each program element, the process or interaction technique designed to bring them about, and criteria tests to evaluate their effectiveness.
6. *Operations planning.* This involves the concrete steps necessary to put the plan into action—purchase of supplies and equipment, assignment of personnel, development of schedules, and similar actions.
7. *Implementation.* The program is put into effect and operated for the specified period of time.
8. *Evaluation.* Each service component is evaluated for effectiveness. Specific elements (behavioral objectives, interaction approaches, or test criteria) may be redesigned at this point for future use.

Feasibility studies. Feasibility studies involve sharply focused examinations of the need for a specific type of facility or program service and the social, economic, or ecological factors that should be taken into account by recreation and parks planners who are considering its implementation. Feasibility studies usually are carried on *before* developing such special facilities as ice rinks, sportsmen's centers, arts complexes, or civic auditoriums. The U.S. Forest Service, in cooperation with the National Ski Areas Association, published a planning manual showing how feasibility studies might be used in the planning process when considering the development of major ski centers and winter resort areas.[9]

Among the specific elements to be examined in depth are (1) the capacity and quality of the land under consideration; (2) the kinds of utility systems that would be needed for water, sewage, power transmission, and telephones, and their effect on the environment; (3) appropriate location and carrying capacity of lifts; (4) effects of wind, sun, and water run-off patterns on sites being considered; (5) skier safety and avalanche control factors; (6) road and development costs; and (7) projected costs for development, balanced against probable user demand and income potential. Similar feasibility study approaches have been developed for many other types of recreation and park facilities.

Facilities evaluation. Planners have also developed detailed methods of examining recreation facilities and have formulated extensive guidelines for their design and construction. As an example, the National Institute of Senior Centers has carried out an extensive study of senior centers throughout the United States under a grant from the Administration on Aging.[10] Based on nine in-depth examinations of leading centers in community centers, housing projects, schools, or separate facilities and thirteen other supplementary site visits, the study attempted to answer the question, "What constitutes a building design, including architectural features, equipment and furnishing, that is most conducive for the optimum functioning of its members and staff?" Directors of the centers were asked to respond to the following questions:

1. From the standpoint of the physical facility, what do you like best about this center?
2. What particular architectural design features do you like best about this center?
3. From the standpoint of the physical planning of this center, what do you think are the worst problems?
4. If you could design this center all over again, what are the first changes you would make?
5. If you could make five rooms in this center larger, which five would you select?
6. If you could add five new rooms to this center, what would you add?
7. If you could add five new pieces of equipment, what would you add?
8. From the standpoint of heating, ventilation or air conditioning, what problems are most troublesome?
9. Would you want to make any changes in the electric lighting or in the electrical outlets in this center?
10. If you could exchange or replace any of your furniture or furnishings, which pieces would you replace?
11. What are good features, and what are the problems that you associate with the following spaces:

a. Hallways	g. Auditorium	m. First aid rooms
b. Multi-purpose room	h. Dining room	n. Storage
c. Entry area	i. Kitchen	o. Offices
d. Quiet lounge	j. Craft rooms	p. Bathrooms
e. Library	k. Meeting rooms	q. Parking
f. Noisy lounge	l. Consultation rooms	r. Outdoor recreation

Based on the information uncovered by the self-assessment and site examinations, the study identified hundreds of guidelines for the design of the various facilities and areas within senior centers. As a single example, the guidelines for entry areas included recommendations for *Arrival and Departure*, covering the following items: (1) storage for car or mini-bus; (2) sheltered and illuminated approach; (3) lever door hardware (avoid heavy doors); (4) automatic doors; (5) entry without steps; (6) vestibule to accommodate wheelchairs; (7) slip-proof pavement; (8) car and bus turnabout; (9) parking area; (10) service entry; (11) loading dock; (12) concealed garbage and refuse storage and pick-up area.[11] Similar recommendations for every other aspect of the centers design can either be used in the planning of *new* facilities, or in the evaluation and possible re-design of existing ones.

Simulation planning methods. A final method of decision-making that is used by planners involves the use of simulation models. These are being used experimentally in large-scale industrial concerns or government projects and involve constructing theoretical models involving the key elements in the organization's operation. Different courses of action are then tested, usually with the help of a computer, and the outcomes are identified. This is too sophisticated a technique to be used by most recreation and park agencies. However, in simplified form, simulation may be extremely helpful to recreation planners and decision-makers by playing administrative games or using psychodramas or sociodramas. They are also useful in the process of conflict resolution, and staff training.

RESEARCH AND EVALUATION IN URBAN RECREATION AND PARK DEPARTMENTS

Apart from the specific function of planning for the intelligent development of recreation and park departments, there has been an increasing interest in more effective research and evaluation processes in many community recreation and park departments. If the field is to justify its claim for support, it is obvious that it will be increasingly necessary to document its values and outcomes. Furthermore, an effective research and evaluation program should lead to a higher level of public understanding of recreation as a significant form of public service.

Few recreation and park departments have made sufficient use of research. Ver Lee writes:

> There are reasons why the research function is treated lightly in many local recreation agencies. Time and money are at the head of the list—time to keep up with rapidly growing demands and money to hire special research personnel or to buy research services. Also, recreation administrators generally are program oriented; hence, departmental financial resources are usually funneled into new program activities rather than into new staff services. . . . In recent years, there appears to have been a shift from this approach. Municipalities, particularly the larger ones, are becoming more research conscious. Help from foundations, the federal and state governments, our own national organizations, and the colleges and universities has been a stimulus. Research in some recreation departments has benefited from this over-all change in approach.[12]

In part, the reluctance of many recreation and park administrators to move more fully into developing effective research programs has not been because of lack of capability but because of a lack of understanding of just what research *is*. For some, it has appeared to be an overly scholarly or intellectual concern, involved with abstractions, and of little practical value in program development or the administrative process. However, the increasing importance being given to social problems in many larger cities has encouraged the use of research techniques to develop meaningful solutions to these problems. The use of systems analysis and the increasingly critical view being taken of the operations of municipal government have made it increasingly necessary to develop sound methods of evaluation and research in public recreation and park departments.

Gradually, a full awareness of the meaning of research has evolved. Today, it is understood as an organized search for knowledge. Its purpose is to discover accurate answers to questions or to test theory, through the application of scientific procedures. Customarily, it involves the following five steps.

1. A concise formulation of a problem or hypothesis to be investigated or tested
2. The development of a study or experimental design appropriate to this problem or hypothesis

3. Carrying out of the study, including establishing test conditions or demonstration programs or simply gathering data
4. Scoring, analyzing, and interpreting data
5. Presentation of conclusions and developing recommendations for action or further study

In general, research in such areas as public administration or educational, rehabilitative, or social work services may be assigned to two possible approaches: pure research and applied research. *Pure research* is largely theoretical in nature. It explores fundamental issues, problems, or hypotheses in an attempt to identify cause-and-effect relationships or basic concepts that need not have any direct connection to action programs or specifically useful purposes. On the other hand, *applied research* is usually directed to finding solutions or information that *can* be applied in meaningful and practical ways. Pure research may prove to be the opening wedge that leads to applied research, and in many ways it can ultimately be of great practical value.

Research may require highly sophisticated techniques for assessing benefits of recreational experience, the costs of programs and facilities, determining appropriate activities for different organizations or populations, and achieving a realistic order of priorities for public and voluntary agencies. Sherwood has written:

> If a growing and more successful evaluation research program is to become part of our social action culture, evaluation research must be recognized as consisting of a broad set of strategies and skills which transcend the narrowly defined technical skills of social research—research design, measurement, statistical inference, and the like. These . . . include elements of sociopolitics . . . strategies for gaining access to the required information, getting and maintaining support for the evaluation effort, and . . . creating a climate for . . . the sometimes slow-to-arrive findings and for the incorporation of these findings in the decision-making process.[13]

Uses of research in recreation and park administration

Typical problem areas to which research may be directed in recreation and park administration include the following:

1. The determination of needs and interests in recreation program development through analysis of user preferences, populations to be served, trends in the field, and similar studies
2. The analysis of personnel policies, including the qualifications of personnel, staff functions and roles, job titles, orientation and in-service training, the assignment of staff members, channels for communication and problem-solving, and the meaningful evaluation of performance
3. Gathering information needed for the acquisition of open space and the development of recreation and park facilities, structures, and other physical resources; this may include developing experimental designs and testing out new kinds of equipment or facilities
4. Evaluation of participation: numbers and types of participants, forms of play behavior or use of facilities or programs, and the measurement of outcomes of participation

5. Program evaluation: the review of a single event, specialized services, or a total program
6. Development of efficient services, such as effective maintenance procedures, techniques for controlling vandalism, research into useful publicity or public relations methods, budgetary control systems, or management of a special type of facility
7. Research leading to the formulation of social policy having to do with working with special populations, establishing community priorities, developing decentralized administrative structures, and similar problems

Many interesting examples of research related to recreation and park administration have been published in *Parks and Recreation, The Journal of Leisure Research, The Therapeutic Recreation Journal,* and *Recreation Canada.* As a single example, Byerts and Teaff used a number of social research techniques in studying MacArthur Park in Los Angeles and developing recommendations for its redesign. Briefly summarized, the study involved

> . . . collecting historical, physical, and demographic information, taking inventory on existing park facilities, and interviewing and observing park users in the field. The study then related the research findings to design recommendations applying specifically to MacArthur Park and generally . . . to inner-city parks.[14]

Categories of research designs and methods[15]

In general, all research may be assigned to two broad categories: (1) the type that gathers *quantifiable data,* which may be reported arithmetically or treated statistically; and (2) the type that deals essentially with *nonquantifiable data,* which may be presented in other ways than with numbers. These, in turn, are broken down into four major approaches to the processing of data:

Historical research customarily makes use of nonquantifiable data in the study of the past; typically, it might rely on eyewitness accounts, diaries, letters, newspapers, reports, political documents, or similar sources of evidence.

Critical research usually relies on nonquantifiable data and is involved with such elements as esthetic theory, literary or philosophical discussion, or psychological or sociological analysis.

Analytical research may involve the use of quantifiable data, but it is more commonly concerned with the structure of a subject, such as an analysis of behavior, the structure of games or social relationships, or the processes existing within an organization or community.

Empirical research is concerned with the gathering of data, usually quantifiable, dealing with the study of institutions, organizations, social processes or services, programs, needs, attitudes, or similar subjects.

These categories may be further subdivided into six major types of research designs: case-study, comparative, evaluative, experimental, longitudinal, and historical-philosophical.

Research designs. The *case-study design* is usually used when the problem is to investigate a single organization, community, club, agency, or culture. It implies intensive study making use of a variety of methods over a period of time.

The *comparative or cross-sectional design* involves the analysis of two or more populations, processes, organizations, or social systems and comparing them to each other.

The *evaluative design,* as described earlier, involves the analysis or appraisal of an existing program, service, or administrative process, policy, or method, with the purpose of measuring its effectiveness or outcome—based in terms of predetermined goals, criteria, or standards.

The *experimental design,* most commonly employed in the physical sciences, may be used in exploring new techniques or administrative devices or in testing out a hypothesis related to cause and effect. It usually involves establishing an experimental program or environmental condition and comparing its effects with those found in a carefully selected control situation in which the experimental factors are not present.

The *historical-philosophical design* is usually used in studying events that have occurred in the past or in the analysis of theoretical concepts or structures.

The *longitudinal or trend-analysis design* is usually employed in the study of quantifiable data over a period of time.

Tools for gathering data. The tools, or actual methods, for gathering data in research studies may include any or all of the following.

In *artifact analysis,* such elements as games, folk dances, drawings, songs, sayings, or similar items are studied.

Content analysis is a systematic approach to studying documents, reports, the reporting of events, or similar sources of information, in which their elements are carefully categorized and quantified.

A *controlled experiment,* as described previously, involves the setting up of an artificial or laboratory situation or a demonstration project and evaluating its outcomes in comparison to a control situation or to past processes.

The *critical incident* method involves the intensive study of one or more significant episodes or incidents, from which information may be gathered to provide generalizations about a broader problem.

Documentary analysis, as used in historical and philosophical research, involves the study and systematic interpretation of documents of various types.

Field study involves observation of various types in an actual field setting; it may include actual participation in activity or group processes or simply observing, interviewing, and recording data of many kinds.

Judges' appraisals, customarily used in evaluative study, consist of reliance on the judgment of qualified experts in measuring the effectiveness of a process or program, the value of a principle, administrative technique, or the rank order of priorities or goals.

Rating scales and checklists are specific devices used to gather information systematically or to get responses from individuals in a precoded or closed-end way.

Statistical methods represent a wide variety of methods for treating quantitative data. They consist of two basic types: *descriptive* statistics, which are primarily concerned with developing a statistical picture of an organization, program, population, or other subject, and *inferential* statistics, which include a variety of sophisticated methods for determining relationships among variables and establishing cause-and-effect relationships or possible predictive statements on the basis of data gathered.

Survey methods are widely used in social science and public administration studies. They may include observational surveys, mailed questionnaires, interview schedules, opinion polls, and similar devices.

Tests of behavior or performance tend to be used in measuring change, either physical, mental, or attitudinal, in performance of individuals who have been involved in an experimental or demonstration project.

Normally, in preparing any research effort, whether it is an informal, in-house study or a project that will require special approval or funding by a foundation or branch of government, it is necessary to develop a proposal or outline of the research that is to be done. When the research study is to be carried on within a college or university or as part of a funded program, it must be rigorously prepared and subjected to careful critical analysis before being submitted for approval.

Elements of a research proposal. The elements of such a proposal normally include the following:

It is essential that the *title of the study* be precise and fully descriptive of the study.

The *statement of the problem* states the problem area or focus of the proposed study: what it seeks to discover or investigate.

The *background of the study* provides a historical background of the problem, places it in a social context, and presents the importance of, or need for, the study. It may include a section on related literature consisting of other research or published writings on the subject; this may also be provided as a separate element in the proposal.

The *statement of purposes and/or hypotheses* include a concise statement of exactly *what* a research study is intended to find out—either the questions to be answered or the hypotheses (major theoretical statements) to be tested. In some studies, a rationale for the hypotheses or questions should be presented.

The *basic assumptions* consist of a statement of the fundamental, underlying principles essential to the rationale of the study and its underlying procedures. They may also be presented as a conceptual framework, which consists of the underlying concepts supporting the study approach.

The *definitions of terms* include a concise definition of each of the major terms that are essential to an understanding of the study proposal—particularly those that may be ambiguous or used in a way peculiar to the study.

In the *limitations* it is essential to make clear aspects of the study that will *not* be explored or any restrictions that are deliberately imposed or inherent in the study situation.

The explanation of the *procedures* represents a major element in study proposals. It should include such sections as:

1. Population or sampling to be studied
2. Development of testing or survey instruments, either those used in previous studies or developed for this one (with, if necessary, procedures for determining validity and reliability of instruments)
3. Pilot testing or pretesting of population groups to determine feasibility of the study and usefulness of the instrument
4. Obtaining needed permissions, approvals, or cooperation to carry out the major study
5. Setting up the experimental situation, or organizing the survey and carrying out the actual data-gathering procedures
6. Recording methods and grouping of data for analysis
7. Analysis of data; indication of how this will be done
8. Interpretation of findings

Although it is not possible to state fully in advance what *conclusions* will be reached or the nature of *recommendations* that will be made, some indication should be given of possible types of conclusions or recommendations for further research, policy development, program changes, and the like.

The *preliminary outline of the report* might show how the final report will be organized in terms of chapters, major sections, or other elements.

Particularly in the case of funded research proposals, it is important to present a realistic and accurate *proposed schedule* for the various stages and conclusion of the study.

A preliminary *bibliography*, including relevant books, reports, articles, or research summaries, should be presented; this would normally be expanded during the course of the study.

In reviewing any research proposal, it is important to ask oneself the following kinds of questions:

Am I—as the researcher—genuinely interested in the problem but free from strong biases that might imperil my objectivity?

Do I possess or can I acquire the necessary skills, abilities, and background knowledge to carry out the study—or can I, or my department, obtain the needed assistance to carry it out?

Have I access to the equipment, laboratories, subjects, or other resources needed to carry out the study?

Will it be possible to obtain the accurate data in sufficient scope needed to validate findings?

Can administrative support, guidance, and cooperation be obtained to carry out the study successfully?

Will the solution of the problem either advance knowledge appreciably in the field or be of practical value to other professionals or agencies?

Will the investigation duplicate the work that has been done or is being done by other individuals or organizations?

Collaboration in research. Many recreation and park departments carry out limited forms of research with respect to evaluation procedures, reporting on programs, attendances, cost-benefit analysis, and similar tasks. However, comparatively few actually initiate full-scale research efforts that might be extremely valuable in improving their operations and determining program priorities and outcomes. As ver Lee points out, most departments are limited in their research resources. Therefore it is necessary to promote more collaboration in planning research projects. The following types of organizations should join together in such studies:

Professional organizations. These organizations, either national, regional, or state, sponsor studies, hold conferences or symposiums on research and publish research findings. Typically, the National Recreation and Park Association publishes the *Journal of Leisure Research,* and a number of other journals published by its branches also disseminate research findings.

Colleges and universities. Institutions of higher learning not only sponsor much research in leisure or various branches of recreation and park development directly, through graduate theses and dissertations, but also provide faculty personnel to assist in research projects sponsored by other agencies. Often, college professors are highly skilled in the needed areas of planning, statistical analysis, psychology, sociology, or various forms of natural science needed to guide research in this field.

State and federal agencies. In increasing numbers, state and federal agencies concerned with parks, open space, recreation, and economic development have been sponsoring research studies. In many cases, they are providing funding for other organizations to carry out the studies on a contractual basis.

Recreation and park agencies. More and more public and voluntary social agencies or recreation departments are carrying on their own research projects today or, in many cases, providing the setting or subjects through which other researchers can carry on meaningful studies.

Need for familiarity with principles and methods

How important is it for recreation and park administrators to be familiar with basic principles and methods of research? Staley suggests that, if they are to be most effective, they must be able to evaluate programs effectively and to use research results intelligently. In addition, the astute administrator must be able to judge, in Staley's view, whether a study has been carried out in such a way that he can have reasonable confidence in its findings and their applicability. He writes that administrators should be actively urged to:

1. Encourage other staff members to use a scientific or documentation approach in gathering information or solving on-the-spot recreation problems

2. Foster among other staff members skill in the use of research results

3. Cooperate with universities and other groups and disciplines in providing the laboratory for a wide variety of research problems requiring actual program situations

4. Actively pursue foundation and government grants for research, demonstration, experimental, and pilot programs (In the last few years there has been a major spurt of action in federal and foundation research in social welfare, education, poverty, science, environment, health, and urban affairs. New grants ranging over a broad subject matter are an accepted expression of government concern. Alert agencies are challenged to conceive new ways in which their particular services can attack major social problems and to actively seek research funds for planning and for pilot or experimental projects.)

5. Assist in identifying problems in the field that require research and share these with colleagues who may be in a better position to follow up on them

6. Budget for staff to carry on the research function (These staff members could be on the payroll as a part-time or full-time function, depending on the size of the department, or they could be hired on an ad hoc basis from the local college or university, community planning council, or private firms.)[16]

Information retrieval

During the past several years, an increasing number of such studies have been carried out, either with problems directly related to recreation or in areas of the physical or natural sciences, or social sciences, with strong implications for recreation. Thousands of studies relating to outdoor recreation primarily have been summarized in *Outdoor Recreation Research,* a reference catalogue published regularly by the Bureau of Outdoor Recreation of the Department of the Interior, in cooperation with the Smithsonian Institution's Science Information Exchange. This effort to identify ongoing research in outdoor recreation has been supplemented by a number of other major bibliographies and literature retrieval projects. For example, Betty van der Smissen and Donald V. Joyce have compiled a 555-page volume, *Bibliography of Theses and Dissertations in Recreation, Parks, Camping and Outdoor Education—1970,* which is published by the National Recreation and Park Association. This document and *Recreation and Leisure Information Systems: Status and Priorities,* compiled and edited by Betty van der Smissen, Diana R. Dunn, and Neil J. Stout, are included in the Educational Resources Information Center (ERIC) clearinghouse retrieval system.

Increasing efforts are being made to develop more effective retrieval systems for recreation literature, publications, and research. The major problem today is still to bridge the gap between the researcher and the practitioner. As in so many fields, a considerable amount of extremely useful research is carried on—much of which finds its way only to college instructors or other researchers in the field. Efforts must be made to have a much wider dissemination of data being gathered to assist recreation and park administrators and other key public officials in the development of policies and the improvement of programs.

Beyond this, it will be essential to develop new and more sophisticated techniques for gathering the kinds of information that will be useful to professionals in this field. Means of assembling great bulks of statistical data, of analyzing and storing information, and of making sophisticated judgments must be improved. Shafer predicts that recreation research is on the verge of a revolution. He comments that the traditional methods of the social sciences are proving inadequate to the task of dealing effectively with the growing complexity of recreation problems.

These problems range from forecasting the consequences of alternative recreation policies to furnishing useful planning data to recreation decision-making, both public and private. However, the inadequacies are now being remedied by new developments in the physical and biological sciences. Revolutionary developments include such things as systems-analysis techniques, new mathematical concepts, simulation procedures, and new ways to manage the natural environment. In addition, automated access to central data banks in computers will provide the social and behavioral sciences with massive data processing capability. . . .[17]

Use of computers in recreation and park management and research

Computers have become extremely widely used in business and government administration. Electronic data processing offers tremendous possibilities for speeding up the collection, sorting and analysis of information, and for carrying out routine business operations related to payroll computation, inventory accounting, production scheduling, customer billing, and similar functions. It is also used, in a more sophisticated way, for problem-solving or decision-making, through the use of simulation models and advanced mathematical techniques. Certainly, in much social science research, computers are essential in the rapid analysis of data and in storage and retrieval systems.

However, how widely used is electronic data processing in recreation and park agencies today? Dunkel and van Doren reported in 1974 that a study of 142 recreation and park departments throughout the United States revealed that 54% of the responding agencies made use of computers.[18] In general, the larger its population, the more likely a department was to use computers. Most of the departments responding positively to the survey reported that they made multiple use of computers for accounting and budget reports, inventory control, payroll, and surveys and research. The use of computers for recreation-related tasks was comparatively rare. For example, only 8% of the agencies used them for purposes such as program scheduling, performance evaluation, or tree inventories.

It was also found that recreation and park management personnel had rarely been responsible for initiating or actively supporting the introduction of electronic data processing in their agencies. Although computer-using agencies reported distinct values, in terms of the computer's improved and expanded data analysis, resulting in more accurate and up-to-date information, reduction in personnel hours and costs, and increased convenience in data storage, many administrators tended to have only superficial knowledge of the computer and to be distrustful of it. Dunkel and van Doren comment that many recreation and park administrators seem ill-prepared to deal with this vital tool of modern management and research, stating:

> . . . active support and participation by all levels of management in the computer effort is one of the most important factors of success. If the output is to satisfy the information needs of management, systems design and implementation must evolve from a cooperative effort combining the management expertise of the administrator and the computer expertise of the data processing personnel. When an agency's personnel are involved in the computer conversion effort, and workshops are conducted to explain the purposes, procedures, and output of computer processing, most employees will work toward the goals set for EDP, and cooperation will increase.[19]

Recognizing the trend toward computer use, it is still crucial that the recreation and park administrator keep in mind the limitations of electronic data processing systems. They can gather, record, and analyze quantitative data and can predict the outcomes of alternative courses of action. They can assemble an amazingly complex mass of information and yield information regarding relationships, correlations, and similar information. However, they can never make judgments, and they cannot interpose values. This function must be reserved for people—and, to the extent that recreation and park administration is rooted in the base of constructive and meaningful human relations processes, electronic data processing and, indeed, the entire research effort must be regarded as a tool, not as a master.

Suggested assignments for student reports or projects

1. Select a specific planning study that was carried out in your community or region several years ago. If none is available, select one in a nearby community, county, or township. Analyze it critically, and determine the extent to which its recommendations have been carried out.

2. Using published guidelines in this field, develop a fairly brief instrument for the evaluation of community recreation and parks. As a team assignment, this might actually be applied to a specific department, with a final report developed of the department's strengths and weaknesses.

3. Based on the recommended format in the text, develop an outline of a research proposal to investigate a specific problem in recreation and parks. Place emphasis on two elements: definition of the problem and recommended research procedures.

REFERENCES

1. Goodman, W. I., editor: *Principles and Practices of Urban Planning*, Washington, D.C., 1968, International City Managers Association, p. 349.
2. Schatz, Walter C.: "Comprehensive Planning for Community Recreation Services," unpublished paper, New York, 1968, Teachers College, Columbia University, pp. 55-56.
3. *Basic Policies for the Comprehensive Plan of Chicago*, Chicago Department of City Planning, 1964, p. 3.
4. Schatz, *op. cit.:* p. 28.
5. Bureau of Outdoor Recreation: *How Effective Are Your Community Recreation Services?*, Washington, D.C., 1973, Department of the Interior.
6. "Program Evaluation in a Boys' Club," New York, 1967, National Manual of Boys' Clubs of America.
7. Peterson, Carol A.: "Applications of Systems Analysis Procedures to Program Planning in Therapeutic Recreation Service," in: Avedon, Elliott M.: *Therapeutic Recreation Service*, Englewood Cliffs, N.J., 1974, Prentice-Hall, Inc., p. 131.
8. *Ibid.:* pp. 137-149.
9. U.S. Forest Service: *Planning Considerations for Winter Sports Resort Development*, Washington, D.C., 1973, Department of Agriculture.
10. Jordan, Joe I.: *Senior Center Facilities*, Washington, D.C., 1975, National Institute of Senior Centers.
11. *Ibid.:* p. 164.
12. ver Lee, J.: "The Role of Research in Recreation Services in the Urban Complex," in *Recreation Research*, Washington, D.C., 1966, American Association for Health, Physical Education, and Recreation, p. 12.
13. Sherwood, C. C.: "Issues in Measuring Results of Action Programs," *Research Letter*, National Recreation and Park Association, October, 1967, p. 1.
14. Byerts, Thomas O., and Teaff, Joseph D.: "Social Research as a Design Tool," *Parks and Recreation*, January, 1975, p. 34.
15. Based on research guidelines developed for doctoral candidates in recreation at Teachers College, Columbia University, in the late 1960s, chiefly by Prof. Elliott M. Avedon.
16. Staley, E. J.: "Function of Research in Recreation Administration," in *Recreation Research, op. cit.*, pp. 108-109.
17. Shafer, E. L., Jr.: "Recent Recreation Research: Implications from the Physical and Biological Sciences," *Parks and Recreation*, August, 1968, p. 22.
18. Dunkel, Margot S., and van Doren, C. S.: "Computers," *Parks and Recreation*, October, 1974, p. 42.
19. *Ibid.:* p. 86.

CHAPTER 11

DEPARTMENTAL MANUALS, RECORDS, AND FORMS

All government departments and voluntary agencies rely to some extent on manuals, records, and forms as a means of providing control of their operations and making sure that their policies are carried out correctly.

Manuals represent sets of printed guidelines that are used to give the vital facts of an organization to its staff and that present in concise and accurate form the policies they are expected to obey or the schedules, responsibilities, and methods that are essential in efficient program operation.

Records consist of information kept on file, usually in the agency's central office, within several important areas of administrative responsibility: (1) legal authorization, charter, ordinance, or other laws bearing on the agency's existence and function; (2) official statement of philosophy and management policies; (3) minutes of board or commission meetings and actions; (4) maps, blueprints, and lists of properties and facilities owned by the department; (5) personnel records, including applications, regular evaluation reports, statements of personnel actions, and commendations for past and present employees; (6) budgetary and financial records; and (7) program records, brochures, reports, and a wide variety of other administrative information, such as public relations releases or clippings, intradepartmental and extradepartmental communications, permits and reservations, contracts and bids, and similar printed materials.

Forms are the means through which reports of various kinds or requests for funds, equipment, material, facilities, transportation, or other forms of assistance are made. By outlining exactly the type of information that must be provided, they provide a precise, systematic record of many happenings or transactions within the department. In addition, they ensure that policies are carried out correctly by mandating that certain actions receive official approval by the appropriate administrator or supervisor.

Taken all together, manuals, records, and forms are essential to the properly managed recreation and park department or agency. They are part of efficient office management and ensure that employees are given appropriate information to help them perform their jobs properly. They help the administrator carry out his various tasks effectively and provide him or her with needed backup information. However, they also represent an ever-present danger. The tendency to require reports, memorandums, requisitions, and other forms of written communication—usually in triplicate—sometimes results in a situation in which an agency winds up swimming in paper. Staff members can be kept so busy filling out and shuffling documents that they have little time to do their job. Therefore the intelligent administrator will keep manuals, records, and forms to a minimum, using or requiring only those which make a real contribution or which are required by law or other municipal authority.

DEPARTMENTAL MANUALS

A manual is a printed booklet, large or small, that is used to provide important information and assistance to staff members. In recreation and park departments, there are several different types of manuals:

Personnel manuals. These provide essential details of employment within a department, such as working hours, holidays, vacations, sick leave, salary and pay periods, overtime and time cards, employee benefits, retirement policies, and similar information. They may also include specific information about job responsibilities, key personnel and offices in the department, rules relating to behavior, dress, personal habits, use of department vehicles, and such matters.

Administrative policy manuals. These include all formally approved statements of departmental policy, either as passed by the board or commission or as issued by the administrator. In most cases, copies are given to all supervisors or other management personnel and kept on file in the office. They must be kept up to date with new entries from time to time. In some departments, they include not only major policy statements but also procedural guidelines on all levels and are issued to *all* employees.

Program manuals. These are manuals that present goals, methods, materials, schedules, and responsibilities of actual programs. They take many forms: (1) a seasonal manual, such as a summer program manual, which is given to all summer employees; (2) a recreation leader's manual, which provides not only personnel information but also guidelines for effective leadership and examples of useful activities; or (3) manuals covering major areas of activity, such as a separate set of guidelines for arts and crafts, aquatic programs, or sports.

General maintenance manuals. Maintenance manuals include precise statements of maintenance responsibilities on all levels, usually including operations calendars, suggested work plans and work sheets, lists of supplies and equipment, inventories of tools, inspection forms and check lists, and detailed statements as to how specific tasks are to be carried out.

Facility manuals. These are specialized manuals that deal with a single major type of facility, such as a senior center, ice rink, or swimming pool. Frequently they include both program guidelines and recommendations for leadership personnel and maintenance schedules and responsibilities.

In larger departments, several different kinds of manuals may be used. In smaller programs, it would not be uncommon to find only one manual combining many of the above elements. Manuals should be carefully designed and prepared and kept up to date with new policies and procedures as these change. In some cases, new manuals are produced each year; in others, a manual may be used for several years with only minor revisions or inserts. Manuals should represent a team effort, with several staff members sharing in their production, rather than be the work of a single individual.

To illustrate the nature of public recreation and park department manuals, the following outline indicates the major sections that might be included in a manual intended primarily for summer recreation leaders.

Outline of suggested recreation leader's manual

Foreword	Letter of introduction from department administrator or mayor
Chapter I	Statement of department philosophy and objectives
Chapter II	Department organization chart and list of key administrators or division heads with offices and telephone numbers
Chapter III	Goals of playground program; listing of playgrounds and centers with map of city or district
Chapter IV	Responsibilities of recreation leader
Chapter V	Suggestions for program planning, including daily and weekly schedules, rainy-day programs, trips, and special events
Chapter VI	Leadership methods and activities, with sample games, dances, music, arts and crafts, and nature activities
Chapter VII	Discipline and control on the playground: typical problems and policies, regulations for penalties or use of police
Chapter VIII	Accident and first aid policies and procedures; safety guidelines for playground equipment and activities; handling emergencies
Chapter IX	Publicity responsibilities of leader: bulletin board, fliers, departmental releases
Chapter X	Use of neighborhood volunteers
Chapter XI	Equipment and supplies: inventory, care of materials, locks and keys, requisitioning procedures
Chapter XII	Care and maintenance of grounds: daily inspections and clean-up, work-order procedure
Chapter XIII	Other department regulations: personal dress, smoking and drinking, solicitation of prizes and contributions, handling of monies, lost and found, visitors on playground, use of personal car, use of telephone, animals on playground, off-grounds trips
Chapter XIV	Personnel policies: required staff meetings and in-service training sessions; hours of work; sick days or inability to report to work; payroll procedures; change of address; other departmental regulations
Appendix	Departmental forms: playground registration cards, attendance forms, petty cash vouchers, time reports, forms for permission to go on trips, equipment requisition forms, accident report forms, program reports, discipline problem forms, seasonal evaluation form

To illustrate the nature of manuals further, this chapter presents excerpts taken from manuals of a number of different recreation and park departments. It cannot cover the full range of all subjects dealt with in every type of departmental manual. However, it *does* show the kinds of guidelines that are found most typically in such manuals.

Summer playground manuals

The following sections are taken from the summer playground or recreation leadership manuals of several cities.

General responsibilities of summer playground leaders. Source: Evansville, Indiana, Public Recreation Commission.

General duties

A playleader's duties are numerous and varied. He must plan, organize and conduct the program in such a manner that the playground is an asset to the neighborhood and not a liability. He will:

1. Encourage patron's good personal habits by setting a good example himself.
2. Maintain order and discipline by enforcing the Department's rules and regulations.

3. Make an effort to know his neighborhood so as to plan a program that meets the recreational needs and desires of that neighborhood.
4. Encourage participation by planning and organizing a program that is attractive.
5. Plan and organize activities through which values, skills, attitudes, and knowledges may be developed for future leisure time.
6. Teach games, both old and new, and promote the special activities scheduled at his playground.
7. Make his playground a safe place to play by enforcing safety rules and by elimination of all types of hazards.
8. Curb and discourage undesirable activities, such as gambling, vandalism, rowdyism, and profane language.
9. Keep the ground clean.
10. Develop in all patrons a respect for both public and private property.
11. Maintain good public relations and be an enthusiastic supporter of the Recreation Commission and its programs.
12. Cooperate with his co-workers and with the administration.
13. Keep accurate records and file reports as required by the Department.

The first day on the playground. Source: Albuquerque, New Mexico, Parks and Recreation Department.

A successful first day is of great importance as it provides the basis or foundation on which the remainder of the playground season is built. If the first day results in a happy and enjoyable experience for the children, they will be enthused about their playground and their leaders. They will tell their parents and other children; they will want to come back. A bad start will handicap the leaders for many days to come. The following suggestions should be helpful in making the first day a successful one:

1. Registration of any new youngster is important and should be handled as soon as possible. The registration should be delegated to one of the Junior Leaders. The Senior Leaders' time will be better spent organizing groups and activities.
2. Meet the children *with a smile* and ask their names. Tell them your name. Tell them about some of the interesting things that they can look forward to (what their playground has in store for them this summer).
3. Be kind and friendly with the children but let them know at the outset that you expect them to conduct themselves as ladies and gentlemen.
4. Get some games or activities going immediately. Kids want ACTION! They want to do things. Start a volleyball or softball game, or a singing activity. Gradually introduce other activities until everyone is doing something. PROVIDE ACTIVITIES FOR ALL AGES.
5. Avoid long-drawn-out presentations of games and rules before allowing the kids to play. Present just enough rules so that play may get started. The rules may be discussed in detail later.
6. Start immediately to instill in the children a sense of pride in their playground. Explain to them how important the playground is, and then show them what they can do to make it the best playground in town. One of the first things that can be done to develop the idea of service is to organize a clean-up squad. They can help pick up broken glass, paper, or other debris that may have accumulated since the last usage.
7. The activities for the week should be posted on the bulletin board. KEEP AN ATTRACTIVE BULLETIN BOARD THAT IS UP-TO-DATE.

Game leadership on the playground. Source: Edmonton, Alberta, Canada, Parks and Recreation Department.

Purposes of playground games

1. Games provide enjoyable group activity.
2. Games provide opportunity for competition under supervision. Children need to test their agility, strength, etc.
3. Supervised games help to develop desired social traits such as self-control, friendliness, courtesy, obedience to officials, and habits of fair play.
4. Games permit economical use of space and equipment with a large number of participants in a limited area.
5. Games help to increase playground attendance and hold the child's interest, encouraging attendance at specified times of the day or week.

Guidelines for teaching games

1. Preparation
   a. Know your game.
   b. Have all equipment ready to use.
   c. Mark play spaces beforehand.
   d. Use method of selecting teams so they are even in ability, and weaker players are not left until end in selection, or left out.
2. Procedure in teaching a new game
   a. Give the name of the game.
   b. Explain objectives of the game.
   c. Explain major rules, and *start playing the game.*
   d. Give further details of rules as needed.
3. Explanation
   a. Unless formation is scattered, it is best to get the group into the proper formation for the game before instruction is given.
   b. Avoid talking too much and give brief, clear and simple directions.
   c. Use a demonstration if necessary to help make the game clearer.
   d. Ask for questions after you have explained the game.
4. Playing the game
   a. Use an alert child to start the game.
   b. If the game is going badly and you cannot correct it while it is going on, it is better to stop it and straighten out the difficulty.
   c. Be interested in the game; teach with enthusiasm and sincerity; don't let it drag.
   d. Strive for 100% participation.
   e. Always be in position to supervise the activity. Coach as well as referee.
   f. Play with the group some of the time.
5. Discipline
   a. Have the attention of the whole group; don't allow talking while you are teaching.
   b. Don't over-direct the game, but keep the group under control.
   c. Teach children to respond to a whistle or some other means of control.
   d. Allow some noise and shouting; they signify that your games session is successful.

Safety and accident prevention. Safety is a topic dealt with in most departmental manuals, both to protect participants from accidents and to avoid lawsuits that may stem from negligence. Source: Oklahoma City, Oklahoma, Department of Parks and Recreation, Recreation Leader's Manual. (For an example of a disciplinary action report form, see Fig. 11-1.)

Safety suggestions
General safety

1. Safety is a basic consideration in playground and pool operation and the well-managed recreation facility is a safe place for people to play.
2. Remember that *all* accidents have a cause and might have been prevented. Prevention of accidents is one of the basic rules of first aid training.

```
┌─────────────────────────────────────────────────────────────────┐
│                                                                   │
│                    LOUISVILLE, KENTUCKY                           │
│                 Department of Parks and Recreation                │
│                    Disciplinary Action Report                     │
│                                                                   │
│                                  Date: _____            │
│                                                                   │
│   It was necessary to take disciplinary action against            │
│   NAME: _____                         │
│   ADDRESS: _____ AGE: _____               │
│   for the following reasons: _____  │
│   _____ │
│   _____ │
│   _____ │
│                                                                   │
│   The following action was taken: _____  │
│   _____ │
│                                                                   │
│   The name of the individual's parent or guardian is _____  │
│   _____ , residing at _____  │
│   Name of person reporting this action: _____  │
│   Recreation location (playground, center, etc.): _____  │
│   Action taken by Superintendent on above: _____  │
│                                                                   │
└─────────────────────────────────────────────────────────────────┘
```

Fig. 11-1

3. Be sure that you are a safety-conscious person yourself and that you attempt to instill this attitude in others through your safety program.
4. All staff members at pools or playgrounds should know the procedure for handling cases involving serious accidents or injuries. Discussion of these procedures should take place in one of your first staff meetings.
5. Each playground and pool should have a listing of emergency numbers near their telephone, if they have one. Included should be the Fire and Police Departments and the Central Office. Playgrounds that do not have telephones should have access to two or more telephones within the immediate neighborhood.
6. Know the location of your first aid kit and keep it well stocked. Brush up on your first aid methods.
7. Be sure that all staff members are aware of the areas on a park or playground where accidents generally occur. (Please check list on Guides to Safety to help your program of safety.)

Playground safety

1. Check apparatus and equipment daily. If it is not in working condition or is dangerous, place it OUT-OF-ORDER and notify the office immediately.
2. Teach children the correct methods of using the apparatus and insist that they be followed.
3. Prepare, post and enforce simple rules of safety for your playground.
4. Know where accidents are liable to happen and be alert to these areas.
5. Enforce ordinances involving dogs and the riding of bicycles on the playground to the best of your ability.
6. Motor scooters and other types of motorized vehicles are not allowed on parks or playgrounds. Contact police at once if this occurs.

```
                    PUBLIC RECREATION COMMISSION
                        2 S. E. Eighth Street
                        Evansville, Indiana

                       ACCIDENT REPORT FORM

  1.  Name_____  Address _____
  2.  Location_____ Sex:  M___; F___; Age_____
  3.  Time accident occurred:  Hour _____a.m.;_____p.m.; Date_____
  4.  Place of accident:  Building _____Playground_____Beach_____
                          Swimming Pool_____Camp_____Elsewhere _____
  5.  Witnesses:  Name_____Address_____
                  Name_____Address_____
                  Name_____Address_____
                                                Description of Accident
Nature of Injury                            How did accident happen?  What was patron
  6.  Abrasion  _____      Bruise _____    doing?  Where was patron?  List specifically
      Amputation_____      Burn   _____    unsafe acts & unsafe conditions existing.
      Laceration_____      Cut    _____    Specify any tool, apparatus, equipment
      Concussion_____      Sprain _____    involved.  Give your opinion as to cause of
      Fracture  _____                       accident._____
      Scratches _____                       _____
      Puncture  _____                       _____
      Other (Specify)_____        _____

Part of Body Injured                        _____
      Ankle  _____         Face  _____     _____
      Finger_____          Foot  _____     _____
      Scalp _____          Nose  _____     _____
      Tooth _____          Leg   _____     _____
      Wrist _____          Knee  _____     _____
      Elbow _____          Eye   _____     _____
      Back  _____          Arm   _____     _____
      Hand  _____          Other_____      _____
  7.  Leader in charge when accident occurred_____
                                                   (Enter Name)
Immediate Action Taken
  8.  First Aid Treatment      _____  By (Name)_____
      Sent Home                _____  By (Name)_____
      Taken to Hospital        _____  By (Name)_____
      Contact Emergency Vehicle_____  By (Name)_____
      Were parents notified: Yes____No_____
Location                                              Remarks
  9.  Athletic Field_____   Game Room _____  What recommendations do you have for pre-
      Auditorium   _____    Home Ec   _____  venting other accidents of this type?
      Locker Room  _____    Pool      _____  _____
      Playground   _____    Beach     _____  _____
      Craft Room   _____    Camp      _____  _____
      Gymnasium    _____    Stairs    _____  _____
      Corridor     _____    Showers   _____  _____
                             Other     _____

      This report must be sent to office within 24 hours after accident.

          Signed:  Director _____

                   Leader   _____
```

Fig. 11-2

Apparatus

Slides

1. Do not permit crawling or running up slides.
2. Do not allow children to stand up when sliding down.
3. Do not permit children to slide down backwards.
4. Do not permit hanging of feet over sides when sliding.
5. Caution children to observe that all persons are clear of the chute before they slide.
6. Do not permit wrestling on the ladder. See that they wait their turn.
7. Generally do not allow children over 12 years of age to use slides.

See-saws

1. Do not allow children to jump or slide off while another person is up in the air on the other end.
2. Do not permit bumping see-saws on the ground.
3. Caution children to keep their feet from under the board at all times.
4. Do not permit standing on see-saws.

Swings

1. Do not allow more than one person on a swing at a time.
2. See that persons use swings that are for their size.
3. Caution children about standing in swings and do not allow jumping from swings.
4. Caution children about running in front of swings.
5. Do not allow children to run under swings when they are pushing another person.
6. Do not permit children to climb on swings.

Climbing apparatus

1. Do not allow children to stand on top of any climbing equipment.
2. Caution children about holding to horizontal ladders, chinning bars and jungle gyms with both hands.
3. Do not allow overcrowding.
4. Be sure that persons who are waiting, stand far enough away so that they will not be struck by the feet of a swinging child.
5. Do not allow pushing, shoving, or dangerous stunts.

First aid procedures. Source: Huntington Beach, California, Recreation and Parks Department. (For an example of an accident report form, see Fig. 11-2.)

I. Emergency procedure
  A. Serious injury
    1. Apply immediate first aid.
    2. Keep the child quiet.
    3. Call the RESCUE SQUAD (536-2—).
    4. Notify the child's parents.
    DO NOT call an ambulance or attempt to take the child home. Notify the Recreation Supervisor (536-5—) and fill out an Accident Report Form (to be turned in to the Recreation Supervisor within 24 hours).
  B. Minor accident
    Apply first aid if needed. A first aid kit is included with your program equipment.
    1. General first aid directions
      a. Lay the victim down; keep him warm and quiet.
      b. Examine for injuries, bleeding, and breathing first.
      c. Give immediate first aid.
      d. If a serious injury, call the RESCUE SQUAD (536-2—).
      e. Notify the child's parents and the Recreation Supervisor.
      f. Complete an Accident Form, and, if possible, include at least two witnesses, their addresses and phone numbers.
    2. Mouth to mouth resuscitation
      a. Lay the victim on his back.
      b. Clear the mouth of foreign particles.
      c. Lift up on the back of the neck and extend the head. This allows a direct open air passage.
      d. Pinch the nostrils shut and place your mouth firmly over the victim's mouth.
      e. Blow your breath into the victim's mouth. You must blow hard enough to see a slight rise in the victim's chest.
      f. Remove your mouth to permit exhalation. Watch the victim's chest come back down.
      g. Repeat this every 3 to 5 seconds until the victim is again breathing under his own control.
      h. If unable to gain an air exchange, turn the victim over and slap him

sharply between the shoulder blades to dislodge any foreign matter stuck in his throat.

3. Bleeding

Arterial bleeding is bright red and comes in spurts. This is severe bleeding and pressure must be directly applied:

a. Directly on the wound—use the most sterile material available. Wrap tightly.

b. If direct pressure doesn't slow down the amount of bleeding, then apply pressure at the pressure point between the wound and heart.

c. If direct pressure fails, apply a tourniquet.

4. Eye wounds

a. Do not try to remove an object from the eye. If the wound is serious, call the RESCUE SQUAD (536-2—) and call the Recreation Supervisor.

b. If the injury is minor, call the child's parents and fill out an Accident Report. Small objects are usually washed out of the eye by the child's own tears.

5. Leg or arm injuries

Follow general first aid directions. Do not attempt to transport the child, but call the RESCUE SQUAD (536-2—) if the child (victim) is *seriously injured*. Do not attempt to put a dislocated or broken bone back in place, in any situation.

II. Additional pointers

A. DO NOT lift a gasping person by the belt.

B. Have a reason for what you do. *Do not guess!*

C. Do not attempt to diagnose.

D. DO NOT DISCUSS ACCIDENT WITH ANYONE.

Publicity methods

Specific guidelines are given here with respect to two types of publicity devices: bulletin boards and posters. Source: Oakland, California, Recreation Department. (For an example of a playground news form, see Fig. 11-3.)

Bulletin boards

Make wide use of bulletin boards! They should be attractive, colorful, and in a good location. They should be up-to-date! Plan frequent changes. Use signs, posters, schedules, and other information. Don't overlook the WHY, WHEN, WHAT, WHERE, WHO, AND HOW.

Suggested rules for maintaining an attractive bulletin board

1. Keep it clean, up-to-date, and attractive.

a. Lettering should be neat and easily read.

b. Add something new each day—a motto, a joke, a drawing, or a handicraft project.

2. Make your notices a bit startling. "Did you know that . . . ," or "Here's something you don't want to miss—," or "Jim is a winner at horseshoes. . . ."

3. Have a plan.

a. Playground rules in one corner.

b. New events in upper right-hand corner.

c. A place for an unexpected contribution from just anyone.

More on bulletin boards

1. They are a must for every gathering place.

2. Select a popular and permanent location. Change items frequently—inspect often.

3. Use to announce activities, events, elections—to display clippings, photographs, project results.

AUSTIN, TEXAS
Department of Recreation and Parks
Playground News Form

Playground: _____ Name of event: _____

Time of event: _____ Date of event: _____

Place: _____ Participants: _____

Coming event: _____Past event: _____Spectators: _____

GIVE DETAILS AND NAMES IN FULL:

_____

_____

_____

Note: Use other side to complete story. _____

Playground Leader

Fig. 11-3

4. Encourage people to watch for new postings.
5. Give only a few messages at a time.
6. Assign care of the board to one with sense of design.
7. Edge photos with color—arrange attractively. Do not bunch.
8. Construction or cork board makes a durable background.
9. Colored tape borders add eye appeal.
10. USE YOUR IMAGINATION!
PROS—Seen by many; decorative; stable and continuing source of information.
CONS—Time-consuming; requires constant care.

Posters

There are two ways to make a poster:
1. Displaying a minimum of information so that the patron will want to know more about the activity.
2. Displaying everything about the activity.
You may use either method, depending on your needs, but they both must be neat, well-balanced, interesting, readable, colorful, and eye-catching.

Other things to know about making posters

1. Arouse interest with well-made eye-catching pieces.
2. Make design bold and direct—to hold that passing glance.
3. Have ONE message to a poster.
4. State event, time, place, and date in the least number of words.
5. Use capital and small letters for contrast—and to make the message STAND OUT.
6. Make lettering for quick reading and understanding.
7. Brush lettering is rapid and easy. Allow generous margins.
8. Add coloring in lettering, background, pictures and/or borders.
9. Silk screen process is ideal for a small quantity.
10. Window card size—11″ × 14″—is best for general distribution.
11. In the language of colors and their power to attract—black on yellow leads, then green on white, red on white, blue on white, white on blue.

12. How about a three-dimensional poster?
13. How about having a poster contest?
Materials to use. A poster can be made on almost anything (not just paper). Paint, ink, crayons, rope and cord, pins and tacks, raffia, cotton, and wood are just a very few of the materials at your disposal.

There are many places to put posters. Just remember to place them where they will be seen best!

PROS—Reach out to wide audience; distribution leads to community contacts.

CONS—Expense; impersonal.

Special events management

Source: Nassau County, New York, Department of Recreation and Parks.

Special events

Special events are the icing on the recreation cake and often the events that stand out most prominently in the minds of the participants and the public in general. Therefore, careful consideration must be given to this area of programming. Employ the following ground rules:

1. All plans for special events must be screened by the Assistant to the Superintendent for Program Development. The clearance of these plans is the responsibility of the Park Director.
2. Carefully plan out each step of your program, using a map of your park area. (Copies may be secured through your Park Director.)
3. Be sure to consider the age and sex of participants, probable number of participants, the possibility of adverse weather (have an alternate plan), leadership needed, facilities, supplies and equipment needed, the aims to be achieved, possible hazards, and finances needed.
4. Make sure the public is fully aware of the event and that photo coverage requests are made when appropriate. (Special events are usually a prime opportunity for this purpose.) Make sure that special signs or posters are ordered well in advance. Use directional signs within the park so that the public can reach the site of the event. When ordering signs, include all information to be printed on signs, as well as specific details regarding construction of signs—size, color, size of lettering, etc.
5. Crowd control must be given careful attention to assure the safety of the participants and the success of the event. Make arrangements for necessary equipment such as stanchions, rope, and other appropriate control barriers.
6. Include provision for traffic and pedestrian control with the local police precinct. (Be sure to keep police informed whenever you expect a crowd so that they can provide the proper traffic coverage.)
7. Remember, you can control the crowd only as far as your voice will carry. Therefore, arrange for the necessary sound equipment through your Park Director. Depending on the size of the event, this may be anything from a whistle to a sound truck. The success of the event will depend on the appropriate piece of equipment. Advance planning is necessary as many times other sections of the Division will be involved. If special items of equipment, such as the traveling stage, podium, etc. will be needed, give as much time as possible (a minimum of 2 weeks). The traveling stage is generally scheduled 4 to 6 months in advance.
8. Make sure you have adequate first aid and emergency coverage. Arrangements should be made with the Specialist Unit for special first aid coverage. When large crowds are expected arrangements can be made for the Red Cross Mobile Safety Unit to be present.
9. Make sure additional staff has been secured if necessary.
10. The day before the event, be sure all items you plan to use are available. Special materials such as pennants, banners, etc. may be secured through

your Park Director. Be sure you have sufficient seating and have made arrangements for musical accompaniment if necessary (piano, records, etc.). Plan to have any necessary construction done well in advance of the event. Work orders should be in early to give sufficient notice for maintenance support.

11. Make use of volunteers—help them to feel like a part of the recreation staff. Use name tags or other means of identification to set them apart. Give volunteers specific assignments and check on them periodically.

12. Make a complete report on the special event in terms of contacts used. A Special Events Evaluation Form for this purpose is to be filled out and forwarded to the Special Events Director at the Specialist Unit through the Office of the Park Director. This form will be kept on file for future reference and follow up.

13. Determine whether pre-registration is necessary and plan accordingly. If there is any registration at the event, make the necessary arrangements for tables, personnel, etc.

14. Contact local experts to act as judges, when necessary. In major events, if notables are desired as judges, this request should be made to the Office of Program Development.

15. Have a run-through of the event prior to the actual event with park personnel and volunteers so that everyone understands his job and the way the event is to be handled.

Guidelines for specific facility: swimming pool

Many manuals deal with program operation and maintenance procedures within a single type of facility. The following sections from departmental manuals provide guidelines for swimming pool operation and maintenance.

Responsibilities of lifeguards. Source: St. Louis, Missouri, Department of Parks, Recreation, and Forestry: Aquatic Program Manual.

Specific rules

1. While on duty, a Guard SHOULD:
   a. Report, ready for duty, at least 15 minutes before assigned shift and be in proper position when his shift starts.
   b. Be professional, alert, courteous, and always tactful.
   c. Maintain an erect and alert position while on the stand so he can observe signals from the other guards and note anything unusual in the water area he is guarding.
   d. Refrain from unnecessary talk or visiting with the public. If talk is necessary, do so while keeping assigned area under observation.
   e. Make requests and issue orders in a COURTEOUS and DETERMINED manner. If orders are not executed in full and at once, report the incident to the Senior Guard on duty.
   f. ON STAND DUTY, take the proper position in the seat. ON WALKING PATROL, concentrate primarily on the water area.
   g. Always have a whistle and wear an approved type of identification.
   h. Keep swimmers and bathers from congregating on walk area in the immediate vicinity of the guard stands.
   i. Refer detailed inquiries to the Pool Manager or Aquatic Program Supervisor.
   j. Pool Manager or assistant will be responsible for clearing all swimmers out of water during an electrical storm.
   k. Not only guard the lives of the patrons, but also maintain discipline among the more active ones so as to ensure the comfort and pleasure of others. Do not tolerate any rowdyism.

    l. Promptly enforce all facility rules.

    m. Keep the facility fit for inspection at all times; keep all litter picked up and keep all life guard, life saving, and first aid equipment in readiness.

    n. At the time each shift ends, make a survey of the bottom of pool and then the entire locker room. Make sure everyone is out of the building.

    o. Know your specific duties in the event of a major emergency.

    p. Check to make certain all doors and gates to facility are locked when a life guard is not on duty.

Some don'ts

2. While on duty a GUARD SHOULD NOT:

    a. Gather with other guards. (If there is a surplus of guards, as is indicated by grouping, an elimination of this surplus could take place.)

    b. Play musical instruments, smoke, read or indulge in byplay.

    c. Teach swimming or diving (unless pool is specifically restricted for instruction, or following clearance with proper authority).

    d. Swim unless there is a specific relief for this purpose except for rescue purposes.

    e. Store anything execpt his own personal belongings in guard room.

    f. Leave his post except in cases of emergency or when properly relieved.

    g. Use the life guard stands for checking articles of clothing, radios, etc.

    h. Use abusive language or profanity in the execution of his duties.

Rules for the public

1. No one will be admitted under the influence of alcohol.
2. Patrons should be required to take showers before entering the pool or pool area.
3. Women should be required to wear bathing caps at pools.
4. Patrons with open sores or any infectious disease, such as athlete's foot, are not permitted in the pool or pool area.
5. No smoking in pool area and entire building.
6. No eating in pool area or entire building.
7. Profanity, improper behavior and vulgar remarks are prohibited.
8. Running within the pool area or within the pool building is forbidden.
9. Shallow diving into 2½ or 3 feet depth from the pool edge should be prohibited.

REMEMBER: ALERTNESS is the key to life saving.

Pool maintenance requirements. Source: Las Vegas, Nevada, Recreation Department: Public Pool Operations Manual.

    Maintenance duties are divided into areas such as water maintenance, deck maintenance and grounds maintenance. Usually full-time city employees will be assigned such duties as gardening, plumbing and electrical work.

    Pool managers should not overlook the use of full-time maintenance people in the emergency procedures. Maintenance people should assist lifesaving personnel to clear the pool, control the crowd and bring emergency equipment to the victim.

A. Public health requirements

    1. A free chlorine residual minimum of 0.25 PPM with a maximum of 1.0 PPM must be maintained throughout the pool at all times when the pool is in use.

    2. The water should be maintained at all times in an alkaline condition indicated by a pH of not less than 7.2 and not more than 8.2.

    3. The water should have sufficient clarity to make readily visible a black disc 6 inches in diameter at the deepest point of the pool, from a distance of 30 feet.

    4. Not more than 15% of water samples covering any considerable time period either (a) contain more than 200 bacteria per milliliter by agar plate count, or (b) show positive test for coliform organisms in any of the five 10 ml. portions of a sample or more than 1.0 coliform organisms per 50 ml by membrane filter test.

B. Water maintenance

Routine water maintenance is necessary and must be assigned to a member of the staff as a regular duty. A checklist similar to the following should be prepared to meet Public Health Requirements and the standards of particular pool programs.

1. Check the condition of the water at specified intervals. Check the temperature of the air and water. Test the water for chlorine residual, pH and clarity. Record the findings on the daily water condition report. The chlorine residual should meet local and state requirements. If the water is over-chlorinated or under-chlorinated, steps must be taken to correct the condition in accordance with procedures established for the specific pool. Adjustments to the water and chlorinating systems should be done only by personnel who have been trained in such procedures. Caution should be taken when hand feeding chemicals to pool, that no patrons are in the water. Similar steps should be taken to adjust pH.

2. See that all automatic filtering and chlorinating systems are working and not overheated. If the pumps are not working, notify the aquatic supervisor, who will take proper steps to correct the situation. Do not turn off any pump systems at any time unless instructed to do so by the aquatic supervisor.

3. Clean lint and hair traps.

4. Check the clarity of the water. If a black 6-inch disc cannot be seen on the bottom of the deepest point from a distance of 10 yards away on deck, close the pool for repairs and notify the aquatic supervisor through the pool manager.

5. Remove all debris, sputum and foreign matter from the pool surface, bottom, drains, scuppers and deck.

6. Brush, vacuum and chlorinate the pool in accordance with an approved schedule.

7. Maintain the water level at the high water line as marked on the sides of the pool.

8. Control algae by use of algaecide or superchlorinating the pool once each week after the pool is closed in the evening.

C. Building and deck maintenance

The aquatic supervisor should arrange to have the pool facilities clean and in readiness upon the arrival of the pool patrons. Trees shedding leaves into the pool area should be cut back; shrubs blocking safety view sight lines should be removed or trimmed. Grass growing through safety expansion joints should be treated with weed killers; debris outside the fence should be cleared. Furniture, equipment, and supplies should be in ample quantities and in good condition.

The daily checklist of building and deck maintenance shall include the following:

1. Sweep and clean all decks and drains to remove debris before washing.

2. Hose down decks and disinfect all areas.

3. Maintain clean walkways and areas adjacent to the pool.

4. Clean toilets, urinals, and showers.

5. Mop floors with antiseptics, such as ½ cup of sodium hypochlorite solution to a bucket of water.

6. Polish metal fixtures.

7. Clean windows and walls.

8. Report defective electrical equipment to the pool manager for repair by a qualified electrician.

9. Remove accumulated oil rags, dust cloths, and inflammable liquids to prevent possible fires.

10. Turn in items found during maintenance and cleanup periods to the pool office.

General maintenance manuals

As indicated earlier, many recreation and park departments provide their custodial or maintenance staff with manuals covering their varied responsibilities. As an illustration, three excerpts are provided from the Oak Park, Illinois,

Recreation Department's maintenance manual. These are *selected* guidelines from much fuller sets of instructions. They illustrate how some responsibilities are seasonal, normally being performed only once a year, whereas others are carried out at more frequent intervals, or even on a weekly or daily basis.

Maintenance operation calendar

January   Check storage areas—clean, repair, paint.
Take down Christmas displays.
Repair and paint summer outdoor equipment.
Maintain ice rinks.

February   Repair and construct program items—Nok Hockey, preschool equipment, etc.
Repair playground apparatus.
Check and repair lawn mowers.
Repair and paint trash receptacles.
Evaluate winter operation.
Order plant materials.

March   Strip and wax floors.
Clean fans and vents.
Inspect, repair, and paint all benches and picnic tables.
Prune trees and shrubs.
Aerate, cut grass short, roll areas, apply weed killer and fertilizer.
Fertilize bushes and flower beds.

April   Clean all drains and catch basins.
Clean equipment sleeves and install summer equipment, including tennis nets, repair court areas.
Clean and put away snow blowers and snow equipment.
Clean sand boxes and add sand where needed.
Install new apparatus and inspect other apparatus for winter breakage and damage.
Take tumbling mats for repair.
Plant grass.
Plant new plant materials not affected by frost.
Replace wood chips where needed.
Prepare ball diamonds.
Clean out winter protection materials.

Similar tasks must be carried out throughout each month of the year, geared both to program needs and to climatic and growing factors.

The following are examples of work to be done at more frequent intervals.

Cleaning control schedule

Work to be done twice a year. Clean and lubricate space heaters, motors, and ventilating fans. Clean and lubricate heating system pumps and motors. Clean ventilation screens or grates. Check plumbing fixtures for leaks; repair if necessary.

Work to be done every three months. Wash light fixtures. Clean ceilings. Wash walls. Strip and apply floor finish. Wash and apply finish to baseboard moldings.

Monthly work. Wash windows. Wash walls as necessary. Wet-mop floors and polish. Clean storage closets. Keep soil around bushes loose and free from weeds. Edge grass areas along walks, brush areas, and flower beds.

Weekly work. Clean and disinfect toilet bowls and urinals. Clean and polish mirrors, hand driers, and fixtures. Vacuum, sweep or shake rugs. Clean counters, sinks, range, refrigerator, cabinets, desks, etc. Clean under and behind Coke machines, range, and refrigerator. Cut grass areas and hand trim. Plant and weed flower beds as needed.

Daily work plan—center custodian. Specific tasks of opening and inspecting the building are described, along with detailed listings of cleaning or polishing activity rooms and lobbies, washrooms, kitchens, offices, and outside areas. In addition, other guides are given for replacing light bulbs, filling out special work orders, keeping storage, maintenance, and boiler rooms clean, checking fire extinguishers, noting and correcting safety hazards, keeping curbs and parkways clean, and similar functions.

Manuals in other agency settings

In other types of voluntary or therapeutic agencies, manuals may assume somewhat different forms. In psychiatric hospitals, for example, departmental manuals may place considerable stress on describing the function of the recreation or activity therapy service within the total departmental structure of the institution. As an illustration, the Penetanguishene Mental Health Centre, Ontario, Canada, provides staff members with detailed information regarding (1) the hospital setting, structure, and administrative units; (2) the functions of recreational services in relation to vocational services and occupational therapy and as part of the clinical effort; (3) layout of recreation facilities and areas; (4) staff roles of recreation therapists; (5) specific descriptions of recreation programs serving geriatric, alcoholic, adolescent, and other special groups of patients; (6) special services dealing with patient assessment, recreational counseling, research, and community-related programs; and (7) hospital policies concerned with use of facilities, staff parking, payroll procedures, and similar matters.

As a single example of guidelines found in a hospital manual, the following excerpt deals with procedures for transportation and community trips.

Transportation and community trips. Source: Spring Grove State Hospital, Maryland: Procedures Manual of Rehabilitation Therapy Department.

Transportation—Bus

Bus rides will be carried out in the following manner:
1. A written 2-week advance notice. Plans for bus rides will be submitted in duplicate 2 weeks in advance to the Rehabilitation Bus Driver in charge of Transportation in the Rehabilitation Building.
2. There will be NO SMOKING ON THE BUSES. Signs stating this will be on all buses.
3. Groups using the buses will have some responsibility for helping to keep the bus clean.
4. The bus will be available only on the days and times specified by the Bus Driver in Charge of Transportation.

NOTE: Directions should be clearly stated; give shortest route and/or the most direct route. A chauffeur's license is required to drive the bus.

Transportation—Station wagon

The Rehabilitation Department has been asssigned a station wagon primarily for use in Rehabilitation programs. If you have a need for this vehicle in your program, request it through your supervisor and the Supervisor of Special Services or Rehabilitation Secretary.

This vehicle is for our use and convenience and it behooves each of us to take as good care of it as if it were our own.

1. There is a travel log kept in the glove compartment on which you must record your *beginning and ending* MILEAGE AND PLACE VISITED.
2. There is a special parking place in the Foster-Wade area parking lot designated for this vehicle. It must be kept there at all times when not in use.
3. Personnel using this vehicle must turn keys in to the switchboard after 4:30 P.M.
4. Check the vehicle *before and after* using it. Report any malfunctioning or damage to the vehicle in writing, whether you are or are not responsible for said damage or malfunctioning. *Duplicate* reports should be submitted to the Supervisor of Special Services.
5. When transporting patients, be certain that all doors are properly closed.
6. Make sure there is gas in the vehicle.

NOTE: You are not to schedule, without permission from the Director, trips beyond the Baltimore-Towson-Annapolis-Columbia area. Trips to points beyond these distances should not be planned.

Community trips

Make certain adequate Nursing or Rehabilitation coverage is available for all community trips. Patients are to be properly dressed and neat in appearance. Personnel planning trips to the community should make periodic checks to insure patients have proper clothing through Volunteer Services or other channels.

Personnel assigned by the office of Supervisor of Special Services to be in charge of off grounds trips will be in charge of both staff and the total patient group for the duration of the trip and will assume the following responsibilities:

1. The person in charge is responsible for the safety and comfort of all attending patients and has the authority to establish procedures regarding patient limits and instructions to accompanying personnel on the assigned activity.
2. The person in charge has the authority to refuse to admit on the bus any patients inappropriately dressed for the activity and/or inappropriate in behavior.
3. The person in charge will assume the responsibility for reporting on the trip to both the Supervisor of Special Services and Volunteer Services when so indicated.
4. The person in charge has the final authority in making all decisions regarding the following situations that might arise.

   Return of patient to hospital: If it becomes necessary to return a patient to the hospital before the trip is over, the person in charge will notify the hospital General Supervisor, who will arrange transportation. The person assigned in charge will arrange the pick-up place. Dependent upon the pick-up place, he will assign one accompanying personnel to remain with the patient.

   Combative patient: The person in charge will assign 1:1 ratio with this patient and shift the coverage of the remaining accompanying personnel. If this is not adequate, notify the police *if they are available on the premises,* and follow the same procedure for *return of patient to hospital.*

   Sick or injured patient: The person in charge will assign 1:1 ratio with this patient and shift the coverage of the remaining accompanying personnel. Notify assigned Nursing Service personnel, if present on outing, and/or notify the First Aid Station on the premises. If additional action needs to be taken, notify the hospital General Supervisor, who will arrange transportation to return to the hospital. An accident or injury report must be filed immediately upon return to the hospital and left in duplicate with the Ward Charge; an additional copy is to be submitted to the supervisor of Special Services.

   Lost patient: Assign one employee to search for the patient and shift the coverage of the remaining accompanying personnel. If necessary, inform

the manager on the premises and the police, *if available on the premises.*
Notify the hospital General Supervisor, and *upon return to the hospital,*
notify the building supervisor and one of the following in this order: your
immediate supervisor, the Supervisor of Special Services, the Director of
Rehabilitation Therapies.

Incident reports: Any involvement, i.e., illness or injury, accident, stealing,
fighting, lost patient, etc., must be reported in writing. Unless otherwise
specified above, submit incident reports in duplicate to the Ward Charge
and a copy to the Supervisor of Special Services immediately following
the activity.

DEPARTMENTAL RECORDS

The general purpose of manuals is to provide needed information to staff
members and to indicate how various functions should be carried out. The purpose of records is to gather complete and accurate information as to how they
have been carried out. Records provide a permanent source of readily available
information that can be used by the recreation and park administrator for the
following purposes: (1) give details of the department's operation to the general public or to other agencies or administrators; (2) demonstrate compliance
with state or municipal regulations governing the operation of public departments; (3) protect against possible charges of misfeasance (in the handling
of money, for example), or against lawsuits; (4) serve as a basis for reviewing
the department's operations and evaluating either its overall performance or
specific programs; (5) assist in the formulation of policies or making needed
decisions; or (6) follow up with needed data on any aspect of administrative
responsibility, such as facilities planning or management, or fiscal administration.

Records normally fall into several major categories, including the following.

Legal documents. These include copies of all relevant state or municipal
laws, charters or ordinances that affect the department, as well as other legal
opinions, records of lawsuits, contracts, or information affecting the formal
authorization of the department, and policy development.

Statements of philosophy and policy. Formal statements of departmental
philosophy, goals, and objectives should be kept in the records, as well as policy
statements, usually in manual form.

Board or commission records. Assuming that the department operates under a board or commission, full records should be kept of its minutes, policy
actions, decisions, reports, correspondence, and memoranda. Similarly, if the
department does not have a formal board or commission but has a city-wide
advisory council, records of that body's action should be kept.

Facilities and equipment. Records should be maintained of all department-
owned properties and facilities, including copies of legal deeds and easements,
maps, blueprints and working drawings of facilities, and similar information.
Inventories of equipment and supplies should be kept, along with specifications
for purchase, maintenance schedules and standards, and other records related
to the physical operation of the department.

Personnel information. General information regarding personnel policies and
procedures should be kept in the file, such as job descriptions, in-service educa-

---

ST. LOUIS, MISSOURI
Daily Swimming Pool Report and Cash Receipt Form
Department of Parks, Recreation and Forestry

Date: _____

NAME OF POOL: Fairgrounds ( ) Marquette ( ) Vashon ( )

SESSION: Afternoon ( ) Evening ( )

WEATHER CONDITION: Hot ( ) Mild ( ) Cloudy ( ) Cold ( ) Rain ( )

	Adult	Child
Ticket number at finish:	_____	_____
Ticket number at start:	_____	_____
Tickets sold:	_____	_____
Amount due:	_____	_____

Total amount: $ _____

Petty cash on hand: $ _____

Rain checks (by number):

Issued _____

Received _____

In the event the pool is closed, please give reason why in red ink.

_____
Cashier

_____
Aquatic Program Supervisor

_____
Pool Manager

_____
Cash received by Clerk II

Received: $ _____

Date: _____

Fig. 11-4

tion schedules and events, and procedures for promotion, transfer, or disciplinary action. In addition, individual personnel folders for all past and present staff members should include full records of each individual's application, assignments, time records, civil service status, disciplinary action or commendations, and similar data.

Financial records. Copies of past and present budgets, sources of revenue, and other relevant budgetary information should be kept systematically. This includes current reports of encumbrances and expenditures, cash receipts and totals (Fig. 11-4), cash transmittal forms, payroll figures, and all other information dealing with the budgetary status and financial transactions of the department.

Program reports. Summaries of past programs, along with detailed schedules, descriptions, and brochures for present programs, should be carefully kept.

EDMONTON, ALBERTA
Department of Parks and Recreation
Report of Daily Attendance

Play area: _____   Date: _____

Statistics of		Age groups						
		Under 6	6 to 12	Teen-age	Adult	Volun-teers	Spec-tators	Total
Estimate attendance at play area	Morning							
	Afternoon							
	Evening							
Handicrafts								
Sports								
Active games								
Drama, story hour								
Dancing								
Special events (name)								
Volunteers								
Meetings								

_____   _____
Sessions   Leader

Fig. 11-5

This would include calendars of major events, attendance reports for playgrounds and centers (Fig. 11-5), systematic reports of city-wide, district, and individual programs, and other relevant information.

Filing records. Other miscellaneous records might include public relations releases or clippings, departmental memoranda and communications, copies of contracts and bids, facilities permits and reservations (Fig. 11-6), accident or incident reports, and other records that do not fit into the above categories. A convenient and efficient filing system must be developed with a master index that will permit prompt retrieval of needed records. In most offices, one or two members of the clerical staff are assigned filing responsibilities and are most skilled at finding needed records. However, in emergencies, other secretaries or professional staff members should be familiar enough with the filing system to quickly locate needed materials.

Since an active department is likely to pile up a large bulk of records and reports each year, three categories should be established: (1) active files, which should be kept on hand and ready for use; (2) inactive files, which may be

State of California — The Resources Agency

DEPARTMENT OF PARKS AND RECREATION

CAMPSITE RESERVATION REQUEST
1975

Please include middle initial in your name.

Your name and address

_____

_____

_____

_____

IMPORTANT

You may obtain faster reservation service if you apply in person to a ticket outlet operated for the State by Ticketron, Inc. For outlet locations phone:

Los Angeles Area	(213) 670-1242
San Diego Area	(714) 565-9947
San Francisco Area	(415) 788-2828
Sacramento Area	(916) 445-8828

If there is no Ticketron outlet location convenient to where you live, you may mail your request to:

RESERVATION OFFICE
DEPARTMENT OF PARKS AND RECREATION
P.O. Box 2390
Sacramento, California 95811

A. Name of Park See Inside for Types of Facilities and List of Parks	First Choice		Second Choice		Third Choice	
	Arrival Date	Nites	Arrival Date	Nites	Arrival Date	Nites

Check this box ☐ if we may use our judgment in substituting other nearby parks.

LIMIT 2 RESERVATIONS PER PERSON FOR SAME PARK AND SAME DATES

B. √ Check   **Type of Camping Equipment**

1	1 Tent or No Equipment
2	2 Tents
3	Large Tent (over 9' x 12')
4	Tent Trailer
5	Van or Bus w/Side Tent
6	Camper/Motorhome thru 18 ft.
7	Camper/Motorhome thru 21 ft.
8	Camper/Motorhome thru 24 ft.
9	Camper/Motorhome thru 27 ft.
10	Camper/Motorhome, over 27 ft., ____ ft.
11	Trailer thru 15 ft.
12	Trailer thru 18 ft.
13	Trailer thru 21 ft.
14	Trailer thru 24 ft.
15	Trailer thru 27 ft.
16	Trailer, over 27 ft., ____ ft.
	Other (Explain)
	Boat Trailers are considered Trailers

C. Pets   Yes_____ No_____   *Dog fee payable with proof of valid rabies inoculation at park.*

D. Number of Persons _____

E. Computation of Fees

The $1.50 reservation fee is required for each period and/or campsite requested. Maximum period for any reservation is 15 days.

1. *Camping Fees:*

   (D) Developed Sites _____ nites @ $3.00 _____

   (P) Primitive Sites _____ nites @ $1.50 _____

   (H) Hookup Sites _____ nites @ $4.00 _____

2. *Reservation Fees:*

   Reservation Fee(s) _____   _____ @ $1.50 _____

Total Camping and Reservation Fees (1 + 2) = $_____

Make check or money order for this amount to Department of Parks and Recreation.

Your Daytime Phone_____

BE SURE YOU COMPLETE SECTIONS A THRU E AND ENCLOSE FULL PAYMENT OF CAMPING AND RESERVATION FEES. INCOMPLETE OR INCORRECT FORMS WILL BE RETURNED.

Fig. 11-6

suggested form for parents' permission for troop camping and trips

Troop No. _____ is planning a troop camp ☐, camping trip ☐

Plans have been approved by _____
(council or troop committee)

Mrs.
Miss _____ is chairman of the group directly responsible for this camp.
She will be glad to have you call if you have any questions.

Her telephone number is _____

Mrs.
The leader in charge of the camp will be Miss _____

The group will be gone _____, leaving on _____, from _____
(number of days)   (date)   (place)

at _____o'clock and returning on _____to _____at _____o'clock.

The cost for each girl will be _____ for _____

This is to be paid one week before the departure. _____

Each girl will bring _____
(list necessary equipment and explain program or use back
of this section or another page for this information)

Mrs.
In case of emergency, the leaders will call Miss _____
(name, address, phone)

who will immediately get in touch with parents.

Troop Leader _____

— —

(Tear off and return to troop leader.)

My daughter _____ is in good physical condition at present and has
had no serious illness or operation since her last health examination. I shall make sure that she does not attend if
she is not feeling well.

I understand the cost will be _____

During the camp period, I may be reached at:

_____   _____
(address)   (phone)

Any remarks: _____

_____

_____

_____

_____
Signatures—(Parents or Guardian)

Fig. 11-7. Courtesy Girl Scouts of the U.S.A., New York, N.Y.

stored in a less convenient location where they are available for reference; and (3) files that include records that are no longer needed, which may be disposed of periodically or kept in dead storage if space is readily available. A final question regarding files is the issue of confidentiality. Although departmental files and the records kept in them are normally made accessible to all staff members for departmental use or to provide needed information to the public or to civic groups, some material should be kept confidential. Thus the direct correspondence of the administrator, the minutes of closed board meetings, some forms of personnel records, and other designated files may be kept under lock and key and opened only to key individuals or with special permission.

DEPARTMENTAL FORMS

Departmental forms represent the means through which various procedures are carried out in a consistent, uniform, and approved way. They are of many different types: program or attendance report forms (Fig. 11-5), requisition forms, worksheets or job checklists, parental permission forms (Fig. 11-7), accident report forms (Fig. 11-2), and many others. Several sample forms for various purposes appear throughout this chapter.

Forms vary widely from department to department both in length and in amount of detail required. Ideally, forms should be as brief and concise as possible; however, to gather all the essential information, it is often necessary to make them rather lengthy. As much as possible, forms should have coded sections that merely require numbers or check marks to be entered. However, it is often necessary to ask for anecdotal or narrative information, as in the case of accident reports. Often it is possible to simplify forms by having directions or explanations for them on another page of the departmental manual. One of the important responsibilities of supervisors is to make sure that all leaders understand the forms they are required to fill out and that they do this promptly and accurately and submit them without delay.

This chapter has provided a number of varied illustrations of administrative, supervisory, and leadership guidelines taken from the actual manuals of recreation and park departments, hospitals, or voluntary agencies in the United States and Canada. Each agency should develop its own manuals, based on its unique circumstances, needs, and administrative policies. Similarly, it should institute effective record-keeping systems and develop forms for all important procedures and situations. Although paperwork and record keeping are not exciting or inspirational tasks, they are essential to a smoothly functioning organization.

CHAPTER 12

THE EFFECTIVE EXECUTIVE

This book has described, in the preceding chapters, the major functional areas of recreation and park administration. Finally, however, when all is considered, the key element that makes for success or failure on the job is the extent to which the recreation and park executive has mastered the challenge of being an effective administrator.

Does the administrator possess that curious combination of prescience, chemistry, leadership, dynamism, perception, and judgment that tends to be found in outstanding executives? Or is he or she one of the many who display an impressive array of physical attributes, fine speech, and polished skills—but who lack drive and initiative? This could be the most important message of this book for the reader in terms of understanding effective executive leadership.

There are several key elements in this analysis. They include (1) the qualities, such as intelligence and drive, that make for success in positions of executive responsibility; (2) specific knowledge of the recreation and park field; (3) knowledge of the roles played by administrators and the ability to fill these roles; (4) human relations skills and the ability to work with people; (5) the capacity for sound decision-making; (6) effective communication skills; (7) a personal philosophy that permits the executive to flourish in a world of practical politics; and (8) an understanding of effective executive practices.

QUALITIES AND SKILLS UNDERLYING SUCCESS AS AN EXECUTIVE

The successful recreation and park administrator must have certain key qualities, such as intelligence, motivation, drive, willingness to work hard and to communicate effectively with others, and planning and organizing ability. However, such traits by themselves will not ensure success. Peter Drucker, a leading consultant to American business firms, comments that high intelligence is common enough among executives. However, he writes, brilliant men are often strikingly ineffectual—they have never learned that insight and knowledge are transformed into effectiveness only through unremitting work and self-discipline.

> Among the effective executives I have known and worked with, there are extroverts and aloof, retiring men, some even morbidly shy. Some are eccentrics, others painfully correct conformists. . . . Some are scholars and serious students, others almost unlettered. Some have broad interests, others know nothing except their own narrow area and care for little else. . . . [T]here are people who use logic and analysis and others who rely mainly on perception and intuition. There are men who make decisions easily and men who suffer agonies every time they have to move.[1]

He concludes that success in an executive role is certainly not due to any single basic personality type. Instead, it is the result of a complex of habits or practices of self-management in effective executive behavior. These habits or practices are described later in this chapter.

Specific knowledge of the recreation and park field. The successful recreation and park administrator must deal first with an intangible—the process of determining what provides pleasure and healthy social outcomes for community residents in their leisure time. He or she must also deal with such concrete factors as payrolls, annual budgets, fees and charges, blueprints, and earth-moving machines. The administrator must face city councils and the demands of neighborhood associations as well as a host of other problems large and small in which knowledge and experience are essential if he or she is to be successful.

The executive must also be adaptable to constantly changing challenges. The 1940s and 1950s represented an era of newly developing departments. In the 1960s, there was great expansion, side by side with new problems of vandalism, crime and civic disturbance, and increased emphasis on community involvement and socially oriented programs. In the 1970s, recreation and parks have been assigned new and varied community roles, but administrators have been faced, in many communities, by critical budgetary problems. What will the 1980s bring? The key point is that no matter how knowledgeable he or she was in the past, the executive must be adaptable, alert, flexible, and ready to meet new problems with innovative and intelligent solutions. In part this depends on his understanding his essential organizational roles.

Understanding administrative roles. What are the key roles of administrators? In addition to their professional responsibilities, effective administrators recognize that they must play certain symbolic roles within organizations. Among others, they are actors, catalyzers, disciplinarians, friends, guardians, innovators, model figures, spokesmen, and technicians.

Actor. This term is intended in two senses: (1) the administrator must *act* rather than be passive, and (2) he must be acutely aware of the *image* he portrays on the public stage and must consciously present himself in positive and effective ways.

Catalyzer. The administrator must be a person who makes things happen, who brings diverse individuals and groups together, and who facilitates community processes and programs.

Disciplinarian. It is the responsibility of the administrator to make sure that others in the organization obey its policies and carry out their assigned functions.

Friend. In addition to his professional functions, the effective executive is also a friend in that he may have a close and warm personal relationship with many of his co-workers.

Guardian. The administrator must guard and husband the resources of his department—both in the sense of physical resources and public funds and as far as its reputation is concerned.

Innovator. The effective manager must be a person who can create new ideas and projects or who is receptive to the innovative ideas of others.

Model figure. The administrator must be able to define the fundamental values and objectives of the department and must personally command respect and support; he should be able to serve as a model for others in the department.

Spokesman. In both a literal and figurative sense, the administrator speaks for the department in the press and other media, at city council meetings and similar events, and in all public interchange.

Technician. Finally, in many practical ways, the administrator must be a master of the practical processes of management and must be skilled at carrying these out himself or directing subordinates in them.

As he fulfills these varied roles, the administrator recognizes that he has separate sets of responsibilities: (1) to himself, in the sense that he must satisfy his own professional values and personal needs, both financial and in terms of job satisfaction; (2) to the community at large or to the specific population served by an agency in terms of their recreational and social needs; (3) to the owners, either the municipal government, the controlling board or commission, the trustees, or others to whom he is formally responsible; (4) to the profession of recreation and parks, in terms of representing its interests, goals, values, and standards of ethical practice; (5) to his co-workers in municipal government or the voluntary agency or therapeutic field and to employees in his own department; (6) to those who participate directly in his program activities; and (7) finally, to the overall society and, particularly for park managers or resource planners, to the environment, in the sense that his department must follow policies that preserve and enhance rather than destroy or abuse nature.

Ideally, the effective executive is able to recognize and blend these separate sets of responsibilities in a harmonious way. A key aspect of this process involves his ability to work effectively with people.

Human relations skills. Earlier sections in this book describe current trends in personnel management and supervision. The hard taskmaster or play-it-by-the book executive can no longer function effectively in today's climate of management-worker relations.

To maximize his departmental output, the effective administrator today must maximize interdepartmental communication, create an atmosphere of trust and high morale, and encourage the kinds of self-motivated work attitudes that make for maximum job performance. This can best be accomplished when the following conditions prevail: *understanding, mutual agreement, and identification* with respect to the task of the team; *open communications,* in which not only ideas, facts, and arguments are fully aired, but also feelings; *mutual trust* that each member of the team is valued and will be treated with real regard for his needs; *mutual support,* which frees individuals from the need to be self-protective so that they may contribute more fully to the task facing the team; *management of mutual differences,* the ability to resolve conflicts constructively; and *selective use of the team,* in which team members are used either individually or in groups according to the nature of the tasks to be accomplished and their own skills.[2]

The ability to be sensitive to people and their needs is essential to the effective executive. He cannot always be a "soft" administrator, as McGregor characterizes one style option. When faced by a political threat to his department, when involved in interdepartmental infighting, when confronted with other deliberate challenges to his authority or the work of his department, the administrator may have to be forceful in his approach. At all times, however, he should have control of his emotions, should be able to understand both himself and those he is working with, and should strive to play an interpersonal role that is constructive and creative. This will contribute immeasurably to his success.

Despite the vast difference in the nature of the work and the setting, the recreation and park administrator must project an image not unlike that of the combat military leader. Under pressure, he must demonstrate to his subordinates courage, resourcefulness, intuition, and, above all else, consideration for his troops. Staff and line personnel will perform at a superior level if they are following a strong and thoughtful leader. This is particularly true in moderate- and large-sized departments where intimate, day-to-day contacts are impossible. Charisma, a difficult-to-describe aura that surrounds certain exciting leaders and public figures, is simply a word describing some combination of these leadership qualities in one dynamic personage.

Intelligent decision-making. Decision-making is a key aspect of the work of the typical executive in business or public administration. According to Drucker:

> Effective executives do not make a great many decisions. They concentrate on the important ones. They try to think through what is strategic and generic, rather than "solve problems." They try to make the few important decisions on the highest level of conceptual understanding. . . . They want to know what the decision is all about and what the underlying realities are which it has to satisfy. They want impact rather than technique, they want to be sound rather than clever.[3]

He goes on to suggest five basic points that are important in the decision-making process.

1. Problems should be understood as being primarily generic—that is to say, part of a fairly typical pattern and subject to solution through the application of a rule or principle. Only a few problems are unusual enough to require original analysis and fresh decision-making.

Since this is the case, the intelligent executive does not attempt to develop fresh, imaginative solutions for every problem that comes across his desk. He gives his major energies to developing sound principles of administration and attempts to apply them where possible, rather than to solve many problems with different solutions.

2. A second important element in decision-making is to determine the boundary conditions of the decision. What goals must it achieve? What conditions must be satisfied? If a decision falls short of accomplishing its minimum objectives, it is a failure—but these objectives must be determined in advance and reasonable assurance gained that the decision will achieve them.

3. It is essential, Drucker believes, to start out with what is right, rather than what is acceptable. Ultimately, compromise may be necessary, but concern at the outset about anticipated obstacles and objections tends to negate positive, clear action.

4. Decision-making must also include a workable plan for converting the decision into action. If it does not, the decision will not be an effective one.

5. Finally, Drucker suggests, a feedback mechanism should be built into the decision to determine, over a period of time, whether the actual events that occur are in line with the expectations held at the time of decision-making. Continuous

testing as to whether the concepts and assumptions on which a decision is made are still valid or becoming obsolete may require that a decision be reversed.

Various methods used in decision-making all involve a similar series of stages: (1) recognizing and defining the problem or issue; (2) exploring its causes and gathering information about all relevant factors or influences; (3) defining possible alternatives or courses of action; (4) attempting to measure in advance the outcomes of each possible decision, taking into account the known variables and environmental factors; (5) arriving at a preferred recommendation or solution; and (6) implementing the decision. Most administrators do not go through a complicated process of decision-making but rather rely on the close-at-hand evidence and on their own common sense or judgment as the basis for taking action.

It should be recognized that all decisions do not flow from a single omnipotent authority, the departmental administrator. A leader makes many quick decisions on the job. Some must, however, be pushed up to the supervisor for resolution or approval. In turn, although supervisors make many decisions themselves, they must clear more crucial or difficult ones with their administrators. In turn, administrators may seek the advice or approval of their boards with respect to controversial or extremely important policy-related decisions.

There are several major constraints or difficulties in the path of effective decision-making. First, it should be recognized that administrators are able to devote only a limited portion of their time to this task and that the information placed before them is only a portion of all the potential data that might be relevant to solving the problem. Thus, in many cases, decisions are made on an off-the-cuff basis, without sufficient consideration of all the facts and alternatives.

Many pressures may be placed on the administrator, both from sources inside his organization and from outside groups. Often, when these pressures are political in nature, it becomes a matter of horse-trading, such as giving up a present point to obtain a future benefit.

The element of political impact must be realistically weighed in the decision-making process. Often surprisingly small issues are at stake. The quirks of political pressure will sometimes find a mayor or cluster of city councilmen badgering a recreation and park superintendent over the transfer of a park attendant or the official naming of a new wading pool. It is necessary for the administrator—while adhering to his professional beliefs and basic principles—to thread a careful path through the political flak thrown up by emotional, short-sighted, but well-intentioned public officials. The transfer of a laborer may result later in a massive budget approval; the delay in scheduling the opening of a new ice rink to suit the schedule of a traveling mayor may expedite the subsequent purchase of ten new trucks. Trade-offs of this kind are logical and ethical so long as basic principles are not compromised.

To ensure that there is full input of all relevant information and views, many successful administrators develop a participative management approch in which supervisors and other personnel affected by decisions play an active role in considering alternatives and providing relevant information and views. It is also helpful to bring in groups of constituents, community representatives, other professionals, or officials in city government or voluntary agencies to consult them on problems.

So-called sunk costs, referring to the previous investment of money, time, and other resources in a given program or project, often act as a barrier preventing decisive and intelligent action. If a program is under way and has already cost a substantial sum, it is often easier to let it continue rather than expend the energy and suffer the disruptions that will occur if a hard decision to end it by reversing policy is made. Some analysts of public administration have concluded that in every bureau there is a strong, inherent pressure on the vast majority of officials that prevents them from making radical changes or shaking up the system by innovative decisions. Nigro[4] suggests the following guidelines for effective decision-making:

1. "Cognitive nearsightedness," defined as the tendency to make decisions that satisfy immediate needs but do not deal with long-range concerns, should be avoided. Instead, decisions should be based on fundamental principles, rather than expediency, and should come to grips with long-range effects.

2. It is important to recognize and deal with the fundamental causes or roots of a problem rather than its symptoms. Only if this is done can a decision have a meaningful effect.

3. Decision-makers should not rely excessively on their own experience or the preconceived notions of the executive but should gather contrary evidence or points of view to put the problem into the fullest possible perspective.

4. Finally, the decision-making responsibility must be accepted. In many organizations there is a tendency to pass the buck and avoid the risk-taking involved in tackling a problem head on. The effective administrator is not reluctant to make courageous decisions and exercises this power willingly and intelligently.

Effective communication. Communication is the process of expressing, transmitting, and receiving messages in verbal, written, or visual form. Within recreation and park departments, as in all kinds of organizations, communication is constantly at work. It occurs in staff meetings, personnel conferences, training workshops, formal speeches, annual reports and newsletters, meetings with citizen groups, and policy statements. It may even take place through acts, as in the firing of an employee for cause, which deliver a message to all other employees. It may be transmitted through gestures or body language that deliver ideas in forms that are often more eloquent than words.

But it is in the media of verbal and written communications that most administrators need to be skilled. To make sure that they express their views, ideas, requests, or orders clearly and concisely, the administrator should consider carefully the content and style of his or her communications. It is helpful first to understand the basic elements of communication. Belasco, Hampton, and Price have identified five distinct steps in this process:

1. *Formulation of sender's thoughts.* It is necessary for the would-be communicator to decide exactly what it is that he or she wants to say, and what its impact or effect should be.

2. *Encoding.* This technical term simply means the way in which thoughts are translated into language for effective communication—using the most clear, simple, unambiguous language possible—that will be non-threatening and constructive.
3. *Transmitting.* What will be the most effective means of delivering the message—in writing, in verbal form, and in what setting or format? The clarity of the delivery is also important: is one's speech too fast, or one's handwriting or typing illegible?
4. *Reception.* Are those receiving the message in a situation where it will reach them accurately, and where they will be attentive to it?
5. *Decoding.* Are all the words or other elements in the message clearly understood? This can be checked by follow-up questions, discussions, or monitoring methods.[5]

There are many barriers to effective communication—either in the way the message is framed and delivered or in structural obstacles, such as the inability of employees on one level to communicate directly with supervisors or administrators who are several layers above them in the chain of command. Often emotions such as anger or antagonism prevent people from delivering their messages accurately. In other cases, listening becomes selective, in that people may tend to hear only what they want to hear and to reject other messages. In some cases, messages may be contradictory, in that administrators may say one thing but actually carry out actions that say something else.

To overcome these barriers to effective communication, administrators must first decide exactly what it is they want to say and then determine the most effective channel, medium, or technique for communicating it. There should be a careful, clear, unmistakable transmission of the message that invites a follow-up or response. Communication *must* be understood as a two-way process if it is to be most meaningful. Finally, it should be recognized that communication is a form of action and that it should be honest, consistent, and part of the administrator's total approach to employees, the public, or governing bodies.

Meeting the challenge of practical politics. In addition to having the skills described here, successful administrators must have certain other qualities or competences. Research has shown that they tend to be individuals who enjoy accepting personal responsibility for solving problems and that they set goals for themselves and their agencies that are ambitious yet possible to attain. To reach these goals, they are prepared to take calculated risks. They welcome feedback from others, and they use this feedback in guiding their own actions. They have a high personal need for achievement, and they are skilled in dealing effectively with conflict situations, resolving them in ways that contribute to the health of their organizations.

Finally, they are able to meet the challenge set by practical politics, either in a governmental situation or in the voluntary, therapeutic, or other agency structure where they hold responsibility. The term *practical politics* may be interpreted in a variety of ways. To some, it may refer to the need to deal with political officials, neighborhood organizations, legislators, or state and federal departments in constructive and professionally sound ways to gain support for one's department. To others, it may suggest a chameleon-like maneuvering, in which the department head sacrifices his professional ideals to the demands or pressures of harassed politicians.

If he sees the problem in the latter sense, the practical politics player is a loser. The recreation and park administrator who capitulates to political pressures at every turn, who hires strictly on the basis of party affiliation, and who gives top priority to serving those neighborhoods that vote right is not a true professional. He cannot provide a full measure of service to the overall community, he tends to be regarded strictly as a mayor's man, and he is subject to easy dismissal with a turnover in political fortunes or even with less provocation.

The realistic position, then, is that the recreation and park executive who seeks to work in the world of politics must understand the political structure and the channels for getting things done. He must be loyal to the mayor and the party in power and not seek to undermine it. But he must also maintain his professional ideals and must seek at every turn to let his on-the-job decisions be guided by the weight of the evidence in terms of the legitimate priorities and standards that apply. If he cannot survive in a given situation and maintain his service credo, he should look elsewhere; in the long run, his career will benefit from such a change.

Throughout, he must maintain his credibility. This can only be done by behaving consistently in the following ways: (1) keeping every commitment and backing up each statement, promise, or threat, whether made in public or private; (2) acting in predictable rather than irrational or on-again-off-again ways; (3) following a legitimate and carefully articulated philosophy of recreation and public service; and (4) encouraging the airing and sharing of dissent.

Finally, he must be able to manage himself in terms of effective executive practices.

EFFECTIVE EXECUTIVE PRACTICES

As indicated earlier, Drucker has found that successful administrators generally have one thing in common—a core of habits or practices that seem to make for effective administration in a variety of settings, whether public service, higher education, or business. These practices can be learned and must be repeated until they become firmly ingrained in the day-by-day behavior of the individual. They are within the grasp of any reasonably capable administrator and add immeasurably to his overall effectiveness.

Effective executives know where their time goes. The use of one's time is a key factor in an administrator's effectiveness. Typically, many top executives are harassed, under constant demand, constantly torn among responsibilities and use their time in a variety of nonessential ways. Drucker suggests that they should:

1. *Record* their time, by finding out where it actually goes
2. *Manage* it, by cutting back unproductive demands on it
3. *Consolidate* discretionary time (that is, time that can be freed from routine responsibilities to tackle major tasks) into the largest possible blocks

The managing of one's time by cutting out unnecessary or nonproductive responsibilities is essential. The executive must ask himself: "Are these jobs I must personally be responsible for?" "Are these meetings really necessary?" or "Must I write this speech or make this appearance?" When he is able to prune such time-wasters and make sure that his time is most productively employed, he is on his way to becoming more fully effective.

Querulous alibis about "I'm too busy" or "I don't know where my times goes" identify the speaker as a weak or ineffective administrator. One elementary technique to make certain that time does not simply disappear or to guarantee that periodic opportunities are available for quiet thinking and planning is as follows:

1. The administrator studies his diary or schedule book at the end of each month. He selects a day in the coming month and marks in clearly, "All-day planning session." His secretary is informed that absolutely no appointments are to be made on this date.

2. The executive arranges a comfortable retreat (a hotel room, university lounge or isolated classroom, unused summer cottage, or similar location) where he will have tables, chairs, space—and above all, privacy and quiet.

3. He asks his secretary not to call him at this location except for the most extreme emergency. Needless to say, he is not to be visited by other staff personnel unless he has asked them to join him in a thinking and planning all-day session.

Effective executives focus on outward contribution. Drucker points out that the prime focus of the executive should be on accomplishing results, rather than on the effort he expends. This means that he must think in terms of what it is he is trying to achieve rather than the functions he carries out, day by day.

When he takes this stance and is primarily concerned with the way his own contribution can significantly affect the overall performance of his department, the executive turns away from a concern with his own narrow skills or those of his subordinates and looks at his entire organization and its purpose. It also moves him in the direction of the outside world—the various publics he serves—to measure and improve the results of his department's work. He is minimally concerned with techniques and tools and maximally concerned with impact and accomplishment.

Effective executives build on strengths. It is essential that executives make use of all the strengths available to them in themselves, their ultimate superiors, and their entire staff. Although they cannot overcome weaknesses, they can make them irrelevant. In assigning a subordinate, for example, the administrator does not try to determine his weaknesses and then assign him to a post where he can stay out of trouble. Instead, he should ask, "What *can* he do well?" and then make sure that he is productively used in such a role.

In part, this is a matter of carefully examining the jobs to which people are assigned and making sure that they *can* be performed within reason. This involves not so much the technical difficulty of the work to be done as the temperament the job calls for. Jobs *should* be made big and challenging, so that all employees have the opportunity to use their talents to the fullest and to grow within the organization. This implies that they must know that the executive is fully receptive to their creative efforts.

Effective executives do first things first. The successful administrator concentrates his energies on the few major efforts where his superior performance will produce key results. He forces himself to select priorities for himself and to stay with these priorities. Such concentration is essential because there are so many possible tasks demanding the attention of the typical executive in government or business. In Drucker's view, for him to disperse his energies among all of these, giving a modicum of time and energy to each, means that little can be accomplished.

> The more an executive focuses on upward contribution, the more will he require fairly big continuous chunks of time. . . . Yet, to get even that half-day or those two weeks of really productive time requires self-discipline and an iron determination to say "No."[6]

In selecting priorities, it is essential to aim at the future rather than to be conditioned by the past, to focus on opportunities rather than problems, and to aim high rather than at goals that can easily be accomplished. The truly effective executive, in Drucker's view, actually commits himself to *one* major task at a time; thus he becomes the "master of time and events, instead of their whipping boy."

THE CREATIVE EXECUTIVE

Many recreation and park executives are capable, respected leaders in their communities and in the profession, but only a few emerge as outstanding professionals.

The key factor here is their ability to be creative, to be open and responsive to the crucial challenges of the present day, to develop exciting and innovative programs and concepts, and—above all—to see beyond the traditional, to envision new roles and solutions for recreation and parks. We live in an era of immense change in terms of technology, international affairs, social values and relationships, medicine, education, population trends, family life, career choices, business practices, mobility—and leisure. The rate of change is constantly accelerating, and it is impossible to deal with it effectively using the formulas of yesterday.

It is essential to be *visionary*, to *anticipate the future*, to *speculate* about it, to *be ready* for it before it confronts us with seemingly unanswerable challenges. Toffler writes:

> Instead of deriding the "crystal-ball gazer," we need to encourage people, from childhood on, to speculate freely, even fancifully, not merely about what next week holds in store for them but about what the next generation holds in store for the entire human race. We offer our children courses in history; why not also courses in "Future," courses in which the possibilities and probabilities of the future are systematically explored, exactly as we now explore the social system of the Romans or the rise of the feudal manors?[7]

Ultimately, the most successful recreation and park executives will be those men and women who are able to *shift into the future tense*, who are able to read and understand social change as it occurs—rather than to resist it—and to clearly anticipate the leisure and social needs of their nation and communities in radically new ways. Recreation and park administrators must be trend-setters and not simply followers of the traffic flow! Only under this kind of creative and imaginative leadership will the broad field of recreation and parks be able to establish itself fully as an integral aspect of government and community life. This, then, is the ultimate challenge facing recreation and park administrators, both in the present and in the decades that lie ahead.

Suggested examination questions or topics for student reports

1. Write a brief essay on the effective executive based on the text and on administrators you have known. In your discussion, deal both with personal traits of the executive and with administrative practices that promote or detract from his effectiveness.
2. Present a description of a significant problem in recreation and park administration, supervision, or leadership. Analyze the problem, show how it was solved, and evaluate the outcome. In this description, present the principles that should have been used to deal with the problem, and show how special circumstances may have been responsible for modifying their application.
3. Analyze your own use of time. Applying principles presented in the text based on Drucker's recommendations, develop a set of personal recommendations as to how you could become more effective in terms of work productivity.

REFERENCES

1. Drucker, Peter F.: *The Effective Executive,* New York, 1967, Harper & Row, Publishers, p. 22.
2. McGregor, Douglas: *The Professional Manager,* New York, 1967, McGraw-Hill Book Co., pp. 162-166.
3. Drucker, *op. cit.:* pp. 113-114.
4. Nigro, Felix: *Modern Public Administration,* New York, 1970, Harper & Row, Publishers, p. 170.
5. Belasco, James A., Hampton, David R., and Price, Karl F.: *Management Today,* New York, 1975, John Wiley & Sons, Inc., pp. 115-118.
6. Drucker, *op. cit.:* pp. 100-101.
7. Toffler, Alvin: *Future Shock,* New York, 1971, Bantam Books, Inc., p. 424.

BIBLIOGRAPHY

Artz, Robert M., and Bermont, Hubert: *Guides to New Approaches to Financing Parks and Recreation*, Washington, D.C., 1970, National Recreation and Park Association and Acropolis Books Ltd.

Avedon, Elliott M.: *Therapeutic Recreation Service: An Applied Behavioral Science Approach*, Englewood Cliffs, N.J., 1974, Prentice-Hall, Inc.

Ball, Edith L.: *Hosteling: The New Program in Community Recreation*, New York, 1971, American Youth Hostels.

Bannon, Joseph, J.: *Problem Solving in Recreation and Parks,* Englewood Cliffs, N.J., 1972, Prentice-Hall, Inc.

Bannon, Joseph, J.: *Leisure Resources: Its Comprehensive Planning*, Englewood Cliffs, N.J., 1976, Prentice-Hall, Inc.

Belasco, James, Hampton, David, and Price, Karl: *Management Today*, New York, 1975, John Wiley & Sons, Inc.

Bengtsson, Arvid: *Environmental Planning for Children's Play*, New York, 1970, Praeger Publishers, Inc.

Bittel, Lester R.: *What Every Supervisor Should Know*, New York, 1974, McGraw-Hill Book Co.

Brightbill, Charles K.: *Man and Leisure: A Philosophy of Recreation*, Englewood Cliffs, N.J., 1971, Prentice-Hall, Inc.

Bucher, Charles A., and Bucher, Richard D.: *Recreation for Today's Society*, Englewood Cliffs, N.J., 1974, Prentice-Hall, Inc.

Buechner, Robert D., Editor: *Recreation and Open Space Standards*, Washington, D.C., 1969, National Recreation and Park Association.

Bureau of Outdoor Recreation: *Outdoor Recreation Planning for the Handicapped*, Washington, D.C., 1967, U.S. Government Printing Office.

Butler, George D.: *Introduction to Community Recreation*, New York, 1976, McGraw-Hill Book Co.

Butler, George D.: *Recreation Areas: Their Design and Equipment*, New York, 1958, The Ronald Press Co.

Carlson, Reynold, Deppe, Theodore, and MacLean, Janet: *Recreation in American Life*, Belmont, Calif., 1972, Wadsworth Publishing Co., Inc.

Dattner, Richard: *Design for Play*, New York, 1969, Van Nostrand Reinhold.

Dimock, Marshall E., and Dimock, G. O.: *Public Administration*, New York, 1969, Holt, Rinehart & Winston, Inc.

Doell, Charles E., and Twardzik, Louis F.: *Elements of Park and Recreation Administration*, Minneapolis, 1973, Burgess Publishing Co.

Drucker, Peter F.: *The Effective Executive*, New York, 1967, Harper & Row, Publishers.

Dunn, Diana, R., Editor: *Guidelines for Action Developing Opportunities for the Handicapped in Recreation, Parks, and Leisure Services*, Washington, D.C., 1971, U.S. Dept. of Health, Education, and Welfare and National Recreation and Park Association.

Ellis, M. J.: *Why People Play*, Englewood Cliffs, N.J., 1973, Prentice-Hall, Inc.

Ezersky, Eugene M., and Theibert, P. Richard: *Facilities in Sports and Physical Education*, St. Louis, 1976, The C. V. Mosby Co.

Friedberg, M. Paul, and Berkeley, Ellen P.: *Play and Interplay: A Manifesto for New Design in Urban Recreational Environment*, New York, 1970, Crowell, Collier & Macmillan.

Frieswyk, Siebolt H.: *Mobile and Portable Recreation Facilities in Parks and Recreation: Current Design and Operation*, Washington, D.C., 1966, National Recreation and Park Association.

Frye, Virginia, and Peters, Martha: *Therapeutic Recreation: Its Theory, Philosophy and Practices*, Harrisburg, Pa., 1972, Stackpole Books.

Gold, Seymour M.: *Urban Recreation Planning*, Philadelphia, 1973, Lea & Febiger.

Godbey, Geoffrey, and Parker, Stanley: *Leisure Studies and Services: An Overview*, Philadelphia, 1976, W. B. Saunders Co.

Gray, David, and Pelegrino, Donald A.: *Reflections on the Recreation and Park Movement*, Dubuque, Iowa, 1973, William C. Brown Co., Publishers.

Guggenheimer, Elinor C.: *Planning for Parks and Recreation Needs in Urban Areas*, New York, 1969, Twayne Publishers, Inc.

Hatry, Harry P., and Dunn, Diana R.: *Measuring the Effectiveness of Local Government Services: Recreation*, Washington, D.C., 1971, The Urban Institute.

Hines, Thomas I.: *Revenue Sources Management in Parks and Recreation*, Arlington, Va., 1971, National Recreation and Park Association.

Hjelte, George, and Shivers, Jay S.: *Public Administration of Recreational Services*, Philadelphia, 1972, Lea & Febiger.

Jensen, Clayne R.: *Outdoor Recreation in America*, Minneapolis, 1970, Burgess Publishing Co.

Jubenville, Alan: *Outdoor Recreation Planning*, Philadelphia, 1976, W. B. Saunders Co.

Kando, Thomas M.: *Leisure and Popular Culture in Transition*, St. Louis, 1975, The C. V. Mosby Co.

Kaplan, Max: *Leisure: Theory and Policy*, New York, 1975, John Wiley & Sons, Inc.

Kavanaugh, J. Michael, Marcus, Morton J., and Gay, Robert M.: *Program Budgeting for Urban Recreation: Current Status and Prospects in Los Angeles*, New York, 1973, Praeger Publishers, Inc.

Kast, Fremont E., and Rosenzwieg, James F.: *Organization and Management: A Systems Approach*, New York, 1970, McGraw-Hill Book Co.

Kraus, Richard: *Recreation Today: Program Planning and Leadership*, Santa Monica, Calif., 1977, Goodyear Publishing Co., Inc.

Kraus, Richard: *Recreation and Leisure in Modern Society*, Santa Monica, Calif., 1971, Goodyear Publishing Co., Inc.

Kraus, Richard: *Urban Parks and Recreation: Challenge of the 1970's*, New York, 1972, Community Council of Greater New York.

Kraus, Richard: *Therapeutic Recreation Service: Principles and Practices*, Philadelphia, 1973, W. B. Saunders Co.

Kraus, Richard, and Bates, Barbara: *Recreation Leadership and Supervision: Guidelines for Professional Development*, Philadelphia, 1975, W. B. Saunders Co.

Lutzin, Sidney G., and Storey, Edward H., Editors: *Managing Municipal Leisure Services*, Washington, D.C., 1973, International City Management Association.

McFarland, Dalton E.: *Management: Principles and Practices*, New York, 1970, Macmillan, Inc.

McGregor, Douglas: *The Professional Manager*, New York, 1967, McGraw-Hill Book Co.

Millar, Susanna: *The Psychology of Play*, Baltimore, 1968, Penguin Books, Inc.

Murphy, James F.: *Concepts of Leisure: Philosophical Implications*, Englewood Cliffs, N.J., 1974, Prentice-Hall, Inc.

Murphy, James F.: *Recreation and Leisure Service: A Humanistic Perspective*, Dubuque, Iowa, 1975, William C. Brown Co., Publishers.

Murphy, James F., Williams, John G., Niepoth, E. William, and Brown, Paul D.: *Leisure Service Delivery System: A Modern Perspective*, Philadelphia, 1973, Lea & Febiger.

Musselman, Virginia, and Frieswyk, Siebolt, Editors: *Guidelines for the Organization and Administration of a Cultural Program in Community Recreation*, Washington, D.C., 1965, National Recreation and Park Association.

National League of Cities: *Recreation in the Nation's Cities: Problems and Approaches*, Washington, D.C., 1968, Department of Urban Studies of National League of Cities, for Bureau of Outdoor Recreation.

Neal, Larry L.: *Recreation's Role in the Rehabilitation of the Mentally Retarded*, Eugene, Oregon, 1970, University of Oregon Press.

Nesbitt, John A., Brown, Paul D., and Murphy, James F.: *Recreation and Leisure Service for the Disadvantaged*, Philadelphia, 1971, Lea & Febiger.

Nigro, Felix A.: *Modern Public Administration*, New York, 1970, Harper & Row, Publishers.

O'Morrow, Gerald S.: *Therapeutic Recreation: A Helping Profession*, Reston, Va., 1976, Reston Publishing Co.

Pomeroy, Janet: *Recreation for the Physically Handicapped*, New York, 1964, Macmillan, Inc.

Public Health Service: *Activity Supervisor's Guide, A Handbook for Activities Supervisors in Long-Term Nursing Care Facilities*, Washington, D.C., 1969, U.S. Dept. of Health, Education, and Welfare.

Rodney, Lynn S.: *Administration of Public Recreation*, New York, 1964, The Ronald Press Co.

Rutledge, Albert S.: *Anatomy of a Park: The Essentials of Recreation Area Planning and*

Design, New York, 1971, McGraw-Hill Book Co.

Sessoms, H. Douglas, Meyer, Harold D., and Brightbill, Charles K.: *Leisure Services: The Organized Recreation and Park System,* Englewood Cliffs, N.J., 1975, Prentice-Hall, Inc.

Shivers, Jay S.: *Principles and Practices of Recreational Service,* New York, 1967, Macmillan, Inc.

Shivers, Jay S., and Calder, Clarence R.: *Recreational Crafts: Programming and Instructional Techniques,* New York, 1974, McGraw-Hill Book Co.

Shomon, Joseph J.: *Open Land for Urban America: Acquisition, Safekeeping, and Use,* Baltimore, 1971, The Johns Hopkins University Press.

Stein, Thomas A., and Sessoms, H. Douglas, Editors: *Recreation and Special Populations,* Boston, 1973, Holbrook Press, Inc.

Timms, Howard L.: *Introduction to Operations Management,* Homewood, Ill., 1967, Richard D. Irwin, Inc.

van der Smissen, Betty: *Evaluation and Self-Study of Public Recreation and Park Agencies: A Guide with Standards and Evaluative Criteria,* Arlington, Va., 1972, National Recreation and Park Association.

van der Smissen, Betty, Editor: *Indicators of Change in the Recreation Environment: A National Research Symposium,* University Park, Pa., 1975, Pennsylvania State H.P.E.R. Series.

van der Smissen, Betty, Editor: *Recreation Research,* Washington, D.C., 1966, American Association for Health, Physical Education and Recreation and National Recreation and Park Association.

Weiskopf, Donald C.: *A Guide to Recreation and Leisure,* Boston, 1975, Allyn & Bacon, Inc.

Whitaker, Ben, and Browne, Kenneth: *Parks for People,* New York, 1973, Shocken Books, Inc.

Wiemer, David L.: *Private Funds for Parks and Recreation,* Long Island City, N.Y., 1969, Playground Corp. of America.

Management Aids Bulletins

These booklets, published by the National Recreation and Park Association, contain valuable administrative guidelines relating to a wide variety of functions in parks and recreation. In addition to the bulletins cited in this text, the series includes such titles as:

No. 13	A Safety Guide for Park and Recreation Employees.
No. 26	A Manual on Concession Contracts.
No. 32	Park Police.
No. 34	Guidelines for Campground Development.
No. 40	Creative Playground Equipment.
No. 43	Day Camping for Park and Recreation Departments.
No. 46	Budgeting for Parks and Recreation.
No. 49	Swimming Pool Management.
No. 54	Litter Control Handbook.
No. 63	Personnel Policies.
No. 65	In-Service Training Manual.
No. 72	Administering Admissions to Events and Programs in the Park and Recreation Field.
No. 76	Sample Leases, Licenses, Permits.
No. 79	Publicity Handbook.
No. 81	Public Employee Unions—Organizations.
No. 82	School-Community Park and Recreation Operations.
No. 86	Community Instrumental Music Programming.
No. 88	Recreation in Nursing Homes.

AUTHOR INDEX

SUBJECT INDEX